Born in The Wilderness

A Book of Mormon Commentary

Volume One

The First Book of Nephi
thru
The Words of Mormon

Philip M. Hudson

"Our lives passed away like as it were unto us a dream, we being a lonesome and a solemn people, wanderers, cast out from Jerusalem, born in a wilderness". (Jacob 7:26).

"I will proceed to do a marvellous work among this people, even a marvellous work and a wonder: for the wisdom of their wise men shall perish, and the understanding of their prudent men shall be hid."
(Isaiah 29:14).

Copyright 2023 by Philip M. Hudson.
Published 2023.
Printed in the United States of America.
All rights reserved.

No portion of this book may be reproduced,
stored in a retrieval system, or transmitted
in any form or by any means, mechanical,
electronic, photocopy, recording, scanning,
or other, except for brief quotations in
critical reviews or articles, without
the prior written permission
of the author.

ISBN 978-1-957077-50-5

Illustrations - Google Images.
This book may be ordered from
online bookstores.

Publishing Services
by BookCrafters, Parker, Colorado.
www.bookcrafters.net

Joseph Smith "has translated the book, even that part which I have commanded him, and as your Lord and your God liveth, it is true." (D&C 17:6).

"And I saw another angel fly in the midst of heaven, having the everlasting gospel to preach unto them that dwell on the earth, and to every nation, and kindred, and tongue, and people."
(Revelation 14:6).

The light of the Gospel endows us with the capacity to love ourselves, as well as the Savior. As we embrace its principles, the Lord blesses us. Illumination dissipates the cobwebs of doubt, smooths out the rough edges of testimony, builds our self-confidence to tackle the tough questions, and provides the self-assuredness we require to exercise our agency wisely. Light bestows upon us the gifts of harmony, comfort, and a clear conscience. It illuminates the Gospel as the ultimate measure of truth. Light exerts a liberating influence, as it releases us from apprehension, despair, doubt, fear, ignorance, hesitancy, unsteadiness, and worry while empowering us to keep that which we hold near and dear protected from those who scurry about within the shadows just waiting for an opportunity to ransack our treasury. As our learning style embraces the Spirit, we discover a pattern that soon becomes our norm, as we draw closer and closer to the perfect day.

"And if ye shall
believe in Christ ye will believe in
these words, for they are the words of
Christ, and he hath given them unto me;
and they teach all men that they should do
good. And if they are not the words of Christ,
judge ye - for Christ will show unto you, with
power and great glory, that they are his words,
at the last day; and you and I shall stand
face to face before his bar; and ye shall
know that I have been commanded
of him to write these things."
(2 Nephi 33:10-11).

"Take thee one stick, and write upon it, for Judah, and for the children of Israel his companions: then take another stick, and write upon it, For Joseph, the stick of Ephraim, and for all the house of Israel his companions. And join them one to another into one stick; and they shall become one in thine hand." (Ezekiel 37:16-17).

Our greater understanding of the Plan of God that is revealed in The Book of Mormon blesses our lives in many ways. Its power creates the opportunity for dynamic change, as wisdom flows along established channels. Moreover, personal accountability, responsibility, and commitment to obedience expand. The humble need to serve strengthens connections of brotherhood and sisterhood while it generates interdependency within a community of true believers in which any cultural differences are effectively expunged. We are no longer strangers or foreigners. We've become fellowcitizens with the Saints, within the household of God.

When we
open up The Book
of Mormon for the first
time, there will be revealed
a strait and narrow path that
stretches away to a soft glow of
light on the eastern horizon.
At that very moment, our
real journey to Christ
will only have just
begun.

Table of Contents

"Scripture consists not in what we read, but in what we understand."
(St. Hilary).

Acknowledgements

Acknowledgements..1

Preface

Preface..3

Introduction

Introduction..5

The First Book of Nephi
His Reign and Ministry
Around 600 B.C. to 588 - 570 B.C.

Chapter 1	17
Chapter 2	19
Chapter 3	23
Chapter 4	25
Chapter 5	27
Chapter 6	29
Chapter 7	31
Chapter 8	33
Chapter 9	37
Chapter 10	39
Chapter 11	41
Chapter 12	45
Chapter 13	49
Chapter 14	53
Chapter 15	57
Chapter 16	61
Chapter 17	65

Chapter 18..69
Chapter 19..73
Chapter 20..79
Chapter 21..83
Chapter 22..87

The Second Book of Nephi
About 588 - 570 B.C. to 559 - 545 B.C.

Chapter 1..91
Chapter 2..95
Chapter 3..99
Chapter 4..103
Chapter 5..109
Chapter 6..113
Chapter 7..117
Chapter 8..119
Chapter 9..123
Chapter 10..129
Chapter 11..133

Introduction to
The Isaiah Chapters
Second Nephi 12 - 24

Introduction to The Isaiah Chapters..135

The Second Book of Nephi
About 588 - 570 B.C. to 559 - 545 B.C.
Chapters 12 - 33

Chapter 12	139
Chapter 13	143
Chapter 14	145
Chapter 15	147
Chapter 16	151
Chapter 17	155
Chapter 18	157
Chapter 19	161
Chapter 20	165
Chapter 21	169
Chapter 22	173
Chapter 23	175
Chapter 24	179
Chapter 25	185
Chapter 26	189
Chapter 27	193
Chapter 28	199
Chapter 29	207
Chapter 30	211
Chapter 31	215
Chapter 32	221
Chapter 33	225

The Book of Jacob
The Brother of Nephi
About 544 B.C. to 421 B.C.

Chapter 1..229
Chapter 2..235
Chapter 3..239
Chapter 4..241
Chapter 5..247
Chapter 6..255
Chapter 7..259

The Book of Enos
About 420 B.C.

Chapter 1..263

The Book of Jarom
About 399 B.C. to 361 B.C.

Chapter 1 267

The Book of Omni
About 323 B.C. to 130 B.C.

Chapter 1 271

The Words of Mormon
About 385 A.D.

Chapter 1 279

Observations

Observations..285

Author's Note

Author's Note..469

Addendum
A sampling of scriptures
(1 Nephi – Words of Mormon)

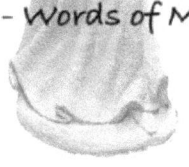

Addendum – A sampling of scriptures (1 Nephi – Words of Mormon)..477

Commentary and Compendium Index

Commentary and Compendium Index..553

Acknowledgements

The creation of my Commentary would have been impossible without stability and support on the home front. In the early years of its genesis, my children Tara, Joanna, Christopher, Patrick, Elizabeth, Kathryn, and Andrew tolerated the late hours when their sleep must have been interrupted many times by the incessant tapping on my keyboard. Later, when I was preoccupied with endless revisions, their insight and suggestions helped to define and refine the work. I will always remember the conversations we had concerning the lessons we learned from the scriptures. Often, listening to their perspective propelled me in new directions that expanded my appreciation of themes that I would have otherwise only narrowly or superficially addressed. Their example always gave me courage and the inspiration to make the study of The Book of Mormon relevant to our family's circumstances.

Throughout the process, my wife Jan has stood by my side and put up with my fixation on this project in countless ways. Without her constant support, my efforts would have fallen far short of my envisioned goal. She became the rudder of my ship, guiding me past unseen rocks and reefs. She has been my helm, holding steady when winds of adversity blew, and has been my telltale, who always alerted me to threatening squalls. She has been my keel, who helped me to move against the current and the wind, and my mainsheet, who held firm with just enough pressure to prevent me from capsizing when I was dangerously heeled over. She has been my safety-line, providing security when my footing was unsure and the foaming sea was streaming across my deck. She has been my compass, showing me the way, especially when the course was unclear, my chart, warning me of hidden dangers, and my barometer, cautioning me to take heed of impending storms. She has always been my lookout, standing as my faithful sentinel whenever I became distracted by trivial concerns. It was she who held the line that trailed in my wake, offering the promise of safety whenever I slipped and fell overboard. She has been and ever will be the wind that fills my sails. Jan and I may be partners in this great adventure, but she is my better half.

Those
timid souls of
weak character and
vacillating faith in the
life-changing lessons that
we glean The Book of Mormon
frequently think that they can
side-step both the requirements
of repentance and the demands
of discipleship. But it is because
that have never experienced the
freedom enjoyed by those who
move with willpower and grit
along the strait and narrow
path, due to the liberating
influence generated by
the covenants made
with our Lord and
Savior, Jesus
Christ.

Preface

I have always wanted to write a Commentary on The Book of Mormon. In 1981, when the New English Language Edition of the Standard Works was published, I began to comprehensively organize my card files and correlate them with the marginal notations that I had made over the years in my copies of the scriptures. These references became the foundation of my written impressions in this Commentary.

Collating my source material was daunting, especially before the age of word processing began in earnest, with the introduction of personal computers in the early 1980s.

I have attributed quotations to original authors whenever possible, as well as when I have editorialized the thoughts expressed by others. In many cases, however, the language in my Commentary will naturally reflect the teachings of leaders in The Church of Jesus Christ of Latter-day Saints. Of course, I alone am responsible for the content of these volumes. I hope my interpretation of the teachings of The Book of Mormon will cultivate your interest to dig deeper into the themes woven into its tapestry. My only goal is to help you to expand your insights into the foundation truths, core doctrines, and eternal principles that are the celestial guideposts embedded within its verses.

Hugh Nibley observed: "Men fool themselves, when they think for a moment that they can read scripture without ever adding something to the text or omitting something from it". Therein lies the power inherent in its study. We glean insight and understanding every time we investigate the word of God. I have learned to love the scriptures, and I often think of St. Hilary, who wrote: "Scripture consists not in what we read, but in what we understand". In my Commentary, I have consistently tried to anchor to the scriptures the ideas swirling around in my head.

Utilization of a Commentary does not replace personal scripture study. The spiritual awakening that accompanies prayerful efforts to understand the mysteries of God through the study of His word cannot be achieved through another person's interpretation. Perhaps, though, my own perspectives on the eternal themes expressed within The Book of Mormon will be helpful to you as you read and seek your own guidance. It is my hope that you will use this Commentary only to assist you in your own personal journey to Christ.

Our challenge is to enlist the aid of the Holy Ghost as we process the world around us. Many years ago, Dallin Oaks said: "Latter-day Saints know that learned or authoritative commentaries can help us with scriptural interpretation, but we maintain that they must be used with caution. Commentaries are not a substitute for the scriptures any more than a good cookbook is a substitute for food. When I refer to "commentaries", I mean everything that interprets scripture, from the comprehensive book-length commentary to the brief interpretation embodied in a lesson or an article, such as this one".

"One trouble with commentaries", he continued, "is that their authors sometimes focus on only one meaning to the exclusion of others. As a result, commentaries, if not used with great care, may illuminate the author's chosen and correct meaning but close our eyes and restrict our horizons to other possible meanings. Sometimes, those other less obvious meanings can be the ones most valuable and useful to us as we seek to obtain answers to our own questions. This is why the teaching of the Holy Ghost is a better guide to scriptural interpretation than is even the best commentary".

I could not agree more heartily with these wise words of counsel from President Oaks. As a matter of fact, every time I proofed a chapter (and I did this many times) I found myself scribbling additional notes in the margins and thinking to myself, "Why didn't I see that before?". That is precisely what I hope will be the experience of everyone who takes the time to read my Commentary. I trust the process will motivate you to search the scriptures more carefully and to be instructed by the Spirit, as you do so, that you might be led in directions that will prove to be personally illuminating.

I would expect that my older grandchildren who read this Commentary will be impacted in ways that are different from my adult children or my contemporaries. I hope that my observations will touch you differently each time you read them. When I am long-gone, perhaps the considerable thought that went into its production will generate a palpable bond that will span the years separating us. Maybe, the gulf that then divides us will not be as great, and our shared energies will pave the way to an eventual joyous reunion.

Know that I have been exhilarated when I have found wisdom and great treasures of knowledge, even hidden treasures, in the scriptures. These doctrinal themes have become pearls that I might have overlooked had I taken only a cursory glance. I hope that I am planting seeds so that you might harvest greater understanding, as well.

I had the opportunity to visit the Holy Land many years ago. We stopped, too briefly, at Qumran. The Dead Sea Covenantors lived there, and in the ruins of their library, I was able to pause and reflect upon their Eleventh Hymn that had been recovered from parchments hidden within caves high above their community. The translation reads, in part: "Behold, for mine own part I have reached the intervision, and through the spirit thou hast placed within me, come to know Thee, my God". In similar fashion, Moses wrote: "But now, mine own eyes have beheld God; but not my natural, but my spiritual eyes, for my natural eyes could not have beheld; for I should have withered and died in his presence; but his glory was upon me; and I beheld his face". (Moses 1:11)

I am continually reminded of Nephi's counsel to press forward with complete dedication and steadfastness, or confidence and a firm determination in Christ, having a perfect brightness of hope, or perfect faith, and charity, or a love of God and of all men. If we do this, he promised, feasting upon the word of Christ, or receiving strength and nourishment from the scriptures, and endure to the end in righteousness, we shall have eternal life, that is the greatest gift God can bestow upon His children. (See 2 Nephi 31:20). It is with love that I extend to you the invitation to enjoy my Commentary.

Introduction

Cicero wrote: "The first law for the historian is that he shall never dare utter an untruth. The second is that he shall suppress nothing that is true. Moreover, there shall be no suspicion of partiality or of malice in his writing". The accounts in The Book of Mormon abridged by the prophet-historian Mormon were true to the mandate given by Cicero. Although, as Washington Irving brooded: "It is the rule that history fades into fable; fact becomes clouded with doubt and controversy; the inscription moulders, and columns, arches, and pyramids are but heaps of sand, and their epitaphs, nothing but characters written in the dust", yet The Book of Mormon stands as a shining example of the divine model.

The Book of Mormon "is the witness that testifies to the passing of time. It illuminates reality, vitalizes memory, provides guidance in daily life, and brings us tidings of antiquity". It is the "evidence of time, the light of truth, the life of memory, the directress of life, committed to immortality". (Cicero, "De Oratore", ii, 36). In its pages, "the centuries roll back to the ancient age of gold". (Horace, "Odes", IV, ii, 39).

Those who read The Book of Mormon undertake an incredible journey through thousands of years of history as the pages of a profound text unfold before the panorama of great civilizations. Within its pages lies the intrigue of ancient Asia, as warlords battle for supremacy, the tension in Jerusalem mounts as rival empires of the Near East struggle for power, and the faithful prepare for a journey to a land of promise beyond the horizon of their vision.

The Book of Mormon may be devoured as if it were literally the bread of life, and those who read it feast upon the word of God and feel exhilaration as prophets counsel us from the dust. We seek, and yearn, and strive, and wrestle for our blessing, realizing that "unto some it is given by the Holy Ghost to know that Jesus Christ is the Son of God, and that he was crucified for the sins of the world", while "to others it is given ... the word of knowledge". (D&C 46:13 & 18).

The Book of Mormon makes the bold claim that its pages contain "the fulness of the Gospel". (D&C 42:12). Even members of The Church of Jesus Christ of Latter-day Saints sometimes misinterpret this to mean that there will be found within its pages detailed instructions regarding every doctrinal principle that governs our lives in the last days, and that the Nephite Saints participated in every ordinance of the Gospel as we know it. But it is we, and not they, who live in the Dispensation of The Fulness of Times, when the knowledge of the ages is being revealed. The Book of Mormon Saints only received "the fulness of the Gospel", in the sense that they were given instruction for their own needs, and sufficient for their own salvation.

The Title Page of The Book of Mormon is an overview of its history, and was written by the Prophet Mormon who inserted it into the last leaf of the collection of plates. (See H.C., 1:71). It was translated by Joseph Smith and moved by him to the beginning of the book. It forthrightly explains that the book was written for doubters, "to the convincing of the Jew and Gentile" that Jesus is The Christ. But it also makes the astounding acknowledgement that it might contain mistakes. This admission, however, refer to faults other than theology. Joseph Smith assured the Saints that "The Book of Mormon (is) the most correct of any book on earth, and the keystone of our religion, and a man (will) get nearer to God by abiding by its precepts, than by any other book". (H.C., 4:461).

Most evidence suggests that he and Oliver Cowdery "began their work of translation" in April 1829, beginning with The Book of Mosiah, and that during the month of May they translated to the end of The Book of Moroni. They then translated the Title Page, and finally The Small Plates of Nephi and The Words of Mormon before the end of June. The text of the Title Page was used as the book's description on the copyright form filed on June 11, 1829. (See "Encyclopedia of Mormonism", V. 1, Book of Mormon Translation by Joseph Smith, John Welch).

The translation was unlike that of any other text, inasmuch as it was accomplished "through the mercy (and) power of God". (D&C 1:29). This is as specific an explanation as is found regarding just how Joseph created an evenly flowing and coherent narrative spanning a thousand years of history, that stands revealed today without the benefit of subsequent editorial revision. During his lifetime, he tended to let the record speak for itself. With an understanding of the revelatory process, we are drawn to the book itself rather than to the specific means of translation, and without distraction we focus on the challenge left by Moroni: "And when ye shall receive these things, I would exhort you that ye would ask God, the eternal Father, in the name of Christ, if these things are not true; and if ye shall ask with a sincere heart, with real intent, having faith in Christ, he will manifest the truth of it unto you, by the power of the Holy Ghost". (Moroni 10:4, see verse 5).

Jesus Christ Himself testified of the book's historical and doctrinal accuracy. Joseph Smith "translated the book, even that part which I have commanded him, and as your Lord and your God liveth, it is true". (D&C 17:6, see D&C 19:26). For emphasis, the Savior used an ancient Hebrew oath in His witness. "Because he could swear by no greater, he sware by himself". (Hebrews 6:13).

Sometimes, those who are learning about the Restoration of the Gospel ask why the Church does not still possess the plates from which the Nephite history was translated. But as Hugh Nibley pointed out: "The presence of the plates would only prove that there are plates, and no more. It would not prove that Nephites wrote them, or that an angel brought them, or that they had been translated by the gift and power of God. A far more impressive claim is put forth when the whole work is given to the world as a divinely inspired translation". (Hugh Nibley, "An Approach to The Book of Mormon", p. 17-18).

Thus, The Book of Mormon stands on its own merits, in sharp contrast to the confusion surrounding most biblical scholarship. For example, "there are so many Greek New Testament manuscripts (over 5,000) that effective management and citation in a critical text amount to highly selective and careful genealogical classification into families, so that over 150,000 alternative readings can be grouped and profiled in a useful way. Also, the American Bible Society has counted over 24,000 differences among only six separate pre-1830 editions of the 1611 King James Version of the Bible". (FARMS Report).

No wonder that, in the Sacred Grove, Joseph Smith learned of the sects of Christendom that "they were all wrong" and that "all their creeds were an abomination". (J.S.H. 1:19). Organizations or teachings that do not lead us clearly and unambiguously toward salvation and exaltation in the Celestial Kingdom are abominable in the sight of God because they thwart the stated purpose of The Plan of Salvation, which is to guide us unerringly and bring to pass our immortality and eternal life. (See Moses 1:39). It was such confusion, in Joseph Smith's mind, that led to his Theophany and introduced the world to the Dispensation of The Fulness of Times.

Today, there is remarkable harmony within the Church regarding the dogma embedded within The Book of Mormon. Every day throughout the world, millions of Latter-day Saints open their translations of this scripture and are exposed to the same identical doctrinal themes. Contrast this unity of the faith with the thousands of denominations that interpret, with significant differences and sometimes-heated discussions, hundreds of variants of single biblical verses of scripture. It is far better that the Church proclaims that The Book of Mormon has been translated by the gift and power of God through the Prophet Joseph Smith. This leaves little room for conflicting doctrinal interpretation either within or outside the Church.

So important is The Book of Mormon, that right after its publication on March 26, 1830, the faithful met in Fayette, New York, and officially organized The Church of Jesus Christ of Latter-day Saints on April 6, 1830. Fully ten years earlier, Joseph Smith had communed with The Father and The Son in the Sacred Grove. Three years after that theophany, he received several documented visits from the Angel Moroni. Between 1823 and 1830, he became personally acquainted with all of the important characters in The Book of Mormon and enjoyed additional visits from Moroni. Still, the Church could not be organized until the Nephite scriptures that had been miraculously handed down to us were ready for publication.

Joseph Smith is listed in that first edition as the books' "author and proprietor". Thus, enemies of the Church have claimed that he wrote it, but the truth is simply that in accordance with the copyright laws of the State of New York at the time, someone had to be listed as author and proprietor of a text, and Joseph Smith was the logical choice.

In the past, paragraph two in the Introduction invited misunderstanding, because Lamanites were identified therein as the "principal" ancestors of the American Indians. (This introduction was written by Bruce R. McConkie in 1981, and was not part of the original translation of the text). Archaeological, anthropological, and genetic research suggests that the civilizations whose histories are recorded in The Book of Mormon lived in rather narrowly defined geographical areas in Meso-America. Certainly, there are many Native Americans today whose lineage may be traced to peoples other than Nephites and Lamanites who co-inhabited the Americas two thousand years ago. In any event, the 2007 change of one word in the Introduction, eliminating the word "principal" from the phrase "the principal ancestors of the American Indians..." and rendering it "among the ancestors of the American Indians..." invites a clearer understanding of the intent of the Introduction that was originally written by McConkie.

In their written testimony found at the beginning of the text, three witnesses accorded honor to the "Father, and to the Son, and to the Holy Ghost, which is one God". Better than other Christians, Latter-day Saints understand the nature of the Godhead. They recognize the individuality of each member of the Holy Trinity, while acknowledging the spiritual rapport between the Father, Son, and Holy Ghost, and between Them and true believers who enjoy a Holy Communion as they have become "one" in a spiritual sense.

Eight additional witnesses saw and handled the plates and described them as "having the appearance of gold". (See J.S.H. 1:34). We really do not know how many of the plates were actually made of gold. The 24 Gold Plates of Ether are the only ones that are identified in the text of The Book of Mormon as having been made of gold. (See Mosiah 8:9). We do know, however, that they were heavy. These witnesses "hefted" the bound plates that are estimated to have weighed in the neighborhood of 36 kilograms. The plates from which Joseph translated The Book of Mormon may have been thin sheets of gold, (see "Testimony of Joseph Smith", J.S.H., 1:34) but the text itself suggests that, in general, the Nephite prophets engraved their records on a variety of metals.

The Three Witnesses to The Book of Mormon wrote only that they had "seen the plates which contain this record" without reference to the specific composition of the metal, although they went into great detail to describe the engravings themselves and their purpose to benefit humanity. Various record-keepers referred to "plates of ore". (See

1 Nephi 19:1, Mosiah 21:27, and Mormon 8:5). When the prophets referred to a specific material, it was generally to "brass". (See 1 Nephi 3:3, 3:12, 3:24, 4:16, 4:24, 4:28, 5:10, 5:14, 5:18-19, 13:23, 19:21-22, 22:1, 22:30, 2 Nephi 4:2, 4:5, 5:12, Omni 1:14, Mosiah 1:3, 1:16, 10:16, 28:11, 28:20, Alma 37:3, 3 Nephi 1:2 & 10:17). "Plates of gold" are mentioned only in Mosiah 8:9 and 28:11, where they specifically refer to the 24 Gold Plates of Ether. Mormon, who had access to all the records and who abridged many of them, never referred to plates of gold.

His son Moroni twice referred to the plates, but only in reference to hiding them in the earth. (See Ether 15:11 & Mormon 8:4). Likewise, "Ammaron, being constrained by the Holy Ghost, did hide up the records which were sacred, yea, even all the sacred records which had been handed down from generation to generation, which were sacred". (4 Nephi 1:48-49). It may simply be that the custodians of the record were more focused on the message than on the material.

Because gold itself was much more plentiful in the Lands of The Book of Mormon, it many have not mattered to them of what material the plates were crafted. Jacob reported that his people, who still had an "Old World" mindset, had "begun to search for gold, and for silver, and for all manner of precious ores". Note that Jacob qualified as "precious" the ore his people sought. "In the which," or in these precious materials, he continued, "this land … doth abound most plentifully". (Jacob 2:12). In the same vein, Mormon reported: "Both the Lamanites and the Nephites … did have an exceeding plenty of gold, and of silver, and of all manner of precious metals". (Helaman 6:9). As had Jacob before him, Mormon characterized the hoarded materials as "precious metals".

We do know that the Eight Witnesses to The Book of Mormon testified that the plates they were shown and "hefted" had "the appearance of gold" and that Joseph Smith wrote in his History that Moroni told him that the book that was hidden in the Hill Cumorah was "written upon gold plates". (J.S.H. 1:34). But The Book of Mormon record itself does not corroborate Moroni's characterization of the gold composition of the plates. In the Church, however, it is commonly accepted that the records, other than The Plates of Brass, were "gold plates". Gold has always denoted value, and at the very least, the precious gift of The Book of Mormon is equivalent to the gifts of gold, frankincense, and myrrh, traditionally bestowed by the Wise Men of the East upon the Christ child in Bethlehem.

Interestingly, however, none of The Book of Mormon chroniclers describe their records as "gold plates," with the prominent exception of the Plates of Ether, that are specifically characterized as being of "pure gold". (Mosiah 8:9). Nephi's record was engraven upon "plates of ore". (1 Nephi 19:1). It was the record upon these plates that was pleasing to Mormon, and not the plates themselves. (The Words of Mormon, 1:4). As a matter of fact, when occasion arose, the various record keepers in The Book of Mormon almost pointedly described only the intrinsic quality of the plates entrusted to their care, while pointedly and characteristically ignoring the temporal value of the metals upon which the records were engraven.

The Testimony of the Prophet Joseph Smith is also interesting because his account of the initial appearance of the angel who delivered the plates is unique. (See J.S.H. 1:29-43). Joseph wrote that late one evening a light started to appear in his bedchamber and grew brighter and brighter until it was lighter than at noonday. Suddenly the Angel Moroni appeared before him, standing in the air. Clearly, Moroni came from another realm or dimension. He did not come through the door to enter the room. Rather, he just "appeared".

After he had delivered a detailed message, the light began to gather up around Moroni, and he ascended in a conduit right into heaven. This remarkable description is alien to our experience. None of us has ever seen light gather around an individual in this manner, presumably leaving the rest of the room in enveloping darkness, and none of us has ever seen such a light surround an individual who is then sucked up into the heavens as though the ceiling of the room were non-existent. The events of that evening are more remarkable when we realize that they were repeated, for emphasis, two more times.

On the following day, and in broad daylight, Moroni again appeared to Joseph in a field near his home. Once more, this resurrected being was described as being surrounded by an unearthly light that transcended the brilliance of the sun itself.

Just how important is it for us to read, understand, and apply the principles contained in this book that was heralded by this heavenly angel? Joseph Fielding Smith, Jr. stated: "No member of this Church can stand approved in the presence of God who has not seriously and carefully read The Book of Mormon". (C.R., 10/1961). The witness of the divinity of Jesus Christ gained through study of The Book of Mormon is an invaluable aid for those who desire to be valiant in the testimony of Jesus. Often, we marvel at the care with which the foundation was laid for the Restoration of the Gospel and the translation and publication of The Book of Mormon. Sometimes, however, we are guilty of carelessness in the diligence with which we actually study its pages. President Smith's statement is a reminder that we all need to sharpen our scholarship to a fine point.

Moroni's challenge, therefore, should be thoughtfully pondered. Every day, in fact, thousands put his promise to the test. When Heavenly Father placed His spirit children on the earth, he anticipated their initial ignorance of the saving principles of the Gospel. But His nurture of our spirits in the pre-earth existence had endowed each of us with a solid understanding of Gospel principles. It was only when we could learn no more in that setting, that we welcomed the opportunity to come to the earth to continue our education. (See Abraham 3:26, & Titus 1:2). We left our heavenly home with the assurance from our Father that, while on earth, we would have the Light of Christ and the influence of the Holy Ghost, and that heavenly power would help us to recognize the truth when we heard it. (See D&C 84:46, & 93:2). As Brigham Young declared: "Every Gospel principle carries within it a witness that it is true". In fact, Joseph Fielding Smith, Jr. who, like President Young, was a prophet, seer, and revelator, said that the witness of the Holy Ghost is more powerful than a vision or even the manifestation of heavenly messengers.

This concept is one of the beautiful simplicities of the Gospel. The Plan allows all of us to enjoy the same access to the simplest, and yet most powerful, witness to the truth. In an inarticulate voice softer than the faintest whisper of sweet breath on the cheek, the Holy Ghost gently testifies, or bears witness, of truth. As Moroni 10:5 teaches (in a verse that is often overlooked, in favor of the previous verse): "By the power of the Holy Ghost ye may know the truth of all things".

The Holy Ghost has revealed all that is true, and has illuminated every eternal principle that has guided the minds of men and women since the dawn of history. We constantly benefit from that which He reveals. In the Last Days, when the Spirit is "poured out upon all flesh, and when "young men see visions, and old men dream dreams", it will be the Holy Ghost Who provides the creative drive. (Joel 2:28). The irony is that many will fail to recognize the source of their inspiration. Job did not. He wrote: "For God speaketh once, yea twice, yet man perceiveth it not. In a dream, in a vision of the night, when deep sleep falleth upon men, in slumberings upon the bed; then he openeth the ears of men, and sealeth their instruction." (Job 33:14-16). We cannot help but think of the experience of Joseph Smith in his bedchamber, when we read Job's description of how Heavenly Father communicates with His children.

Of course, Jesus Christ wants us to have a testimony of the divine authenticity of The Book of Mormon. It has come to us through thousands of years of effort on the part of ancient prophets and after the personal sacrifice of countless individuals who have passed through the refiner's fire. The prophet Isaiah foresaw a "marvelous work and a wonder" that would not come to pass for another 2,700 years (Isaiah 29:14), and in the apocalyptic vision of John, another angel was seen "in the midst of heaven, having the everlasting Gospel to preach unto them that dwell on the earth, and to every nation, and kindred, and tongue, and people". (Revelation 14:6).

Precisely because The Book of Mormon is another testament, or second witness, of Jesus Christ, missionaries use it to great effect as a principal tool of conversion. The organization of the book is divinely inspired to assist Heavenly Father in His work to bring to pass our immortality and eternal life, by teaching us the principles of faith, repentance, baptism, and the ordinances of the priesthood. (See Moses 1:39).

All who desire to have a sure personal witnesses must carefully and prayerfully read The Book of Mormon, and then ask in faith if what they have studied is true. They will then receive the testimony of the Holy Ghost to motivate them to seek out the Priesthood and to enter into sacred covenants with God. It will be as it was on the Day of Pentecost, when Peter and others were preaching to a multitude whose hearts and minds were open and receptive to the truth. The words of the Apostles carried the weight of authority, and penetrated the hearts of their listeners to the end that they asked: "Men and brethren, what shall we do? Then Peter said unto them, Repent, and be baptized every one of you in the name of Jesus Christ for the remission of sins, and ye shall receive the gift of the Holy Ghost". (Acts 2:37-38). On that day, there were about 3,000 souls added to the kingdom of God on earth. (See Commentary Reference to 3 Nephi 15:21-24).

A similar scenario exists today. Since the Restoration of the Gospel, there has been a Pentecostal outpouring of the Spirit, and those with a sincere desire to understand the will of God bring the same humble petition to the doorstep of the missionaries: "Now that we have heard your message, have put it to the test of prayerful inquiry, and have received a witness of the Spirit, what shall we do?" The response of the servants of the Lord is unequivocal: "You must exercise saving faith that leads to the waters of baptism and to continuing commitment, dedicated discipleship, selfless service, and sustained spirituality".

Members of the Church believe they "must be called of God, by prophecy, and by the laying on of hands, by those who are in authority, to preach the Gospel, and to administer the ordinances thereof". (5th Article of Faith). The first ordinance of the Gospel following baptism is confirmation as a member of the Church together with the bestowal of the Holy Ghost. Even though many individuals receive their testimony of The Book of Mormon before becoming members of the Church, their expanding understanding will be further enhanced following their baptism as the Spirit unfolds to them the mysteries of the kingdom. As Joseph Smith wrote of his own experience almost two years after the organization of the Church: "By the power of the Spirit our eyes were opened and our understandings were enlightened, so as to see and understand the things of God". (D&C 76:12).

Critical to comprehension of the monumental themes contained within The Book of Mormon is familiarity with the underlying structure of the text. It is not too difficult to understand, as long as we remember that Mormon was the prophet who gathered all the records together and who then abridged certain of these into The Plates of Mormon. (See Mormon 1:1). This is the main reason why the text is called The Book of Mormon. In a larger sense, though, it is not really his book, alone.

The scope of its 531 pages is far-reaching, and its literary style was intentionally designed to focus on the core material rather than on its various authors. It is remarkable, however, that 15 major writing styles and personalities survived both abridgment and translation. The working vocabulary of 1 Nephi alone has 23% more words than comparable Old Testament sections, and although there are only 2,696 root words in the entire book, or only 10% of Shakespeare's working vocabulary, its depth is breathtaking. Sometimes, less is more.

Mormon said that he could not write "the hundredth part of the things of (his) people". (Words of Mormon 1:5, see Jacob 3:13, & Helaman 3:14). Even though Joseph Smith wrote in his history that the plates at the Hill Cumorah were deposited in the earth in a box fashioned out of stone, other sources indicate that there were many more plates in the collection at that site. (See Helaman 3:15). Brigham Young said that there was a whole room, with plates stacked high against the walls. Together, he said that they would comprise several wagon loads.

What we do have, swells in significance when we realize that the body of the records included in The Book of Mormon is a condensation of that which had been considered to be of most importance in the eyes of a long line of Nephite prophet-historians. Hugh Nibley rightly called the book "a blueprint for survival in the Last Days". As such, it is a detailed and accurate representation of a much larger structure. He said: "The events and situations that not many years ago seemed to some as wildly improbable and greatly overdrawn, have suddenly become the story of our times, and we see and shall see the words of the prophets who speak to us from the dust fearfully and wonderfully vindicated". ("The World and The Prophets", p. 196).

Nephi only started writing 30 years after leaving Jerusalem, which might give solace to those of us who have trouble maintaining the continuity of our own personal journals. He had plenty of time, beforehand, to distill in his mind just what he would include and how he would do it. Writing from the perspective of middle age might also have been an advantage, for hindsight always seems to be 20 / 20, and maturity often gives us a mentally, emotionally, and spiritually stable perspective that is too frequently lacking in youth.

First, he abridged the writings of his father that were collectively called The Book of Lehi, and then he made his own carefully constructed record. It took Nephi 10 years just to write the first 25 chapters, possibly because he wrote in a very stylized Hebraic pattern, the first nine chapters of 1 Nephi comprising a complex chiasm. Then, in chapters 10-22 he worked out a second, parallel chiasm. Note that Chapter 9 and Chapter 22 each end with a formal "Amen", signifying the end of that distinctive Hebraic literary device.

The Small Plates of Nephi in their entirety include the First and Second Books of Nephi, the Books of Jacob, Enos, Jarom, and Omni, and the Words of Mormon. These plates were placed in the repository at Cumorah for a reason that was unclear to Mormon. The Small Plates included a duplication of The Book of Lehi, an abridgement of which was written on The Large Plates of Nephi. The reason for their preservation became obvious only when Martin Harris lost the initial 116 pages of manuscript translation, forcing Joseph Smith to turn to The Small Plates of Nephi in order to translate a parallel history of the early Nephite record to be used as a substitute for the missing and potentially corrupted text.

The Small Plates of Nephi are always called "these plates". They were translated in the first-person tense, inasmuch as they came, not from an abridgement, but directly from the record of Nephi and his descendants, up to and including Omni. The period of history covered by these plates is slightly less than half of the Nephite history, or 470 out of a total of 1,021 years.

The Words of Mormon that follows Omni is an editorial insert written by Mormon in 385 A.D. and inserted by him in the record, to bridge the gap between The Small Plates of Nephi and The Plates of Mormon (his abridgement of the balance of The Large Plates of Nephi) that follow.

The literary labor of Mormon, called The Plates of Mormon, comprises The Books of Mosiah, Alma, Helaman, Third Nephi - The Book of Nephi, Fourth Nephi - The Book of Nephi, and The Book of Mormon chapters 1-7. When reading from the translation of The Plates of Mormon, the text is generally in the third person tense, inasmuch as it is an abridgement from The Large Plates of Nephi. When Mormon inserted editorial comments throughout his abridgement, it was written in the first-person tense., often accompanied by the phrase "and thus we see." When reading 1 Nephi through Omni, "those plates" means The Large Plates of Nephi that follow The Words of Mormon in the format of The Book of Mormon. The Plates of Mormon also included writings of Mormon's son Moroni. These are found in The Book of Mormon Chapters 8 & 9, and in The Book of Moroni.

The Book of Ether is an abridgment from an ancient record that was written upon 24 gold plates found by the people of King Limhi in the days of King Mosiah. At least a portion of these plates was abridged by Moroni, either from Mosiah's earlier translation or directly from The Plates of Ether. Moroni inserted editorial comments of his own, and included this record in a general history under the title "The Book of Ether". (See Ether 1:1-2).

At great expense and personal risk, Lehi's sons retrieved The Plates of Brass from Jerusalem. They contained "the five books of Moses (or the first five books of the Old Testament), and also a record of the Jews from the beginning down to the commencement of the reign of Zedekiah, king of Judah; and also, the prophecies of the holy prophets". (1 Nephi 5:11-13). Consequently, many of the writings of the prophet Isaiah are prominently found upon The Plates of Brass.

"The version of Isaiah in the Nephite scripture hews an independent course for itself, as might be expected of a truly ancient and authentic record. It makes additions to the present text in certain places, omits material in others, transposes, makes grammatical changes, finds support at times for its unusual readings in the ancient Greek, Syriac, and Latin Versions, and at other times no support at all. In general, it presents phenomena of great interest to the student of Isaiah". (Sydney B. Sperry, "Book of Mormon Compendium", p. 512).

"The text of Isaiah in The Book of Mormon is not word for word the same as that of the King James Translation. Of 433 verses of Isaiah in the Nephite record, Joseph Smith modified 234. Some of the changes were slight, while others were radical. However, 199 verses are word for word the same as the K.J.T. We, therefore, freely admit that Joseph Smith may have used the K.J.T. when he came to the text of Isaiah on the plates. As long as the K.J.T. agreed substantially with the text on the plates, he let it pass; when it differed significantly, he translated the Nephite version and dictated the necessary changes". (Sydney B. Sperry, "Book of Mormon Compendium", p. 507-508).

As Hugh Nibley has pointed out: "Resemblances between the Bible and The Book of Mormon are not hard to explain and are confirmation of authenticity. If The Book of Mormon is what it says it is, we should expect to find within its pages a strong biblical influence. Its prophets sound like those of the Old Testament because they studied and consciously quoted the words of those prophets, and all prophets moreover are programmed to sound alike, being called for the same purpose, under much the same conditions". ("Churches in The Wilderness").

The Plates of Brass were the Nephite scriptures, and included therein was the written record of their family histories and genealogies. They were revered by the Nephites, as evidenced by frequent quotations from and references to them throughout The Book of Mormon. As Nephi explained: "And I did read many things unto them which were written in the books of Moses; but that I might more fully persuade them to believe in the Lord their Redeemer I did read unto them that which was written by the prophet Isaiah; for I did liken all scriptures unto us, that it might be for our profit and learning". (1 Nephi 1:23).

The "books of Moses" to which Nephi referred concern the Pentateuch, Torah, or The Law. These are not to be confused with The Book of Moses in The Pearl of Great Price. Nephi's books of Moses were, in fact, the principal scriptures of the Jews. From these books of The Law, there sprang up an encyclopedic interpretation by the Jews at Jerusalem called The Talmud.

Readers of The Book of Mormon will repeatedly encounter direct references to Isaiah in its text. As a matter of fact, 32% of The Book of Isaiah is quoted in The Book of Mormon, while 3% is paraphrased. Following the pattern established earlier in The Book of Mormon, in the New Testament there are more quotations attributable to Isaiah than to all other Old Testament prophets combined. It is little wonder that The Book of Mormon should rely so heavily on Isaiah, however, since his prophecies not only reflect Old World religious philosophy, but also a latter-day world view and testament of Jesus Christ.

Nephi delighted in the words of Isaiah, and recorded 2 Nephi Chapters 12-24 in an effort to prove the truth of Christ's coming, and that save He should come, we must perish. Isaiah was what we call a "Messianic Prophet" whose principal mission was to point us toward the Savior, to His teachings, and to salvation through obedience to the principles of His Gospel.

During the ministry of Isaiah, the Ten Tribes were taken captive and later fled to the north where they were swallowed up and lost to history. But they carried with them the words of Isaiah, just as Lehi did in his journey to the Promised Land. (See D&C 133:26 & 2 Nephi 29:13-14). The Jews also retained Isaiah's words, and today, Covenant Israel, or the Church, has them. His is a very diversified audience.

Nephi knew that the words of Isaiah would be as a pearl of great price in the Last Days, and to those who would suppose that they are not, he said "I (will) speak particularly, and confine the words unto mine own people; for I know that they shall be of great worth unto them in the last days; for in that day shall they understand them; wherefore, for their good have I written them". (2 Nephi 25:8). Nephi considered the writings of Isaiah, who had lived just over a century earlier, to be scripture. Clearly, he understood that whatsoever the prophets speak when moved upon by the Spirit, "shall be the will of the Lord, shall be the mind of the Lord, shall be the word of the Lord, shall be the voice of the Lord, and the power of God unto salvation". (D&C 68:4).

Today, it is the clear responsibility of members of the Church to carefully and prayerfully study the prophecies of Isaiah, for they were meant for our generation. His language might be veiled in symbolism and shadows of meaning with which we are not superficially familiar. Nevertheless, we have been commanded by the Savior Himself "Seek ye out of the best books words of wisdom; seek learning, even by study and also by faith" (D&C 88:118) and "live by every word that proceedeth forth from the mouth of God". (D&C 84:44).

Nephi recognized Isaiah's witness of the Lord Jesus Christ as pre-eminent among the testimonies of the prophets. It should be no surprise that the Savior declared to the Nephite Saints: "And now, behold, I say unto you, that ye ought to search (his teachings). Yea, a commandment I give unto you that ye search these things diligently; for great are the words of Isaiah". (3 Nephi 23:1). The main reason for the scriptures, after all, is to persuade us to believe in Christ. This is why the prophets all seem to sound alike. They all draw upon the same eternal truths to prove their points. Theirs is not vain repetition, but rather theatrical encore. "The prophets do have much the same message, and the now recognized practice by the prophets of giving out the words of their predecessors as their own receives its first clear statement and justification in The Book of Mormon". (Hugh Nibley, "Since Cumorah", p. 40-41).

Shakespeare wrote: "The past is prologue". ("The Tempest", Act 2, scene 1, 245-254). The phrase was intended to imply that our past is merely a prologue, or an introduction, to the great adventure upon which we will embark if we follow through on our plans. This original interpretation teaches that what has come before on our journey through life doesn't matter in the grand scheme of things, because a new future lies before us, subject to the choices we will yet make. The human condition does not change much over time, which is one reason why the Lord has revealed The Book of Mormon in the Last Days, so that we might profit from the experiences of the Nephites who are distant from us in time and yet are so like us.

Hugh Nibley observed: "The tragedy of the Nephites, who brought destruction by war upon their own heads, was not what became of them, but rather what they themselves became". ("Since Cumorah", p. 425). "A man's character is his fate", wrote the Greek philosopher Heraclitus. The Nephite scriptures are a study in human frailties, and the epic drama that unfolds before our minds' eye strengthens and clarifies our moral and ethical values.

In The Book of Mormon, "we are not laying down ground rules for taste, or saying that it is good because some people like it, or bad because others do not. What we are saying is that whatever one may think of it, is one of the great realities of our time, and that what makes it so is that millions of people believe it. Its literary or artistic qualities do not enter into the discussion. It was written to be believed. It's one and only merit is truth. Without that merit, it is all that non-believers say it is. With it, it is all that believers say it is". (Hugh Nibley, "Of All Things", p. 93). With this historical perspective, an abiding testimony in the divinity of the work, and an anticipation of enlightenment throughout the journey, let us commit and re-commit ourselves to a lifetime study of this keystone text.

To rely
upon our own
impotent efforts
to improve the quality
of our lives, instead of upon
the boundless grace of God that
is evident throughout The Book of
Mormon, reduces the Plan of God
to a crude caricature that is
without meaning and
substance.

"Those who gain (a) divine witness
from the Holy Spirit will also come to know
by the same power that Jesus Christ is the Savior
of the world, that Joseph Smith is His revelator and
prophet in these last days and that The Church of
Jesus Christ of Latter-day Saints is the Lord's
kingdom once again established on the
earth, preparatory to the Second
Coming of the Messiah."
(Introduction).

The First Book of Nephi
His Reign and Ministry
Around 600 B.C. to 588 - 570 B.C.

First Nephi
Chapter 1

"I, Nephi, having been born of goodly parents, therefore I was taught somewhat in all the learning of my father". (V. 1). In this, the opening verse of The Book of Mormon, Nephi gave tribute to both of his parents, although his father received the credit for his education. It must have been intellectually stimulating growing up in the home of a prosperous merchant with international connections. Actually, Lehi was a product of three cultures: Hebrew, Egyptian, and the desert. In time, his familiarity with life in the wilderness along the caravan routes would prove invaluable to his family's welfare.

Nephi revealed that his father was schooled in "the learning of the Jews and the language of the Egyptians". (V. 2). Lehi's commercial interests would have required him to converse fluently with his Egyptian trading partners; nevertheless, his native tongue was Hebrew. The record of Nephi, referred to in this verse, referred to his abridgement of The Book of Lehi that comprises the first 9 chapters of The First Book of Nephi. It was written in the words of his father in his native Hebrew. The stylized and abbreviated "reformed Egyptian" to which Moroni referred a thousand years later, was only developed by later Nephite historians. (See 1 Nephi 3:15, Omni 1:17, & Mormon 9:32).

With his family, Lehi dwelt "at Jerusalem" or in the land of Jerusalem, but probably not in the city itself. (V. 4). Nevertheless, he was a contemporary of, and probably was acquainted with, the prophet Jeremiah, as well as Habakkuk, Zephaniah, and Nahum, all of whom preached in the city at about the same time. Lehi shared the apprehension of all these prophets regarding Israel's apostasy.

"And in that same year there came many prophets, prophesying unto the people that they must repent, or the great city Jerusalem must be destroyed". (V. 4, see Commentary Reference to 2 Nephi 6:8). As the Bible records: "Howbeit I sent unto you all my servants the prophets ... But (Israel) hearkened not, nor inclined (her) ear to turn from (her) wickedness ... Wherefore my fury and mine anger was poured forth, and was kindled in the cities of Judah and in the streets of Jerusalem". (Jeremiah 44:4-6).

Lehi's concern prompted him to pray "unto the Lord, yea even with all his heart, in behalf of his people". (V. 5). As a result, he had a "Theophany" comparable to that of Joseph Smith in the Sacred Grove. "And it came to pass as he prayed unto the Lord, there came a pillar of fire and dwelt upon a rock before him; and he saw and heard much; and because of the things which he saw and heard he did quake and tremble exceedingly". (V. 6).

He "saw One descending out of the midst of heaven, and he beheld that his luster was above that of the sun at noonday". (V. 9). Nine verses in this chapter summarize the experience of his father, and Nephi concluded them by writing: "And after this manner was the language of my father in the praising of his God". (V. 15). We can only guess how descriptive Lehi's own narrative must have been. Unfortunately, that first person account was part of the 116 pages of manuscript lost by Joseph Smith during the translation of Mormon's abridgement of The Book of Lehi. At least the Prophet Joseph had the opportunity to enrich his own personal understanding of the record of Father Lehi and enjoy a familiarity with his writings that has been denied to the rest of us.

Nephi explained that he would not make a full account, but only an abridgement of his father's record. 1 Nephi Chapters 1-8, recorded on The Small Plates of Nephi, are that abridgement of The Book of Lehi. As Nephi wrote: "Behold, I make an abridgment of the record of my father upon plates which I have made with mine own hands; wherefore, after I have abridged the record of my father, then will I make an account of mine own life". (V. 17). Chapter 9 is a transitional chapter, and 1 Nephi 10 through 2 Nephi 33 is Nephi's own account.

Having received a divine commission to prophesy to the people, Lehi returned to the city of Jerusalem. He likely counseled against an alliance with Egypt, which was the direction in which the rulers in Jerusalem were leading the country. At that time, Judah was a vassal state of Babylonia, and Lehi correctly foresaw that an alliance with Egypt would bring the wrath of Babylon down upon Judah.

But "it came to pass that the Jews did mock him because of the things which he testified of them". (V. 19). They rejected his message, and tried to stone Lehi for prophesying not only of the fate of Jerusalem, but also of the Messiah Who was to come. "They were angry with him; yea, even as with the prophets of old". (V. 20). In a similar fashion, the Second Book of Chronicles reveals that the people "mocked the messenger of God, and despised his words, and misused the prophets, until the wrath of the Lord arose against his people, till there was no remedy". (2 Chronicles 36:16).

The same conditions exist today, as the Lord's servants try to warn the people. They are generally ignored, often mocked and despised, and sometimes persecuted for their efforts. When Lehi delivered his message to a hostile audience in Jerusalem, his life was put in jeopardy, setting a pattern for the treatment of Nephite prophets over the next thousand years.

In his record that follows, Nephi went to great lengths to compile approximately 30 proofs that the Lord will deliver those who obey Him and endure in faith. "But behold, I, Nephi, will show unto you that the tender mercies of the Lord are over all those whom he hath chosen, because of their faith, to make them mighty even unto the power of deliverance". (V. 20). Throughout its pages, The Book of Mormon illustrates time and again how this is the case.

First Nephi
Chapter 2

Nephi had no use for "the Jews at Jerusalem". (V. 3, see 2 Nephi 30:4, Alma 11:4, & 4 Nephi 1:31). Consequently, his record wastes no time in shifting its focus of attention. Because there was no other remedy or option, the Lord directed Lehi to depart with his family from the land of Jerusalem into the wilderness. He was given assurances that the forced exodus would be in its best interest, for the Lord told him: "Blessed art thou Lehi, because of the things which thou hast done", and He continued: "Because thou hast been faithful and declared unto this people the things which I commanded thee, behold, they seek to take away thy life". (V. 1). Truly, "the guilty taketh the truth to be hard, for it cutteth them to the very center". (1 Nephi 16:2). But ironically, speaking with such power that mob action is incited can actually be a measure of one's honesty, integrity, and obedience.

Being a trader, Lehi was accustomed to pulling up stakes on a moment's notice, and Nephi accepted the sudden departure of his family without surprise or comment in the record. "And it came to pass that he departed into the wilderness. And he left his house, and the land of his inheritance, and his gold, and his silver, and his precious things, and took nothing with him, save it were his family, and provisions, and tents, and departed into the wilderness". (V. 4, see Commentary Reference to 3 Nephi 6:2). Lehi never looked back as he left forever the land of his birth. He would never again have use for the telestial trinkets he had accumulated. There is no record that his family questioned their departure at this time. If Nephi or any of the other children had asked about the family's welfare, Lehi might have simply responded as Father Abraham had answered his son Isaac, as they readied for sacrifice upon Mount Moriah: "God will provide". (Genesis 22:8).

The party struck out into the "wilderness", which was the uninhabited land of the Arabian Peninsula. This area is even today called the Rub al Khali, or "Empty Quarter". It was inhospitable, and the only road through it was the caravan route that was even then called the Frankincense Trail. As Lehi's party entered the Rub al Khali, it was swallowed up and disappeared in a matter of days without leaving a trace.

The group consisted of Lehi, Sariah, their sons Laman, Lemuel, Sam, and Nephi, and an unspecified number of daughters. In fact, Sariah is one of only three women mentioned by name in the Book of Mormon. The others are Abish (Alma 19:16) and Isabel (Alma 39:3).

Laman and Lemuel are Arabic names, reflecting Lehi's ties to the desert, and Sam, which is an Arabic form of Shem, is an Egyptian name, consistent with Lehi's economic relationship with that country.

It is in this chapter that we encounter the first cultural details that mark The Book of Mormon with the indelible stamp of authenticity. For example, the party stopped "in a valley by the side of a river of water." (V. 6). The Semitic phraseology is striking, for in the desert, it was noteworthy when one actually encountered running water. The contrasting term in Arabic, which is the equivalent of a dry gulch, is "wadi".

The time-honored tradition in ancient times was to commemorate the establishment of an encampment, so Lehi "built an altar of stones, and made an offering unto the Lord, and gave thanks." (V. 7). Such rock cairns, dating from before the time of Christ, are still found throughout the Arabian Peninsula.

Then Lehi, according to custom, named the river after his eldest son, and entreated Laman to be like unto it, "continually running into the fountain of all righteousness!" (V. 9). As a desert dweller, he was naturally concerned that a water source might dry up, and he used the figure of speech to powerful effect, with dramatic imagery that could not have been lost on both Laman and Lemuel.

Then Lehi employed a typical Arab vocative, "Ya Laitaka", as he encouraged his second son. "O that thou mightest be like unto this valley, firm and steadfast, and immoveable in keeping the commandments of the Lord!" (V. 10, see Commentary Reference to 3 Nephi 6:14). To the Western mind, this seems all wrong, for since when were valleys firm and steadfast? Surely, Lehi must have meant to liken his son to the mountains, which we all know are solid and enduring. But no, the valleys have always been the routes of travel for the caravans of the Near East, and have made passage through the rugged mountains possible. From Lehi's perspective, the simile is absolutely correct.

His concern for Laman and Lemuel was well-founded, because in the next few verses, we encounter the first rumblings of discontent from these sons. "And thus, Laman and Lemuel, being the eldest, did murmur against their father." (V. 12). That they had neither paid the price to develop independent testimonies of the principles of the Gospel nor had learned the language of the Spirit, was now coming back to haunt them. In straitened circumstances, they did not have the solid foundation upon which independent witnesses are grounded.

Murmuring is the subdued and continually repeated expression of indistinct or inarticulate complaint or grumbling. Like an earthquake, murmuring can build into harmonic waves with the power to undermine the foundation of relationships and institutions. Because those who murmur expect results without responsibility, it is a cowardly act. While it is often conducted anonymously or within the cloak of secrecy, its effect is felt publicly. Those who murmur want a tangible return without having made a legitimate initial investment. (See Essay: "Speak Kind Words To Each Other").

Later in The Book of Mormon, the prophet historian Mormon wrote of the many thoughtless words that the people did "imagine up in their hearts, which were foolish and vain; and they were much disturbed, for Satan did stir them up to do iniquity continually; yea, he did go about spreading rumors and contentions upon all the face of the land, that he might harden the hearts of the people against that which was good and against that which should come." (Helaman 16:22). We see in the murmuring of Laman and Lemuel these very seeds of apostasy.

Lehi's elder sons had stood to inherit all that they had left behind in Jerusalem. They resented the fact that their father "had led them out of the land of Jerusalem, to leave the land of their inheritance, and their gold, and their silver, and their precious things, to perish in the wilderness." (V. 11). They were so focused upon their worldly goods that they failed to recognize the hand of the Lord working in their behalf. The same Spirit that had confirmed Lehi's blessing for obedience could not penetrate the sclerotic souls of Laman and Lemuel to bear the same sure witness. They only saw before them an old man who had been led astray by "the foolish imaginations of his heart," and they murmured "because knew not the dealings of that God Who had created them." (V. 11-12). To their ears, the voice of the Spirit spoke in a foreign tongue, incomprehensible and nonsensical to their carnal minds.

Thus, Lehi exhorted his elder sons in the only way that they could understand. "With power, being filled with the Spirit", he reasoned with them, "until their frames did shake before him. And he did confound them, that they durst not utter against him; wherefore, they did as he commanded them." (V. 14). When their physical senses were stimulated, they recognized the power, if not the authority, of their father's words. For Nephi's part, he simply wrote: "And my father dwelt in a tent." (V. 15). He needed to say no more, for Lehi was a sheik of the desert, and when he sat in his tent, he was the family's absolute and undisputed ruler.

Nephi was grieved, however, by the behavior of Laman and Lemuel, and he sought his own confirmation from the Spirit, that his father was indeed a capable and inspired patriarch. "Having great desires to know of the mysteries of God ... I did cry unto the Lord; and behold he did visit me, and did soften my heart, that I did believe all the words which had been spoken to my father; wherefore, I did not rebel against him like unto my brethren." (V. 16). After he had received this witness, he testified to Sam, who also believed. (V. 17).

Nephi was also told other important things by the Spirit. First, he learned that the party would be led to a "land of promise." (V. 20). This is the first time such a land had been mentioned, and it may have come as a great surprise to Nephi. However, many groups over the years had left Jerusalem in search of lands of promise. The Dead Sea Covenanters who lived at Qumran near the shores of the Salt Sea are today the most conspicuous. Certainly, there were righteous families other than Lehi's who were led by the Spirit to forsake the degenerating conditions in Israel.

Secondly, Nephi learned that he would become a "ruler and a teacher" over his brethren. (V. 22). Because he was the younger son, this must have come as quite a shock. It definitely ran counter to the normal order of things, and would later prove to be a major point of contention for Laman and Lemuel.

At this time, Nephi also learned that he and his brethren would have a great posterity. The Spirit suggested that his descendants would be righteous, and those of Laman and Lemuel would not. "For behold, in that day that they shall rebel against me, I will curse them even with a sore curse, and they shall have no power over thy seed except they shall rebel against me also." (V. 23, see Commentary Reference to 1 Nephi 3:29). But he also learned that the Lord would use the descendants of his brethren to "be a scourge unto (the seed of Nephi), to stir them up in the ways of remembrance." (V. 24). As we read The Book of Mormon, we see that this was repeatedly the case.

"The Lord spake unto my father, yea, even in a dream, and said unto him: Blessed at thou Lehi, because of the things which thou hast done; and because thou hast been faithful and declared unto this people the things which I commanded thee, behold, they seek to take away thy life. And it came to pass that the Lord commanded my father, even in a dream, that he should take his family and depart into the wilderness. And it came to pass that he was obedient unto the word of the Lord, wherefore, he did as the Lord commanded him." (1 Nephi 2:13, see Job 33:15:16).

First Nephi
Chapter 3

Chapters 3-7 chronicle the events that transpired during the year following the party's departure from Jerusalem. At an encampment near the Gulf of Aqaba, "the fountain the Red Sea" aboout 320 kilometers from the city, Lehi revealed the Lord's command that a party return to Jerusalem to secure their family history, the "record of the Jews, and also a genealogy of (their) forefathers", engraven upon The Plates of Brass. (V. 2).

In Semitic languages, the noun always precedes the adjective, and so in The Book of Mormon, we always read about "Plates of Brass", the "Sword of Laban", or "genealogy of our forefathers", etc. and never about "Brass Plates", "Laban's sword", or our forefathers' genealogy, as would be the custom in English.

Inasmuch as The Plates of Brass, containing Lehi's genealogical records, were in Laban's possession, it is possible that he and Lehi were related. "For behold, Laban hath the record of the Jews, and also a genealogy of my forefathers, and they are engraven upon plates of brass." (V. 3, see also 1 Nephi 5:14-16).

Verse 7 reveals the depth of Nephi's faith. We could each inset our own name, and review this verse regularly. "I will go and do the things which the Lord hath commanded, for I know that the Lord giveth no commandments unto the children of men, save he shall prepare a way fore them that they may accomplish the thing which he commanded them."

Accordingly, the brothers returned to Jerusalem, and at this point in the record, we encounter the language found throughout The Book of Mormon when geographical references relating to elevation are made: "And it came to pass that when we had gone up to the land of Jerusalem..." (V. 10). Jerusalem lies in the hill country of Judea, and anyone traveling to that city would naturally gain elevation; hence, the record states that the brothers went "up" on their journey (and down on their return to Lehi's encampment). (See also v. 15, and Commentary References to Omni 1:13 & 27).

Laban was a ruler among the Jews at Jerusalem, and his treasury was the repository of The Plates of Brass. His vile reputation must have been well known, because none of the brothers were anxious to see him. In typical Hebrew practice, they drew lots to determine who would be given the dubious honor. (V. 11). The lot fell upon Laman, who entered the house of Laban and asked if he might be given the records. Laban's response was that of a typical Oriental potentate: "Behold, thou art a robber," he exclaimed, "and I will slay thee." (V. 13).

Laman escaped to tell the tale to his brothers, who, with the exception of Nephi, were inclined to return to camp without the plates. It was Nephi who drew the line, taking an oath that he would not return until he had secured that for which they had come and for which they had risked so much. "But behold, I said unto them that: As the Lord liveth, and as we live, we will not go down unto our father in the wilderness until we have accomplished the thing which the Lord hath commanded us." (V. 15).

Besides, he said, they needed the plates in order to preserve their language. "It is wisdom in God that we should obtain these records, that we may preserve unto our children the language of our fathers." (V. 19, see also 1 Nephi 1:2). Just how important this was would become clear later in the narrative. (See Omni 1:17). It is also possible that the language to which Nephi was referring in this verse was specific doctrinal instruction contained on The Plates of Brass. Nephi wrote in the following verse that it would be important to have the plates in order to preserve "the words which have been spoken by the mouth of all the holy prophets, which have been delivered unto them by the Spirit and power of God, since the world began, even down unto this present time. And it came to pass that after that manner of language did I persuade my brethren." (V. 20-21).

Another attempt was made to secure the plates, this time by purchase with all of the treasures that had been left behind in Lehi's home at Jerusalem. But even this generous offer was rejected, and all the accumulated wealth of the family fell into the hands of the unscrupulous Laban. There was method to the madness, however for Lehi's sons were taught an important lesson, that they might put the value of their worldly goods in its proper perspective. The Lord wanted to emphasize to them that they should rely upon His power alone, and not on the worth of telestial trinkets, to accomplish His purposes.

In any event, Laman and Lemuel became so angry with Nephi that, in frustration, they began beating him and Sam with a rod. (V. 28). At this point, an angel intervened, saying: Why do ye smite your younger brother with a rod? Know ye not that the Lord hath chosen him to be a ruler over you?" (V. 29). This was a most significant declaration, because the staff was a badge of independence and authority in the ancient Near East, and that man who held one thereby demonstrated his position and superiority over his contemporaries. It was the intention of Laman and Lemuel to show Nephi just who was in charge, by hitting him with a rod. But the interceding angel had something else in mind. Did they not know that Nephi was to be a ruler over them, and not the other way around?

Laman and Lemuel quickly reverted to their true form and character, however, because no sooner had the angel departed than they began to murmur anew, "saying, how is it possible that the Lord will deliver Laban into our hands? Behold, he is a mighty man, and he can command fifty." (V. 31). The typical garrison of a city like Jerusalem was 50 soldiers, and the two brothers were in awe of Laban, who was in command of so many troops. This episode is a classic example of the faithless fearing the arm of flesh, rather than trusting in the power of God. It also illustrates the principle that faith precedes the miracle, and that when a sign is given to the faithless, it is shrugged off, its significance is ignored, and they go right on doing as they have always done.

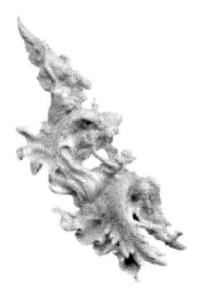

First Nephi
Chapter 4

In this chapter, we see how Nephi's resolute nature fueled his efforts to motivate his brethren to return one more time to Jerusalem, so that with the Lord's help they might accomplish their mission. To reinforce the reality of divine intervention to his brethren, he cited the miracle that had been performed by Moses when he parted the waters of the Red Sea. "Therefore, let us go up", Nephi said. "Let us be strong like unto Moses". (V. 2). Truly, even the elements obey the voice of priesthood authority. "Wherefore can ye doubt?" he asked. (V. 3, see 1 Nephi 17:50, & Jacob 4:6). Certainly, Nephi reasoned, if the brothers would only follow the Spirit, they might secure the records from a wicked man.

Accordingly, late in the evening, Nephi crept into the city alone. In those times, it was very dangerous to be on the streets after dark. Today we take for granted the electrification of our cities, but the Ancients had no such luxuries, and were ever at the mercy of lawless individuals who operated under the cover of darkness. Nephi did have one great advantage, however, for he wrote that he "was led by the Spirit, not knowing beforehand the things which (he) should do". (V. 6).

In Jerusalem, it was the custom to take an armed guard when one had to be out at night. The fact that Nephi encountered Laban, drunk and alone, indicates that things must have been very serious indeed for Judah. Laban had probably been at a clandestine meeting of the leaders of the city to discuss its political crisis, and he had gone alone in order to maintain its secrecy. Perhaps only his servant had known his whereabouts, for Nephi wrote that he later "spake unto (him) concerning the elders of the Jews, he knowing that his master, Laban, had been out by night among them". (V. 22).

Nephi recorded that, once he had discovered the identity of the figure lying prostrate in the street before him, he was constrained by the Spirit to kill Laban. (V. 10). There follows a lengthy justification for doing so. Obviously, Nephi was not comfortable about fulfilling the obligation, for he required 8 verses to explain the action. Nevertheless, when the Spirit told him that "the Lord slayeth the wicked to bring forth his righteous purposes (and) it is better that one man should perish than that a nation should dwindle and perish in unbelief", Nephi carried out the gruesome assignment. (V. 13, see Commentary Reference to Omni 1:17).

Afterward, Nephi donned Laban's clothing and went to the treasury where the records were kept. The servant of Laban must have been anxiously awaiting word of how the meeting had gone, so he inquired of Nephi, supposing it was his master to whom he was speaking. Nephi responded "as if it had been Laban" and ordered the servant to bring the plates and follow. (V. 23).

When Zoram, the servant of Laban, realized what was happening, he was frightened, but Nephi seized him, and in order to calm him, made an oath, whispering forcefully into his ear: "As the Lord liveth, and as I live", your life will be spared. It is a barometer of just how bad things must have been in Jerusalem at this time to see how Zoram immediately transferred his loyalty to the family of Lehi, seeing in them an avenue of escape from an increasingly intolerable situation. Zoram, in turn, made his own oath of fealty to the brothers. It is a measure of the power of the Semitic oath that, as soon as it was made, Nephi reported that their "fears did cease concerning him". (V. 37).

First Nephi
Chapter 5

Meanwhile, back at the camp, Sariah began to complain. She echoed the assessment of Laman and Lemuel, calling Lehi a visionary man. (V. 2). In this moment of faltering faith, she must have been overwhelmed by the prospect of the probable loss of her precious sons. Lehi responded with carefully measured control, agreeing with his wife that he was a visionary man. After all, it had been at the express command of God that he had sent their boys back to Jerusalem to secure The Plates of Brass. Lehi's spiritual sensitivity had also been responsible for the flight of the family into the wilderness while the rest of Judah remained in Jerusalem, ignorantly waiting to be slain or to be taken captive by Babylonian invaders who were even then mustering to do battle.

Only when their sons did return was Sariah comforted. (V. 7). She exclaimed: "Now I know of a surety that the Lord hath commanded my husband to flee into the wilderness; yea, and I also know of a surety that the Lord hath protected my sons". (V. 8). How much better would it have been, however, had she maintained the sustained faith of Lehi and Nephi. Perhaps her fear can be forgiven her when one acknowledges the pressure she must have been under in these unusual circumstances. In any event, when the family was once again reunited, everyone was thrilled, and a sacrifice and, according to Hebrew custom, burnt offerings were made unto the Lord. (V. 9).

Lehi was anxious to examine the recently acquired Plates of Brass, and the balance of this chapter is a discussion of their contents. "He did search them from the beginning. And he beheld that they did contain the five books of Moses, which gave an account of the creation of the world, and also of Adam and Eve, who were our first parents; and also a record of the Jews from the beginning, even down to the commencement of the reign of Zedekiah, (the then current) king of Judah; and also the prophecies of the holy prophets, from the beginning, even down to the commencement of the reign of Zedekiah; and also many prophecies which have been spoken by the mouth of Jeremiah". (V. 10-13). Since the five books of Moses were included, a plausible source for Native American creation stories that parallel Biblical accounts is also established.

Lehi then confirmed from the genealogical records contained on the plates that he was a descendant of Joseph through Manasseh. "And it came to pass that my father, Lehi, also found upon The Plates of Brass a genealogy of his fathers; wherefore he knew that he was a descendant of Joseph. And Laban also was a descendant of Joseph, wherefore he and his fathers had kept the records". (V. 14 & 16, see 2 Nephi 3:4, & Alma 10:3). From this statement, we can logically conclude that Lehi held the Melchizedek Priesthood, inasmuch as he was not a Levite, which was the only tribe in Israel authorized to hold the Aaronic Priesthood. Therefore, the authority held by the Nephites down to the time of Christ must have been Melchizedek Priesthood.

In verse 16, we learn that one of the first things Nephi did after the Great Separation was build a temple. "And I, Nephi, did build a temple, and I did construct it after the manner of the temple of Solomon save it were not built of so many precious things ... But the manner of the construction was like unto the temple of Solomon, and the workmanship thereof was exceedingly fine." "Why gather the people of God into a Church?" asked the Prophet Joseph Smith. He said: "The main object was to build unto the Lord a house whereby He could reveal unto His people the ordinances of His house and the glories of His kingdom and teach the people the way of salvation." (H.C., 5:423). When we have completely internalized the principles of the Gospel so that the conduct of our lives is in complete harmony with the Law of Heaven, we will all be "made free, and partakers of the heavenly gift." (4 Nephi 2-3). This path of discipleship leads to the temple, which "is a machine for the making of gods." (Henri Bergson).

Joseph Smith could have been referring to the teachings of The Book of Mormon, when he wrote: "This is good doctrine. It tastes good. I can taste the principles of eternal life, and so can you. They are given to me by the revelations of Jesus Christ; and I know that ... you believe them. I can taste the spirit of eternal life. I know it is good, and when I tell you of these things which were given me by inspiration of the Holy Spirit, you are bound to receive them as sweet, and rejoice." ("Teachings," p. 355).

Then, in verse 19, Lehi prophesied that the doctrine upon the plates from which The Book of Mormon was translate should never "be dimmed any more by time". Good quality brass contains a high percentage of zinc, but it is difficult to write on such a metal. More zinc produces a brass-like alloy that is soft enough to make inscriptions with a stylus, but is more susceptible to tarnishing. (See Alma 37:5). Perhaps Lehi's figure of speech referred to the physical qualities of The Plates of Brass. But since he was a visionary man, it is likely that he was also referring to the ability of the plates to convey spiritual insight to his descendants who should later possess the records. Being filled with the Spirit, Lehi prophesied: "These plates of brass should go forth unto all nations, kindreds, tongues, and people who were of his seed". (V. 18).

Lehi and his son Nephi "had kept the commandments wherewith the Lord had commanded (them). And (they) had obtained the records which the Lord had commanded (them), and searched them, and found that they were desirable". (V. 20-21). They were flushed with confidence because of their renewed and reinvigorated faith that whenever the Lord would henceforth give the command, they would be ready and able to continue the journey "in the wilderness towards the land of promise". (V. 22).

First Nephi
Chapter 6

Nephi indicated in this chapter that he would not include in his record any of the genealogies found upon The Plates of Brass, because they would take up too much room, and he desired to write only about "the things of God". (V. 3). Besides, he concluded, family histories were included in The Book of Lehi. Unfortunately, these histories were lost when Martin Harris mishandled the first 116 pages of the manuscript translation of The Large Plates of Nephi.

It was Nephi's desire that the content of The Small Plates focus on the religious history of his people, and he was quite specific that those who kept the record after him should pay heed to this instruction. (V. 6). He also reiterated that his full intention was to "persuade men to come unto the God of Abraham, and the God of Isaac, and the God of Jacob, and be saved". (V. 4, see Commentary Reference to 1 Nephi 1:20). Thus, we are given a preview by Nephi of the contents of The Small Plates of Nephi specifically and of The Book of Mormon generally.

These records will not interest the world, whose preoccupation is in the gratification of its physical appetites. Rather, they address the spiritual hunger of the obedient, who exhibit child-like faith. As Nephi wrote: "The things which are pleasing unto the world I do not write, but (I will write) the things which are pleasing unto God and unto those who are not of the world. (V. 5).

The Savior taught: "Except ye be converted, and become as little children, ye shall not enter into the kingdom of heaven". (Matthew 18:3). A righteous descendant of Nephi said of such innocents that a heavenly host descended "out of heaven as it were in the midst of fire; and they came down and encircled (them) about, and ... angels did minister unto them". (3 Nephi 17:24).

Of such experiences, Truman Madsen wrote: "Maybe we are not born an empty tablet upon which the chalk of childhood writes. Maybe a child has swift, untinctured affinity and response to his own burning deeps. He has a whole, happy, healthy relationship with the core of creativity and spirituality, which is his glory-laden spirit. If so, the explicit and expansive messages of the Messiah, 'bringing all things to their remembrance,' would shine more clearly through the boy Samuel, the boy Nephi, or the boy Joseph. That would explain the verse, added by the Prophet to the Biblical account of the youth of Christ Himself: 'He needed not that any man should teach Him.' (J.S.T. Matthew 3:24-26). God, to reveal Himself to Christ, needed only to reveal Christ to Himself, in 'the glory he had with Him before the foundations of the world.' Is it any different with us?" ("Eternal Man", p. 77).

With prophetic insight, Nephi recognized that The Book of Mormon would be a tremendous tool of conversion to bring us to the knowledge of our Redeemer and unfold to our view a more realistic understanding of our own nature.

Ezra Taft Benson echoed Nephi's concern, declaring: "Converts will not survive in the heat of the day unless their taproots go down to the fulness of the Gospel that The Book of Mormon contains. Our Church classes are not as spirit-filled unless we hold it up as a standard. Do eternal consequences rest upon our response to this book? Yes, either to our blessing or our condemnation. Every Latter-day Saint should make the study of this book a lifetime pursuit. Otherwise, he is placing his soul in jeopardy and neglecting that which could gives spiritual and intellectual unity to his whole life". ("Ensign", 5/1975, p. 65).

First Nephi
Chapter 7

In this chapter, we learn about one final mission of Nephi and his brothers to the land of Jerusalem, whose purpose was to recruit the family of Ishmael to go down with them into the wilderness and ultimately to the Promised Land. Once again, it was the Lord speaking through His prophet who issued the instruction; "And it came to pass that the Lord commanded (my father) that I, Nephi, and my brethren, should again return unto the land of Jerusalem, and bring down Ishmael and his family into the wilderness". (V. 2).

They achieved their objective because, as Nephi reported: "The Lord did soften the heart of Ishmael, and also his household, insomuch that they took their journey with us down into the wilderness to the tent of our father". (V. 5). But on their return, Laman and Lemuel again became angry. Nephi recorded that "they did rebel against us; yea, against me, Nephi, and Sam, and their father, Ishmael, and his wife, and his three other (faithful) daughters". (V. 6). Toward Nephi, in particular, "they were exceedingly wroth, and they did bind (him) with cords, for they sought to take away (his) life". (V. 16).

In Nephi's own words, "it came to pass that I prayed unto the Lord, saying: O Lord, according to my faith which is in thee, wilt thou deliver me from the hands of my brethren; yea, even give me strength that I may burst these bands with which I am bound. And it came to pass that when I had said these words, behold, the bands were loosed from off my hands and feet, and I stood before my brethren, and I spake unto them again". (V. 17-18).

The power of this tremendous demonstration of faith was lost on Nephi's older brethren, who were angry with him anew. Another Semitic custom was illustrated when Laman and Lemuel, who would never have yielded to a man, relented only when one of the daughters of Ishmael and her mother intervened in Nephi's behalf. To the brothers, what would have originally been considered to be a weakness was now viewed as merciful, and thus they could save face.

It is an intriguing possibility that the daughter of Ishmael who had defended Nephi later became his wife. (See 1 Nephi 16:7). After all, it was the Lord Himself Who had explained to Lehi that "it was not meet for him, Lehi, that he should take his family into the wilderness alone; but that his sons should take daughters to wife, that they might raise up seed unto the Lord in the land of promise". (V. 1). Three of the daughters of Ishmael had taken the side of Nephi, Sam, and presumably, of Zoram. There is no reason to believe that their allegiance ever wavered, or that their hearts, which had been softened by the Lord, did not welcome the later attention of the righteous young men of the party. (See V. 5 & 6).

In typical fashion, Nephi forgave his brethren for having treated him so badly. (V. 21). Even in his youth, Nephi intuitively knew that "love is never wasted, because at a minimum, it enlarges the capacity of the giver". (Neal A. Maxwell). His love for his brethren was something that could not be hidden. From our distant perspective, as we read of his experiences 2,600 years after they transpired, his noble character continues to be self-evident on every page. Repeatedly, Nephi demonstrated by his actions his allegiance to his Savior.

First Nephi
Chapter 8

The events of The First Book of Nephi Chapters 8-15 took place in the Valley of Lemuel during the eight years that the family group lived there. During this time, Lehi received a revelation from God that he characterized as a dream or a vision. (V. 2). Whether received in this manner, or through the medium of voices, promptings, a burning in the bosom, or a stroke of inspiration, when accompanied by the power of the Holy Ghost, such communication constitutes revelation.

Chapter 8 deals with Lehi's dream, the interpretation of which was revealed to Nephi and recorded by him in Chapters 11 and 25 of The First Book of Nephi. In the dream, Lehi found himself in the midst of a dark and dreary wilderness which is the standard nightmare of the desert traveler. (V. 4). After many hours, he "beheld a large and spacious field". (V. 9). In the midst thereof was a tree "whose fruit was desirable to make one happy". (V. 10). This was a representation of the love of God. (See 1 Nephi 11:21-23 & 25).

Lehi told his family: "I did go forth and partake of the fruit thereof; and I beheld that it was most sweet, above all that I ever before tasted. Yea, and I beheld that the fruit thereof was white, to exceed all the whiteness that I had ever seen". (V. 11). This was a representation of eternal life. In his dream, Lehi was naturally anxious to share this experience with his loved ones, and so he cast his eyes about, looking for his family members. (V. 12-13).

Beside the tree, he beheld a true desert river flowing with muddy, roiling water running in its bed. This represented filthiness, or even the depths of hell. (See 1 Nephi 12:16, & 1 Nephi 15:26-29). A rod of iron that represented the security afforded by the word of God ran from the river to the tree. (V. 19). Adjoining the rod was the safety and stability of a strait and narrow path. (V. 20).

In his dream, Lehi called to Sariah, Sam, and Nephi, "and they did come unto (him) and partake of the fruit also". (V. 15-16). His joy, as he embraced these members of his family, must have been indescribable. But imagine his concern, as he beckoned to Laman and Lemuel, who "would not come unto (him) and partake of the fruit". (V. 18).

In the dream, he beheld many other people on the path who were also attempting to follow the rod of iron. Some of them let go of the rod, lost the security that it offered, and were swallowed up by the mists of darkness swirling about them. These mists represented the temptations of the devil. (See 1 Nephi 12:17).

A great and spacious building, standing as it were in the air, represented the vain imaginations and pride of the world. (See 1 Nephi 12:18). This description precisely matches. The appearance of cities to the Bedouin of the desert.

Those who make their homes in tents have always felt uneasy in cities of stone and mortar, and are often made to feel inferior by their worldly inhabitants.

Other multitudes did manage to catch "hold of the end of the rod of iron; and they did press forward through the mist of darkness, clinging to the rod of iron, even until they did come forth and partake of the fruit of the tree". (V. 24). By continually holding fast to the rod of iron, never letting go with both hands at the same time, but rather moving along steadily with deliberate and measurable progress, they reached the tree that was laden with desirable fruit. (V. 30).

These were contrasted to others who had instead oriented themselves toward the great and spacious building. In their efforts to reach it, some were drowned in the river of filthy water, while others who did reach the building then turned to point the finger of scorn at those still holding fast to the rod of iron. (V. 27 & 33).

The persecution by those who "were in an attitude of mocking and pointing their fingers towards those who had come and were partaking of the fruit" was intense. (V. 27). Consequently, after many "had tasted of the fruit they were ashamed, because of those that were scoffing at them; and they fell away into forbidden paths and were lost". (V. 28).

Of the fate of Laman and Lemuel, Lehi said only that they "partook not of the fruit". (V. 35). Therefore, he feared for his elder sons, "lest they should be cast off from the presence of the Lord. And he did exhort them then with all the feeling of a tender parent, that they would hearken to his words, that perhaps the Lord would be merciful to them, and not cast them off". (V. 36 & 37).

All of these representations were strikingly familiar to desert travelers, and the symbols of the dream must have had a powerful effect on Lehi's family. Therefore, Lehi "bade them to keep the commandments of the Lord; and (then) he did cease speaking unto them". (V. 38).

Even today, a correct understanding and spiritual interpretation of Lehi's dream is culturally relevant and vital to our welfare. As Marion G. Romney said: "If we would avoid adopting the evils of the world, we must pursue a course which will daily feed our minds with and call them back to the things of the Spirit. I know of no better way to do this than by daily reading The Book of Mormon" which is the iron rod of the Latter-day Saints. (C.R., 4/1980).

We have been warned that in the Last Days, "men's hearts shall fail them". (D&C 45:26). Think of this in light of what Jeffrey Holland counseled: "The heart (is) the figurative center of our faith, (and) the poetic location of our loyalties and our values". (C.R., 10/2009). The warning signs of a physical heart attack are shortness of breath, angina, pain in the jaw and in the left arm, and a tightening in the chest. But the warning signs of spiritual arrhythmia and telestial-trauma-induced cardiomyopathy are greater. If we have secular shortsightedness and find ourselves in the tangled web of the Christmas lights of confusion, we lose our focus on celestial sureties as we get caught up in telestial traffic jams and conceptual cul-de-sacs from which there is no retreat but in defeat.

The therapies for spiritual heart failure are equivalent to calling "911", administering CPR, or performing quadruple bypass surgery. Sometimes, radical measures such as a heart transplant, are required. As the Savior said: "They that are whole need not a physician, but they that are sick". (Luke 5:31). We are all beset by mists of spiritual darkness that threaten to descend upon us. These are manifest as negative peer pressures of any kind in any degree, worldliness, affluence, crudity, and treating sacred things profanely. The mists may be disguised as vanity when we engage in activities that have little worth. Idolatry may be our temptation when we are intrigued by gods of wood and stone. The wrong kind of education, or misapplied knowledge, may be our stumbling block. Secular humanism, and all other forms of "isms", may be our pitfall. Focusing on telestial trinkets, being prideful, arrogant, pretentious, or hypocritical may cause us to lose focus. Procrastination, complacency, apathy, and even overzealous behavior can cloud our vision. If our stiff necks prevent us from looking up to God, we will lose our orientation on celestial signposts. In fear, we may trust in false evidence that appears to be real. Then, our shaky knees will no longer support us on our journey along the path.

The formula outlined in Lehi's dream is straightforward and uncomplicated: Hold fast to the Rod of Iron. Regularly participate in Church activities, obey the Word of Wisdom, attend Seminary, receive the endowment, serve a mission, marry in the temple, be temperate in behavior, and honor the Sabbath day. "Press forward" with complete dedication and "steadfastness" or confidence and a firm determination in Christ, "having a perfect brightness of hope" or perfect faith, and charity or "a love of God and of all men". If we "feast upon the word of Christ" and receive strength and nourishment from the scriptures, and endure to the end in righteousness, we "shall have eternal life", which is the greatest gift that God can bestow. (2 Nephi 31:20). The Rod of Iron is the power of Christ to counter adversity and is our one safe haven.

"Whosoever heareth these sayings of mine, and doeth them", said the Savior, "I will liken him unto a wise man, which built his house upon a rock: And the rain descended, and the floods came, and the winds blew, and beat upon that house; and it fell not: for it was founded upon a rock". (Matthew 7:24-25). Think of The Three Little Pigs, who left the security of their mother's home and went out into the world to live independently. One foolishly built a house of straw, and the second a house of sticks. When the Big Bad Wolf came and threatened to devour the little pigs, he huffed and puffed and blew those poorly and thoughtlessly constructed houses down. Only the Little Pig who had prudently built his house out of bricks was able to withstand the onslaught of the wolf. This is the same message that God sent to the family of Lehi in his dream.

"I also beheld a strait and narrow path, which came along by the rod of iron, even to the tree by which I stood."
(1 Nephi 8:20).

First Nephi
Chapter 9

Chapter 9 begins with another simple statement by Nephi that communicates a wealth of information to the insightful and perceptive reader: "And all these things did my father see, and hear, and speak, as he dwelt in a tent, in the valley of Lemuel". (V. 1, see 1 Nephi 4:38, 7:5, & 10:16). What more need he have said?

Nephi explained that "these plates", or The Small Plates of Nephi, contained a record of the religious history of the Nephites. "I should make these plates", he wrote, "for the special purpose that there should be an account engraven of the ministry of my people". (V. 3).

"The other plates", The Large Plates of Nephi, contained an account of the secular history of the people. Upon them, was "engraven an account of the reign of the kings, and the wars and contentions" of the Nephites. (V. 4). Nephi alluded to a hidden reason for making the second record upon The Small Plates of Nephi. "Wherefore, the Lord hath commanded me to make these plates for a wise purpose in him, which purpose I know not". (V. 5).

Twenty-four centuries after Nephi made his record on The Small Plates, Joseph Smith lost the first 116 pages of the manuscript translation of The Large Plates of Nephi. He then translated from a second, parallel record, engraven on The Small Plates of Nephi, rather than re-translating the same 116 pages from The Large Plates. Consequently, in The Book of Mormon, 1 Nephi through Omni is a translation of The Small Plates of Nephi. Truly, "the Lord knoweth all things from the beginning; wherefore, he prepareth a way to accomplish all his works among the children of men, for behold, he hath all power unto the fulfilling of all his words". (V. 6).

The Words of Mormon at the end of The Small Plates of Nephi is a transitional book that links the translation of The Small Plates with that which follows, which is a translation of Mormon's abridgement of The Large Plates of Nephi, written on The Plates of Mormon, comprising the books of Mosiah, Alma, Helaman, 3 Nephi, 4 Nephi, and Mormon chapters 1-7. (See The Words of Mormon 1:3-5 & D&C 10:38-45).

Chapter 9 concludes a nine-chapter chiasmus with a formal ending of the first of two parallel structures in 1 Nephi; "And thus it is. Amen". (V. 6). Chapters 10-22 comprise a second chiasm. For a discussion of chiasmus, see Commentary Reference to 1 Nephi 15. Chapters 10-15 are the spiritual core of the book, and it is in Chapter 10 that Nephi begins his own account.

"The Lord hath commanded me to
make these plates for a wise purpose in
him, which purpose I know not. But the Lord
knoweth all things from the beginning; wherefore,
he prepareth a way to accomplish all his works among
the children of me; for behold, he hath all power
unto the fulfilling of all his words."
(1 Nephi 9:5-6).

First Nephi
Chapter 10

"I must speak somewhat of the things of my father". (V. 1). Thus wrote Nephi following the record of Lehi's vision of The Tree of Life. It was important for him to document his father's prophecy concerning the Jews at Jerusalem, that they would be carried away to Babylon, and that they should later return to the land of their inheritance.

Lehi prophesied that "they should be destroyed, even that great city Jerusalem, and many be carried away captive into Babylon (and) according to their own due time of the Lord, they should return again, yea, even be brought back out of captivity". (V. 3). His emphatic declaration that Jerusalem would be destroyed would by itself have served to justify his decision to lead his family into the wilderness, although, at this point, nobody in the party should have questioned Lehi's authority or his judgment. (See Commentary Reference to 2 Nephi 6:8). In any case, his prophecy would not be validated until his descendants encountered the People of Zarahemla sometime between 279 and 130 B.C. (See Omni 1:15).

In fact, the Babylonian Captivity did take place about 587 B.C. while Lehi's party was establishing itself in the Promised Land. "For, behold, said (Lehi), I have seen a vision, in which I know that Jerusalem is destroyed; and had we remained in Jerusalem we should also have perished". (2 Nephi 1:4, see Commentary Reference to 2 Nephi 6:8).

Lehi also prophesied concerning the coming of the Savior, using the Hebrew term "Messiah", that means "the anointed one". (V. 4, see Commentary Reference to 2 Nephi 3:17). His visions firmly established Lehi as a Messianic Prophet in the best tradition of Isaiah. Nephi then spoke of the great number of prophets who had all testified of the Messiah. (V. 5). Since we do not find these references in the Old Testament, we must assume that their recorded testimonies are among the plain and precious things that were removed from the Bible as we know it. (See 1 Nephi 13:26).

Lehi also testified concerning John the Baptist "who should come before the Messiah, to prepare the way of the Lord". (V. 7). He would baptize in Bethabara in Galilee, south of the Sea of Gennesaret. (V. 9). Clearly, although he would not be born for another 600 years, John's mission was known to the Lord and to his prophet Lehi.

Lehi then spoke very clearly about the sacrifice of the Redeemer of Israel, that He would be slain by His own people, "and after he had been slain he should rise from the dead, and should make himself manifest, by the Holy Ghost, unto the Gentiles". (V. 11). This news must have been startling to his family because the God of Abraham, Isaac, and Jacob was the personal deity of Israel, and they were jealous of their special covenant relationship with Him. To teach that He would reveal himself to the uncircumcised was bold doctrine. They may have also been surprised to hear such unambiguous teaching regarding the doctrine of resurrection.

Then, in the spirit of prophecy, Lehi likened Israel to an olive tree, "whose branches should be broken off and should be scattered upon all the face of the earth". (V. 12). The ancient prophets often metaphorically linked Israel to the olive tree. A good example is The Allegory of Zenos that had been recorded upon The Plates of Brass. (See Jacob 5). Because his family would understand the symbolism, Lehi said: "It must needs be that we should be led with one accord", or in unity with the receipt of an intended blessing, "into the land of promise, unto the fulfilling of the word of the Lord, that we should be scattered upon all the face of the earth". (V. 13).

In his record, Nephi used a number of terms not found in the Old Testament. For example, we read about the "Bible", "Saints", a "Church", the "fulness of the Gospel", "Gospel of Jesus Christ", "Apostles", the "Lord", "Christ", the "Redeemer", the "Son of God", "crucifixion," the "covenant people of the Lord", "Messiah," (used once in the Old Testament and twice in the New Testament), and the "Holy Ghost". These terms and others render the writings of the prophets of The Book of Mormon plain and easily understood, and although the book is contemporaneous to the Old Testament, it flows as if it were a New Testament era opus. These terms provide a clue to what extent the "parts which are plain and most precious" were removed from the canon of scripture by agents of "the great and abominable Church". (See 1 Nephi 13:26).

Nephi testified that he had faith that he might see, hear, and know of the things of God, "by the power of the Holy Ghost, which is the gift of God unto all those who diligently seek him, as well in times of old as in the time that he should manifest himself unto the children of men". (V. 17). He declared that the Holy Ghost has always functioned in our affairs, as the Church so testifies today. (V. 18, see 2 Peter 1:21). The promise has ever been that those "that diligently seeketh shall find; and the mysteries of God shall be unfolded to them, by the power of the Holy Ghost". (V. 19). Nephi knew whereof he spoke, having enjoyed the witness of the Spirit many times in his own life.

He opened the chapter with the explanation: "And now I, Nephi, proceed to give an account upon these plates of my proceedings, and my reign and ministry, wherefore I proceed with mine account". (V. 1). In fact, much of the chapter is a parenthetical aside into the activities of his father, but he ended unequivocally with a declaration that reveals an awakening appreciation of his own mission: "And the Holy Ghost giveth authority that I should speak these things, and deny them not". (V. 22).

First Nephi
Chapter 11

Chapter 11 is Nephi's detailed account of the inspired interpretation of his father's dream, or vision. "For it came to pass that after I had desired to know the things that my father had seen, and believing that the Lord was able to make them known unto me, as I sat pondering in mine heart, I was caught away in the Spirit of the Lord". (V. 1). Nephi not only had the desire to know, but he also had the faith that he could know. Further, he had invested the time to ponder the things about which he had questions. Having paid the price, he received a spectacular answer.

Joseph Smith and Sydney Rigdon described a similar experience with the Spirit, recording that "while we meditated upon these things, the Lord touched the eyes of our understandings and they were opened, and the glory of the Lord shone round about". (D&C 76:19). Joseph also described the voice of the Lord as "the sound of the rushing of great waters". (D&C 110:3). John the Revelator wrote of "his voice as the sound of many waters". (Revelation 1:5). Paul modestly wrote of his own personal experience: "I knew a man in Christ above fourteen years ago ... such an one caught up to the third heaven. And I knew such a man ... how that he was caught up into paradise, and heard unspeakable words, which it is not lawful for a man to utter". (2 Corinthians 12:2).

In his Apocalypse, John wrote: "I looked, and behold, a door was opened in heaven: and the first voice which I heard was as it were of a trumpet talking with me, which said, Come up hither, and I will shew thee things which must be hereafter. And immediately I was in the spirit". (Revelation 4:1-2). Clearly, Nephi, Paul, Joseph, Sydney, and John shared experiences that are difficult to describe. The one thing that they had in common was that they were taught by "the Spirit of the Lord". (V. 11). However, none of them clearly articulated just who this Spirit was.

Nephi was also "caught away in the Spirit of the Lord, yea, into an exceedingly high mountain". (V. 1). The word "mountain" is used in the scriptures in different allegorical or figurative senses. Here, it might refer to a high place of God, that is to say, a place of revelation.

It is interesting that, given the transcendent experience in which he was participating, Nephi did not lose his faculties or forget the purpose for his mighty prayer. When the Spirit asked him: "Behold, what desirest thou?" he was able to answer, "I desire to behold the things which my father saw". (V. 2-3). In much the same way, Joseph Smith, who was probably about the same age as Nephi was at this time, remembered the purpose of his prayer in the Sacred Grove, and wrote of the experience: "My object in going to inquire of the Lord was to know which of all the sects was right, that I might know which to join. No sooner, therefore, did I get possession of myself, so as to be able to speak, than I asked the Personages who stood above me in the light, which of all the sects was right". (J.S.H. 1:18).

When Nephi confirmed his belief in all that his father had spoken, "the Spirit cried with a loud voice, (as it were a trumpet?) saying, Hosanna to the Lord, the Most High God; for he is God over all the earth, yea, even above all. And blessed art thou, Nephi, because thou believest in the Son of the Most High God". (V. 6). As a Testator, the Spirit confirmed to Nephi the reality of God the Father, the Lord Who rules over all, as well as the reality of His Son, Who rules by divine investiture of authority.

Faith precedes the miracle, and signs follow those who believe. (See Mark 16:17). Thus, Nephi would now receive The Vision of The Tree of Life as a sign, and he was commanded that afterward he should stand as a witness of the Savior and "bear record that (He) is the Son of God". (V. 7).

Therefore, in remarkable detail, the Spirit unrolled a panorama before the eyes of Nephi. This, he recorded in the next 124 verses that comprise the balance of Chapter 11 and all of Chapters 12, 13, and 14. Once again, The Book of Mormon is startling in its clarity, for the ingenuity with which it weaves together ancient and modern history, for the freshness with which it treats events distant from its own time and place, and for the bold manner in which it addresses issues of relevance in the Last Days.

Nephi had written that he "was desirous also that (he) might see, and hear, and know of these things, by the power of the Holy Ghost, which is the gift of God unto all those who diligently seek him". (1 Nephi 10:17). His righteous desire was granted, to enjoy companionship with that very member of the Godhead, for he wrote: "I spake unto him as a man speaketh; for I beheld that he was in the form of a man; yet nevertheless, I knew that it was the Spirit of the Lord; and he spake unto me as a man speaketh with another". (V. 11). This is the only place in all of scripture where the Holy Ghost is characterized as being in the form of a man. (See D&C 130:22-23).

Verses 13-23 concern the birth of the Savior and compliment the Christmas story found in the New Testament. Nephi "beheld the city of Nazareth; and in the city ... a virgin" who is now familiar to all Christians of faith. (V. 13).

The condescension of God in verse 16 refers to the fact that although He was Lord God Omnipotent and the Father of our spirits, He became the Father of mortal offspring born of a mortal woman. "Knowest thou the condescension of God?" asked the angel. "Behold, the virgin whom thou seest is the mother of the Son of God, after the manner of the flesh". (V. 18).

The condescension of God in verse 26 refers to the fact that although He was Lord God Omnipotent and Creator of the Earth, God the Son submitted to all the trials of mortality and finally suffered an ignominious death upon the cross. "Look, and behold the condescension of God!" declared the angel again. "And I looked and beheld the Redeemer of the world. And the Lamb of God went forth and was baptized. And I beheld that he went forth ministering unto the people". (V. 27). "And I, Nephi, saw that he was lifted up upon the cross and slain for the sins of the world". (V. 33).

The interpretation of the symbolism of the tree was given to Nephi when the Spirit asked: "Knoweth thou the meaning of the tree which thy father saw? And I answered him, saying: Yea, it is the love of God". (V. 21-22). "And it came to pass that I beheld that the rod of iron, which my father had seen, was the word of God, which led to the fountain of living waters or to the tree of life, which waters are a representation of the love of God; and I also beheld that the tree of life was a representation of the love of God." (V. 25).

Verse 27 tells us that at the baptism of the Savior, the Holy Ghost would descend "in the form of a dove". This would be the "sign of the dove" that Joseph Smith explained is an emblem or token of truth and innocence. (H.C., 5:261). Through the power of the Spirit, Nephi learned that the sick and afflicted would be "healed by the power of the Lamb of God, and that the devils and the unclean spirits (would be) cast out". (V. 31).

Nephi saw the future as if it were a present reality, and that the Savior "was taken by the people; yea, the Son of the everlasting God was judged of the world. And I, Nephi, saw that he was lifted up upon the cross and slain for the sins of the world". (V. 32-33). Certainly, Nephi could now better understand the condescension of the Son of God, mentioned by the Spirit in verse 26.

In vision, Nephi saw not only the persecution of the "apostles of the Lamb", but also of the righteous of all ages. He wrote that "the multitude of the earth was gathered together; and (he) beheld that they were in a large and spacious building". (V. 34-35). This represented "the pride of the world; and it fell, and the fall was exceedingly great". (V. 36). The angel wanted Nephi to know that he was given the interpretation of his father's vision, in part, so that he would know that "thus shall be the destruction of all nations, kindreds, tongues, and people, that shall fight against the twelve apostles of the Lamb". (V. 36). In this way, the Spirit charged Nephi with a most solemn missionary responsibility, to bear witness of the Lord and Savior of the world and to preach the first principles and ordinances of the Gospel, namely faith, repentance, baptism, and the receipt of the Holy Ghost.

"The Spirit cried with a loud voice, saying: Hosanna to the Lord, the most high God; for he is God over all the earth, yea, even above all. And blessed art thou, Nephi, because thou believest in the Son of the most high God; wherefore, thou shalt behold the things which thou hast desired. And it came to pass that the Spirit said unto me: Look! And I looked and beheld a tree; and it was like unto the tree which my father had seen; and the beauty thereof was far beyond, yea exceeding of all beauty; and the whiteness thereof did exceed the whiteness of the driven snow."
(1 Nephi 11:6 & 8).

First Nephi
Chapter 12

In Chapter 12, Nephi foresaw that God would provide a land of promise for his posterity, but that warfare would be the dominant interaction between his descendants and those of Laman and Lemuel. "I looked and beheld the land of promise; and I beheld multitudes of people, yea, even as it were in number as many as the sand of the sea". (V. 1). "And I beheld wars, and rumors or wars, and great slaughter with the sword among my people". (V. 2). When Mormon abridged the record of the Nephite prophets, he wrote that in the years 19-21 A.D., in the battles between the Nephites and the Lamanites "there never was known so great a slaughter among all the people of Lehi since he left Jerusalem". (3 Nephi 4:11).

Nephi also saw in vision the events surrounding the crucifixion. "And it came to pass that I saw a mist of darkness on the face of the land of promise; and I saw lightnings, and I heard thunderings, and earthquakes, and all manner of tumultuous noises; and I saw the earth and the rocks; that they rent; and I saw mountains tumbling into pieces; and I saw the plains of the earth, that they were broken up; and I saw many cities that they were sunk; and I saw many that they were burned with fire; and I saw many that did tumble to the earth, because of the quaking thereof". (V. 4). As Mormon reported after these events had actually taken place: "The face of the whole earth became deformed, because of the tempests, and the thunderings, and the lightnings, and the quaking of the earth". (3 Nephi 8:17). In fact, "the whole face of the land was changed" during the destruction "that did last for about the space of three hours". (3 Nephi 8:12 & 19).

Then Nephi recorded: "After I saw these things, I saw the vapor of darkness". (V. 5). Mormon reported that "there was thick darkness upon all the face of the land, insomuch that the inhabitants thereof who had not fallen could feel the vapor of darkness. And there could be no light, because of the darkness, neither candles, neither torches; neither could there be fire kindled with their fine and exceedingly dry wood, so that there could not be any light at all". (3 Nephi 8:20-21).

Then, in vision, Nephi's descendants beheld "the Lamb of God descending out of heaven". (V. 6). "And behold", wrote Mormon, "they saw a Man descending out of heaven; and he was clothed in a white robe; and he came down and stood in the midst of them. And it came to pass that he stretched forth his hand and spake unto the people, saying: Behold, I am Jesus Christ, whom the prophets testified shall come into the world". (3 Nephi 11:8-10).

Nephi also beheld the ministry of the Nephite Twelve, who were not called "Apostles" in The Book of Mormon. (V. 7-8). Nevertheless, they "were Apostles to the Nephite race" according to Joseph Fielding Smith, Jr. ("Doctrines of Salvation",

3:158-159). They held the authority of the Melchizedek Priesthood and were legal administrators who were empowered to bestow upon their people the blessings of the fulness of the Gospel.

The Angel of the Lord explained to Nephi that the Twelve "are righteous forever; for because of their faith in the Lamb of God their garments are made white in his blood". (V. 10). Symbolically, all those whose sins are forgiven through the sacrifice of the Savior have garments made white in His cleansing blood. Nephi may have understood at this time that his own calling and election was made sure, inasmuch as the Holy Spirit of Promise had given him a sure witness Christ and of His Infinite Atonement.

Nephi was given to understand that after the appearance of the Savior among his descendants, three generations would pass away in righteousness. "The love of God which did dwell in the hearts of the people" during that time would be so great that Mormon would be impressed to write: "Surely there could not (have been) a happier people among all the people who had been created by the hand of God". (4 Nephi 1:15-16). These were they who would be "made white in the blood of the Lamb, because of their faith in him". (V. 11).

The next sweeping panoramic view that Nephi beheld was that of "the people of (his) seed gathered together in multitudes against the seed of (his) brethren; and they were gathered together to battle". (V. 15). As a matter of fact, in the days of the prophet Mormon, around 330 A.D., there would be "one complete revolution throughout all the face of the land". (Mormon 2:8). He described "a continual scene of wickedness and abominations (that) has been before mine eyes ever since I have been sufficient to behold the ways of man". (Mormon 2:18).

Satan never sleeps, and "death stands at attention, obedient, expectant, ready to serve, ready to shear away the people en masse; ready, if called upon, to pulverize, without hope of repair, what is left of civilization. He awaits only the word of command". (Winston Churchill, "The Gathering Storm", p. 37). Death is eager to drag its victims into "the fountain of filthy water which (Lehi) saw, yea, even the river of which he spake; and the depths thereof are the depths of hell". (V. 16).

"And the mists of darkness are the temptations of the devil, which blindeth the eyes, and hardeneth the hearts of the children of men, and leadeth them away into broad roads, that they perish and are lost". (V. 17). In fact, "heaven lies about us in our infancy. Shades of the prison-house begin to close upon the growing boy; but, behold, he sees the light, and whence it flows. He sees it in his joy. The youth, who daily farther from the east must travel, still is nature's priest, and by the vision splendid, is on his way attended. At length, the man perceives it die away, and fade into the light of common day". (William Wordsworth, "Ode: Intimations of Immortality from Recollections of Early Childhood").

Nephi saw that a principal distraction from activities of eternal significance in the Last Days would be the "vain imaginations and the pride of the children of men". (V. 18). These are worthless, useless, and of no effect or power. Sin is waste. It is doing one thing, when something else of far greater significance could be done in its stead. It is settling for mediocrity when the more difficult road leads to greater heights. It is a capitulation to spiritual stagnation rather than an acceptance of the challenges related to eternal progression. It is nothing more than an overnight stay in a second-class hotel. It is trading a mess of pottage for an eternal birthright. It is eating garbage and drinking sewage instead of the cornucopia that is before you.

Vanity and pride distract disciples from a determination to concentrate on eternal values. Double mindedness is repeatedly condemned in the scriptures. James pointed out a number of cases: faith versus lack of confidence in prayers (James 1:6-7); blessings versus cursings from the same tongue (James 3:10); devotion to God versus allegiance to Babylon (James 4:1-4), being subject to one lawgiver versus judging the law and others (James 4:11-

12); and submitting to God versus yielding to the influences of the devil. (James 4:6-7). Truly, there is "a great and a terrible gulf" that divides the righteous from the wicked. (V. 18).

With chilling clarity, Nephi saw the double-minded individuals who overcame his own people because of their pride and their capitulation to the wiles of the worldly. (V. 19). The ancient Church in the New World was, in fact, ultimately destroyed by the internal dissension of uncommitted members. In the end, so great would be the apostasy of their Lamanite brethren that the spirit of contention would not leave them even after the destruction of their Nephite enemies. "Gathered together in multitudes, (Nephi) saw wars and rumors of wars among them". (V. 21). Consequently, he saw in vision that they would "dwindle", or waste away and decline "in unbelief", and become dark, loathsome, and filthy. That is to say, they would become morally corrupt or polluted, with an inclination to vileness and wickedness. (V. 22). A profound change of heart would be necessary before they would again return to the covenants made anciently by their forefathers.

"And it came to pass that I saw
a mist of darkness on the face of the
land of promise; and I saw lightnings, and
I heard thunderings, and earthquakes, and all
manner of tumultuous noises; and I saw the plains
of the earth, that they were broken up; and I saw many
cities that they were sunk; and I saw many that were burned
with fire; and I saw many that did tumble to the earth, because
of the quaking thereof. And it came to pass after I saw these
things I saw the vapor of darkness, that it passed from off
the face of the earth; and … I saw the heavens open, and
the Lamb of God descending out of heaven; and he
came down and showed himself unto them."
(21 Nephi 12:3-6).

First Nephi
Chapter 13

In this chapter, Nephi was given in vision a broad view of the state of the world in the Last Days. He clearly saw "the great persecutor of the Church, the apostate, the whore, even Babylon, that maketh all nations to drink of her cup, in whose hearts the enemy, even Satan, sitteth to reign". (D&C 86:3).

Nephi wrote: "And it came to pass that I saw among the nations of the Gentiles the formation of a great Church". In this verse, we encounter a typesetting change that was made in the 1981 English language edition of The Book of Mormon. Oliver Cowdery's original manuscript read "formation", but in 1830 the typesetter misread that word as "foundation", that for 150 years had remained incorrectly incorporated into the text.

When we encounter the "great and abominable Church" in The Book of Mormon, we should be careful not to read in too much literal significance. In 1 Nephi 14:10, Nephi correctly taught that there are really only two Churches. So, the great and abominable Church should not refer specifically to one Church of Christendom, although it has been common among members of The Church of Jesus Christ of Latter-day Saints to label the Holy Catholic Church as such. But to do so would be technically incorrect.

Verse 12 refers to the prompting Christopher Columbus received to cross the Atlantic Ocean on his voyage of discovery. Nephi wrote: "And I looked and beheld a man among the Gentiles, who was separated from the seed of my brethren by the many waters; and I beheld the Spirit of God, that it came down and wrought upon that man". Whether this was the Light of Christ, or the Holy Ghost is irrelevant. Of the experience, Columbus simply wrote: "God gave me fire for the deed". As a result of his "discovery", others were able to free themselves from spiritual and intellectual captivity by coming to the New World to worship God according to the dictates of their own conscience. (V. 13).

We also learn in this chapter that God takes sides in some conflicts. During the Revolutionary War in the British Crown Colonies, "the power of the Lord" was with the rebels, and they were delivered "out of the hands of all other nations". (V. 16 & 19). The Church that gained a foothold in the new nation supported and upheld "that law of the land which is constitutional". (D&C 98:5). In this sense, the revolutionaries within the British colonies were justified in their armed opposition to the tyrannical rule of Great Britain. Besides, to fully express the spirit of the Reformation that presaged the Restoration of the Gospel, a new and fertile field was needed where the infant Church of Christ could take root in nurturing soil.

Nephi also beheld the Bible, or "a record of the Jews". (V. 23). At the time that "it proceeded forth from the mouth of a Jew, it contained the fulness of the Gospel of the Lord". (V. 24). In older editions of The Book of Mormon, this verse was rendered "the plainness of the Gospel of the Lord". The Plan of Salvation, however, is the fulness of the Gospel, and that is a more accurate description of the Bible before the plain and most precious parts were removed. (See 2 Nephi 28:30).

In this chapter, we also learn why the Church of the devil is abominable. "For behold, they have taken away from the Gospel of the Lamb many parts which are plain and most precious; and also many covenants of the Lord have they taken away". (V. 26). Sometimes knowingly, and at other times unwittingly, the covenant has been changed, and the Old Testament has been effectively eliminated as a witness for Christ. This is an abomination because such actions stop the potential progression of those caught in the snares of the Church of the devil, and the purpose of mortality in the great Plan of Salvation is destroyed. With this in mind, the Church News reported that "the witness for Christ was the most important thing in that ancient record". (1/1966). Without the testimony of Christ, the Old Testament loses much of its purpose and power.

"And all this have they done that they might pervert the right ways of the Lord", wrote Nephi, "that they might blind the eyes and harden the hearts of the children of men". (V. 27). This prophecy has largely been fulfilled. Were it not for the plain and precious parts that have been taken away from that record, the Old Testament might read like its contemporary text The Book of Mormon. Instead, "an exceedingly great many do stumble, yea, insomuch that Satan hath great power over them". (V. 29). These verses underscore the power of the word of God to help all of mankind to conduct itself righteously and to resist the temptations of the devil, and conversely they warn that without the rod of iron, wandering off into mists of darkness is more likely. (See 1 Nephi 12:17).

Verse 30 reinforces our understanding that by the time of the last great battles in The Book of Mormon in the 5th century A.D., the distinctions between Nephite and Lamanite were social, political, cultural, and economical, rather than genealogical. There was "a mixture of (Nephi's) seed, which (was) among (the Lamanites)". In verse 35, the Lord spoke of the destruction of the descendants of Nephi in the sense that they would be rendered to no avail, and that their influence would be neutralized, rather than that they would be literally annihilated, as had been the wicked inhabitants of Ammonihah. (See Alma 16:9).

By divine investiture of authority, the angel promised Nephi that the Lamb of God would visit the remnant of the House of Israel represented by the seed of Lehi, saying: "I will bring forth unto them, in mine own power, much of my Gospel, which shall be plain and precious, saith the Lamb". (V. 34). The reason for the preservation of an unambiguous record was made clear to Nephi. "For behold, saith the Lamb: I will manifest myself unto thy seed, that they shall write many things which I shall minister unto them, which shall be plain and precious; and after their seed shall be destroyed, and dwindle in unbelief, and also the seed of thy brethren, behold, these things shall be hid up, to come forth unto the Gentiles, by the gift and power of the Lamb. And in them shall be written my Gospel, saith the Lamb, and my rock and my salvation." (V. 35 & 36).

Nephi must have been encouraged to learn that the Lord would remember his descendants, the Children of the Covenant, in the Last Days. Because of this prophecy, those who were later charged with the preservation of the record would have received a powerful witness of their tremendous responsibility.

This chapter promises that through the Gentiles, the remnant of Lehi's descendants in the land would be instruments in bringing forth a great body of scripture, "other books", which would also stand as witnesses of the Bible. These are The Doctrine and Covenants and The Pearl of Great Price, in addition to The Book of Mormon. "These last records", said the angel, "shall establish the truth of the first, which are of the twelve apostles of the Lamb" in the Holy Land. (V. 40). They were to go initially to the Gentiles, because Israel had first rejected the Lord in former days. (V. 42).

The words of Christ were to be made known in The Book of Mormon as well as in the Bible, "wherefore they both shall be established in one". (V. 41). This verse is reminiscent of the prophecy of Ezekiel, wherein he wrote: "Moreover, thou son of man, take thee one stick, and write upon it, for Judah, and for the children of Israel his companions then take another stick, and write upon it, for Joseph, the stick of Ephraim, and for all the House of Israel his companions. And join them one to another into one stick; and they shall become one in thine hand". (Ezekiel 37:16-17).

It is important that we responsibly care for the precious gift of The Book of Mormon. Ezra Taft Benson said that "every Latter-day Saint should make the study of this book a lifetime pursuit. Otherwise, he is placing his soul in jeopardy and neglecting that which could give spiritual and intellectual unity to his whole life". (C.R., 4/1975). As Nephi clearly understood, there is a difference between a convert who holds fast to the rod of iron, and one who does not.

The "great and abominable church, which is most abominable above all other churches, (has) taken away from the gospel of the Lamb many parts which are plain and most precious; and also, many covenants of the Lord have they taken away."
(1 Nephi 13:26).

First Nephi
Chapter 14

In Chapter 14, the angel to whom we were introduced in Chapter 11 promised Nephi that those Gentiles who would hearken to the Lamb in the Last Days would become adopted Children of the Covenant of Abraham and would enjoy all the blessings reserved for the faithful. The angel told Nephi: "They shall be numbered among the seed of thy father; yea, they shall be numbered among the House of Israel". (V. 2).

On the other hand, he warned that those whose allegiance was to the great and abominable Church of the devil would find their souls in hell or in the spirit prison of the disobedient. "For behold, this is according to the captivity of the devil, and also according to the justice of God, upon all those who will work wickedness and abomination before him". (V. 4). Clearly, the captivity of the devil brings us into spiritual bondage and estrangement from God. When we deny the Atonement, mercy cannot prevail on our behalf and our claim to the cleansing effect of the blood of Christ is forfeit. Justice must then prevail. Consequently, "the souls of (those individuals are led away) down to hell - yea, (to) that great pit which hath been digged for the destruction of men (and which) shall be filled by those who digged it, unto their utter destruction". (V. 3). Their progression grinds to a halt, because The Plan of Salvation is, for them, no longer operative. For, "whoso repenteth not must perish". (V. 5).

Nephi learned these principles from the angel, as well as through his study of The Plates of Brass. He also discovered that the Restoration of the Gospel in the Last Days would have eternal consequences. "For the time cometh, saith the Lamb of God, that I will work a great and a marvelous work among the children of men; a work which shall be everlasting". (V. 7).

The scriptures characterize the Last Days as "very great, and very terrible". (D&C 97:18). This is because Christ is the Messenger of the Covenant, and His Word will be so powerful that it will be "either to the convincing of them unto peace and life eternal, or unto the deliverance of them to the hardness of their hearts and the blindness of their minds unto their being brought down into captivity, and also into destruction, both temporally and spiritually, according to the captivity of the devil". (V. 7).

The angel asked Nephi: "Rememberest thou the covenants of the Father unto the House of Israel?" (V. 8). He was speaking of The Abrahamic Covenant that has been preserved for those in the Last Days, and that has been articulated within The Pearl of Great Price. "My name is Jehovah", the Savior had explained, "and I know the end from the beginning; therefore, my hand shall be over thee. And I will make of thee a great nation, and I will bless thee above measure, and make thy name great among all nations, and thou shalt be a blessing unto thy seed after thee, that in their hands they shall bear this ministry and Priesthood unto all nations; And I will bless them through thy name;

for as many as receive this Gospel shall be called after thy name, and shall be accounted thy seed, and shall rise up and bless thee, as their father; And I will bless them that bless thee, and curse them that curse thee; and in thee (that is, in thy Priesthood) and in thy seed (that is, thy Priesthood), for I give unto thee a promise that this right shall continue in thee, and in thy seed after thee (that is to say, the literal seed, or the seed of the body) shall all the families of the earth be blessed, even with the blessings of the Gospel, which are the blessings of salvation, even of life eternal". (Abraham 2:8-11).

Nephi remembered these promises and knew that the battle lines between the righteous and the wicked would be drawn around Covenants. It would be a great day for those who would choose to claim the blessings related to obedience, but it would be a terrible day for those who would deny the power of God. "I, Nephi, beheld the power of the Lamb of God, that it descended upon the saints of the Church of the Lamb, and upon the covenant people of the Lord, who were scattered upon all the face of the earth; and they were armed with righteousness and with the power of God in great glory. And it came to pass that I beheld that the wrath of God was poured out upon that great and abominable Church, insomuch that there were wars and rumors of wars among all the nations and kindreds of the earth". (V. 14 & 15, see 1 Nephi 17:48, Jacob 6:2, & Ether 2:9).

There are, after all, "save two Churches only; the one is the Church of the Lamb of God, and the other is the Church of the devil; wherefore, whoso belongeth not to the Church of the Lamb of God belongeth to that great Church, which is the mother of abominations; and she is the whore of all the earth". (V. 10, see Commentary Reference to 2 Nephi 9:37, & 2 Nephi 10:16).

In the Last Days, society is becoming increasingly polarized. On the one hand is the kingdom of God and on the other hand is the kingdom of the devil. Satan's kingdom is typified as the whore of the earth in the sense that it is a corrupt or idolatrous community. It was Wycliff (in 1302) and Tyndall (in 1530) who first applied the epithet to the Church of Rome, but we should not specifically do so. From our perspective, we can see that any organization, society, or system of beliefs that leads the children of God away from Christ or hinders or prevents them from accepting the Gospel is "the Church of the devil".

That the "whore" is powerful today is attested in 1 Nephi 14:11 wherein we learn that she "sat upon many waters". Revelation 17:5 teaches us that "the waters ... are peoples, and multitudes, and nations, and tongues". Her "dominion" is the power, control, and influence of government.

Zion will ultimately be redeemed from the "whore of the earth" by the power of the priesthood. (V. 14). D&C 1:9 teaches that the wrath of God is reserved for the wicked, and that the fulness of His wrath requires their destruction. We are witnessing a significant sign of the times as we see this occur. "And when the day cometh that the wrath of God is poured out upon the mother of harlots, which is the great and abominable Church of all the earth, whose founder is the devil, then, at that day, the work of the Father shall commence, in preparing the way for the fulfilling of his covenants, which he hath made to his people who are of the House of Israel". (V. 17, see 3 Nephi 21:20-29).

The angel taught Nephi that the Apostle John wrote many things that were to transpire in the Last Days right up to the end of the telestial existence of the earth. "Behold, he shall see and write the remainder of these things; yea, and also many things which have been. And he shall also write concerning the end of the world". (V. 21 & 22, see v. 27). He indicated that these teachings were "plain and pure, and most precious and easy to the understanding of men" at the time they were recorded. (V. 23, see 1 Nephi 13:26).
But what happened to the clarity of these teachings. Surely it is the responsibility of the prophets to bless us with the eternal truths of the Gospel in plainness and simplicity so that all might understand and take appropriate action. The very nature of the Apostolic calling is to bear witness to all the world of the divinity of Jesus Christ, and to teach

the path to salvation and exaltation in a way that is easily understood. Today, since the Bible is ambiguous, unclear, confusing, and even contradictory, its lack of lucidity must be the result of errors of omission or commission introduced by uninspired or ill-intentioned copyists over the years.

The angel assured Nephi that these truths would come forth by the power of God via a number of avenues. "And also, others who have been, to them hath he shown all things, and they have written them; and they are sealed up to come forth in their purity, according to the truth which is in the Lamb, in the own due time of the Lord, unto the House of Israel". (V. 26). Who are these "others?"

To Joseph Smith was given "the keys of the mystery of those things which have been sealed, even things which were from the foundation of the world, and the things which shall come from this time until the time" of the coming of the Lord. (D&C 35:18). Of him, Wilford Woodruff declared: "He lived until he received every key, ordinance, and law given to any man on this earth, from Father Adam down, touching this dispensation". (J.D., 16:27).

Nephi saw the dawning of the millennial era, when "there is nothing which is secret save it shall be revealed; there is no work of darkness save it shall be made manifest in the light, and there is nothing which is sealed upon the earth save it shall be loosed". (2 Nephi 30:17). The Lord Himself declared: "Know ye not that there are more nations than one? Wherefore, because that ye have a Bible ye need not suppose that it contains all my words; neither need ye suppose that I have not caused more to be written. For I command all men, both in the east and in the west, and in the north, and in the south, and in the islands of the sea, that they shall write the words which I speak unto them ... For behold, I shall speak unto the Jew, and they shall write it; and I shall also speak unto the Nephites, and they shall write it; and I shall also speak unto the other tribes of the House of Israel, which I have led away, and they shall write it; and I shall speak unto all nations of the earth, and they shall write it". (2 Nephi 29:7, 10 & 12).

When we realize that God is no respecter of persons, we must accept as an article of our faith that He has in the past revealed many things, that He does so now, and that He will continue to do so in the future. (See the 9th Article of Faith). With this acceptance comes the realization that the word of God has been recorded in scripture other than the Bible. (See the 8th Article of Faith). Nephi boldly testified of this truth to whomever was willing to listen, in the closing verse of this chapter. "And thus, it is. Amen". (V. 30).

"For the time cometh, saith the Lamb of God, that I will work a great and a marvelous work among the children of men." (1 Nephi 14:7).

First Nephi
Chapter 15

In the last few chapters, we have learned about Nephi's wonderful spiritual manifestations and have seen how his faith was validated by the appearance of an angel of God. At this point in the text, however, he returns to a narrative of the apostasy of Laman and Lemuel. These two elder sons "disputed" or actively contended against their father's teachings. (V. 2). They resisted his counsel because they were "hard in their hearts;" that is to say, their souls were inflexible, resistive, and unteachable. (V. 3).

Contention is often the result of frustration that comes from a lack of understanding. "Behold", complained the brothers, "we cannot understand the words which our father hath spoken". (V. 7). It is also the raw and highly abrasive edge to interpersonal relationships that is the result of sin. (See 1 Nephi 16:1-2).

With humility, Laman and Lemuel might have been able to overcome their spiritual stagnation and move on to greater heights of comprehension and commitment. As Isaiah had written: "Come now, and let us reason together, saith the Lord: though your sins be as scarlet, they shall be as white as snow; though they be red like crimson, they shall be as wool. If ye be willing and obedient, ye shall eat the good of the land: But if ye refuse and rebel, ye shall be devoured with the sword: for the mouth of the Lord hath spoken it". (Isaiah 1:18).

Nephi asked his brethren if they had inquired of the Lord, so that they might understand and be as one. (V. 8). Their response, written in the form of a four-part chiasm, comprises verses 10-11. Included in this parallel structure is his quotation of a verse of scripture that was contained within The Plates of Brass. It reads: "If ye will not harden your hearts, and ask me in faith, believing that ye shall receive, with diligence in keeping my commandments, surely these things will be made known unto you". (V. 11).

The chiasm itself is as follows:

A: "The Lord maketh no such thing known unto us.
B: How is it that ye do not keep the commandments of the Lord? How is it that ye will perish, because of the hardness of your hearts?
B: If ye will not harden your hearts, and ask me in faith, believing that ye shall receive, with diligence in keeping my commandments
A: Surely these things will be made known unto you".

Nephi constructed chiasms in his record because it was part of the familiar Hebraic literary style to do so. It was fashionable, as Elizabethan sonnets were in England 300 years ago, and just as Rap lyrics in songs became popular in the 1990s. More importantly, because a chiasm is a clever literary device, it was more impressive to the listener, or reader, and was therefore more likely to be remembered.

The style is called a chiasm because of the Greek letter chi, which is an X, suggesting parallel thoughts. In their simplest structure, these thoughts form the pattern represented by A-B-B-A. A contemporary chiasm with which we might be familiar is the nursery rhyme: "Old King Cole was a merry old soul, and a merry old soul was he". (See. 2 Nephi 4:16).

Because they were incapable of independent understanding, Nephi explained to his elder brethren the meaning of their father's teachings, reciting from The Plates of Brass: "Do ye not remember the things which the Lord hath said? If ye will not harden your hearts, and ask me in faith, believing that ye shall receive, with diligence in keeping my commandments, surely these things shall be made known unto you". (V. 11). We who read The Book of Mormon become beneficiaries of Nephi's inspired interpretations of Gospel principles.

He revealed that in the Last Days the Gentiles would receive the fulness of the Gospel of the Messiah, and that from them it would be carried to the remnant of the seed of Lehi. (V. 13). At that day, the remnant would learn that they were the Covenant People of the Lord and of the House of Israel, and they would be taught the very points of doctrine that would enable them to come unto the Lord, enjoy the blessings of the Abrahamic Covenant, and be saved. (V. 14 & 18).

Nephi also spoke to his brethren about the restoration of the Jews in the Last Days, and that they would return both to their homeland and to the true Church. He quoted Isaiah to them to prove his points. "I spake unto them concerning the restoration of the Jews in the latter days. And I did rehearse unto them the words of Isaiah, who spake concerning the restoration of the Jews, or of the House of Israel; and after they were restored they should no more be confounded, neither should they be scattered again". (V. 19 & 20). Isaiah was a Messianic prophet who primarily wrote of the coming of the Redeemer. Therefore, he was a favorite of Nephi, and later of his brother Jacob, and he is the prophet most quoted by them from The Plates of Brass. The best commentary and guide to understanding much of Isaiah, therefore, is The Book of Mormon. The chapter ends with Nephi rehearsing his father's dream of the Tree of Life with his brethren. They had asked him: "What meaneth this thing which our father saw in a dream? What meaneth the tree which he saw?" (V. 21). Nephi explained that it "was a representation of the love of God". (V. 22).

Then they asked: "What meaneth the rod of iron which our father saw, that led to the tree?" (V. 23). Nephi responded: "It was the word of God". Then he taught them: "Whoso would hearken unto the word of God, and would hold fast unto it, they would never perish; neither could the temptations and the fiery darts of the adversary overpower them unto blindness, to lead them away to destruction". (V. 24). Having explained these things, he exhorted his brethren to "give heed to the word of God and remember to keep his commandments always in all things". (V. 25).

The importance of this counsel was underscored by his response to the next question posed by Laman and Lemuel: "What meaneth the river of water which our father saw?" (V. 26). Nephi revealed that it was filthiness, and that so much was the mind of Lehi "swallowed up in other things" at the time he received the vision, "that he beheld not the filthiness of the water". (V. 27, see 1 Nephi 12:16).

This river of filthy water "was an awful gulf, which separated the wicked from the tree of life, and also from the saints of God". (V. 28). It was a representation of hell, which is the destination of the wicked. (V. 29). Nephi taught that it is Satan who "is the preparator of it". (V. 35). The divine justice of God, he reasoned, requires that all "must be brought to stand before God, to be judged of their works; and if their works have been filthiness they must needs be filthy; and if they be filthy it must needs be that they cannot dwell in the kingdom of God; if so, the kingdom of God must be filthy also". (V. 33).

Nephi explained that the kingdom of God cannot be polluted by the presence of the wicked, who are represented as being filthy. Lehi had seen in vision that "the justice of God did also divide the wicked from the righteous; and the brightness thereof was like unto the brightness of a flaming fire, which ascendeth up unto God forever and ever, and hath no end". (V. 30). The Plan of Salvation requires that there must always exist a barrier of separation between the spirits of the righteous and the spirits of the unrighteous as both groups await the Resurrection. All who die during the temporal existence of the earth will pass through the Spirit World, the righteous to receive a glorious resurrection as they claim mercy through the grace of their Savior and Redeemer, and the unrighteous to receive their reward only after they have personally paid the uttermost farthing for their sins and have satisfied the demands of the Law of Justice. All will be accomplished in harmony with the Plan of the Father, that was ratified by His spirit children in the Grand Council before the world was created. (See D&C 121:32, 138:55-56, Alma 13:3 & Abraham 3:22).

Therefore, Nephi must have meant that Satan is the "preparator" of hell in the sense that "it is he who is the author of all sin", just as Christ is "the author and finisher of our faith". (Helaman 6:30 & Hebrews 12:2; see Moroni 6:4). Hell is understood by the Latter-day Saints to be the torment of the wicked in the sense that it is the temporary abode in the spirit world of those who were disobedient in this mortal life. Thus, The Book of Mormon speaks of spiritual death as hell. (See 2 Nephi 9:10-12). So defined, hell will have an end when all its captive spirits have paid the price of their sins and enter into a degree of glory after their resurrection. Statements about an everlasting hell should be interpreted in their proper context, in the light of D&C 19:4-12 that defines, and qualifies, eternal and endless punishment.

On the other hand, "the devil and his angels are condemned to a place spoken of as a lake of fire - a figure of eternal anguish. This condition is sometimes called hell in the scriptures. This kind of hell, that is after the resurrection and judgment, is exclusively for the devil and his angels, and is not the same as the period between death and resurrection. The one group is redeemed from hell and inherits some degree of glory. The other receives no glory. They continue in spiritual darkness. For them the conditions of hell remain". ("Bible Dictionary", p. 699-700).

It is we who make the choice. These are our "days of probation", our time of testing or putting to the proof. (V. 32). We can be as the merchant "who, when he had found one pearl of great price, went and sold all that he had, and bought it". (Matthew 13:46). Or, we can procrastinate the day of our repentance, relying upon the false, vain, and foolish doctrine that urges us to "Eat, drink, and be merry, for tomorrow we die; and it shall be well with us". (2 Nephi 28:7).

In Lehi's dream, those who sought the tree of life and endured to the end in righteousness found the reward for their effort to be a prize that was "most precious and most desirable above all other fruits, yea, and (was) the greatest of all the gifts of God". (V. 36). The Doctrine & Covenants confirms that the fruit of the Tree of Life is the gift of eternal life. (See D&C 14:7 & 88:4).

"They shall
come to the knowledge
of their Redeemer and the
very points of his doctrine,
that they may know how to
come unto him and be saved."
(1 Nephi 15:14).

First Nephi
Chapter 16

It was difficult for Laman and Lemuel to listen to Nephi's interpretation of their father's dream because the truth hurt their guilty conscience. "Thou hast declared unto us hard things", complained Laman and Lemuel, "more than we are able to bear". (V. 1). As therapy, Nephi encouraged them to walk uprightly, and to engage in spiritually aerobic exercise. "And it came to pass that I, Nephi, did exhort my brethren, with all diligence, to keep the commandments of the Lord". (V. 2). He wanted them to prepare for the banquet of consequences, where the blameless will bow their heads in reverence, rather than hang them in shame, in the presence of God Who will be there.

He knew how destructive the murmuring of Laman and Lemuel would be. Murmuring is the subdued and continually repeated expression of indistinct or inarticulate complaint or grumbling. It is the disobedient who murmur against the teachings of the prophets. Murmuring by otherwise active members of the Church is very detrimental to individuals, families, wards, and stakes. Therefore, Nephi was encouraged when his brethren "did humble themselves before the Lord; insomuch that (he) had joy and great hopes of them, that they would walk in the paths of righteousness". (V. 5). This, in spite of his vision of the destiny of the descendants of Lehi. (See 1 Nephi 12:19-23).

Nephi reminded us that "all these things were said and done as (his) father dwelt in a tent in the valley which he called Lemuel". (V. 6). It seems strange to us that the valley was not called by the same name as the river, for this is our custom. But to the desert dweller, a river could dry up and disappear without warning. It was the valley that endured and made passage through inhospitable mountains possible, and thus, it was to the valley that geographical and symbolical references were made by the ancients.

Ishmael had five daughters who became the wives of the young men in the camp. (V. 7). Perhaps the same daughter who had intervened on Nephi's behalf outside Jerusalem became his wife. (See 1 Nephi 7:19). We do not know who the sons of Ishmael married, but it must have been daughters of Lehi who remain unidentified in the text, for we know of no other young women in the party. We do know that "Zoram took the eldest daughter of Ishmael to wife", and that his family later followed Nephi into the wilderness. (V. 7, see 2 Nephi 5:6). Since they had kept all the commandments that had been given to them up to this time, Lehi's little band was permitted by the Lord to move on. (V. 8-9). Just as Israel had been led by a pillar of fire during its forty years of wandering in the wilderness following their exodus from Egypt, the Lord now led Lehi's party through the medium of "a round ball of curious workmanship; and it was of fine brass. And within the ball were two spindles; and the one pointed the way whither (they) should go into the wilderness". (V. 10, see Exodus 13:21).

This was the "Liahona". (See Commentary Reference to Alma 37:38). It was a true "compass" that consisted of a pair of spindles in motion, the nature of that motion being a circle. (Hugh Nibley, "Since Cumorah", p. 296). This compass functioned according to faith, and was divinely provided to guide the way. The transliteration from Hebrew suggests that the term "Liahona" means "God gives light, as does the Sun". This is certainly an appropriate description of the device used by Lehi's party as it traveled through the wilderness to the Land Bountiful and beyond. (See 1 Nephi 17:5).

The Liahona was actually a "type" of Christ. As Alma taught Corianton: "And now, my son, I would that ye should understand that these things are not without a shadow; for as our fathers were slothful to give heed to his compass they did not prosper; even so it is with things which are spiritual. For behold, it is as easy to give heed to the word of Christ, which will point to you a straight course to eternal bliss, as it was for our fathers to give heed to this compass, which would point unto them a straight course to the promised land. And now I say, is there not a type in this thing?" An outward observance without any real inward meaning is only a ceremony. But a rite that has a present spiritual meaning is a symbol; and if, besides, it also points to a future reality, conveying at the same time, by anticipation, the blessing that is yet to appear, it is a type.

"For just as surely as this director did bring our fathers, by following its course, to the promised land, shall the words of Christ, if we follow their course, carry us beyond this vale of sorrow into a far better land of promise. O my son, do not let us be slothful because of the easiness of the way; for so was it with our fathers; for so was it prepared for them, that if they would look they might live; even so it is with us. The way is prepared, and if we will look we may live forever". (Alma 37:43-46).

After a journey of four days, Lehi's party reached a place that they called "Shazer". (V. 13). In Arabic, "Shajer" or "Shazher" means either "a clump of trees" or "a seepage of water". Both may be correct, for Lehi's party could hardly have picked a better name for their first suitable stopping place.

As they traveled on, they stopped "in the most fertile parts of the wilderness, which were in the borders near the Red Sea". (V. 14). They were likely able to plant, cultivate, and harvest crops, for we read that they stockpiled seeds during these prolonged encampments. (V. 17, see v. 11). They also depended upon food obtained as they hunted animals, and so it was a real calamity when Nephi broke the only steel bow in their arsenal. (V. 18). Critics have claimed that this reference to steel is a technical flaw in The Book of Mormon, asserting that steel was unknown at this early date, but Hugh Nibley has pointed out that "steel may be taken to mean any form of very tough iron, and the correct chemical formula for it is found in objects from Ras Shamra, dating back to the 14th century B.C". ("Lehi in The Desert", p. 212).

This was a critical moment for the party, because without this bow, it was unable to obtain food at a time when all were fatigued and in need of sustenance. For not only had Nephi broken his bow, but the wooden bows of his brethren had lost their "springs" and were useless. (V. 21). Note the peculiar Semitic use of the plural form of a noun of quality. At this point, even Lehi was discouraged and began to murmur against the Lord his God. (V. 20).

Nephi took stock of the situation and made a new bow out of wood. (V. 23). To go from a steel bow to a wooden bow was quite an achievement, and in the record, Nephi was justly proud. He also made an arrow. His hand-made wooden bow would have had nowhere near the strength of his treasured metal bow, and so he would have needed new arrows matched to its replacement. Hence, it is appropriate that Nephi should mention that he made an arrow, as well as a bow.

This would have been the ideal moment for the "heir apparent" to step in and take charge, just when the old man was wavering in his faith. In a pulp novel, this is exactly what would have happened. After all, had not an angel already declared that Nephi would rule over his brethren? (See 1 Nephi 3:29). But at this pivotal time, Nephi continued without wavering to honor his father, even though he had received his own powerful spiritual manifestations and confirmations. He simply asked his father: "Whither shall I go to obtain food". (V. 23).

With renewed faith, Lehi "did inquire of the Lord". (V. 24). His voice came to Lehi, "and he was truly chastened because of his murmuring against the Lord, insomuch that he was brought down into the depths of sorrow". (V. 25). It was "Godly sorrow" that Lehi felt for his sins, and the depth and quality of his feeling was a critical step in his process of true repentance. This is an excellent example of God's purpose for the chastisement of those whom He loves. Such experiences bring repentant souls into attitudes of holiness and acceptance before God.

At the direction of the Lord, Lehi consulted the Liahona, and it is possible that a warning was written upon it, for afterward he "did fear and tremble exceedingly". (V. 27). "And it came to pass that I, Nephi, beheld the pointers which were in the ball, that they did work according to the faith and diligence and heed which we did give unto them. And there was also written upon them a new writing, which was plain to be read, which did give us understanding concerning the ways of the Lord; and it was written and changed from time to time, according to the faith and diligence which we gave unto it". (V. 28-29).

Elsewhere in scripture, we learn that Alma saw in the Liahona a type or a symbol of the Word of God, or the Gospel. In time, the Liahona was passed on with the plates and other emblems of authority, and may have been deposited with them in the Hill Cumorah, for it was shown to the Three Witnesses. (See D&C 17:1). In any event, Nephi was able to obtain meat for the party by following the instructions that were given to Lehi via the Liahona.

Thus invigorated, the group resumed its travels, but after many days Ishmael died. Perhaps the strain of the sustained journey was too much for him. He must have been put to rest in an established burial ground, because the name of the place "was called Nahom". (V. 34). The Arabic root "NHM" means "to sigh, or to moan". Among dwellers of the desert, such expressions of grief are a monopoly of women, and Lehi's group fit the pattern exactly. "And it came to pass that the daughters of Ishmael did mourn exceedingly, because of the loss of their father". (V. 35).

Ishmael's death was a convenient pretext for his sons, as well as for their kindred spirits Laman and Lemuel, to renew their murmuring against Nephi. (V. 35-36). They also charged that Nephi had taken it upon himself to be their ruler and teacher, although they were his elder brethren. They did this in spite of the fact that the angel had already declared to them that Nephi would, in time, lead the family. (See 1 Nephi 3:29 & 2 Nephi 5:19).

There might be significance to the timing of this latest round of murmuring on the part of Laman and Lemuel. An article in the Jewish Quarterly Review (N. 69, p. 82-83) discusses the symbolic meaning attached to the breaking of a bow. Kings would break the bows of disobedient vassals, the bow being a symbol of power and leadership. Laman and Lemuel may have seen the breaking of Nephi's bow in the context of their Near Eastern background. It was immediately after this event when Nephi made another bow and thus had the only functional bow in camp, that they complained that he had "taken it upon himself to be their ruler". (V. 37).

Laman and Lemuel now denied that Nephi had seen an angel who had ministered unto him, although they had witnessed the event themselves. This is a classic example of the wicked declaring that black is white. They also denied the divine source of the many miracles that they had witnessed. Faith, it would seem, always precedes the recognition and acceptance of miracles. Belief, without the moral element of responsibility we call faith, often crumbles in the face of adversity.

Their anger took a murderous turn, when "Laman said unto Lemuel and also unto the sons of Ishmael: Behold, let us slay our father, and also our brother Nephi". (V. 37). Thus, the pattern was set for ongoing fratricidal conflict between the descendants of Laman and Lemuel and Nephi, when Laman complained of Nephi that "he worketh many things by his cunning arts, that he may deceive our eyes". (V. 38).

But even in their ignorance, and in spite of their denial of divine intervention in the party's behalf, the Lord was merciful to Laman and Lemuel. His voice came unto them, spoke many words to them, and chastened or disciplined them with the purpose of effecting moral improvement. (V. 39). Those who are "chaste" are virtuous, morally pure, innocent, and free from guilt. In the brothers' case, they were not yet completely spiritually bankrupt. They still had the opportunity to recognize the foolishness of their behavior and conform their lives to principles that would bring them peace, spiritual security, and happiness. In fact, this chastisement of the brothers did bring about positive change, however transient it might later prove to be, and the party was consequently again blessed with the temporal necessities of life.

First Nephi
Chapter 17

This chapter provides insight into the lengthy preparation of the group for the colonization of a new world. It would appear that as they "did travel and wade through much affliction in the wilderness", they were fortified and refined. (V. 1). Even the women and children "began to bear their journeyings without murmurings". (V. 2). "And thus, we see", wrote Nephi, "that if it so be that the children of men keep the commandments of God he doth nourish them, and strengthen them, and provide means whereby they can accomplish the thing which he has commanded them". (V. 3, see 1 Nephi 3:7).

They lived on raw meat, because they did not often dare to make fires. (V. 2 & 12). This might have been for protection, for a fire would have served as a beacon for bandits roaming the area. Becoming accustomed to raw meat might also have prepared them for life aboard ship, where routine cooking fires would have been hazardous

Nephi related that eight years were spent in the wilderness before they came to a beautiful oasis beside the sea that they called Bountiful, "because of its much fruit and also wild honey". (V. 4-5). One possible location for this land is Salalah in Oman, on the southern tip of the Arabian Peninsula. A description of this area by an explorer in 1846 described it as "a land of groves, well watered, with lush vegetation".

They rested there for "many days" before Nephi was again instructed by the Lord. (V. 7). It must have been unsettling for him when he was told to construct a ship. (V. 8). An ancient proverb goes: "Show an Arab the sea, and a man of Sidon the Desert". In other words, the desert is the home of the Arab, while the ocean is familiar territory to the seafaring people of the port city of Sidon. As a matter of fact, Nephi's brothers called him a fool when he told them of his plans, because they knew that oil and water don't mix.

But Nephi's reaction to the Lord's command was simply to ask where he might go to find the necessary materials for construction. (V. 9). His faith was implicit, and he did not question the Lord's judgment or wisdom. The Lord, in turn, promised that He would be their "light in the wilderness", as He led them toward the promised land. (V. 13, see v. 30). They had the Liahona, that being interpreted, means "God gives light, as does the sun", and they might have recognized their wanderings in the wilderness as a type and a shadow of the similar Exodus of Israel from Egypt. (V. 30, see Jacob 7:26, Book of Mormon Symposium Series, 1988).

The hearts of Laman and Lemuel, on the other hand, had not softened during their years of hardship in the wilderness. When they were asked to work on the construction of the ship, they complained bitterly. (V. 17-18). After reaching Bountiful, life must have been easy for them, and well suited to their inherent laziness.

They would have seen Nephi's shipbuilding plans as another postponement of their quest for temporal prosperity. They felt that they had been robbed of a very comfortable lifestyle in the land of Jerusalem, having been forced to give up all their possessions before embarking upon an arduous journey into the desert wastes of Arabia. "Behold, these many years we have suffered in the wilderness", they declared, during "which time we might have enjoyed our possessions and the land of our inheritance; yea, and we might have been happy". (V. 21). Now, having found a fruitful land, just when they were again comfortably situated, their plans for the good life were again frustrated. They would not believe that Nephi had been "instructed of the Lord". (V. 18).

Sweet irony was manifest when Laman and Lemuel complained: "Thou art like unto our father". (V. 20). How true was this statement. Both Lehi and Nephi were visionary, whereas Laman and Lemuel were congenitally shortsighted. There is literally a world of difference between the two perspectives. The two elder brothers thought that their possessions in the land of Jerusalem would have brought them happiness. But while they were complaining in Bountiful, Jerusalem was under siege by Babylonia, and after two and a half years of privation, the people of the city would even resort to cannibalism. So much for temporal security.

We find in Laman and Lemuel's argument the standard line of the Jews of that time: "And we know that the people who were in the land of Jerusalem were a righteous people; for they kept the statutes and judgments of the Lord, and all his commandments". (V. 22). We know better, for Nephi had written that "there came many prophets, prophesying unto the people that they must repent, or the great city Jerusalem must be destroyed". (1 Nephi 1:4, see Commentary Reference to 2 Nephi 6:8). Nevertheless, Laman and Lemuel murmured against their father, complaining that "he hath judged them". (V. 22). In fact, even after the chastening experience of the Babylonian captivity, the Jews at Jerusalem in general felt no guilt for their sins, but remained unrepentant.

In order to exhort his brethren to righteousness, Nephi quoted from The Plates of Brass, citing Exodus, that chronicled the liberation of their ancestors from Egyptian captivity and their subsequent journey to the Promised Land. (V. 23-32). In doing so, he confirmed the authenticity of these ancient stories from the Bible. The Book of Mormon is truly a witness of the Bible. Nephi reminded his brethren of the water ordeal experienced by the Israelites who had fled Egypt under the leadership of Moses. (V. 26-27). This "water ordeal" was an ancient pattern, and Nephi might have anticipated that theirs was soon to come. (See 1 Nephi 18).

He also rehearsed for his brethren the miraculous feeding of the Israelites with manna from heaven, and recited to them the manner in which God had provided water, "that the children of Israel might quench their thirst". (V. 28-29). As Nephi recounted these stories from the scriptures to his family, they must have recognized the hand of the Lord in their own experiences, for He had comforted them with the assurance: "I will make thy food become sweet, that ye cook it not". (V. 12). For eight long years in the wilderness, as they sat together at mealtime, that promise was repeatedly validated.

Having previously received a vision wherein he saw the apostasy of the "Lamanites", it must have been with a heavy heart that Nephi reminded his brethren how the Israelites had "hardened their hearts and blinded their minds, and reviled against Moses, and against the true and living God". (V. 30). The experience of Israel would prove to be a prologue of the drama that would unfold over the course of the next millennium in the New World.

Nephi then taught the very important principle that righteousness, and not lineage, is important to God. (V. 33). "The Lord esteemeth all flesh in one; he that is righteous is favored of God". (V. 35). He "loveth those who will have Him to be their God". (V. 40). He also taught the converse of this principle, that the destruction of the wicked is required when God's wrath is full, when the people have lost their desire to repent. (See 1 Nephi 14:15).

Nephi asked the rhetorical question: "Do ye suppose that the children of this land, who were in the land of promise, who were driven out by our fathers, do ye suppose that they were righteous?" (V. 33). He was referring to the Canaanites whom the Israelites had been commanded to drive out. "And the Lord spake unto Moses in the plains of Moab by Jordan near Jericho, saying, speak unto the children of Israel, and say unto them, When ye are passed over Jordan into the land of Canaan; Then ye shall drive out all the inhabitants of the land from before you, and destroy all their pictures, and destroy all their molten images, and ... pluck down all their high places: And ye shall dispossess the inhabitants of the land, and dwell therein: for I have given you the land to possess it". (Numbers 33:51-53, see Deuteronomy 7:2 & 9:3).

Nephi said of the Canaanites that they "had rejected every word of God, and they were ripe in iniquity; and the fulness of the wrath of God was upon them; and the Lord did curse the land against them, and bless it unto our fathers; yea, he did curse it against them unto their destruction, and he did bless it unto our fathers unto their obtaining power over it". (V. 35). The Book of Mormon repeatedly illustrates the tremendous significance of this principle and lesson from the scriptures, and it does so here chiastically. Nephi explained that the circumstances of the Israelites at the time of the Exodus were "straitened", or were rendered strict and rigorous, "for they hardened their hearts, even as ye have, and the Lord straitened them because of their iniquity". (V. 41). Thus, they were limited in their range of power and action. When they were taught to look to the brazen serpent, which was a type of Jesus Christ, "because of the simpleness of the way, or the easiness of it, there were many who perished". (V. 41, see Alma 33:19, Alma 37:45, & Helaman 8:14). When Nephi related this story to his family, it must have made quite an impression on Laman and Lemuel as they recognized its inherent symbolism. The image of the Serpent God had such an effect, in fact, that it endured for well over a thousand years as a representation of God in Pre-Columbian American cultures.

Nephi continued to exhort his brethren, and the next few verses provide a brief character sketch of Laman and Lemuel. Nephi accused them of being murderers in their hearts who quickly and easily sinned, and who were slow to remember God, notwithstanding their sacred experiences. (V. 44). He said that they must certainly have lost the ability to feel, for the Lord had to speak to them "like unto the voice of thunder; before they could hear. (V. 45).

Unfortunately, Laman and Lemuel had only been theologically titillated by the miracles they had witnessed. Their experiences did not result in lasting conversion, whereas Nephi was "so full of the Spirit of God" that he was moved to declare: "My frame has no strength". (V. 47). In much the same way, Joseph Smith once declared: "Yea, thus saith the still small voice, which whispereth through and pierceth all things, and often times it maketh my bones to quake while it maketh manifest". (D&C 85:6).

Laman and Lemuel were outraged by what Nephi said, because the "guilty take the truth to be hard, for it cutteth them to the very center". (1 Nephi 16:2). They desired to subject Nephi, at that very moment, to his own water ordeal, but instead, it was they who felt the effects. (V. 48, see v. 49-55). He recorded: "I spake unto them, saying: 'In the name of the Almighty God, I command you that ye touch me not, for I am filled with the power of God, even unto the consuming of my flesh; and whoso shall lay his hands upon me shall wither even as a dried reed; and he shall be as naught before the power of God, for God shall smite him". (V. 48). Laman and Lemuel were such spiritual lightweights that "they were confounded and could not contend against (Nephi); neither durst they lay their hands upon (him) nor touch (him) with their fingers, even for the space of many days". (V. 52). In fact, they shook and trembled in his presence. (V. 54).

Consequently, they declared that they now recognized the hand of God in Nephi's actions, and they attempted to fall down and worship him. But did they have a newfound faith? Paul taught that faith is "the substance of things hoped for, the evidence of things not seen". (Hebrews 11:1). Laman and Lemuel wanted to worship the man with the power, rather than God, Who is the source of all power. Their faith was all form and no substance. They really had no saving faith whatsoever. They believed, but they lacked the moral element of responsibility we call faith. Nephi would have none of it, of course, reminding his brethren: "I am thy brother, yea, even thy younger brother; wherefore, worship the Lord thy God, and honor thy father and thy mother, that thy days may be long in the land which the Lord thy God shall give thee". (V. 55).

These principles are very important, and so in verses 36-39, Nephi's summary was conveyed in chiastic language:

A: The Lord created the earth.
B: The Lord raises up a righteous nation, and destroys the wicked.
B: He leads away the righteous to precious lands, and destroys the wicked.
A: He rules in the heavens, and the earth is his footstool.

We learn in this chapter that the purpose of the creation of the earth was so that it might be inhabited. But the wicked are often quarantined or separated from the righteous. In fact, the Lord has many times led away His people to their lands of promise. (See 3 Nephi 15:20). IV Ezra, an ancient apocryphal book, states that the Ten Tribes of Israel, "in order to be able to live the law without molestation, resolved to depart from the society of mankind and migrate to the other world in a land beyond, where no member of the human race had ever before lived". (See Hugh Nibley, "An Approach to The Book of Mormon", p. 120, & Commentary Reference to 2 Nephi 20:21).

Nephi taught his brethren that if they would value their spiritual welfare, love the Lord, and keep His commandments, they would find the happiness they craved. Heber J. Grant once said: "I bear witness to you as an Apostle of the Lord Jesus Christ, that material and spiritual prosperity is predicated upon the fulfilment of the duties and responsibilities that rest upon us as Latter-day Saints". (C.R,. 10/1889). Similarly, Joseph Smith taught: "Happiness is the object and design of our existence and will be the end thereof, if we follow the path that leads to it. And this path is virtue, uprightness, faithfulness, holiness, and keeping all the commandments of God. In obedience there is joy and peace ... and as God has designed our happiness ... He never has, He never will, give a commandment to His people that is not calculated in its nature to promote that happiness which He has designed."" (History of the Church, 5:134-135.)

First Nephi
Chapter 18

Nephi's rebellious brothers "worship(ed) the Lord, and did go forth" with him by the shores of Bountiful to complete a ship of unusual design and superior workmanship. (V. 1 & 4). After all, the Lord was its architect. (V. 2). We do not know what this craft looked like, but it was "not after the manner of men". (V. 2). It is of interest that four times Nephi described going "down into the ship" and sailing "before the wind". (V. 8).

Laman and Lemuel, who had at first mocked Nephi and called him a fool for even thinking of building a ship, again saw the light. As long as they had visible proof before them, they were willing to concede, however grudgingly, the Lord's Hand in their affairs. Because they beheld "that it was good, and that the workmanship thereof was exceedingly fine; wherefore, they did humble themselves again before the Lord". (V. 4).

Patriarch Lehi continued to receive most of the revelations concerning the party, and so it was to him that the Voice of the Lord came, commanding them to pack their belongings, board the vessel, and set sail. (V. 5, see V. 22). According to the ancient law of primogeniture, they went "down into the ship ... every one according to his age". (V. 6).

Two more children had been born to Lehi and Sariah in the wilderness, and these undertook the journey with their family. (V. 7). When these two sons, named Jacob and Joseph, grew to manhood, it is reasonable to assume that they married daughters of Zoram, who had himself married a daughter of Ishmael.

Their ship put forth "into the sea" and was "driven before the wind towards the promised land". (V. 8). Leaving the southeastern coast of the Arabian Peninsula, they would have crossed the Arabian Sea in a southeasterly direction, taking advantage of the Northeast Monsoon Drift, which would have taken them past the Maldives and the tip of the subcontinent of India. Then, they would have picked up the Equatorial Counter Current, which would have carried them further east through the islands of Indonesia.

Passing north of the continent of Australia, they would have then negotiated Melanesia and Micronesia, crisscrossing the equator, before heading into the open ocean of the South Pacific. Taking a southerly route, they would have battled the South Equatorial Current, and if they went to the north, they would have faced the North Equatorial Current. As they neared the Western Hemisphere, they would have run into the Peru Humboldt Current. Landfall would reasonably have been along the western coast of Meso-America.

Laman and his soulmates set the stage for further chastisement when, not long into the voyage, "they were lifted up unto exceeding rudeness". (V. 9). Their behavior was graphic evidence that they had forgotten by what power they had been sustained in the wilderness, blessed beside the seashore in Bountiful, and watched over on the vast ocean. The party continued to be guided by the Liahona, which only operated by faith, but Nephi worried because they were always in jeopardy of losing the Lord's protection during their long voyage. He wrote: "And I, Nephi, began to fear exceedingly lest the Lord should be angry with (all of) us, and smite us because of our iniquity". (V. 10). In fact, Laman and Lemuel's faithlessness reached the boiling point when they declared: "We will not that our younger brother shall be a ruler over us". (V. 10). This would prove to be the repetitive argument of Laman and Lemuel and their descendants during the entire course of Book of Mormon history.

When Nephi was bound with cords by his brethren following a mutiny aboard the ship, the compass immediately stopped working. (V. 11-12). Consequently, without direction from the Lord, the vessel wandered off course into stormy latitudes and encountered a vicious cyclone. Even with this immediate manifestation of the withdrawal of the guidance of the Spirit, the hearts of Laman and his followers were not softened. They would not release Nephi, although the very real possibility existed that the ship might founder, and all aboard drown. (V. 13). Because of their iniquity, the entire ship's company was "brought near even to be carried out of this time to meet their God". (V. 18).

Nephi remained bound for 4 long days while Lehi and Sariah pleaded for his release. (V. 17). During this time, Laman and Lemuel "began to see that the judgments of God were upon them, and that they must perish save that they should repent of their iniquities". (V. 15, see v. 19). In general, though, they stared uncomprehendingly with slit eyed skepticism at the manifestations of God that lay before them.

In all ages, the disobedient have crowded against each other, elbowing their way to the best vantage point on the balcony of "the large and spacious building which ... is the vain imaginations and the pride of the children of men". (1 Nephi 12:18). Thinking they stand on a solid footing, their position is in reality strategically vulnerable, so that "a great and a terrible gulf divideth them" from the righteous, which is the manifestation of "the word of the justice of the Eternal God, and the Messiah who is the Lamb of God". (1 Nephi 12:18).

Because of their spiritual stagnation, Laman and Lemuel "did breathe out much threatenings against anyone that should speak for (Nephi)". (V. 17). So often, the disobedient try to stifle every expression of indignation against their sinful behavior. Even so, Nephi's righteous family members rallied in his behalf, and begged for his release. (V. 18-19).

In verse 19, we find a rare direct reference to Nephi's family: "My wife with her tears and prayers, and also my children, did not soften the hearts of my brethren that they would loose me". (See 1 Nephi 7:17 & 16:7). They finally released Nephi, but only because they began to see that God's judgments were upon them because of their wickedness. (V. 15 & 20, see Commentary Reference to 1 Nephi 7:19). "And there was nothing save it were the power of God, which threatened them with destruction, could soften their hearts; wherefore, when they saw that they were about to swallowed up in the depths of the sea, they repented of the thing which they had done". (V. 20).

But was this true repentance? A thousand years later, Mormon's second epistle described the behavior of his brethren in these words: "Behold, I am laboring with them continually; and when I speak the word of God with sharpness they tremble and anger against me; and when I use no sharpness they harden their hearts against it, wherefore, I fear lest the Spirit of the Lord hath ceased striving with them". (Moroni 9:4). Nephi warned of the consequences of this same intransigence among his brethren, when he wrote: "For the Spirit of the Lord will not always strive with man. And when the Spirit ceaseth to strive with man, then cometh speedy destruction". (2 Nephi 26:10).

After Nephi regained his freedom, the compass once again became operative. The Liahona was not a nautical compass that showed the way one was going, but was a spiritual compass that showed the way one should go. Marco Polo brought nautical compasses back to Europe from Asia in the 14th century. Before that time in the Near East and Europe, only crude sunstones that polarized sunlight had been used by seafarers such as the Vikings on the open ocean.

Nephi also "prayed unto the Lord". (V. 21). Certainly, "the effectual fervent prayer of a righteous man availeth much", for it was only after he had thus prayed that "the winds did cease, and the storm did cease, and there was a great calm". (James 5:16 & v. 21). Figuratively and literally speaking, heart-felt and ardent prayer can have dramatic effects.

Elaine Cannon, a General President of the Relief Society, related a story about prayer. She said: "Last month in our fast meeting a young woman stood up under great difficulty, the first time she had been able to do so since her husband had passed away. They hadn't been married very long, she said, before he became critically ill. In the last stages of his illness, he was suffering beyond belief, and she was really desperate. She knelt one night by the side of his bed and cried out to the Lord as only a woman can do, full of anxiety, full of demands, pleading, almost scolding the Lord to hear her and answer her prayers and help her husband, to heal him. She was near hysteria. Then she felt a touch on her shoulder, and it was her husband trying to calm her. He said to her, 'Just pray that I may be able to sleep through the night.' She said, 'That sweet sustaining lesson taught me that you don't ask for your will to be done, you just pray that you can meet the challenges of the day. And that lesson from my husband just before he died has helped me to sleep through the night, as well.'"

Because of the focused faith of Nephi, their ship was guided across hostile oceans to a likely landfall on the Pacific coast of the Western Hemisphere, that they called "the promised land", suggesting that there are many such lands of promise. (V. 23, see 2 Nephi 9:2). It was a land of abundance with animals of every kind. It is possible that some of these were not indigenous to the Western Hemisphere, but were descendants of animals that had been brought to the New World hundreds of years earlier by the Jaredites. It is possible that the hand of the Lord had driven these animals from the north countries, into the land southward. (See Ether 9:32). In fact, physical evidence of varied types of wildlife of Pre-Columbian North America can be observed today at the La Brea Tar Pits, in Southern California.

It is interesting that Lehi's party also found gold, silver, and copper to be plentiful. (V. 25). Nephi made mention of it almost as an aside, although these metals were the essence of the treasures the family had left behind in Jerusalem. In the Promised Land, among the early Nephites, they must have had little appeal other than for ornamental purposes. However, during the ensuing thousand-year history of Book of Mormon peoples, the accumulation of gold that has always been the physical evidence of temporal prosperity and the worldly standard of wealth commanded the attention of those who strayed from the Rod of Iron.

"And it came to pass after we had all gone down into the ship, and had taken with us our provisions and things which had been commanded us, we did put forth into the sea and were driven forth before the wind towards the promised land." (1 Nephi 18:8).

First Nephi
Chapter 19

Nephi wrote that he was commanded by the Lord to make plates of ore upon which he was to write the record of his people. These became The Large Plates of Nephi. Both his and his father's prophetic callings were quietly validated when Nephi explained that their prophecies were to be included in that record.

Students of The Book of Mormon sometimes speak of The Book of Lehi, that was a part of the record Nephi made upon The Large Plates of Nephi. Nephi wrote: "And upon the plates which I made I did engraven the record of my father". (V. 1). However, the First Book of Nephi as we have it is the translation made from The Small Plates of Nephi that includes Nephi's synopsis of his father's record. We do not have a direct translation from the writings of Lehi, that were recorded on The Large Plates, because it was lost due to the carelessness with which Martin Harris treated the first 116 pages of manuscript at the time Joseph Smith was translating The Book of Mormon from the plates in his possession.

Nephi did not know at the time he engraved The Large Plates of Nephi that he would also be making a companion record on The Small Plates. Whenever he referred to The Small Plates, he identified them as "these plates". Every time there is a reference to The Large Plates, he identified them as "those plates".

"I knew not at the time when I made them", Nephi wrote, "that I should be commanded of the Lord to make these plates; wherefore the record of my father, and the genealogy of his fathers, and the more part of all our proceedings in the wilderness are engraven upon those first plates of which I have spoken; wherefore, the things which transpired before I made these plates are, of a truth, more particularly made mention upon the first plates". (V. 2).

He elaborated on the contents of both sets of records. "And after I had made these plates by way of commandment, I, Nephi, received a commandment that the ministry and the prophecies, the more plain and precious parts of them, should be written upon these plates; and that the things which were written should be kept for the instruction of my people, who should possess the land, and also for other wise purposes, which purposes are known unto the Lord". (V. 3).

This passage reveals why The Book of Mormon has always been such a powerful testament of Christ and tool for conversion. Unlike the Bible, it contains "the more plain and precious parts" of the doctrine of Christ. Its literary style is not unlike the King James Translation of the Bible, but its clarity is unique among ancient texts. As Nephi told his people at the close of his ministry: "Feast upon the words of Christ; for behold, the words of Christ will tell you all things what ye should do. Wherefore, now after I have spoken these words, if ye cannot understand them it will be because ye ask not, neither do ye knock … Behold, this is the doctrine of Christ". (2 Nephi 32:3-4 & 6).

Nephi also hinted at the "other wise purposes" for which the second, parallel, record of his people was made. At this early date, when he undertook to keep the record on The Large Plates, he already understood the scope of future Nephite history, for he had seen it in vision. Those plates give "a greater account of the wars and contentions and destructions" of his people. (V. 4).

But he only began his engravings upon The Small Plates 30 years after leaving Jerusalem, after having been commanded by the Lord to do so. (See 2 Nephi 5:28-30). He wrote: "An account of my making these plates shall be given hereafter; and then, behold, I proceed according to that which I have spoken; and this I do that the more sacred things may be kept for the knowledge of my people. Nevertheless, I do not write anything upon plates save it be that I think it be sacred". (V. 5-6). Even though The Large Plates contained a record more focused on the temporal activities of the Nephites, it was nevertheless envisioned by Nephi to be important to both the temporal and spiritual salvation of his people. We know this to be true, inasmuch as the abridgment made by Mormon from The Large Plates of Nephi, comprising most of The Book of Mormon from The Book of Mosiah onward, is a great spiritual treasure, as well as a window on Nephite and Lamanite culture.

Nephi acknowledged that his record might contain errors. (V. 6). This is not a reference to theological inconsistencies. As Mormon wrote, "And if there be faults they be the faults of a man". (Mormon 8:12). Both Nephi and Mormon apologized for their perceived inability to communicate in writing with as much fluidity as they would have liked. As Moroni explained in The Book of Ether: "We could write but little, because of the awkwardness of our hands. When we write, we behold our weakness, and stumble because of the placing of our words; and I fear lest the Gentiles shall mock at our words". (Ether 12:24-25, see Commentary Reference to Alma 24:19). In our day, we see how prophetic these words have proven to be, when many criticize The Book of Mormon not so much because of its doctrinal content but for its literary style.

In its defense, the book follows closely the vernacular of the King James Translation of the Bible, which was the edition with which Joseph Smith was familiar. "The Book of Mormon makes fittingly few alterations in Bible language. However much consolation such close parallels may give to those cynical of the book's origins, it must be conceded that at least The Book of Mormon knows a good thing when it sees it. Consistency with the peerless King James Version, whatever its implications for originality, is highly stylistic tribute". (Steven C. Walker, "More than Meets the Eye: Concentration of The Book of Mormon", 20:2:199).

Nephi described just how the wicked trample God under their feet. He wrote: "In other words, they set him at naught, and hearken not to the voice of his counsels". (V. 7). This is a most sobering thought to ponder, especially in these pivotal Last Days. "Fools mock, but they shall mourn" warned Moroni. (Ether 12:26). When the faithless reject the Word of God, they place their souls in jeopardy. As Sir Walter Scott wrote of the Bible, so could we generalize to apply to The Book of Mormon: "Within this awful volume lies the mystery of mysteries. Happiest is he of human race to whom our God has given grace, to read, to fear, to hope, to pray, to lift the latch, and force the way; and better had he ne'er been born, who reads to doubt, or reads to scorn".

Lehi's departure from Jerusalem was established in verse 8 as 600 years before the birth of the Savior. Nephi prophesied that the Savior's ministry would be viewed by the people as a thing of naught, and that they would scourge, smite, and spit upon Him before they crucified Him. Spiritual Babylon is ruled by the Prince of Darkness, and has always both figuratively and literally treated the God of Israel with rudeness and contempt. Especially today, it participates wildly in these activities. Through it all, the Savior has "suffered" this treatment, that is to say, He allows it, submits painfully to it, endures it, and has voluntarily borne the extreme penalty as a result of it. (V. 9).

Verse 10 teaches that there are prophecies that are not currently found in the Old Testament. One plain and precious part of the scriptures that has been lost is the reality that the God of Abraham, Isaac, and Jacob, He Who spoke to Moses on Sinai and led Israel into the Promised Land, is Jesus Christ, the Redeemer of the world. Zenock, Zenos, and Neum were prophets of the lineage of Joseph, and their prophecies were recorded on the family scriptures known as The Plates of Brass, but are not mentioned in the Bible. (See Jacob 5, Alma 33:3-17, & 3 Nephi 10:6).

Zenos, in particular, had prophesied "concerning the three days of darkness, which should be a sign given of his death unto those who should inhabit the isles of the sea, more especially given unto those who are of the House of Israel". (V. 10). His testimony, that is not found in the Old Testament, lends support to The Book of Mormon account in 3 Nephi 8:20-23 of the "thick darkness upon the face of the land" that persisted for three days following the crucifixion.

Zenos prophesied that the Lord God would visit all the House of Israel at the time He was crucified. To some, He would manifest Himself through "his voice, because of their righteousness, unto their great joy and salvation, and (to) others with the thunderings and the lightnings of his power, by tempest, by fire, and by smoke, and vapor of darkness, and by the opening of the earth, and by mountains which shall be carried up". (V. 11). As the Lord told Joseph Smith: "Whosoever believeth on my words, them will I visit with the manifestation of my Spirit; and they shall be born of me, even of water and of the Spirit". (D&C 5:26).

At the same time, "a desolating scourge shall go forth among the inhabitants of the earth, and shall continue to be poured out from time to time, if they repent not, until the earth is empty, and the inhabitants thereof are consumed away and utterly destroyed by the brightness of my coming". (D&C 5:19). The Lord has provided the Gospel as an escape plan, but the prescribed conditions must be obeyed in order to avoid the decreed punishment.

Nephi understood the importance of the message of Zenos not only to those who were "upon the isles of the sea" who were expatriates from the land of Israel, but also to all those who would ever claim membership in the House of Israel, whether by lineage or adoption. (See Commentary References to 1 Nephi 22:4-5, 2 Nephi 8:5, 2 Nephi 10:8, & 21-22, 2 Nephi 21:11, 2 Nephi 29:7-8, & Alma 63:5). "Wherefore, I speak unto all the House of Israel, if it so be that they should obtain these things". (V. 19). This verse stresses the obligation of Latter-day Covenant Israel, or The Church of Jesus Christ of Latter-day Saints, to bring the message of the Restoration to Blood Israel, or the Jews, as well as to the remnant of the seed of Lehi. (See Title Page to The Book of Mormon & Commentary References to 1 Nephi 21:10 & 23, 2 Nephi 30:2, Jacob 5:3-4 & 9, & Jacob 5:67).

The signs given in the New World of the death of Jesus Christ were a foreshadowing of the scourging of Israel because they had crucified their God and had turned their hearts aside, rejecting His power. (V. 10-13). The outward obedience and commitment to the letter of the Law by "the Jews at Jerusalem" was not enough to insure their temporal and spiritual salvation. Their hearts had to be in the right place as well. In fact, a change of heart was required, suggesting the necessity of a rebirth. (See Mosiah 5:7).

God takes no satisfaction in Israel's scourging, but nature must run its course according to the Law of The Harvest. (V. 13). As Mormon wrote: "The judgments of God will overtake the wicked and it is by the wicked that the wicked are punished; for it is the wicked that stir up the hearts of the children of men unto bloodshed". (Mormon 4:5).

"Because they turn(ed) their hearts aside", Israel was to become a "hiss and a by-word, and (would) be hated among all nations". (V. 14). Nevertheless, the Lord would remember them. Mormon wrote: "Ye need not any longer hiss, nor spurn, nor make game of the Jews, nor any of the remnant of the House of Israel; for behold, the Lord remembereth his covenant unto them, and he will do unto them according to that which he hath sworn". (3 Nephi 29:8, see V. 15, & 2 Nephi 29:4-5). Whenever The Book of Mormon speaks of "the remnant of the House of Israel" it is a reference to the descendants of Lehi. In this case, those in the Last Days are particularly cautioned against prejudicial behavior of any kind that is directed toward either the Jews or those who may be descendants of Father Lehi.

In 1921, Heber J. Grant declared; "By the authority of the Holy Priesthood of God that has again been restored to the earth, and by the ministration under the direction of the Prophet of God, Apostles of the Lord Jesus Christ have been to the Holy Land and have dedicated that country for the return of the Jews; and we believe that in the due time of the Lord they shall be in the favor of God again. And let no Latter-day Saint be guilty of taking any part in any crusade against these people". (C.R., 10/1921). Grant delivered this address just a decade before the final solution, the institutional extermination of the Jews as a people, was conceived by the National Socialist Party in Nazi Germany.

At that time, the Latter-day State of Israel was still 27 years from reality. For centuries, it had lived only as a dream of the most devout Jews and ardent Zionists. For almost 2,000 years, there had been no Jewish homeland. Israel existed only in the hearts and minds of the people, in scripture, and in prophecy. Traditionally, Jerusalem had always been sacred to the scattered Jews. Consider the phrase that ends the Seder: "Next year in Jerusalem!" In 1842, Orson Hyde had already dedicated the Holy Land for their return, even though at that time there were less than 7,000 Jews living in Palestine. Surely, it was Latter-day prophets of God and the power of their priesthood authority that facilitated the gathering of the Jews and made possible the miracle that is the modern State of Israel. (See v. 16).

The gathering spoken of in the scriptures is taking place today, not only among the Jews in Israel, but also among the descendants of Ephraim who have been gathering since 1830 by virtue of their membership in The Church of Jesus Christ of Latter-day Saints. Zenos prophesied that "when that day cometh" that Israel no longer turns her heart aside from the Master, "then will he remember the covenants which he made to their fathers. Yea, then will he remember the isles of the sea; yea, and all the people who are of the House of Israel". (V. 15-16). Zenos promised that Israel would be gathered from the four quarters of the earth.

At that day, "all the earth shall see the salvation of the Lord, saith the prophet; every nation, kindred, tongue and people shall be blessed". (V. 17). The members and missionaries of The Church of Jesus Christ of Latter-day Saints will bring the message of salvation to a world in desperate need, and by priesthood authority and ordinance will restore the covenant blessings of Abraham to the nations. They will also provide the Type Joseph blood transfusion needed by the world to restore it to health.

So wrapped up in the prophecies of Zenos and others was Nephi, that he was moved to declare: "For behold, I have workings in the spirit, which doth weary me even that all my joints are weak". (V. 20, see D&C 85:6). As Jeremiah put it: "His word was in mine heart as a burning fire shut up in my bones, and I was weary with forbearing, and I could not stay". (Jeremiah 20:9).

The Spirit then told Nephi that Jerusalem had, in fact, been destroyed. (V. 20, see Commentary Reference to 2 Nephi 6:8). This occurred in 588 B.C. at the hands of the Babylonians. He then acknowledged that the Lord had revealed all things to the prophets of old, including details of Nephite culture. The Lord, he wrote, "did show unto many concerning us". (V. 21). For example, Jacob of old revealed his knowledge of his Lehite posterity when he said: "Joseph is a fruitful bough, even a fruitful bough by a well; whose branches run over the wall". (Genesis 49:22). Ezekiel was given insight into the records of the Nephites, when he wrote: "Moreover, thou son of man, take thee one stick, and write upon it, for Judah, and for the children of Israel his companions: then take another stick, and write upon it, for Joseph, the stick of Ephraim, and for all the House of Israel his companions". (Ezekiel 37:16, see D&C 27:5, & 2 Nephi 3:12).

Today, spiritual realities are hidden only from the wicked, who, having eyes will not see and ears will not hear. The Lord told the Church through Joseph Smith: "Your minds in times past have been darkened because of unbelief, and because you have treated lightly the things you have received". (D&C 84:54). He also revealed that the devil "cometh and taketh away light and truth, through disobedience, from the children of men, and because of the tradition of their fathers". (D&C 93:39). But He also promised that if we would "let (our) bowels also be full of charity towards all men, and to the household of faith", and if we would "let virtue garnish (our) thoughts unceasingly; then (would our) confidence wax strong in the presence of God; and the doctrine of the priesthood (would) distill upon (our) soul(s) as the dews from heaven". (D&C 121:45).

In order to persuade his brethren to believe in the Redeemer, Nephi also quoted passages from the "books of Moses". (V. 23). These scriptures came from The Plates of Brass, but were specifically the Pentateuch, or Torah (The Law), called The Book of Moses by the Jews in the time of the Prophets. Also quoted extensively was Isaiah, whose writings must have comprised a significant portion of The Plates of Brass. The purpose of holy writ is to persuade all mankind to believe in Christ, so Nephi wrote: "I did liken all scripture unto us, that it might be for our profit and learning". (V. 23). This is the reasonable approach taken by the missionaries of The Church of Jesus Christ of Latter-day Saints when they tell people about the wonderful gift of companion scriptures to the Bible that God has given to us. Their message is not intended to detract from the Bible or from the faith of those whom they teach. Its only purpose is "that faith might increase in the earth". (D&C 1:21).

It seems reasonable that we should carefully study the messages of the whole body of scriptures, prayerfully confirm that they harmonize with each other, and then zealously incorporate into our lives the Gospel principles contained therein. Both Paul and Moroni understood that we must "work out (our) own salvation with fear and trembling" before God. (Philippians 2:12 & Mormon 9:27).

Paul exhorted us to "put on the whole armour of God ... having your loins girt about with truth, and having on the breastplate of righteousness; and your feet shod with the preparation of the Gospel of peace; above all, taking the shield of faith, wherewith ye shall be able to quench all the fiery darts of the wicked. And take the helmet of salvation, and the sword of the Spirit, which is the word of God: Praying always with all prayer and supplication in the Spirit, and watching thereunto with all perseverance and supplication for all saints". (Ephesians 6:11-18). In other words, God has provided a variety of means for us to endure to the end in righteousness. Not the least among them have been His words, preserved by the faithful in all ages. "For behold, I shall speak unto the Jews, and they shall write it; and I shall also speak unto the Nephites, and they shall write it; and I shall also speak unto the other tribes of the House of Israel, which I have led away, and they shall write it; and I shall also speak unto all nations of the earth, and they shall write it". (2 Nephi 29:12).

"The rocks of the earth must rend; and because of the groanings of the earth, many of the kings of the isles of the sea shall be wrought upon by the Spirit of God, to exclaim: the God of nature suffers."
(1 Nephi 19:12).

First Nephi
Chapter 20

This chapter corresponds to the 48th Chapter of Isaiah and has significance for us as well as for the Nephites. Isaiah spoke to Israel, the Covenant name of those who had been baptized in the waters of Judah, or in the waters of baptism. (V. 1). This is a plain and precious truth from The Book of Isaiah that is not found in the King James Translation of the Bible.

Chapters 48 and 49 of The Book of Isaiah include one third of all the verses that contain textual changes in the quoted passages from Isaiah in The Book of Mormon. These can be found in Chapters 20 and 21 of The First Book of Nephi, and may be thought of as an inspired commentary when the corresponding chapters of Isaiah are studied.

In this address, Isaiah chastised Israel because although she claimed to be God's chosen people she did not serve Him, nor did she seek Him for spiritual guidance. Nephi recognized the same moral and ethical compromises in the lives of his elder brethren, and quoting the prophet, said: You "swear by the name of the Lord, and make mention of the God of Israel yet (you) swear not in truth nor in righteousness". (V. 1). In all ages, and particularly in The Last Days, there are those who "call themselves of the holy city, but they do not stay themselves upon the God of Israel". (V. 2). The Savior Himself asked: "Why call ye me, Lord, Lord, and do not the things which I say?" (Luke 6:46).

Isaiah was a prophet of God, confirming to all Israel: "Behold, I have declared the former things from the beginning; and they went forth out of my mouth, and I showed them". (V. 3). It is one thing to recount the dealings of God with mankind from the beginning. Those events that have already come to pass that were prophesied long ago serve to confirm our faith and strengthen our testimony that God has maintained an intimate relationship with us. It is quite another thing to witness the prophetic power of the servants of God who reveal truths that have been hidden from the world. (See v. 6). "New things do I declare", wrote Isaiah, and "before they spring forth I tell you of them". (Isaiah 42:9). I declare "the end from the beginning, and from ancient times the things that are not yet done, saying, My counsel shall stand, and I will do all my pleasure. Yea, I have spoken it, I will also bring it to pass; I have purposed it, I will also do it. Hearken unto me, ye stouthearted, that are far from righteousness". (Isaiah 46:10-11). As Pharoah of old declared; "So let it be written, so let it be done". This counsel from Isaiah is appropriate to all ages, and the word of the Lord has been reiterated in our day: "We believe all that God has revealed, all that He does now reveal, and we believe that He will yet reveal many great and important things pertaining to the Kingdom of God". (9th Article of Faith).

Continual spiritual guidance from God, known as revelation, is critical to vital religion, for it "cannot be maintained and preserved on the theory that God dealt with our human race only in the far past ages, and that the Bible is the only evidence we have that our God is a living, revealing, communicating God. If God ever spoke, He is still speaking. He is the great I Am, not the great He was". (Rufus Jones).

Isaiah said that He had revealed things in a particular way because of the spiritual insensitivity of Israel: "I did it because I knew that thou art obstinate, and thy neck is an iron sinew, and thy brow brass". (V. 4). The Lord repeatedly foretold events in Israel's history long before they came to pass, lest in their hardness and obstinacy the people should claim that it was their idols and images that had initiated the chain of events. As Isaiah explained: "I showed them for fear lest thou shouldst say - Mine idol hath done them, and my graven image, and my molten image hath commanded them". (V. 5).

The scriptures stand as a testimony against those who would take credit for the fulfilment of prophecy. Speaking in the name of the Lord, Isaiah declared to an apostate world: "For mine own sake will I do this, for I will not suffer my name to be polluted, and I will not give my glory unto another". (V. 11). Satan is a skillful imitator who successfully distorts our perception of reality until even the very elect may be deceived. "For there shall arise false Christs, and false prophets", warned Jesus, "and shall shew great signs and wonders; insomuch that, if it were possible, they shall deceive the very elect". (Matthew 24:24). When He taught this principle, the Savior did not say that He would leave His sheep without a Shepherd, or that there would be no-one to guide the people, but only made the distinction between true and false prophets.

He also taught: "Wheresoever the carcass is, there will the eagles be gathered together". (Matthew 24:28). Nephi might have quoted Isaiah because he wanted Latter-day Israel to recognize that where the body of the Church is found, there will be found the priesthood of God, as well. This lesson teaches the Latter-day Saints that they should gather in holy places, "to prepare their hearts and be prepared in all things against the day when tribulation and desolation are sent forth upon the wicked". (D&C 29:8). Through the ages, the prophets have always counseled the world to "Look to God, and live". (Alma 37:47).

Isaiah declared that Israel had been a rebellious nation from its infancy, and in consequence did not understand the prophets. "Yea, and thou heardest not; yea, thou knewest not; yea, from that time thine ear was not opened ... and (thou) was called a transgressor from the womb". (V. 8). But the Lord has never forsaken Israel. He will still fulfil the covenant He made with her, for He is God. He will do so for His own purposes, one of which is to prevent Satan from ultimately prevailing during the battle for spiritual survival, and from sabotaging the great Plan of the Father. (V. 9-11).

The Lord declared that He is Eternal and is our Creator. In the simple declaration "I am he", the Lord testified that it was He who "laid the foundation of the earth, and (whose) right hand hath spanned the heavens". (V. 12-13). The right hand is a symbol of righteousness and of the power that comes through obedience to law. This is why it is appropriate in our day to use the right hand when making covenants and performing ordinances.

All of the Lord's creations will ultimately recognize His power and authority. "I call unto them and they stand up together". (V. 13). "I have sworn by myself, the word is gone out of my mouth in righteousness, and shall not return, that unto me every knee shall bow, every tongue shall swear". (Isaiah 45:24).

The Lord knows each of His children, loves them all, and often uses those who are not of the Covenant to accomplish His purposes. One such individual was Cyrus, King of Elam. "He captured Babylon and overthrew the Chaldean dynasty. He issued a decree allowing the Jews to return to the land of Judah and rebuild the temple". ("Bible Dictionary", p. 651).
Of Cyrus, Isaiah wrote: "The Lord hath loved him; yea, and he will fulfill his word which he hath declared by (the prophets); and he will do his pleasure on Babylon, and his arm shall come upon the Chaldeans". (V. 14). In like

manner, the Latter-day Saints have been and will continue to be aided by friends who are prompted by the Spirit of God to perform acts of charity, kindness, and forbearance, and perhaps of vengeance.

Verse 16 powerfully expresses the witness of Isaiah to the world: "Come ye near unto me; I have not spoken in secret; from the beginning, from the time that it was declared I have spoken; and the Lord God, and his Spirit, hath sent me". (See Isaiah 45:19). In both simile and metaphor, Isaiah whimsically described how wonderful Israel's condition would have been had she only listened to the Lord. "Then had thy peace been as a river, and thy righteousness as the waves of the sea". (V. 18). He urged Israel to flee from her captors, but to remember to flee worldly influences at the same time, so that the Lord might redeem her. "Go ye forth (out) of Babylon, flee ye from the Chaldeans." (V. 20).

He ended the chapter with a Hokmah, or folk saying, that would have struck a resonant and familiar chord in the minds of his listeners: "There is no peace ... unto the wicked". (V. 22). This prophetic warning stands in sharp contrast to the wonderful promises made to all Israel in the preceding verses, and might have been given to prick the hearts of the people, motivating them to make individual and collective course corrections in their behavior.

This chapter is a classic example of the dualistic nature of prophecy characteristic of Isaiah, for he was speaking not only to Israel, but also to the posterity of Lehi and to Latter-day Israel. Certainly, those in The Church of Jesus Christ of Latter-day Saints liken the scripture to themselves and profit thereby from his counsel.

"I have showed thee new things ... even hidden things, and thou didst not know them."
(1 Nephi 10:6).

First Nephi
Chapter 21

This chapter adheres to the pattern of ancient court action followed when a party to a contract had broken its covenant. First, there would be a summons (v. 1-6), and then the plaintiff's charge. (V. 9-13). After that, the defendant would enter his plea (V. 14, 21, & 24), and finally would come the judge's indictment. (V. 15-20, 22 & 23, 25, & 26).

These verses correspond to Isaiah Chapter 49. In 2 Nephi Chapter 6 is found additional commentary by Jacob on several verses from that chapter in Isaiah. The message speaks to all those who desire to be obedient to the Covenant and begs the question; "How can we be true Israelites?"

In The Book of Mormon account, verse 1 specifically addresses scattered Israel, adding to the text of Isaiah the following: "And again: Hearken, O ye House of Israel, all ye that are broken off and are driven out because of the wickedness of the pastors of my people; yea, all ye that are broken off, that are scattered abroad, who are of my people, O House of Israel".

The "pastors" of the people refer to ministers in charge of Church ecclesiastical units. The term does not refer to an ordained office in the priesthood of The Church of Jesus Christ of Latter-day Saints. The experience of Joseph Smith in the Sacred Grove helps us to understand why God would characterize the leaders of Christian denominations as wicked. At that time, he was told of the sects that "they were all wrong; and the Personage who addressed (him) said that all their creeds were an abomination in his sight; that those professors were all corrupt". The Personage then explained to Joseph: "They draw near to me with their lips, but their hearts are far from me, they teach for doctrines the commandments of men, having a form of godliness, but they deny the power thereof". (J.S.H. 1:19).

Insult is added to injury when hypocrisy is accompanied by humanized and spiritually impotent creeds. When a religion does not have the power to save souls, it is an abomination in the sight of God, because it perverts the right way of the Lord. Those who promote such diluted doctrine, whose form is without substance, base their faith on corrupted principles that wither in the harsh light of day. But the Gospel is eternal, and key participants in the earthly implementation of The Plan of Salvation were specifically raised up by God from before their birth to do so. "The Lord hath called me from the womb", wrote Isaiah, "from the bowels of my mother hath he made mention of my name". (V. 1, see v. 6). To Lehi's contemporary Jeremiah, God said: "Before I formed thee in the belly I knew thee and before thou camest forth out of the womb I sanctified thee, and I ordained thee a prophet unto the nations". (Jeremiah 1:5). When Lehi searched The Plates of Brass, he probably came across these words from Deuteronomy, one of the five books of Moses: "Remember the days of old ... when the Most High divided to the nations their inheritance, when he separated the sons of Adam, he set the bounds of the people according to the number of the children of Israel". (Deuteronomy 32:8).

The mouth of Isaiah was to be "like a sharp sword". (V. 2). The word of God separates truth from error and strikes terror in the hearts of the wicked. (See 1 Nephi 16:2, & D&C 6:2). Isaiah was "a polished shaft", an instrument in the Lord's Hand, designed to travel swiftly and truly. (V. 2). In like manner, the prophets of the Last Days have joined all the others of Israel's many representatives through the ages who have served the Lord by delivering His word to a world in crisis. (V. 3, see Jacob 5:61-63).

It is for this reason that the message of Isaiah is important to all of God's children and why the Savior was moved to declare: "A commandment I give unto you that ye search these things diligently; for great are the words of Isaiah. For he spake as touching all things concerning my people which are of the House of Israel; therefore, it must needs be that he must speak also to the Gentiles. And all things that he spake have been and shall be, even according to the words which he spake". (3 Nephi 23:1-3).

However, it was to be the fate of Israel that men would despise her, nations abhor her, and that rulers would press her into servitude. (V. 7). But because of the Messiah, both Israel and her Gentile oppressors would ultimately be blessed. Through Joseph Smith, the servant of the Lord, God's Covenant would be renewed, and the Earth would be established. That is to say, clarity and purpose would be restored to our mortal experience. (V. 8, see 2 Nephi 3:11).

The Priesthood servants of God in the Last Days will say to the prisoners: "Go forth, (and) to them that sit in darkness: Show yourselves". (V. 9). Those who had been in the spiritual bondage of the living and the dead would, in a sudden sunburst of spiritual sensitivity, see Jesus Christ as the Messiah and the Light of the World.

As Joseph Smith exhorted the Saints: "Brethren, shall we not go on in so great a cause? Go forward and not backward. Courage, brethren; and on, on to the victory! Let your hearts rejoice, and be exceedingly glad. Let the earth break forth into singing. Let the dead speak forth anthems of eternal praise to the King Immanuel, who hath ordained, before the world was, that which would enable us to redeem them out of their prison; for the prisoners shall go free". (D&C 128:22). That Joseph who was the last-born son of Jacob, or Israel, "truly said: Thus saith the Lord unto me. A choice seer will I raise up out of the fruit of thy loins, and he shall be esteemed highly among the fruit of thy loins. And unto him will I give commandment that he shall do a work for the fruit of thy loins, his brethren, which shall be of great worth unto them, even to the bringing of them to the knowledge of the covenants which I have made with thy fathers". (2 Nephi 3:7).

So powerful will be the ministry of that choice seer and of the Priesthood army of God in the Last Days that the Children of the Covenant "shall not hunger nor thirst, neither shall the heat nor the sun smite them; for he that hath mercy on them shall lead them, even by the springs of water shall he guide them". (V. 10).

The work begun by Joseph Smith will benefit Blood Israel, Covenant Israel, and Land Israel. "Blood Israelites are the literal descendants of Jacob or Israel. Covenant Israelites are those who accept the God and covenants of Israel. Land Israelites are the inhabitants of the land that was granted to the tribes of Israel in the area called Canaan, the Holy Land, or Palestine". (Victor L. Ludlow, "Isaiah: Prophet, Seer, and Poet", p. 402, see Commentary Reference to 2 Nephi 24:29). When we read Isaiah's words, we need to be very careful that we understand which branch of Israel he is speaking about at any given time. (See Commentary References to 1 Nephi 19:19, 2 Nephi 30:2, Jacob 5:3-4 & 9, & Jacob 5:67).

As we have learned, verses 9 and 10 refer to the spiritual bondage of those who will be gathered in the Last Days. (See

D&C 45:28, & 128:22). They will even come from the land of Sinim, an unknown land identified by some scholars as China. (V. 12). On April 3, 1836, in the Kirtland Temple, Moses restored the keys of the gathering of Israel. (See D&C 110:11). One hundred and thirty-nine years later, Spencer W. Kimball declared: "The brighter day has dawned. The gathering is in progress. May the Lord bless us, as we become nursing fathers and mothers unto our (Israelite) brethren and hasten the fulfillment of the great promises made to them". (C.R., 10/1975).

In answer to the Lord's charge of a broken covenant and in the face of His demonstrated and continuing involvement with her in spite of her offenses, the defendant Israel made three responses, in verses 14-26. In typical fashion, as each defense was answered by the Lord, Israel responded with yet another excuse. Perhaps, it is just human nature to do so, but Israel should have known it would be fruitless to argue with the Lord or to debate with Him the merits of His righteous judgment.

First, Israel protested: "The Lord hath forsaken me, and my Lord hath forgotten me". (V. 14). If this sounds familiar, it is because it is the standard argument of those who have strayed from the principles of the Gospel. But it would be well to remember that when we feel alienated from the Spirit and far from God, it is we, and not He, who have moved.

The Lord's response confirmed that He had not forgotten His people, although they had repeatedly forsaken Him. "For can a woman forget her sucking child, that she should not have compassion on the son of her womb?" V. 15). The nail prints in the palms of His hands would be a token to Israel of the Atonement, and her phylacteries or frontlets would be constant reminders of the Covenant. (V. 16, see 3 Nephi 11:15, & Zechariah 13:6). Israel would yet inherit her former lands in great glory. (V. 18). "For thy waste and thy desolate places, and the land of thy destruction, shall even now be too narrow by reason of the inhabitants; and they that swallowed thee up shall be far away". (V. 19). In 1830, there were fewer than seven thousand Jews living in the Holy Land. In 2022, there were 6.8 million. In 1830, only one in five hundred persons living in the Holy Land was a Jew. In 2022, four out of five were Jewish. The prophecies are literally being fulfilled.

But Israel would again make the defendant's plea, failing to recognize that her gathering in the Last Days would be the result of divine intervention. "Who hath begotten me these ... And who hath brought up these?" she asked. "Behold, I was left alone". (V. 21). In the Last Days, the Gentile nations of the earth shall assist in the gathering. "Thus saith the Lord God: Behold, I will lift up mine hand to the Gentiles, and set up my standard to the people; and they shall bring thy sons in their arms, and thy daughters shall be carried upon their shoulders". (V. 22, see 1 Nephi 22:8). The ensign to which the people would look is the Gospel standard. As the Lord told Joseph Smith: "And even so I have sent mine everlasting covenant into the world, to be a light to the world, and to be a standard for my people, and for the Gentiles to seek to it, and to be a messenger before my face to prepare the way before me". (D&C 45:9).

So thoroughly and convincingly would He touch the hearts of the Gentile nations, that the Lord promised Israel through Isaiah that "kings shall be thy nursing fathers, and their queens thy nursing mothers; they shall bow down to thee with their face towards the earth, and lick up the dust of thy feet; and thou shalt know that I am the Lord". (V. 23). When the governments of the earth bow down in humility and assist the efforts of Blood Israel to gather to the land of her inheritance, she should recognize it as a sign from the Lord that He is God. At the same time, those who have persecuted and oppressed Israel shall be punished. "For I will contend with him that contendeth with thee, and I will save thy children". (V. 25). "For the mighty God shall deliver his covenant people". (J.S.T. Isaiah 49:25). And I will feed them that oppress thee with their own flesh; they shall be drunken with their own blood as with sweet wine; and all flesh shall know that I, the Lord, am thy Savior and thy Redeemer, the Mighty One of Jacob". (V. 25-26, see 1 Nephi 22:13-14).

1 Nephi Chapter 2, together with 2 Nephi Chapter 9, comprises the theological core of The Book of Mormon, and could be studied independently in order to capture the essence of the gospel Plan.

First Nephi
Chapter 22

This chapter is a commentary on the words of Isaiah recorded in the previous chapter. After "Nephi had read these things which were engraven upon The Plates of Brass, (his) brethren came unto (him) and said unto (him): What meaneth these things which ye have read?" (V. 1).

Nephi explained that the spirit of the Holy Ghost reveals all things to the prophets, and that what he had read to his brethren pertained "to things both temporal and spiritual". (V. 2-3). He suggested that a very large portion of the earth's population would ultimately have Israelite blood, and correctly interpreted Isaiah's prophecies to mean that, sooner or later, Israel would be scattered across the face of the earth among all nations to satisfy the purposes of God. (V. 3, see 2 Nephi 10:20-22, 3 Nephi 16:4-5 & 20:13, Ether 13:11, D&C 33:6, & Moses 7:62).

In Nephi's day, the Ten Tribes had already been lost to the knowledge of the Jews at Jerusalem. (V. 4). About 721 B.C., these tribes of the Kingdom of Israel had been led away into captivity by the Assyrians. About a year later, according to tradition, they fled to the north and mysteriously disappeared. (See Commentary Reference to 2 Nephi 19:20).

Ultimately, all 12 Tribes of Israel would be scattered upon "the isles of the sea" and among all nations. (V. 4 & 5). To the Hebrews, the continents of Asia and Africa were "the earth" because they had access to them by land, while those regions to which they sailed, were "the isles of the sea". (See Commentary References to 1 Nephi 19:10, 15-16, 19, 2 Nephi 8:5, 2 Nephi 10:8, & 21-22, 2 Nephi 21:11, 2 Nephi 29:7-8, & Alma 63:5).

The idiom, "the isles of the sea", is just one of many recognizable Semitic characteristics found in The Book of Mormon. An idiom is an expression of thought that is peculiar to a given culture. Some contemporary idioms with which we are familiar include: "Shake a leg", "Kick the bucket", "Pedal to the metal", "Give me five", "Hit the slopes", "Crack the books", "Ace the test", and so on. The list of Indo-European idioms that make perfect sense to us is almost endless. But it would be "Greek" to one unfamiliar with the nuances of our language and its structure.

In The Book of Mormon, semitic idioms that are frequently used include: "stretch forth thy hand", "make bare thy arm", "stiffneckedness", "workers of iniquity", "puffed up in pride", "stripped of pride", "face of the land", "four quarters of the earth", "bread and the waters of life", "fountain of living waters", "fountain of all righteousness", and so on. The ease with which these idioms fit into the narrative suggests that it was the Israelite authors of the record who employed them. It begs credulity to think that young Joseph Smith was adroit enough to create and use them on his own initiative and in perfect context throughout The Book of Mormon.

When we have studied such a list and have become comfortable with the Hebraic literary style, flashes of recognition illuminate our minds, and passages of scripture that beforehand had seemed strangely distant in grammatical style suddenly make perfectly good sense. Idioms can thus become the glue that unifies a narrative and binds us to it.

Nephi foresaw that the Lord would raise up nations who would scatter Israel. But then a marvelous work would take place, beginning at a hill called Cumorah. From that time, the Jews, including the posterity of Lehi, would reap the blessings of the Restoration. "Wherefore, it is likened unto their being nourished by the Gentiles and being carried in their arms and upon their shoulders". (V. 8).

The marvelous work would be of worth "not only unto the Gentiles but unto all the House of Israel, unto the making known of the covenants of the Father of heaven unto Abraham, saying: In thy seed shall all the kindreds of the earth be blessed". (V. 9). Thus, the Children of the Covenant, despised of all nations, cast out of their promised land of inheritance, and characterized by a hiss and a by-word for two millennia, would become the agents through whom the Lord would bless all nations.

The Lord would "make bare his arm in the eyes of the nations". (V. 10). That is to say, He would show His power in order to lead Israel out of captivity, gather her to the lands of their inheritance, and bring her out obscurity and darkness, that she might know that the Lord is her Redeemer. (V. 11-12).

Meanwhile, of the Church and kingdom of the devil, Nephi prophesied that "the blood of that great and abominable Church, which is the whore of all the earth, shall turn upon their own heads; for they shall war among themselves, and the sword of their own hands shall fall upon their own heads, and they shall be drunken with their own blood". (V. 13). The wicked feel neither loyalty nor love for anything or anyone but themselves. They enjoy neither the blessings of unity nor the peace that is the province of the righteous. In unorganized chaos, the father of contention, who is Satan, orchestrates the self-destruction of his children and perversely enjoys the process.

The Lord promised that every nation that fights against Zion will be destroyed, as will the great and abominable Church of the devil. (V. 14). In the Last Days, God will not allow the wicked to destroy the righteous. (V. 16). With the Restoration, He has promised that the Church organization that administers the ordinances of salvation will never again be taken from the earth. Its government will remain throughout the turbulent times ahead, to ensure that the promises that God has made to His Covenant people will come to pass. His words will be fulfilled in every whit.

Although the righteous are sure to be caught up in pre-millennial turmoil, they will be preserved by the power of God, and so they need not fear. (V. 17). Mark E. Peterson declared: "In the midst of all these tribulations, God will send fire from heaven if necessary to destroy our enemies while we carry forward our work". The Master of the Universe would never permit Satan or his legions to thwart His purposes, no matter how hard they might try to interfere. As a matter of fact, those who have "perverted the right ways of the Lord, yea, that great and abominable Church, shall tumble to the dust and great shall be the fall of it". (V. 14).

"For behold, saith the prophet, the time cometh speedily that Satan shall have no more power over the hearts of the children of men; for the day soon cometh that all the proud and they who do wickedly shall be as stubble; and the day cometh that they must be burned". (V. 15). This is the unalterable decree of God, Whose judgments are just. The unrepentant will find that His Word is sharper than a two-edged sword.

Nephi assured his brethren that these judgments would come upon the children of men, "yea, even blood, and fire, and vapor of smoke must come; and it must needs be upon the face of this earth; and it cometh unto men according to the flesh if it so be that they will harden their hearts against the Holy One of Israel". (V. 18). As a result of faithlessness and nonconformity to the prescribed requirements of The Plan of Salvation, "all they who fight against Zion shall be cut off". (V. 19).

For the righteous, though, a way of deliverance will be prepared. "A prophet shall the Lord your God raise up", said the Lord to Moses. (V. 20). "This prophet of whom Moses spake was the Holy One of Israel". (V. 21). In consequence of His ministry, the righteous will not be confounded, or brought to ruin. (V. 22). Because they will listen to the Lord's counsel that is given by revelation to the Prophet and that is found in the scriptures, they will not be destroyed. For their own safety, though, they will need to gather in the wards, stakes, and missions of the Church. "And the time cometh speedily that the righteous must be led up as calves of the stall". (V. 24).

The gathering of the Saints to the stakes of Zion will "be for a defense, and for a refuge from the storm, and from wrath when it shall be poured out without mixture upon the whole earth". (D&C 115:6). Ezra Taft Benson taught that our Church ecclesiastical units have "at least four purposes. One is to unify and perfect the members who live in those boundaries, by extending to them the Church programs, the ordinances, and Gospel instruction. (Secondly), the members of stakes are to be models, or standards, of righteousness. (Third), stakes are to be a defense. They do this as stake members unify under the direction of their local priesthood officers and consecrate themselves to do their duty and keep their covenants. (Fourth), stakes are a refuge from the storm to be poured out over the earth". ("Ensign", 1/1991, p. 2-5).

Nephi said that it is those who are of the "kingdom of the devil" who should fear. They are all those "Churches which are built up to get gain, and all those who are built up to become popular in the eyes of the world, and those who seek the lusts of the flesh, and the things of the world, and to do all manner of iniquity; yea, in fine, all those who belong to the kingdom of the devil are they who need fear, and tremble, and quake". (V. 23).

The institutions that represent the devil's kingdom stand in stark contrast to the Lord's government. The Church of Jesus Christ of Latter-day Saints represents itself as His Church on the Earth. "It is the sacred depository of His truth", declared B.H. Roberts. "It is His instrumentality for the perfecting of the Saints, as well as for the work of the ministry. It is Christ's Church in all these respects, but it is an institution that belongs to the Saints. It is their refuge from the confusion and religious doubt of the world. It is their instructor in principle, doctrine, and righteousness. It is their guide in matters of faith and morals. They have a conjoint ownership in it with Jesus Christ, which ownership is recognized in the latter part of the title. This covenant relationship between the Lord and His Church, manifest in the ordinances of the Gospel performed by His priesthood representatives, is central to the very definition: "Latter-day Saint". Members of the Church who are content to identify themselves as "Mormons", or their Church as "The L.D.S. Church", demean the institution to which they pledge their allegiance". (B.H. Roberts, "Comprehensive History of The Church", 1:393).

The sheep of the Good Shepherd know His voice. When they hear His call, they gather "from the four quarters of the earth; and he numbereth his sheep, and they know him; and there shall be one fold and one shepherd; and he shall feed his sheep, and in him they shall find pasture". (V. 25).

Nephi wrote that, during the Millennium, Satan would lose his power over the people because of their righteousness. (V. 26). In that day of enlightenment, all will know they are white-hot sparks struck off the divine anvil of God. Faith will replace fear, and darkness will be banished from their minds.

For now, "The light shineth in darkness, and the darkness comprehendeth it not; nevertheless, the day shall come when you shall comprehend even God, being quickened in him and by him". (D&C 88:49). As Bagheera, the powerfully built black panther in "The Jungle Book", confided to Mowgli the man-cub: "I had never seen the jungle.

They fed me behind bars from an iron pan till one night I felt that I was Bagheera the Panther, and no man's plaything, and broke the lock with one blow of my paw and came away". (Rudyard Kipling, "The Jungle Book", p. 26).

So too, those holding the fulness of the Melchizedek Priesthood, with the keys of power and blessing, will become kings and priests of the Most High God. "In fact, that priesthood is a perfect law of theocracy, and stands as God to give laws to the people, administered in endless lives to the sons and daughters of Adam". (Joseph Smith, "Teachings", p. 322).

"And because of the righteousness of his people, Satan has no power; wherefore, he cannot be loosed for the space of many years; for he hath no power over the hearts of the people, for they dwell in righteousness, and the Holy One of Israel reigneth". (V. 26). The wording of this verse suggests that Satan will be present as a tempter during the thousand years of peace, but the righteousness of the people will prevent him from exercising the influence he craves. (See 4 Nephi 1:2-3, 1:15 & 1:18). It is also possible that more severe restrictions will be placed on Satan during the Millennium. (See D&C 43:31, 88:110, & 101:28).

Nephi taught that all are welcome to dwell with the Saints in Zion, on the condition of repentance. "All nations, kindreds, tongues, and people shall dwell safely in the Holy One of Israel if it so be that they will repent". (V. 28). To reiterate: "He shall feed His sheep, and in him they shall find pasture". (V. 25).

Nephi declared that he and his father were not the only ones who taught and testified of these principles and events. (V. 31). In time, Nephi's namesake would tell the people: "Moses did not only testify of these things, but also all the holy prophets, from his days even to the days of Abraham. Yea, and behold, Abraham saw of his coming, and was filled with gladness and did rejoice. Yea, and behold I say unto you that Abraham not only knew of these things, but there were many before the days of Abraham who were called by the order of God; yea, even after the order of his Son; and this that it should be shown unto the people, a great many thousand years before his coming, that even redemption should come unto them. And now I would that ye should know, that even since the days of Abraham there have been many prophets that have testified these things; yea, behold, the prophet Zenos did testify boldly; for the which he was slain. And behold, also, Zenock, and also Ezias, and also Isaiah, and Jeremiah". (Helaman 8:16-20). Having declared these truths to his brethren, Nephi ended the complicated chiasmus comprising Chapters 12-22 by copying the literary formula of the Egyptian literary style: "And thus it is. Amen". (V. 31).

The Second Book of Nephi
About 588 - 570 B.C. to 559 - 545 B.C.
Chapters 1 - 11

Second Nephi
Chapter 1

As the Second Book of Nephi opens, Lehi informed his family that he had received a vision in which the destruction of Jerusalem was revealed to him. (See 1 Nephi 17:14). Historians agree that Babylonia overran the city between 586 and 590 B.C., just over a decade after the departure of Lehi and his family.

Then, Lehi reminded his loved ones that Jerusalem's destruction notwithstanding, they had obtained a land of promise. (V. 5). The New World was a spiritually choice land for many reasons. Anciently, it had been the location of Adam Ondi Ahman. (See D&C 107:53-56, & D&C 116). Soon, it would be the setting of Christ's post-mortal ministry. (See 3 Nephi 11). Then, it would provide the backdrop for the Restoration of the Gospel, and finally it would witness the building of the New Jerusalem. (See J.S.H., & Ether 13:4-8).

Lehi reassured the righteous of all ages when he promised that the land would be blessed unto them forever. (V. 7). "And if it so be that they shall keep his commandments they shall be blessed upon the face of this land, and there shall be none to molest them, nor to take away the land of their inheritance; and they shall dwell safely forever". (V. 9). In modern language, Lehi would have said that a strong military-industrial complex does not guarantee security. Rather, it is righteousness that insures temporal well-being.

The dark side of Lehi's prophecy concerning those who would dwell in the land of promise was that because of unrighteousness, his posterity would be scattered and smitten by Gentile nations, who would claim their blessings. "And behold, the Lord hath reserved their blessings, which they might have received in the land, for the Gentiles who shall possess the land." (Mormon 5:19).

Beginning in verse 13, Lehi made a final plea to his wayward sons. He was frightened, and his heart was heavy with sorrow because of his concern for the welfare of Laman and Lemuel. Whereas he was personally assured of eternal life because of his total commitment to the Lord, he knew that God's wrath is reserved for the wicked, and he was certain of the inevitable consequences of his sons' behavior. Unhappily, by this time he recognized the inclination of Laman and Lemuel to turn from the light. Lehi urged them to "put on the armor of righteousness", or in other words, to exercise their priesthood authority. (V. 23). He justified Nephi's boldness when dealing with his brethren as "the sharpness of the power of the word of God". (V. 26). Defending Nephi's righteous indignation at the iniquities of Laman and Lemuel, he reasoned that it was sometimes necessary to reprove "with sharpness, when moved upon by the Holy Ghost; and then showing forth afterwards an increase of love". (D&C 121:43). Lehi cautioned that they mistake neither the wisdom nor the pure intent of their brother's counsel for indiscriminate, uncontrolled, or unwarranted anger.

While they were still within the sphere of his influence, Lehi promised Laman and Lemuel that if they would listen to Nephi, they would yet receive his first blessing. As had been the case with Isaac and his sons Esau and Jacob, Lehi would have desired to leave his first blessing with his elder sons. But if they would not hearken to him by following his counsel, a deserving Nephi would instead receive that blessing. (V. 28-29).

To his everlasting credit Lehi never gave up on Laman and Lemuel, and nor did Nephi or Jacob. In fact, their efforts would bear fruit because at least some of their posterity stood with Nephi at the time of the Great Separation that is documented in 2 Nephi Chapter 5.

In Jacob 1:13, a distinction is made regarding the divisions based on religion among the children of Lehi. "The people which were not Lamanites were Nephites". But within this group of Nephites were "Jacobites, Josephites, Zoramites, Lamanites, Lemuelites, and Ishmaelites". This is a startling declaration, because it leads us to conclude that the ministry that had focused on the elder sons and their posterity and on the posterity of Ishmael had not been entirely in vain. Among the Lamanites were counted those who "were a compound of Laman and Lemuel, and the sons of Ishmael, and all who had dissented from the Nephites". (Alma 43:13). In other words, the ministry that had been oriented toward solidifying the faith and testimony of Lehi's descendants had not been only a qualified success. (See Alma 24:29, 43:13, 55:4 & 56:3).

It is plausible to assume that "all those who would go" with Nephi when he departed into the wilderness from the Land of Their First Inheritance included descendants of Laman, Lemuel, and Ishmael, who are called "Lamanites, Lemuelites, and Ishmaelites" in Jacob 1:13. (2 Nephi 5:5-6). Parenthetically, note the absence of a reference in this verse to "Samites", consistent with the blessing given to Sam by Lehi, wherein he was told his posterity would be included with Nephi's. For Lehi "spake unto Sam, saying ...Thy seed shall be numbered with his seed; and thou shalt be even like unto thy brother". (2 Nephi 4:11, see D&C 3:17).

For additional clarification that reflected the reality of their current and future circumstances, Jacob said: "I shall call them Lamanites that seek to destroy the people of Nephi, and those who are friendly to Nephi I shall call Nephites, or the people of Nephi". (Jacob 1:14, see Commentary Reference to Alma 3:4-12).

Verse 28 through 2 Nephi 4:12 comprise the patriarchal blessing literature of The Book of Mormon. In verse 29, we find only an oblique reference to a blessing for Nephi by his father. To his elder sons, Lehi cautioned: "If ye will not hearken unto (Nephi) I take away my first blessing ... and it shall rest upon him". This chapter ends with the blessing of Zoram, that is an example of how, although adopted, one may still qualify for covenant blessings through faithfulness. "And now, Zoram", said Lehi, "I speak unto you: Behold, thou art the servant of Laban". In a sense, Lehi must have still viewed Zoram in a different light than his own kindred, although between 12 and 20 years had passed since Zoram had joined Lehi's family back in Jerusalem, and later through marriage. One has to wonder why Lehi still referred to loyal Zoram as a servant. Perhaps it was hard for him to let go of old prejudices, but we will never know for sure. "Nevertheless", continued Lehi, "thou hast been brought out of the land of Jerusalem, and I know that thou art a true friend unto my son, Nephi, forever. Wherefore, because thou hast been faithful, thy seed shall be blessed with his seed, that they dwell in prosperity long upon the face of this land; and nothing, save it shall be iniquity among them, shall harm or disturb their prosperity upon the face of this land forever". (V. 30-31).

Three examples in subsequent Nephite history validate the blessing that Zoram received under the hands of Lehi. First, Jacob confirmed that among "the people which were not Lamanites were ... Zoramites". (Jacob 1:13, cited above).

Secondly, in The Book of Alma, we read about Ammoron, "a descendant of Zoram", who had supposedly been "pressed and brought out of Jerusalem" against his will by Father Lehi. In reality, Ammoron was an apostate Nephite, but he claimed that he was "a bold Lamanite" and said that he was fighting the Nephites "to avenge their wrongs and to maintain and to obtain their rights to the government". (Alma 54:23-24).

This was the same tired argument that would be repetitively dragged out like dirty laundry for almost 600 years by apostate Nephites and ignorant Lamanites, but we see in it the prophetic insight of Lehi, that "save it shall be iniquity among them, (no-one should) harm or disturb their prosperity upon the face of (the) land forever". (2 Nephi 1:31). Thirdly, on the bright side, in 4 Nephi 1:37-38, we read the account of "the true believers in Christ, and the true worshipers of Christ" who, around 231 A.D. "were called Nephites, and Jacobites, and Josephites, and Zoramites", while "they who rejected the Gospel were called Lamanites, and Lemuelites, and Ishmaelites".

"And now, Zoram, I speak unto yu: Behold, thou art the servant of Laban; nevertheless, thou has been brought out of the land of Jerusalem, and I know that thou art a true friend untoo my son, Nephi, forever."
(2 Nephi 1:30).

Second Nephi
Chapter 2

This chapter, together with Chapter 9, comprises the theological core of The Book of Mormon, and could be studied independently in order to capture the essence of the Gospel Plan. Later in the chapter, it becomes clear that Lehi's discourse was based upon the writings of an earlier, unnamed prophet. "I have spoken these few words unto you all, my sons, in the last days of my probation", said Lehi. "I have chosen the good part, according to the words of the prophet". (V. 30).

When reading the blessing given to Jacob, it is immediately obvious that he had been a very special young man. He had "beheld that in the fulness of times (the Redeemer would come) to bring salvation unto me". (V. 3). He was one of a select few to be visited by the premortal Savior, having been blessed with a vision while yet in his childhood. (V. 4).

Lehi taught a very important principle when he said that "men are instructed sufficiently that they know good from evil". (V. 5). It is for this purpose that the Spirit of Christ is given to all mankind. (See Moroni 7:16). The Light of Christ is in each of us. (See D&C 88:11-13). This is why Joseph Smith was able to say with such confidence of the membership of the Church: "I teach them correct principles, and they govern themselves".

Lehi then taught that no flesh is justified. (V. 5). That is to say, although we know right from wrong, none of us keeps the laws and commandments in perfection, for to be justified means to stand uncondemned before the God. Therefore, without the grace of a Redeemer, our plight is hopeless, for "by the temporal law (we must be) cut off; and also, by the spiritual law (we) perish from that which is good, and become miserable forever". (V. 5).

But there was an Atonement, and "redemption cometh in and through the Holy Messiah". (V. 6). There was a Redeemer "to answer the ends of the law". (V. 7). Christ has offered Himself as the sacrifice for sin, and only asks that our sacrifice be a broken heart and contrite spirit. For all who follow Him, He has brought to pass resurrection from physical death and salvation from spiritual death. But it is only because of His merits, His mercy, and His grace that this is possible. It is only because "the Holy Messiah ... layeth down his life according to the flesh, and taketh it again by the power of the Spirit, that he may bring to pass the resurrection of the dead". (V. 8).

Because of His intercession on our behalf, all of us will briefly be redeemed from spiritual death, or alienation from God. "All men (shall) come unto God; wherefore, they stand in the presence of him, to be judged of him according to the truth and holiness which is in him". (V. 10). They will be allowed to come into His presence one last time to see how much intrinsic light they have lost through wicked behavior. The judgment that is ultimately rendered will be based on the legal demands of justice, or on our willingness to have met the conditions of obedience during the probationary state of mortality. One way or the other, we will answer the ends of the Atonement" to receive punishment or happiness. (V. 10).

Verses 11 through 25 grow out of Lehi's remarks on the Atonement, are parenthetical, and are set apart at the beginning and the end by hokmahs, which are peculiar Hebrew figures of speech, aphorisms, proverbial statements, or theological profundities.

"For it must needs be that there is opposition in all things". (V. 11). Opposition can lead to both desirable and undesirable consequences. Without it, "righteousness could not be brought to pass, neither wickedness, neither holiness nor misery, neither good nor bad". Without it, there could be "no life neither death, nor corruption nor incorruption, happiness nor misery, neither sense nor insensibility". (V. 11). Without it, the earth itself would "have been created for a thing of naught; wherefore there would have been no purpose in the end of its creation". The "wisdom of God and his eternal purposes, and also the power, and the mercy, and the justice of God" would be destroyed without opposition. (V. 12).

Without law, there could be no sin, reasoned Lehi, and without sin, there could be no righteousness. "And if there be no righteousness there be no happiness. And if there be no righteousness nor happiness there be no punishment nor misery. And if these things are not there is no God. And if there is no God we are not, neither the earth; for there could have been no creation of things, neither to act nor to be acted upon; wherefore, all things must have vanished away". (V. 13). Happiness is central to the purpose of life. It "is the object and design of our existence, and will be the end thereof, if we pursue the path that leads to it, and this path is virtue, uprightness, faithfulness, holiness, and keeping all the commandments of God". (Joseph Smith, "Teachings", p. 255, see Commentary Reference to 2 Nephi 9:43). Someone once wisely observed that happiness is like a butterfly. The more we chase it, the more it eludes us. But if we turn our attention to selfless acts and service on behalf of others, it will come and sit softly on our shoulder.

A correct concept of the Fall of Adam is necessary if we wish to understand the basic claims of Christianity. Verses 14-17 provide a wealth of information on this subject. In the beginning, "to bring about his eternal purposes in the end of man, after he had created our first parents, and the beasts of the field and the fowls of the air, and in fine, all things which are created", God presented Adam and Eve with "the forbidden fruit in opposition to the tree of life; the one being sweet and the other bitter". (V. 15).

"Wherefore, the Lord God gave unto man that he should act for himself. (But) man could not act for himself save it should be that he was enticed by the one or the other". (V. 16). Thus, in the Garden of Eden, God allowed "that the devil should tempt the children of men, or they could not be agents unto themselves; for if they never should have bitter they could not know the sweet. Wherefore, it came to pass that the devil tempted Adam, and he partook of the forbidden fruit and transgressed the commandment, wherein he became subject to the will of the devil, because he yielded unto temptation". (D&C 29:39-40). But Adam was not deceived. His was a conscious decision, the result of a correct understanding of the requirements of the Gospel Plan. "Adam fell that men might be". (V. 25).

Verse 17 is one of the few references in scripture to Lucifer, who fell "from heaven, wherefore he became a devil, having sought that which was evil before God". Joseph Fielding Smith, Jr. taught that the devil and his angels are "banished forever from the presence of God because they have lost the power of repentance, for they chose evil after having had the light. These spirits are known as Sons of Perdition". ("Doctrines of Salvation", 2:218-219). One can see why repentance is the central message of the scriptures, because of the eternal consequences associated with the failure to do so.

Not knowing the mind of God, that there must needs be opposition in all things, Satan sought what he thought would be the misery of all mankind, and with his congenital short-sightedness and his predictable stratagem of promoting half-truths, he offered the forbidden fruit to Eve. "Ye shall be as God, knowing good and evil", he promised. (V. 18, see Moses 4:6).

The Fall resulted, and Adam and Eve "were driven out of the garden of Eden to till the earth". (V. 19). So began "the family of all the earth". (V. 20). The scriptures clearly teach that Adam and Eve were the first of Heavenly Father's children to live on this telestial earth. "Father Adam (was) the Ancient of Days, and father of all, and (husband to) our glorious Mother Eve". (D&C 138:38-39).

Lehi next taught Jacob that the first generations of mankind lived to great age so that they might have time to repent. "And the days of the children of men were prolonged, according to the will of God, that they might repent while in the flesh; wherefore, their state became a state of probation, and their time was lengthened, according to the commandments which the Lord God gave unto the children of men: For he gave commandment that all men must repent". (V. 21). As Hugh Nibley said: "When the day of repentance is past, so is the day of grace. The ominous sign today is not that the children of men do wrong, for they always have, but that they have no intention of repenting". ("Beyond Politics", see Alma 34:34, & Moroni 9:3-4 & 18-22).

Mortality thus became a time of probation, testing, or putting to the proof. At issue is the question: "Will we repent?" If not, we must be lost because of the transgression of Adam and Eve that brought temporal and spiritual death to mankind; temporal death because of the separation of the body from the spirit at the conclusion of our mortal journey, and spiritual death because of our alienation from the Spirit from God in the absence of an Atonement at the time of the Judgment.

Lehi clearly taught that had Adam not transgressed the Law in the Garden, he would have vegetated there forever. "And all things which were created must have remained in the same state in which they were after they were created; and they must have remained forever, and had no end. And they would have had no children; wherefore they would have remained in a state of innocence, having no joy, for they knew no misery; doing no good, for they knew no sin". (V. 22-23). Life in Eden was not an ideal existence, but was instead morally static. Our Father knew that Adam and Eve must fall as a critically necessary part of The Plan of Salvation, for "all things have been done in the wisdom of him who knoweth all things". (V. 24).

The parenthetical discourse begun in verse 11 ends with another Hokmah: "Adam fell that men might be, and men are that they might have joy". (V. 25). It is a grand summary of Lehi's discourse on opposition and the Fall of Adam and Eve. This simple aphorism speaks volumes and is one of the basic messages of the Restoration. When the Fall is considered in conjunction with the Atonement of Christ, it is clear that both are part of God's Plan of Eternal Progression, for we may only attain a fulness of joy in a personal, tangible, resurrection. For we are "spirit, the elements are eternal, and spirit and element, inseparably connected, receive a fulness of joy". (D&C 93:33).

In verse 26, Lehi returned to his original discussion that only makes sense after the explanation offered in the parenthetical aside. Even when reading this verse casually, we are struck by the plainness of the message: "The Messiah cometh in the fulness of time, that he may redeem the children of men from the fall. And because that they are redeemed from the fall they have become free forever, knowing good from evil; to act for themselves and not to be acted upon, save it be by the punishment of the law at the great and last day, according to the commandments which God hath given". (V. 26). The scribes and Pharisees of the New Testament, the descendants of the 'Jews at Jerusalem' that Nephi so often took to task, tried to eradicate every trace of Messianic reference in the scriptures. This is why virtually the entire line of Messianic prophecy disappeared from the writings of the prophets in the Old Testament. (See Helaman Chapter 8).

It is Christ's way for us to act for ourselves. It is Satan's way for us to be acted upon. The "perfect law of liberty" presupposes that we "are free according to the flesh". (James 1:25 & 27). We are "free to choose liberty and eternal life, through the great Mediator of all men, or to choose captivity and (spiritual) death, according to the captivity and power of the devil, for he seeketh that all men might be miserable like unto himself". (V. 27). But unless our actions are carried out within the context of the Gospel and its laws, unbridled freedom will lead to tyranny. We have free will, but we cannot choose to escape the consequences that flow from our poor choices.

Satan's plan, based as it was on compulsion, would have denied agency and required obedience. When we trade our divine birthright for a mess of pottage, we find ourselves in the grip of bad habits, and we are snared by Satan, bound by his strong chains, and the heavy cords around our necks restrict the freedom of our actions and drag us down to hell. It is very hard to break bad habits, because we have surrendered our free will in order to acquire them. (See Commentary Reference to 2 Nephi 9:44).

Heavenly Father does not work this way. He always honors the eternal principle of agency. It is riskier this way, but it is the only way. Rather than enslaving us in good habits, He repeatedly gives us the opportunity to recommit ourselves to our covenants of obedience to true and eternal principles, as we receive the Sacrament on a weekly basis. This is one of the most important reasons why Church membership and faithful attendance are vital to our spiritual well-being.

"The Spirit is pure", taught Brigham Young, and is "under the special control and influence of the Lord, but the body is of the earth, and is subject to the power of the devil, and is under the mighty influence of that fallen nature that is of the earth. If the Spirit yields to the body, the devil then has power to overcome the body and spirit of that man, and he loses both".

Lehi closed his blessing to Jacob by exhorting all of his sons to "look to the great Mediator, and hearken unto his great commandments; and be faithful unto his words, and choose eternal life, according to the will of his Holy Spirit. And not choose eternal death, according to the will of the flesh and the evil which is therein, which giveth the spirit of the devil power to captivate, to bring you down to hell, that he may reign over you in his own kingdom". (V. 28-29).

Father Lehi declared that he had "chosen the good part", meaning that he had elected to use his agency to yield himself to the redeeming power of the Atonement that is the lynchpin of The Plan of Salvation. (V. 30). "All things which pertain to our religion are only appendages to it", declared the Prophet Joseph Smith. ("Teachings", p. 127). In this chapter, Lehi effectively addressed the two truths fundamental to our understanding of the Atonement: 1) the Fall of Adam and Eve, and 2) the Divine Sonship of the Lord. In the preservation of this message, both Lehi and Nephi had "none other object save it be the everlasting welfare of (our) souls". (V. 30).

Second Nephi
Chapter 3

Joseph was the youngest son of Lehi, "born in the wilderness of (his) afflictions; yea, in the days of (his) greatest sorrows". (V. 1). By the time of his birth, it was becoming increasingly clear to Lehi that the rebellious nature of his elder sons would result in their eventual apostasy. The name 'Joseph' means 'Increase' in Hebrew, and the boy was well named, for the son that the patriarch Jacob had named Joseph was the only one of his children righteous enough to bear the Patriarchal Priesthood and perpetuate the covenant that God had made with his fathers.

In this chapter is recorded the patriarchal blessing given to Joseph by his father. In verse 2 Lehi declared: "May the Lord consecrate also unto thee this land, which is a most precious land, for thine inheritance and the inheritance of thy seed with thy brethren, for thy security forever".. This blessing was predicated only upon his ability to "keep the commandments of the Holy One of Israel".

Lehi further promised Joseph that his posterity should not "utterly be destroyed". (V. 3). Even though it is sometimes believed that the Nephites were annihilated down to the last man, woman, and child, when the Lamanites prevailed over them in the final great battles between 385 and 421 A.D., this verse correctly teaches that at least some of the descendants of the righteous children of Lehi would be preserved. The Doctrine and Covenants affirms that the Gospel message in the Last Days shall go "to the Nephites, and the Jacobites, and the Josephites, and the Zoramites, through the testimony of their fathers. And this testimony shall come to the knowledge of the Lamanites, and the Lemuelites, and the Ishmaelites, who dwindled in unbelief because of the iniquity of their fathers, whom the Lord has suffered to destroy their brethren the Nephites, because of their iniquities and their abominations". (D&C 3:16-20, see Mormon Chapters 6-8).

In his blessing, Lehi stated his authority, declaring: "I am a descendant of Joseph, who was carried captive into Egypt. And great were the covenants of the Lord which he made unto Joseph". (V. 4, see 2 Nephi 4:1, & Alma 10:3). Of the ancient covenants, The Book of Mormon teaches, and Genesis confirms, that those made between the Lord and Joseph were remarkable, indeed. The story of Joseph in Genesis 37-50 takes up 26% of the book, and deals with the first 2,300 years following the Fall. Joseph lived to the age of 110, or less than 5% of that time. With his grandfather Abraham, whose life spanned less than 8% of that same period, and whose story in Genesis occupies over 14 full chapters, (Genesis 10-25), their combined story of 13% of the chronological record occupies 54% of the book. In fact, Joseph Smith said that the complete record of these two patriarchs might fill "a volume larger than the Bible". (Cleon Skousen, "The Third Thousand Years", Chapter 9).

Verses 5-17 correspond to J.S.T. Genesis 50:24-28, and it is illuminating to read these verses in conjunction with that inspired text. Lehi declared that it had been revealed to their ancestor Joseph that Lehi's family group would leave the land of Jerusalem and be led to a promised land. Joseph "truly saw our day. And he obtained a promise of the Lord, that out of the fruit of his loins the Lord God would raise up a righteous branch unto the House of Israel; not the Messiah, but a branch which was to be broken off, nevertheless to be remembered in the covenants of the Lord that the Messiah should be made manifest unto them in the latter days, in the spirit of power, unto the bringing of them out of darkness unto light - yea, out of hidden darkness and out of captivity unto freedom". (V. 5). This party would constitute the "fruitful bough by a well, whose branches run over the wall", spoken of by Jacob in the patriarchal blessing given to his son Joseph. (Genesis 49:22).

"Messiah" is an Aramaic term meaning "the anointed one" and is used only once in the Old Testament and twice in the New Testament. (See Commentary Reference to 1 Nephi 10:4). The Savior would not be of this branch, for He was to come through the tribe of Judah. Nevertheless, in the Last Days, the Messiah would be made manifest to Joseph's descendants through Ephraim, whose birthright was to rule in power. Joseph was the firstborn son of Jacob's second wife, and so the birthright was his after Reuben, the firstborn son of Jacob by his first wife Rachel, forfeited it because of incest with Bilah. (Genesis 35:22, 49:4 & 26).

Verses 6-17 are identical to J.S.T. Genesis 50:27-34. This prophecy, written on The Plates of Brass, was heretofore unpublished. It is obvious from reading these verses that Joseph was a far greater prophet than is generally recognized. He saw in vision the Latter-day mission of Joseph Smith, and wrote of it extensively. "Yea, Joseph truly said: Thus saith the Lord unto me: A choice seer will I raise up out of the fruit of thy loins; and he shall be esteemed highly among the fruit of thy loins. And unto him will I give commandment that he shall do a work for the fruit of thy loins, his brethren, which shall be of great worth unto them, even to the bringing of them to the knowledge of the covenants which I have made with thy fathers". (V. 7). Joseph Smith's instrumentality in bringing The Book of Mormon to the knowledge of the descendants of Joseph is clearly established in these verses. As John Taylor declared: "Joseph Smith, the Prophet and Seer of the Lord, has done more, save Jesus only, for the salvation of men in this world, than any other man that ever lived in it". (D&C 135:3).

Of the Latter-day prophet, the Lord revealed: "I will give unto him a commandment that he shall do none other work, save the work which I shall command him. And I will make him great in mine eyes; for he shall do my work". (V. 8). "In the short space of twenty years, (Joseph Smith) brought forth The Book of Mormon (and) sent the fullness of the everlasting Gospel, which it contained, to the four quarters of the earth". (D&C 135:5).

The Lord continued: "He shall be great like unto Moses, whom I have said I would raise up unto you, to deliver my people, O House of Israel". (V. 9). In point of fact, Joseph Smith "gathered many thousands of the Latter-day Saints, founded a great city, and left a fame and name that cannot be slain". (D&C 135:3). His office was "to preside over the whole Church, and to be like unto Moses ... to be a seer, a revelator, a translator, and a prophet, having all the gifts of God which he bestows upon the head of the Church". (D&C 107:91-92).

The person and ministry of Joseph Smith was the fulfilment of the prophecy made to Joseph of old: "A seer will I raise up out of the fruit of thy loins; and unto him will I give power to bring forth my word unto the seed of thy loins - and not to the bringing forth my word only, saith the Lord, but to the convincing them of my word, which shall have already gone forth among them". (V. 11). The Prophet Joseph Smith "brought forth the revelations and commandments which compose (the) book of Doctrine and Covenants, and many other wise documents and instructions for the benefit of the children of men". (D&C 135:5). He was "called and chosen to (translate the plates from which was to come) The Book of Mormon". (D&C 24:1).

One of the classic purposes of The Book of Mormon is identified in verse 12. "That which shall be written (in the Bible and Book of Mormon) shall grow together, unto the confounding of false doctrines and laying down of contentions, and establishing peace among the fruit of thy loins, and bringing them to the knowledge of my covenants, saith the Lord". As Ezekiel prophetically foresaw, the stick of Judah (the Bible), and the stick of Joseph (The Book of Mormon), would be joined "one to another into one stick, and they (would) become one in thine hand". (Ezekiel 37:15-20).

It must have been of great comfort to Joseph Smith to translate verses 13 and 14, that read in part: "And out of weakness he shall be made strong, in that day when my work shall commence among all my people", and "that seer will the Lord bless; and they that seek to destroy him shall be confounded". "Yea, thus prophesied Joseph: I am sure of this thing". (V. 16).

In ancient Jewish tradition, there was to be a Messiah Ben Joseph, literally "The anointed one, son of Joseph", who would bring salvation to the descendants of Joseph. "And his name shall be called after me", declared Joseph, "and it shall be after the name of his father. (V. 15). Lehi prophesied in the name of the Lord that the Latter-day prophet of whom Joseph had written would have a spokesman. "I will give unto him that he shall write the writing of the fruit of thy loins, unto the fruit of thy loins; and the spokesman of thy loins shall declare it. And the words which he shall write shall be the words which are expedient in my wisdom should go forth unto the fruit of thy loins". (V. 18-19). That spokesman was Sidney Rigdon, of whom the Lord said in a Latter-day revelation: "And it is expedient in me that you, my servant Sidney, should be a spokesman unto this people; yea, verily, I will ordain you unto this calling, even to be a spokesman unto my servant Joseph. And I will give unto him power to be mighty in testimony. And I will give unto thee power to be mighty in expounding all scriptures, that thou mayest be a spokesman unto him, and he shall be a revelator unto thee, that thou mayest know the certainty of all things pertaining to the things of my kingdom on the earth". (D&C 100:9-10).

The record hidden in Cumorah would "cry from the dust". (V. 20). "For those who shall be destroyed shall speak unto them out of the ground, and their speech shall be low out of the dust, and their voice shall be as one that hath a familiar spirit; for the Lord God will give unto him power that he may whisper concerning them, even as it were out of the ground; and their speech shall whisper out of the dust". (2 Nephi 26:16).

How joyful Lehi must have been as he read the prophecies of his ancestor Joseph, that were recorded on The Plates of Brass. Particularly, Lehi recognized that because of the covenant between the Lord and Joseph, son of Jacob, his descendants through his own son Joseph would not be destroyed. (V. 23, see Commentary Reference to 2 Nephi 10:2).

A final reference by Lehi to Joseph Smith confirmed the significance of the prophet's mission to the descendants of Book of Mormon peoples: "And there shall rise up one mighty among them, who shall do much good, both in word and in deed, being an instrument in the hands of God, with exceeding faith, to work mighty wonders, and do that thing which is great in the sight of God, unto the bringing to pass much restoration unto the House of Israel, and unto the seed of thy brethren". (V. 24).

This chapter closes with a tender farewell to his young son: "And now, blessed art thou, Joseph. Behold, thou art little; wherefore hearken unto the words of thy brother, Nephi, and it shall be done unto thee even according to the words which I have spoken. Remember the words of thy dying father. Amen". (V. 25).

"Yea, Joseph truly said: Thus saith the Lord unto me: A choice seer will I raise up out of the fruit of thy loins. And unto him will I give commandment that he shall do a work ... which shall be of great worth unto them, even to the bringing of them to the knowledge of the covenants which I have made with thy fathers. And his name shall be called after me; and it shall be after the name of his father. And he shall be like unto me; for the thing, which the Lord shall bring forth by his hand, by the power of the Lord, shall bring my people unto salvation."
(2 Nephi 3:7 & 15).

Second Nephi
Chapter 4

As Lehi continued to give his children and grandchildren patriarchal blessings, he related the promises they were given to those that "Joseph, who was carried into Egypt" had received so long ago. (V. 1). "For behold, he truly prophesied concerning all his seed. And the prophecies which he wrote, there are not many greater. And he prophesied concerning us, and our future generations; and they are written upon The Plates of Brass". (V. 2).

Joseph Smith received the record of Joseph when he obtained the Egyptian mummies, but the only portion of it that has been published is J.S.T. Genesis 50:24-25. It reads, in part: "The Lord hath visited me, and I have obtained a promise of the Lord, that out of the fruit of my loins, the Lord God will raise up a righteous branch (that) shall be broken off, and shall be carried into a far country; nevertheless they shall be remembered in the covenants of the Lord, when the Messiah cometh; for he shall be made manifest unto them in the latter days, in the Spirit of power and shall bring them out of darkness into light; out of hidden darkness, and out of captivity unto freedom".

The record itself has unfortunately been lost. A copy remains engraven "upon The Plates of Brass", which record is currently in the hands of the Lord. (V. 2). It is possible that among other things, Joseph Smith learned of the temple endowment from Joseph's record, for "great were the covenants of the Lord which he made unto Joseph". (2 Nephi 3:4).

The opening verses of this chapter constitute Lehi's patriarchal blessing upon the sons and daughters of Laman and Lemuel. He first stressed to them the principle that recurs throughout The Book of Mormon. "The Lord God hath said that: Inasmuch as ye shall keep my commandments ye shall prosper in the land; and inasmuch as ye will not keep my commandments ye shall be cut off from my presence". (V. 4).

Then he repeated the wonderful promise first recorded in The Book of Proverbs: "If ye are brought up in the way ye should go ye will not depart from it". (V. 5, see Proverbs 22:6). He added that should they be raised improperly, their blessing would remain, and the curse for disobedience would be upon their parents' heads, instead. (V. 6). The Doctrine & Covenants echoes this point: "And again, inasmuch as parents have children in Zion, or in any of her stakes which are organized, that teach them not to understand the doctrine of repentance, faith on Christ the Son of the living God, and of baptism and the gift of the Holy Ghost by the laying on of the hands, when eight years old, the sin be upon the heads of the parents". (D&C 68:25).

As Alma taught: "There are many promises which are extended to the Lamanites; for it is because of the traditions of their fathers that caused them to remain in their state of ignorance; therefore, the Lord will be merciful unto them and prolong their existence in the land. And at some period of time, they will be brought to believe in his word, and to know of the incorrectness of the traditions of their fathers; and many of them will be saved, for the Lord will be merciful unto all who call on his name". (Alma 9:16-17). The power of this inspired blessing given to the children of the rebellious sons of Lehi was such that the Lord would not allow their blameless and guiltless descendants to perish. Lehi promised the sons and daughters of Laman: "Because of my blessing the Lord God will not suffer that ye shall perish; wherefore, he will be merciful unto you and unto your seed forever". (V. 7). Lemuel's children received "the same blessing which (Lehi) left unto the sons and daughters of Laman; wherefore, (neither would they) utterly be destroyed; but in the end (their seed should) be blessed". (V. 9).

His patriarchal blessing to his grandchildren was at least partially confirmed at the time of the Great Separation, when within this group of Nephites who left the Land of their First Inheritance were "Jacobites, Josephites, Zoramites, Lamanites, Lemuelites, and Ishmaelites".. This is a startling declaration, because it leads us to conclude that the ministries that had focused on the elder sons and their posterity and on the posterity of Ishmael had not been entirely in vain. (See Commentary reference to 2 Nephi 1:28).

Sam's blessing was inseparable from Nephi's, and he was promised that his posterity would be numbered with his brother's. "For thou shalt inherit the land like unto thy brother Nephi", promised Lehi. "And thy seed shall be numbered with his seed; and thou shalt be even like unto thy brother, and thy seed like unto his seed; and thou shalt be blessed in all thy days". (V. 11). Consequently, when we read in other scriptures of the various Book of Mormon family groups, e.g., D&C 3:17, there are no references to 'Samites', for they had become Nephites and could rightfully claim his blessings as their own. (See Jacob 1:3). Lehi pronounced these blessings on his children and grandchildren "according to the feelings of his heart, and the Spirit of the Lord which was in him". (V. 12). This is the manner in which all blessings should be administered.

At this stressful time, with his father near death, the continuing hostility of Laman and Lemuel must have been of great concern to Nephi. Perhaps because of the trouble caused by his elder brethren, Nephi only briefly recorded his fathers' passing. "He waxed old", he wrote. "And it came to pass that he died, and was buried". (V. 12).

With what must have been a heavy heart, Nephi then reported that his elder brethren were again angry with him each time he delivered to them "the admonitions of the Lord". (V. 13). They were troublesome, vexatious, and trying, showed resentment toward him, and were enraged, wrathful, and irate. Even more, they bore the physical marks of anger such as angry countenances.

As their spirit of contention increased, they felt even more uncomfortable in the company of the more righteous members of their family. At the same time, as they spiraled slowly downward into the abyss of apostasy, their agency and power to change slipped away. The gates of hell loomed large, and the weight of the chains of Satan became oppressive to bear, as they became more firmly entrenched in sin. Nephi's continual mandate from the Lord, nevertheless, was to admonish his brethren, to counsel them against wrong practices, to give authoritative advice, to warn them, and to offer exhortation and encouragement. He was constrained or forced to speak to them plainly according to the word of the Lord. (V. 14).

In the midst of these difficult times, Nephi recorded a lyrical song of praise in which he poured out the feelings of his heart in beautiful poetic style. He prefaced this psalm that is the only example of this writing style in The Book of Mormon, with a testimony of his love for the scriptures. "I write the things of my soul, and many of the scriptures which are engraven upon The Plates of Brass. For my soul delighteth in the scriptures, and my heart pondereth them, and writeth them for the learning and the profit of my children". (V. 15). The scriptures were obviously tremendously important to Nephi. Not only did he enjoy reading them and sharing them with his family, but he also recognized that as the keeper of the sacred records, he was an author of holy writ.

It is clear that the writings of Nephi made a deep and lasting impression on his descendants who were entrusted with the care of the records. All who have the opportunity to read The Books of Nephi are similarly privileged to have had a glimpse into Nephi's heart and soul, for his words are a tangible testament to his character.

A study of the Psalm of Nephi reveals how all the scriptures on The Plates of Brass must have delighted him. "The influence of the books of Isaiah, Jeremiah, Lamentations, and the Psalms, is very apparent. This is a true psalm in both form and ideas. Its rhythm is comparable to the notable cadence of David's poems. It not only praises God, but lays bare to us the very depths of Nephi's own soul". (Sydney B. Sperry, "Book of Mormon Compendium", p. 153).

Starting in verse 16, note the ingenious parallelism: "My soul delighteth in the things of the Lord; and my heart pondereth continually upon the things which I have seen and heard". What is almost the hallmark of Hebrew poetry in contrast to our own is parallelism, the echoing of the thought of one line of verse, in a second line that is its partner. In this repetition of thought, two lines of poetry are said to be parallel if the component elements of one line correspond directly with those of the other, in a one-to-one relationship.

Parallelism has a dignity and spaciousness that allows time for the thought to sink in and have an effect on the hearer, and it also provides the opportunity to present more than one perspective on the matter. Consequently, gifted writers have used this literary device as a very subtle and yet very persuasive learning tool. (See Numbers 23:19, Proverbs 15:1 & Commentary Reference to 1 Nephi 15:9-10).

"The parallelism of the Psalm of Nephi manages marvelous density through the repetitions of its Hebraic thought rhyme". (Steven C. Walker, "More Than Meets the Eye: Concentration of The Book of Mormon", 20:2:199). This would be of tremendous importance to those who were consciously aware of the limitations of space on plates of ore that had been so laboriously created.

Early on, Nephi had emphasized that the content of The Small Plates of Nephi would focus on the religious history of his people, and he was quite adamant that those who kept the record after him should pay heed to this instruction. He reiterated that his full intent was to "persuade men to come unto the God of Abraham, and the God of Isaac, and the God of Jacob, and be saved". (1 Nephi 6:4). Nephi maintained his focus on this objective in his psalm, for in its brevity the Lord is addressed at least 45 times. He must have taken quite some time to compose the psalm, because not only is it internally parallel, but it is written in chiastic style as well. (See John A. Tvedtnes, "The Psalm of Nephi", BYU Studies, V. 11, N. 1, Autumn 1970, p. 58).

Note in verse 20 the continuation of the beautiful internal parallelism of the thought patterns that were introduced in verse 16: "My soul delights in the things of the Lord / My heart ponders continually the things I have seen and heard / My God has been my support / He has preserved me".

Verses 17 and 18 illustrate the principle that the more righteous we become; the clearer are our perceptions. And yet, Nephi cried out: "Notwithstanding the great goodness of the Lord, in showing me his great and marvelous works, my heart exclaimeth: O wretched man that I am! Yea, my heart sorroweth because of my flesh; my soul grieveth because of mine iniquities. I am encompassed about, because of the temptations and the sins which do so easily beset me".

He grieved because of personal inadequacies not mentioned in The Book of Mormon, but in mid-sentence in verse 19, he hit upon the key to triumphing over despair. He would simply trust in the Lord. "I know in whom I have trusted", he declared. "He hath filled me with his love, even unto the consuming of my flesh". (V. 21). Because of his love of the Lord, Nephi would be consumed in the sense that he would be "sanctified by the Spirit unto the renewing" of his body. (See D&C 84:33). The Holy Ghost would purge or purify his body of the effects of sin.

Appreciate again the internal parallelism of several of the following verses: "He hath confounded mine enemies unto the causing of them to quake before me". (V. 22). In other words, Nephi's adversaries would be utterly defeated and brought to naught by the power of the Spirit as it rested on him. When Joseph Smith was a prisoner in Liberty Jail, incarcerated for months on false charges and the subject of the repeated verbal abuse of the guards, he was finally moved to stand and declare: "Silence, ye fiends of the infernal pit! In the name of Jesus Christ, I rebuke you, and command you to be still. I will not live another minute and hear such language. Cease such talk, or you or I die this instant". "He ceased to speak", related Parley P. Pratt, who was a witness to the scene. "He stood erect in terrible majesty, chained, and without a weapon, calm, unruffled, and dignified as an angel. He looked down upon his quailing guards, whose knees smote together, and who, shrinking into a corner, or crouching at his feet, begged his pardon, and remained quiet until an exchange of guards. I have seen ministers of justice, clothed in ministerial robes and criminals arraigned before them, while life was suspended upon a breath in the courts of England. I have witnessed a Congress in solemn session to give laws to nations. I have tried to conceive of kings, of royal courts, of thrones and crowns, and of emperors assembled to decide the fate of kingdoms, but dignity and majesty have I seen but once, as it stood in chains, at midnight, in a dungeon, in an obscure village in Missouri". ("Autobiography of Parley P. Pratt", p. 210-211).

The Lord "hath heard my cry by day, and he hath given me knowledge by visions in the night-time". (V. 23). As Jeremiah put it: "His word was in mine heart as a burning fire shut up in my bones, and I was weary with forbearing, and I could not stay". (Jeremiah 20:9, see Commentary Reference to 1 Nephi 19:20). Joseph Smith described a similar experience with the Lord in these words: "The veil was taken from our minds, and the eyes of our understanding were opened. We saw the Lord standing upon the breastwork of the pulpit, before us; and under his feet was a paved work of pure gold, in color like amber. His eyes were as a flame of fire; the hair of his head was white like the pure snow; his countenance shone above the brightness of the sun; and his voice was as the sound of the rushing of great waters". (D&C 110:1-3).

Having had equally powerful experiences, Nephi was moved to ask: "Why should I yield to sin, because of my flesh? Yea, why should I give way to temptations, that the evil one have place in my heart to destroy my peace and afflict my soul? (V. 27). The Savior, after all, is the "founder of peace". (Mosiah 15:18). "His peace", Nephi knew, "is not the peace of the world of ease, of luxury, idleness, absence of turmoil and strife, but the peace born of the righteous life, the peace that lifts the soul, that day by day brings us closer to the home of Eternal Peace, the dwelling place of our Father". (J. Reuben Clark, Jr.).

Nephi was familiar with the peace we may receive as our lifestyle conforms to our divine potential. Natural progression dictated that he should "no longer droop in sin". He was full of the hope born of a righteous life. "Rejoice, O my heart", he wrote, "and give place no more for the enemy of my soul". (V. 28). When we droop in sin, it is like being at the Banquet of Consequences where, when we go with our loved ones, there will not be much that is satisfying at the table unless we are able "to bow our heads in reverence, and not hang them in shame, in the presence of God who will be there". (Marion D. Hanks, speeches of The Year, 10/3/1967).

"Do not anger again because of mine enemies. Do not slacken my strength because of mine afflictions". (V. 29). This verse very subtly suggests that when we become angry, even because of the actions of unrighteous enemies, our strength slackens. This is because power and violence are mutually exclusive; where one is present, the other is absent. In fact, "when we undertake to exercise control or dominion or compulsion in any degree of unrighteousness, behold, the heavens withdraw themselves; the Spirit of the Lord is grieved; and when it is withdrawn, Amen to the priesthood or the authority of that man". (D&C 121:37).

In the first 10 verses of the psalm, Nephi provided the key to peace of mind and spiritual power: Begin now to live in a manner that pleases God, so that He will want to travel life's path as your Companion and help you approach perfection.

Nephi characterized the Savior as the rock and chief-corner stone of his salvation. (V. 30, see 1 Corinthians 3:11). Jesus Christ is the foundation. Recognizing the sure footing he had in Christ, Nephi asked "wilt thou make me that I may shake at the (very) appearance of sin". (V. 31). He knew by his own experience that it is better to shake, than to be shock-proof, as were his elder brethren. (See Alma 13:12).

Nephi continued to pray, with exclamation points for added emphasis, repeating five variations on the same theme: "May the gates of hell be shut continually before me, because that my heart is broken, and my spirit is contrite!". The gates of hell mark the entrance to the spirit prison of the unjust, a place of correction for those who have committed all but the unpardonable sin. (See D&C 76:73, 138:8 & 28, Isaiah 61:1, 1 Peter 3:19 & Moses 7:57). The way to block these doors is to offer the Lord the required sacrifice, which is to be broken down with sorrow for sin in an attitude of contrition. "O Lord, wilt thou not shut the gates of thy righteousness before me, that I may walk in the path of the low valley, that I may be strict in the plain road! O Lord, wilt thou encircle me around in the robe of thy righteousness! O Lord, wilt thou make a way for mine escape before mine enemies! Wilt thou make my path straight before me!" (V. 32 & 33). Nephi trusted in the Lord rather than in the arm of flesh. He knew well that the first principle of the Gospel is faith, and not temporal power.

"O Lord, I have trusted in thee", he cried, "and I will trust in thee forever. I will not put my trust in the arm of flesh; for I know that cursed is he that putteth his trust in the arm of flesh. Yea, cursed is he that putteth his trust in man or maketh flesh his arm". (V. 34). As David said to the Philistines: "Thou comest to me with a sword, and with a spear, and with a shield; but I come to thee in the name of the Lord of Hosts, the God of the armies of Israel, whom thou hast defied. This day will the Lord deliver thee into mine hand, and I will smite thee ... that all the earth may know that there is a God in Israel ... and all this assembly shall know that the Lord saveth not with sword and spear, for the battle is the Lord's". (1 Samuel 17:45).

"Yea, I know that God will give liberally to him that asketh", declared Nephi. "Yea, my God will give me, if I ask not amiss; therefore, I will lift up my voice unto thee; yea, I will cry unto thee, my God, the rock of my righteousness. Behold, my voice shall forever ascend up unto thee, my rock and mine everlasting God. Amen". (V. 35).

"I know that God will give
liberally to him that asketh. Yea,
my God will give me, if I ask not amiss;
therefore, I will lift up my voice unto thee;
yea, I will cry unto thee, my God, the rock of
my righteousness. Behold, my voice shall
forever ascend up unto thee, my rock
and mine everlasting God."
(2 Nephi 4:35).

Second Nephi
Chapter 5

This chapter chronicles the event known as The Great Separation, when, out of necessity, Nephi and those family members who supported him departed from the Land of Their First Inheritance. The anger focused on Nephi by Laman, Lemuel, and those who followed them had become so intense that Nephi's life was in constant jeopardy, and so there was no viable alternative but to leave.

The question is sometimes asked, "In consequence of their apostasy, and their actions that followed, did Laman and Lemuel become Sons of Perdition?" Bruce R. McConkie wrote: "Those who in this life gain a perfect knowledge of the divinity of the Gospel cause, a knowledge that comes only by revelation from the Holy Ghost, and who then link themselves with Satan and come out in open rebellion ... become Sons of Perdition". ("Mormon Doctrine", p. 746). The answer to that question thus remains undecided because we do not know the hearts of Nephi's rebellious brothers, nor is it our prerogative to make a judgment.

In any event, by this point in the narrative, the reader can recognize "a polarized world in which two irreconcilable ideologies confronted each other. It is addressed explicitly to our own age, faced by the same predicament and the same impending threat of destruction. It is a call to faith and repentance, couched in a language of history and prophecy. But above all, it is a witness to God's concern for all His children and to the intimate proximity of Jesus Christ to all who will receive Him". (Hugh Nibley, "The Book of Mormon: A Minimal Statement", p. 152).

The immediate problem that Nephi described in the opening verses of this chapter was that the anger of his brethren had reached such a height that they sought his life. (V. 2). They murmured against him, "saying: Our younger brother thinks to rule over us; and we have had much trial because of him; wherefore, now let us slay him, that we may not be afflicted more because of his words. For behold, we will not have him to be our ruler; for it belongs unto us, who are the elder brethren, to rule over this people". (V. 3, see 1 Nephi 16:37). Truly, "the guilty take the truth to be hard, for it cutteth them to the very center". (1 Nephi 16:2).

For Nephi and his brethren, the wandering recommenced. "And it came to pass that the Lord did warn me, that I, Nephi, should depart from them and flee into the wilderness, and all those who would go with me". (V. 5, see Jacob 7:26). So, too, for the Latter-day Saints in the middle years of the Nineteenth Century. The Book of Mormon thus became a training manual for members of the Church in the early years following the Restoration.

"Wherefore, it came to pass that I, Nephi, did take my family, and also Zoram and his family, and Sam, mine elder brother and his family, and Jacob and Joseph, my younger brethren, and also my sisters, and all those who would go with me". (V. 6). This mention of sisters is the only Book of Mormon reference that indicates Nephi had sisters. Joseph Smith said Ishmael's two sons married into Lehi's family. Those two sisters thus sided with the Lamanites, and might be the progenitors of the 'Ishmaelitish women' mentioned in Alma 3:7. Since Nephi recorded that he had "sisters" we can assume that at least two other sisters, and perhaps more, must have stayed with him after their separation from the Lamanites.

The refugees traveled "for the space of many days" before they pitched their tents in the wilderness. (V. 7). The place where they stopped, their future home, they called "Nephi", and all who went with Nephi called themselves "the people of Nephi, (V. 8 & 9), while those who stayed with Laman and Lemuel were called "Lamanites". (V. 14). The terms "Nephite" and "Lamanite" are used throughout The Book of Mormon in a loose and general sense to designate not only racial but also political (Moroni 1:9), military (Alma 43:4), religious (4 Nephi 1:38), and cultural (Alma 53:10 & 15), divisions and groupings of people.

In Jacob 1:13, a distinction is made regarding the early divisions based on religion among the children of Lehi. In his lifetime, "the people which were not Lamanites were Nephites". But within this group of Nephites were "Jacobites, Josephites, Zoramites, Lamanites, Lemuelites, and Ishmaelites". This is a startling declaration, because it leads us to conclude that the ministries that had focused on the elder sons and their posterity and on the posterity of Ishmael had not been entirely in vain. Likewise, among the Lamanites were counted those who "were a compound of Laman and Lemuel, and the sons of Ishmael, and all who had dissented from the Nephites". (Alma 43:13). In other words, the ministry that had been oriented toward solidifying the faith and testimony of the balance of Lehi's descendants had not been entirely successful, either. (See Alma 24:29, 43:13, 55:4 & 56:3).

Inasmuch as 2 Nephi 5:5-6 reports that "all those who would go" went with Nephi when he departed into the wilderness from the Land of Their First Inheritance, it is plausible to assume that this group included descendants of Laman, Lemuel, and Ishmael, who are called "Lamanites, Lemuelites, and Ishmaelites" in Jacob 1:13.

For additional clarification that reflected the reality of their current and future circumstances, Jacob then confirmed the same cultural distinction between the Lamanites and Nephites that Nephi had made. "I, Jacob, shall not hereafter distinguish them by these names, but I shall call them Lamanites that seek to destroy the people of Nephi, and those who are friendly to Nephi I shall call Nephites, or the people of Nephi". (Jacob 1:14, see Commentary Reference to Alma 3:4-12).

The people of Nephi kept "the commandments of the Lord in all things according to the Law of Moses", that testified of Christ. (V. 10, see 2 Nephi 11:4). This would continue to be the key to their prosperity throughout their history. As long as they were obedient, they "did prosper exceedingly" in every spiritual way, and "did reap again in abundance", and were blessed temporally, as the "began to raise flocks, and herds, and animals of every kind". (V. 11).

Nephi had been careful to bring with him "the records which were engraven upon The Plates of Brass; and also the ball, or compass, which was prepared for (his) father by the hand of the Lord". (V. 12). He also brought "the sword of Laban". (V. 14). In time, all these took on the character of emblems of authority, the national treasures that a ruler was required to possess to validate the legitimacy of his power. Thus, throughout their history, the Lamanites were forever trying to wrest these powerful symbolic objects from the Nephites.

The Nephites were craftsmen who knew how to construct "buildings, and to work in all manner of wood, and of iron, and of copper, and of brass, and of steel". (V. 15). The Iron Age dates from around 1,500 B.C. to 1,000 B.C., and the first use of the metal was about 3,000 B.C., around the beginning of the Bronze Age. Nevertheless, steel artifacts have been discovered that are more than 2,000 years old. ("World Book Encyclopedia").

Evidently, the plans for the construction of Solomon's Temple were found on The Plates of Brass, for Nephi built a temple after its manner, although on a less grandiose scale. (V. 16). The Lord's people have always been commanded to build temples, for that is where the faithful go to get their bearings on eternity. (See D&C 124:39). Early on, Nephi's people recognized that the temple would be like a celestial observatory oriented toward the infinite. In all their endeavors, he taught them "to be industrious, and to labor with their hands". (V. 17). His earlier training in the desert wastes of Arabia would now be put to good use.

As soon as they had settled in their new home in the Land of Nephi, his people approached him with the proposal that he become their king. Although he resisted, they still looked upon him as their protector. (V. 18, see 2 Nephi 6:2). A theocracy, with God as Lord and King, is the ultimate manifestation of government. The first government on earth was a kingdom under God in which Adam reigned with divine investiture of authority over his people. (See Abraham 1:26, Mosiah 29:13, & Ether 7:23-27). Nephi, in a sense, did the same thing. He recognized that "the words of the Lord had been fulfilled unto (his) brethren, which he spake concerning them, that (he) should be their ruler and their teacher". In fact, he "had been just that right up to the time that his brethren sought his life. (V. 19).

Laman and Lemuel and those who followed them had forced Nephi's hand, and because "they (would) not hearken unto (his) words, they (were) cut off" from the presence of the Lord. (V. 20). The hearts of the Lamanites had become hard "like unto a flint", that is a typical condition of apostates from the truth. (V. 21). As Mormon commented: "And thus we can plainly discern, that after a people have been once enlightened by the Spirit of God, and have had great knowledge of things pertaining to righteousness, and then have fallen away into sin and transgression, they become more hardened and thus their state becomes worse than though they had never known these things". (Alma 24:30).

In the case of the Lamanites, Nephi addressed a much more obvious consequence of their apostasy. Whereas they had once been a handsome people, Nephi reported that they now were cursed with a skin of blackness, so that they might be repugnant to the Nephites. "Wherefore", he wrote, "as they were white, and exceedingly fair and delightsome, that they might not be enticing unto my people the Lord God did cause a skin of blackness to come upon them". (V. 21). In light of such a startling development, it is surprising that Nephi did not report this phenomenon in more detail.

This is the only reference in the entire Book of Mormon where a definite color adjective is used to refer to this mark, and so we might not want to take it literally. All other references call it a "skin of darkness" or a "dark skin". Interestingly, in Hebrew, the terms "blackness" and "darkness" are interchangeable; perhaps in English we should view both terms similarly. In 2 Nephi 30:6, we read about the Lamanites in the Last Days, when "their scales of darkness shall begin to fall from their eyes" and "they shall be a pure and a delightsome people." Before the 1978 revision of the English language scriptures, this word was rendered "white" as opposed to "pure", to emphasize by contrast the concept of "spiritual blackness". In any event, the quality of darkness seems to apply more to the spiritual condition of the Lamanites than to any physical characteristic they may have had, so we should not think that Nephi, or God for that matter, was guilty of racially prejudicial stereotyping.

The Lamanites were to become a scourge to the people of Nephi, "to stir them up in remembrance" of the Lord. (V. 25). To help his people avoid such unpleasant chastisement, Nephi consecrated Jacob and Joseph to be "priests and teachers" of the people. (V. 26). If these were offices in the Aaronic Priesthood, the terms would have been used in the singular. The fact is that Lehi was of the tribe of Manasseh through Joseph and Ishmael was of Ephraim. (Alma 10:3). There were no Levites in the group, and so it is reasonable to assume that none of them would have held offices within the Aaronic Priesthood.

Until the coming of Christ, the Nephites officiated by virtue of the authority of the Melchizedek Priesthood. They offered sacrifice and performed the duties that in Israel would have been the responsibility of Levitical priests. They observed in every detail the requirements of the Mosaic Law. When Christ came, He gave the Nephites all the authority of the Priesthood that we exercise today. (See 2 Nephi 6:2, Jacob 1:8, Mosiah 6:3, Alma 4:6, 45:22, & 49:30).

Nephi stated that his people lived "after the manner of happiness" by being partakers of the Abrahamic Covenant. (V. 27). The blessings of that Covenant include the priesthood, eternal marriage, and a land of inheritance. With a temple and the authority vested in the Melchizedek Priesthood, the people of Nephi were entitled in every way to receive these blessings. All this occurred while they lived in their promised land just thirty years after they had left Jerusalem. (V. 28).

Nephi continued to keep the records of his people on The Large Plates of Nephi. He also was commanded to make those "other plates" that are familiar to us as The Small Plates of Nephi. (V. 30). "Wherefore ... to be obedient to the commandments of the Lord, (Nephi) went and made these plates upon which (he engraved) that which is pleasing unto God". (V. 31-32). The Lord told Joseph Smith that upon The Small Plates of Nephi was engraven specific information "concerning the things which (He) would bring to the knowledge of the people". (D&C 10:40).

Nephi must have been preoccupied with the establishment of his new settlement, as well as with its defense, for just six verses after stating that thirty years had elapsed since leaving Jerusalem, he reported that now a full "forty years had passed away, and we had already had wars and contentions with our brethren". (V. 34). The scale of these conflicts is hard to estimate because the opposing populations of the contestants could not have been great by today's standards. Suffice to say that communication had effectively broken down between the parties such that there was no hope of a peaceful or negotiated resolution in the foreseeable future.

Second Nephi
Chapter 6

In The Second Book of Nephi, Jacob is the author of Chapters 6 through 10, that are several in a series of discourses given to the People of Nephi. Perhaps these chapters were included in Nephi's record because Jacob was also a witness of the Redeemer, who delighted in the scriptures. (See 2 Nephi 11:3, & 2 Nephi 4:16).

Jacob was "called of God and ordained after the manner of his holy order" to the Melchizedek Priesthood, and was consecrated to be a teacher by his brother Nephi. (V. 2, see 2 Nephi 5:26). Thus, he taught with power and authority. The Plates of Brass were the reference and foundation of his message, and from that record he spoke to the people "concerning all things which (were) written, from the creation of the world". (V. 3). He also spoke "concerning things which are, and which are to come", and had evidently been given a specific topic for a "General Conference" style address. (V. 4, see D&C 93:4). "They are the words which my brother has desired that I should speak unto you", he explained, "and I speak unto you for your sakes, that ye may learn and glorify the name of your God". (V. 4). Jacob relied on the words of Isaiah as he sought to teach the People of Nephi, and so there is an application in his message for Latter-day Israel, as well. "The words which I shall read are they which Isaiah spake concerning all the House of Israel. Wherefore, they may be likened unto you, for ye are of the House of Israel. And there are many things which have been spoken by Isaiah which may be likened unto you, because ye are of the House of Israel". (V. 5, see 3 Nephi 23:1-3).

"And now these are the words: Thus saith the Lord God. Behold, I will lift up mine hand to the Gentiles, and set up my standard to the people; and they shall bring thy sons in their arms, and thy daughters shall be carried upon their shoulders". (V. 6). The Lord told Joseph Smith: "I came unto mine own, and mine own received me not; but unto as many as received me gave I power to do many miracles, and to become the sons of God; and even unto them that believed on my name gave I power to obtain eternal life. And even so I have sent mine everlasting covenant into the world, to be a light to the world, and to be a standard for my people, and for the Gentiles to seek to it, and to be a messenger before my face to prepare the way before me". (D&C 45:8-9). Elsewhere, He declared: "And for this cause, that men might be made partakers of the glories which were to be revealed. The Lord sent forth the fulness of his Gospel, his everlasting covenant, reasoning in plainness and simplicity - To prepare the weak for the things which are coming on the earth, and for the Lord's errand in the day when the weak shall confound the wise and the little one become a strong nation, and two shall put their tens of thousands to flight. And by the weak things of the earth, the Lord shall thrash the nations by the power of his Spirit". (D&C 133:57-59).

It shall come to pass in the Last Days, that "kings shall be thy nursing fathers, and their queens thy nursing mothers; they shall bow down to thee with their faces towards the earth, and lick up the dust of thy feet; and thou shalt know that I am the Lord; for they shall not be ashamed that wait for me". (V. 7). Verse 13 is Jacob's commentary on this verse: "Wherefore, they that fight against Zion, and the covenant people of the Lord shall (figuratively) lick up the dust of their feet; and the people of the Lord shall not be ashamed. For the people of the Lord are they who wait for him; for (in the Last Days) they still wait for the coming of the Messiah", having missed Him the first time around.

The verses just cited, verses 6-7, and 16-18, are verbatim quotations from Isaiah 49:22-23, & 24-26. The rest of this chapter is Jacob's own commentary on these verses. Today is the day when Isaiah's great prophecies concerning Israel are being fulfilled. With a sense of urgency, we need to be certain that we are working with the Lord in establishing His word as it has come to us through Isaiah. (See 1 Nephi 19:16, & 3 Nephi 29:4-9).

Putting Isaiah's prophecy into historical context, Jacob explained: "I ... would speak somewhat concerning these words. For behold, the Lord has shown me that those who were at Jerusalem, from whence we came, have been slain and carried away captive". This is the second Book of Mormon confirmation that Jerusalem had been destroyed. (V. 8, see 1 Nephi 19:20, 2 Nephi 6:8 & 25:10, Ezekiel 23:25 & 2 Kings 24:14). "Nevertheless, the Lord has shown unto me that they should return again. (Maher-shalal-hashbaz / a remnant shall return). And he also has shown unto me that the Lord God, the Holy One of Israel, should manifest himself unto them in the flesh; and after he should manifest himself they should scourge him and crucify him, according to the words of the angel who spake it unto me. And after they have hardened their hearts and stiffened their necks against the Holy One of Israel, behold, the judgments of the Holy One of Israel shall come upon them. And the day cometh that they shall be smitten and afflicted". (V. 9-10).

Verse 11 makes the point that many of the House of Israel will come to a knowledge of the Redeemer before the Millennium. "Wherefore, after they are driven to and fro ... they shall be scattered, and smitten, and hated; nevertheless, the Lord will be merciful unto them, that when they shall come to the knowledge of their Redeemer, they shall be gathered together again to the lands of their inheritance". Consider the acceptance today of the Savior by Lamanitish peoples in Central and South America, the Pacific Isles, Australia, and New Zealand, and witness the presence of temples in these lands. In addition, the verse clearly teaches that these people will be gathered to their respective lands of inheritance. In other words, there is more than one land of inheritance, for Zion is where the pure in heart dwell. (See D&C 97:21).

"According to the words of (Isaiah), the Messiah will set himself again the second time to recover (his people); wherefore, he will manifest himself unto them in power and great glory, unto the destruction of their enemies, when that day cometh when they shall believe in him". (V. 14). Joseph Fielding Smith, Jr. felt; "Not many of the Jews will believe in Christ before He comes". ("Doctrines of Salvation", 3:9). However, the sentiment of the Jew's concerning Jesus Christ has shifted considerably over the years. For example, at the time of the Restoration of the Gospel in 1830, if a Jew had mentioned the name of Christ in synagogue, he would have been rebuked. Had a rabbi referred to him, the congregation would have arisen and left the building.

The hearts of Heavenly Father's children will softened, "and blessed are the Gentiles, they of whom the prophet (Isaiah) has written; for behold, if it so be that they shall repent and fight not against Zion, and do not unite themselves to that great and abominable Church, they shall (also) be saved; for the Lord God will fulfil his covenants which he has made unto his children; and for this cause the prophet has written these things". (V. 12).

"Now is the time of the Jew", declared Spencer W. Kimball in October 1975, and we can expect great things to happen among those of the House of Israel in the near future. As Isaiah asked: "For shall the prey be taken from the mighty, or the lawful captive delivered?" (V. 16). In other words, shall the righteous, the Covenant People of the Lord, be delivered from their enemies? The answer is a resounding "Yes!" For "they that believe not him shall be destroyed, both by fire, and by tempest, and by earthquakes, and by bloodsheds, and by pestilence, and by famine. And they shall know that the Lord is God, the Holy One of Israel". (V. 15). "For the mighty God shall deliver his covenant people". (V.

17). Isaiah 49:25 continues: "For thus saith the Lord: I will contend with them that contendeth with thee, and I will save thy children".

So important are these two verses that for added emphasis both Isaiah and Jacob structured them as a chiasm. Verse 16 is a complaint, or question from Israel, about how the great Restoration can take place. Verse 17 is the Lord's response, and His promise to Israel:

A: Shall the prey be taken captive?
B: Shall the lawful captive be delivered?
B: The captive of the mighty shall be taken away.
A: The prey of the terrible shall be delivered.

Then, verse 18 very forcefully reaffirms the power of God: "And I will feed them that oppress thee, with their own flesh; and they shall be drunken with their own blood as with sweet wine; and all flesh shall know that I the Lord am thy Saviour and thy Redeemer, the Mighty One of Jacob". (See Isaiah 49:26). Thus did Isaiah testify of Christ. No wonder Jesus Christ Himself declared: "Great are the words of Isaiah!" (3 Nephi 23:1).

"And blessed are the Gentiles,
they of whom the prophet had written
for, behold, if it so be that they shall repent
and fight not against Zion and do not unite
themselves to that great and abominable church,
they shall be saved, for the Lord God will fulfil
his covenants which he has made unto his
children." (2 Nephi 6:12).

Second Nephi
Chapter 7

Within this chapter that parallels Isaiah 50, is a promise of the Savior's redemption, a foreshadowing of His mission and His suffering, and a terse reminder to Israel to trust in the Lord. It is critical that it be read in its historical context, because only then will it make sense. Under Mosaic Law, a marriage could not be legally dissolved unless the wife received a 'bill of divorcement.' In the opening verses, the Lord argued that, in spite of her apostasy, He could take Israel back because she had never been legally separated from Him. Moreover, because the Lord had no creditors, His sovereign rights over His children had not been jeopardized. In ancient times, children might be sold into slavery or indentured for a fixed number of years in order to satisfy a debt.

In verse 1, the Lord rhetorically asks if He had initiated the estrangement between Himself and Israel, and He answers His own question by stating that it is she, and not He, who has done so. "Yea, for thus saith the Lord: Have I put thee away, or have I cast thee out forever? ... Where is the bill of your mother's divorcement? To whom have I put thee away, or to which of my creditors have I sold you? Behold, for your iniquities have ye sold yourselves, and for your transgressions is your mother put away".

Verse 2 promises redemption based on the merits of the Savior, but acknowledges that in spite of His gift, the Jews did not receive him as the Messiah. "When I came, there was no man, none to answer. O House of Israel, is my hand shortened at all that it cannot redeem, or have I no power to deliver?" Israel could have been redeemed at any time, if only she had asked for the Lord's help. As He explained in a Latter-day revelation: "In that day when I came unto mine own, no man among you received me, and you were driven out. When I called there was none of you to answer; yet my arm was not shortened at all that I could not redeem, neither my power to deliver". (D&C 133:66-67).

Verse 2 also illustrates that although we are powerless to control the seas and the heavens, the Lord can easily do so. "At my rebuke, I dry up the sea, I make their rivers a wilderness and their fish to stink because the waters are dried up, and they die because of thirst". In that same context, verse 3 refers to Egypt at the time of the Exodus, and also to the Second Coming of the Savior. "I clothe the heavens with blackness, and I make sackcloth their covering". In our day, we have become jaded to such manifestations, because illusions and caricatures of power are so prevalent in the visual media, but these reminders of God's power must have made quite an impression on the Nephites.

Verses 4-11 comprise a Servant Song wherein the Lord speaks to Israel through Isaiah. These verses should be read with this in mind. "The Lord God hath given me the tongue of the learned", said the prophet, "that I should know how to speak a word in season unto thee, O House of Israel. (V. 4). He "hath opened mine ear, and I was not rebellious, neither turned away back". (V. 5).

Verse 6 is written in the first-person tense for emphasis, and is a foreshadowing of the mission and suffering of the Savior: "I gave my back to the smiter, and my cheeks to them that plucked off the hair. I hid not my face from shame and spitting". To pluck the hair from one's beard was a terrible form of degradation in ancient times.

Isaiah recognized the source of his power. "The Lord God will help me", he wrote, "therefore, shall I not be confounded. Therefore, have I set my face like a flint, and I know that I shall not be ashamed". (V. 7). In the next verse, Isaiah assured us that God will uphold His servants. "The Lord is near, and he justifieth me. Who will contend with me? Let us stand together. Who is mine adversary? Let him come near me, and I will smite him with the strength of my mouth". Verse 8 is reminiscent of the Lord's counsel to Joseph Smith: "Neither take ye thought beforehand what ye shall say; but treasure up in your minds continually the words of life, and it shall be given you in the very hour". (D&C 84:85)

"For the Lord God will help me. And all they who shall condemn me, behold, all they shall wax old as a garment, and the moth shall eat them up". (V. 9). As Paul asked the Romans, "What shall we then say to these things? If God be for us, who can prevail against us?" (J.S.T. Romans 8:31). When we love the Lord, and obey the voice of His servants, it is impossible for us to walk in darkness without the light of Gospel knowledge. (V. 10). "If your eye be single to my glory", promised the Savior to Joseph Smith, "your whole bodies shall be filled with light, and there shall be no darkness in you, and that body which is filled with light comprehendeth all things". (D&C 88:67, see 3 Nephi 13:22).

Verse 11 is a terse reminder to trust in the Lord. "Behold all ye that kindle fire, that compass yourselves about with sparks, walk in the light of your fire and in the sparks which ye have kindled. This shall ye have of mine hand – ye shall lie down in sorrow". We cannot generate our own light. We can only hope to be like white hot sparks struck off the divine anvil of God Himself. One reason the inhabitants of the earth were under condemnation before the Restoration of the Gospel in 1830 was because "they (sought) not the Lord to establish his righteousness, but every man walk(ed) in his own way, after the image of his own god, whose image (was) in the likeness of the world". (D&C 1:6, see D&C 59:21, & 88:35). Some things never change, and history tends to repeat itself.

Second Nephi
Chapter 8

This chapter returns to the address that was interrupted by the Servant Song in Chapter 7, verses 4-11. Verse 1 employs the imagery of a rock quarry. "Look unto the rock from whence ye are hewn, and to the hole of the pit from whence ye are digged". Abraham is the rock, and his wife Sarah is the pit. "Look unto Abraham, your father, and unto Sarah, she that bare you; for I called him alone, and blessed him". (V. 2). Abraham was called when he was yet without children. He and Sarah are our greatest ancestral examples of faithfulness to God.

Note the parallelism of verse 3, where the idea is repeated for added emphasis: "For the Lord shall comfort Zion, he will comfort all her waste places; and he will make her wilderness like Eden, and her desert like the garden of the Lord. Joy and gladness shall be found therein, thanksgiving and the voice of melody".

Three times in this chapter, the Lord urged Israel to hearken unto him. "Give ear unto me", he pleaded, "for a law shall proceed from me, and I will make my judgment to rest for a light for the people". (V. 1, 4 & 7). Three times, He urged Israel: "Awake, awake". (V. 9, 17 & 24). In the Last Days, Isaiah foresaw that "many people shall go and say, Come ye, and let us go up to the house of the God of Jacob; and he will teach us of his ways, and we will walk in his paths; for out of Zion shall go forth the law, and the word of the Lord from Jerusalem". (Isaiah 2:3).

"The isles shall wait upon me, and on mine arm shall they trust". (V. 5). If those upon the "isles of the sea" is a reference to the Nephites, then Jacob may have particularly emphasized this verse because he recognized that Isaiah was referring to his own people. To the Hebrews, the continents of Asia and Africa were "the earth" because they had access to them by land, while those regions to which they sailed were "the isles of the sea". (See Commentary References to 1 Nephi 19:10, 15-16, 19, 1 Nephi 22:4-5, 2 Nephi 10:8, & 21-22, 2 Nephi 21:11, 2 Nephi 29:7-8, & Alma 63:5).

Isaiah's special talent was to create vivid imagery in the mind's eye of the people, utilizing metaphor and simile that make lasting impressions on us: "Lift up your eyes to the heavens, and look upon the earth beneath; for the heavens shall vanish away like smoke, and the earth shall wax old like a garment; and they that dwell therein shall die in like manner. But my salvation shall be forever, and my righteousness shall not be abolished". (V. 6).

Israel was familiar with the requirements of righteousness, for the law was written in their hearts. Therefore, Isaiah urged them: "Fear ye not the reproach of men, neither be ye afraid of their revilings. For the moth shall eat them up like a garment, and the worm shall eat them like wool". (V. 7). But the righteousness of the Lord would be forever, and his salvation from generation to generation.

However, it would be necessary for Israel to awaken from the deep sleep of apostasy and recover the power of her former glory. "Awake, awake! (Repeated two times). Put on strength, O arm of the Lord; awake (a third time) as in the ancient days". (V. 9, see Ezekiel 29:3). When Israel is exhorted to put on her strength as she did in days past at the time of the Exodus, a reference is made to Rahab, which is a poetical name of Egypt, and to the dragon, which also refers to Egypt. For did not the Lord show forth His power at the time of the Exodus from Egypt, when He "cut Rahab, and wounded the dragon?" Is He not the same God who "hath dried the (waters of the Red) sea, the waters of the great deep; that hath made the depths of the sea a way for the ransomed to pass over" on dry land? (V. 10).

Isaiah was speaking of the Last Days, when he foresaw that "the redeemed of the Lord shall return, and come with singing unto Zion; and everlasting joy and holiness shall be upon their heads; and they shall obtain gladness and joy; sorrow and mourning shall flee away". (V. 11).

Verse 12-16 urge Israel to trust in the Lord, rather than in the arm of flesh. "Who art thou, that thou shouldst be afraid of man, who shall die? (V. 12). I am the Lord thy God, whose waves roared" during Israel's passage through the Red Sea. "The Lord of Hosts is my name". (V. 15). I may plant the heavens and lay the foundations of the earth, and say unto Zion: Behold, thou art my people". (V. 16). Speaking of the Latter-days, Isaiah reminded Israel that for almost 2,000 years she will have drunk of the cup of the Lord's fury, and "drunk of the dregs of the cup of trembling (with) none to guide her". (V. 17-18).

Beginning in verse 19, mention is made of two Latter-day prophets who will minister to Israel with great power before being martyred in the streets of Jerusalem. They will "lie at the head of all the streets; as a wild bull in a net, they are full of the fury of the Lord". (V. 20). Perhaps these are the witnesses described in Revelation 11:1-6. (See D&C 77:15). Bruce R. McConkie was of the opinion that "these two prophets will be Latter-day Saints, most likely members of the Quorum of The Twelve Apostles, or of the First Presidency". ("Doctrinal New Testament Commentary", 3:507-511).

The cup of the Lord's fury from which Israel will have drunk for so long will be taken from her hand and will pass to her oppressors. (V. 22-23). The Lord "shall thoroughly plead their cause, that he may give rest to the land, and disquiet the inhabitants of Babylon". (Jeremiah 50:34). For many years, these oppressors have said to Israel: "Bow down, that we may go over", and Israel had been resigned to lie down "as the ground and as the street to them that went over". (V. 23). This is a reference to the ancient custom of forming a footpath of the bodies of prostrate prisoners of war, over whom the conquerors walked!

The events of the Last Days will allow Israel to "put on (her) strength" by exercising the authority of the Holy Priesthood of God. She shall awaken and put on her beautiful garments. (V. 24). Joseph Smith explained that this verse "had reference to those whom God should call in the last days, who should hold the power of priesthood to bring again Zion, and the redemption of Israel; and to put on her strength is to put on the authority of the priesthood, which she, Zion, has a right to by lineage; also, to return to that power which she had lost". (D&C 113:8). Jerusalem will loose herself "from the bands of (her) neck", that is, be freed from the curses of God. (V. 25). Of this verse, the Prophet said: "We are to understand that the scattered remnants are exhorted to return to the Lord from whence they have fallen; which if they do, the promise of the Lord is that he will speak to them, or give them revelation ... The bands of her neck are the curses of God upon her, or the remnants of Israel in their scattered condition among the Gentiles". (D&C 113:10).

Moroni spoke to Latter-day Israel, in similar fashion: "Awake, and arise from the dust, O Jerusalem; yea, and put on thy beautiful garments, O daughter of Zion; and strengthen thy stakes, and enlarge thy borders forever, that thou mayest no more be confounded, that the covenants of the Eternal Father which he hath made unto thee, O House of Israel, may be fulfilled". (Moroni 10:31).

"For the Lord shall comfort Zion,
he will comfort all her waste places,
and he will make her wilderness like
Eden, and her desert like the garden
of the Lord. Joy and gladness
shall be found therein."
(2 Nephi 8:3).

Second Nephi
Chapter 9

This chapter, together with the discourse by Lehi in 2 Nephi Chapter 2, is one of the most important in all scripture. It is an inspired commentary on Isaiah in which Jacob approached each subject in terms of God's goodness and greatness, relating the covenants of God to all the House of Israel, and generalizing when he spoke of the 'Jews.' (V. 1-2). Even though Jacob and Nephi were of Manasseh through Joseph, (Alma 10:3), they thought of themselves as 'Jews.' "I say Jew", explained Nephi, "because I mean them from whence I came". (2 Nephi 33:8).

The peoples of whom Jacob spoke were to be gathered in the Last Days to lands of inheritance and lands of promise. (V. 2). Note the plural quality of the noun. "Every nation is the gathering place for its own people", explained Bruce R. McConkie at the first Area Conference of the Church, in South America, in 1972.

Verses 4-27 comprise a discourse on the Atonement and correspond to Isaiah 50:4-9 and 2 Nephi 7:4-9. Jacob began by declaring that with the great gift of a body come serious liabilities, behooving the Creator to "become subject unto man in the flesh, and die for all men". (V. 4 & 5). Then, verses 6-15 comprise one of the most important discussions to be found in all scripture relating to the necessity of the Resurrection and the power of the Atonement. Death, after all, is part of the "merciful Plan of the Great Creator". (V. 6). After the Fall, and because of the requirements of the Law of Justice, mankind suffered not only physical death, but also spiritual death which is alienation from the Spirit of God occurring when we die "as to things pertaining unto righteousness". (Alma 12:16). The first individual spiritual death occurs when we commit sin after reaching the age of accountability. In the scriptures, this is called "the first spiritual death". (See D&C 29:41). After repentance and baptism of water, we can then be spiritually born again through the cleansing action of the baptism of fire and the Holy Ghost. (See Mosiah 5:7).

Jacob understood all these things, and so taught in verse 6 that an Atonement would be required to vitalize the Plan. "For as death hath passed upon all men, to fulfil the Merciful Plan of the Great Creator, there must needs be a power of resurrection, and the resurrection must needs come unto man by reason of the fall; and the fall came by reason of transgression; and because man became fallen they were cut off from the presence of the Lord". The Atonement reconciles the Fall with eternal life by removing the permanent effects of physical death, and giving all of Adam and Eve's posterity the opportunity to have the effects of spiritual death eliminated through repentance. The Atonement nullifies Satan's efforts to sabotage the Plan and saves us from becoming devils or angels to devils. The Atonement gives the Savior the power to crush the head of Satan by bringing into operation the Law of Mercy, which mitigates for those who conform to its requirements the effects of the first Law that demands Justice. Having explained this to his congregation, Jacob was enraptured by God's mercy and grace. As the Apostle Paul confirmed; "By grace ye are saved, thru faith, and that not of ourselves; it is the gift of God". (Ephesians 2:8).

The alternative is frightening. Concerning conditions in the Last Days, Isaiah wrote: "Darkness shall cover the earth, and gross darkness the people". (Isaiah 60:2). Without the Atonement, we are subject to the devil, "to rise no more". (V. 8). He is Perdition, and we would have become his sons and daughters had no Atonement been made, for we would never have had the opportunity to repent. (V. 9).

We would have been in the grasp of that "awful monster" death and hell, or physical and spiritual death. (V. 10). But the Holy One of Israel overcame temporal (v. 11) and spiritual (v. 12) death because He has the power and authority to exercise the keys of resurrection. There is a difference between priesthood power and priesthood authority. The one comes from the laying on of hands and the other comes through righteousness. The Savior, Who lived a perfect life and atoned for our sins, acted in complete obedience to law in bringing into play His power over the Law of Mercy. He literally bought our sins with the Atonement.

Joseph Fielding Smith, Jr. taught that it is contrary to the law of God for the heavens to be opened and messengers to come and do anything for us that we can do for ourselves. Since we cannot redeem ourselves from the effects of sin, a Savior had to be provided. It was determined in the Grand Council in Heaven that He would be the "lamb slain from the foundation of the world". (Revelation 13:8).

In verse 13, Jacob explained that "the paradise of God" in the spirit world is the abode of the righteous. The unrighteous go instead to the spirit prison of the unjust to await their day of redemption. The Spirit Prison of The Unjust is a place of correction for those who have committed all but the unpardonable sin. (See D&C 76:73, 138:8 & 28, Isaiah 61:1, 1 Peter 3:19 & Moses 7:57). That day will come if they accept the Gospel of Jesus Christ and when necessary vicarious priesthood ordinances have been performed for them. We can literally become "saviours on Mount Zion" to our kindred dead as they are brought through the veil of the temple into the presence of the Lord. (Obadiah 1:31). Those in the Spirit Prison of the Unjust, however, who have rejected the Gospel, meaning the power of the Atonement and salvation through Jesus Christ, will have to pay for their sins themselves and will not be redeemed from the Fall until they have personally "paid the uttermost farthing". (Matthew 5:26).

Jacob then explained that because of the resurrection of Christ, we will pass from physical death to immortality, or the condition of our bodies when reunited eternally with our spirits. "And it shall come to pass that when all men shall have passed from this first death unto life, insomuch as they have become immortal, they must appear before the judgment-seat of the Holy One of Israel; and then cometh the judgment, and then must they be judged according to the holy judgment of God". (V. 15). Immortality will come as a free gift to all who have ever lived on the earth.

In addition, all mankind will at least briefly pass from spiritual death when they meet God at the Judgment Bar. Thus, the Resurrection completely overcomes the effects of the Fall, which are physical death and spiritual alienation from God. For a fleeting moment, all mankind will come back into His presence to be judged. Those who have refused to repent will speedily be banished from heaven, for they would not long endure the glory of His celestial abode. But for the righteous, the place of judgment will be "the pleasing bar of the great Jehovah". (Moroni 10:34). The doors will swing open to reveal the household of God bathed in the light of a dazzling vista with limitless potential.

Those who have not been cleansed in the blood of the Lamb or taken the opportunity to rely on the merits of Christ and the power of His Atonement through the first principles and ordinances of the Gospel, are described by Jacob as being "filthy". (V. 16). Sadly, they are beyond the reach of the Atonement to pay the penalty for their sins. Therefore, the Law of Mercy is of no effect for them. They must submit themselves to the Law of Justice as if there had been no Atonement made, and their torment that follows is symbolically described "as a lake of fire and brimstone, whose flame ascendeth up forever and ever and has no end". (V. 16).

In spite of the horror we feel when visualizing the plight of the unrepentant, we must give God credit for even-handedness. Jacob affirmed His justice when he said: "He executeth all his words, and they have gone forth out of his mouth, and his law must be fulfilled". (V. 17). His mercy and His holiness are also validated, for "he delivereth his saints from that awful monster the devil, and death, and hell, and that lake of fire and brimstone, which is endless torment". (V. 19, see D&C 19:11-12).

Consistent with Psalms 149:1, wherein ancient Israel was described as "a congregation of Saints", Jacob used the term "saints" to describe the righteous who believe in the Holy One of Israel. (V. 18, see Commentary Reference to 1 Nephi 10:13). These are they who have "endured the crosses of the world". Christ identified what it means to "take up our cross". "For a man to take up his cross is to deny himself all ungodliness, and every worldly lust, and keep my commandments". (J.S.T. Matthew 16:25-26, see Jacob 1:8, D&C 23:6, 55:2, & 112:14). Paul used the "cross of Christ" to impress upon our minds the doctrine of the Atonement. The symbolism of the cross is more properly found in the ordinance of the Sacrament, where we take upon ourselves the name of Christ, and promise to always remember Him and to keep His commandments.

God knows everything. "There is not anything save he knows it." (V. 20). If He did not have all knowledge, He would cease to be God, and we could not have faith in Him. God progresses by increasing His creations, worlds without number, and by bringing to pass the immortality and eternal life of these creations. (See Moses 1:39). As the Grand Architect of our universe and of eternal worlds, His unimpaired innocence, spirituality, holiness, and virtue allow Him to use principles as if they were foundation building blocks.

His efforts to create "new creatures in Christ" are facilitated by the commandments to repent, to be baptized, and to have perfect faith. (V. 23). These are the basic entrance requirements that qualify us to join Him in His Celestial Kingdom. (See John 3:5). Perfect faith impels us to action as though we had perfect knowledge.

The early Nephites clearly taught that baptism is an essential ordinance of the Gospel. "If (we) will not repent and believe in his name, and be baptized in his name, and endure to the end, (we) must be damned; for the Lord God, the Holy One of Israel, has spoken it". (V. 24, see Moses 5:58, & 6:52).

Verses 25 and 26 explain that the Law of Mercy satisfies the demands of Justice for those who have lived without the knowledge of God's laws. Nevertheless, all those who reach the age of accountability have the light of Christ that allows them to have a foundation appreciation of what is good and what is evil. (See Moroni 7:15-18).

Because of the Atonement, we all have equal opportunity before the Lord. "All men may have the privilege, living or dead, of accepting the conditions of the Great Plan of Redemption provided by the Father, thru the Son, before the world was". (John Taylor, "Mediation and Atonement", p. 181). But "wo" unto those who have the law, if they transgress. "Wo" is a condition of deep suffering from misfortune, affliction, grief, and calamity. Our lives are probationary, when we are tested to see if we will be true to our declared values.

With two exclamation points for emphasis, verse 28 explains that access to the Spirit must accompany true learning. "O that cunning plan of the evil one! O the vainness, and the frailties, and the foolishness of men! When they are learned they think they are wise, and they hearken not unto the counsel of God, for they set it aside, supposing they know of themselves, wherefore, their wisdom is foolishness and it profiteth them not. And they shall perish". (See 1 Corinthians 2:24, 2 Timothy 3:7, D&C 3:4, 88:4, & 123:12). This verse tells us that an appeal to vanity is the devil's way of turning our minds against The Plan of Salvation. (See 2 Nephi 14:27, 28:4, & 28:14). It is a warning against the pitfalls of intellectual apostasy and the snares of secular humanism. (See V. 42, & Colossians 2:8). The next verse is a hokmah employed by Jacob to drive home his point: "But to be learned is good, if they hearken unto the counsels of God". (V. 29).

Verse 30 parallels Isaiah 50:11 and 2 Nephi 7:2-11 and concerns the Final Judgment. "Wo unto the rich, who are rich as to the things of the world. For because they are rich they despise the poor, and they persecute the meek, and their hearts are upon their treasures; wherefore, their treasure is their god. And behold their treasure shall perish with them also". (V. 30). Satan's Golden Question is and always has been: "Do you have any money?" Then, he plants the seeds of apostasy: "You can have anything in this world for money." He uses telestial toys that are the treasures of the earth as counterfeits for God. Jeremiah asked the question: "Shall a man make gods unto himself, and they are no gods?" (Jeremiah 16:20, see Deuteronomy 4:28, 28:36 & 64, 2 Kings 19:18, 1 Chronicles 29:2, Daniel 5:4 & 23, Isaiah 37:19, & Abraham 1:11). In His Preface to the Doctrine and Covenants, the Lord declared of those who lived at the time of Joseph Smith: "They seek not the Lord to establish his righteousness, but every man walketh in his own way, and after the image of his own god, whose image is in the likeness of the world, and whose substance is like that of an idol, which waxeth old and shall perish in Babylon, even Babylon the great, which shall fall". (D&C 1:16).

"Wo unto the deaf that will not hear; for they shall perish. Wo unto the blind that will not see; for they shall perish also. Wo unto the uncircumcised of heart, for a knowledge of their iniquities shall smite them at the last day". (V. 31-33). Such are terrestrial and telestial individuals. (See D&C 76). Truly; "Circumcision is that of the heart, in the spirit, and not in the letter". (Romans 2:29).

Verse 34 parallels Proverbs 19:9. "Wo unto the liar, for he shall be thrust down to hell". Those who bear false witness qualify only for the telestial kingdom. (See D&C 76).

"Wo unto the murderer who deliberately killeth, for he shall die". (V. 35). This sin places the transgressor beyond the power of the Atonement. In obedience to the demands of Justice, the transgressor must atone with his own blood for his sins.

"Wo unto them who commit whoredoms, for they shall be thrust down to hell. Yea, wo unto those that worship idols, for the devil of all devils delighteth in them". (V. 36-37). The worship of idols of any kind is a whoredom and is adulterous in a figurative sense. (V. 37, see Jeremiah 3:8). In the classical sense, a "whore" is "a corrupt or idolatrous community". (O.E.D., see 1 Nephi 14:10). For a member of the Church to worship idols and thereby turn his or her back on the sacred covenants of the Priesthood is akin to infidelity. The devil rules in the earth by the manipulation of those who worship idols. He thus delights in both the idols and the idol worshippers. (V. 37). John Taylor taught: "Priesthood is the legitimate rule of God and is the only power that has a right to rule upon the earth, and when the will of God is done on the earth, as it is done in heaven, no other power will bear rule". (J.D., 5:187).

"Wo unto all those who die in their sins", without repentance. (V. 38). The "enticements" of the devil are powerful. (V. 39). His offers of pleasure or advantage are insidiously and adroitly alluring, for he is a master seducer. The Atonement of Christ considered the fact that we would yield in varying degrees to his temptations. But the Gospel provides a way for us to learn from our mistakes by relying upon the sacrifice of the Savior so that we may be justified by the Spirit. That is to say, we may be found worthy to enter into God's rest even after having repeatedly fallen short of the mark, as long as we repent.

Repentance is our critical activity and the focus of our attention. The earth is a wonderful learning laboratory; indeed, as Henri Bergson so astutely observed, it "is a machine for the making of Gods". The Gospel Plan transforms mortality into a majestic clockwork rather than an evil trap and snare of Satan. This is why Jacob drove home the point: "Remember, to be carnally minded is death, (but) to be spiritually minded is life eternal". (V. 39). This hokmah is the summary of previous verses and focuses our attention on the theme of the entire chapter that is oriented to "the greatness of the Holy One of Israel". (V. 40). To deny that is to "revile" against, or to degrade and minimize, the truth. (V. 40).

Jacob urged his listeners to "come unto the Lord". (V. 41). He acknowledged that the way is narrow, meaning that the broad avenues of Idumea are poor alternatives. The way lies in a "straight course" in contrast to Satan's devious roadmap. At heaven's gate, the keeper will not be Saint Peter but Christ himself, for "He employeth no servant there". (V. 41). There will be no opportunity there for the deception of Satan or his angels.

In verse 42, Jacob summarized the teachings of verses 28-38. "And whoso knocketh, to him will he open; and the wise, and the learned, and they that are rich, who are puffed up, because of their learning, and their wisdom, and their riches - yea, they are they whom he despiseth; and save they shall cast these things away, and consider themselves fools before God, and come down in the depths of humility, he will not open unto them". (See J.S.T. Matthew 7:32-33 / K.J.T. Matthew 7:22-23).

Blessings are predicated upon obedience to law, and when we keep the statutes taught by Jacob to his congregation, we will experience the "happiness which is prepared for the saints". (V. 43, see Alma 40:12, & 41:10). "Happiness is the object and design of our existence and will be the end thereof, if we follow the path that leads to it. And this path is virtue, uprightness, faithfulness, holiness, and keeping all the commandments of God. In obedience there is joy and peace .... and as God has designed our happiness ... He never has, He never will, give a commandment to His people that is not calculated in its nature to promote that happiness which He has designed."" (History of the Church, 5:134-135, see Commentary Reference to 2 Nephi 2:13).

Jacob knew he had been obedient to God's commandments and so he confidently taught the people boldly and plainly. Even though he had solemn responsibilities as their priest and teacher, he was free from their sins. (v. 44, see v. 48). He asked them: "Is it expedient that I should awaken you to an awful reality of these things? Would I harrow up your souls if your minds were pure? Would I be plain unto you according to the plainness of the truth if ye were freed from sin? Behold, if ye were holy I would speak unto you of holiness; but as ye are not holy, and ye look upon me as a teacher, it must needs be expedient that I teach you the consequences of sin". (V. 47-48).

He was concerned that the "chains" of the devil might shackle the Nephites. Hundreds of years later, the prophet Alma explained what these chains are. "And they that will harden their heart, to them is given the lesser portion of the word until they know nothing concerning his mysteries; and then they are taken captive by the devil, and led by his will down to destruction. Now this is what is meant by the chains of hell". (Alma 12:11, see Commentary Reference to 2 Nephi 2:26-27).

This dire warning applies equally and without qualification to members and non-members of The Church of Jesus Christ. When our hearts are hardened against the scriptures and the message of salvation proclaimed by the servants of the Lord, it is as though our portion is diminished further and further, until we are without defense against the aggressive tactics of the devil. Left to ourselves, we are more susceptible to be influenced by his lies, rather than by the illuminating truths of the Spirit, and we risk being dragged down to hell.

The Day of Judgment will be glorious for the righteous, because the Holy Ghost will justify them. Therefore, Jacob exhorted his brethren: "Turn away from your sins; shake off the chains of him that would bind you fast; come unto that God who is the rock of your salvation. Prepare your souls for that glorious day when justice shall be administered unto the righteous, even the day of judgment, that ye may not shrink with awful fear; that ye may not remember your awful guilt in perfectness, and be constrained to exclaim: Holy, holy are thy judgments, O Lord God Almighty

– but I know my guilt; I transgressed thy law, and my transgressions are mine; and the devil hath obtained me, that I am a prey to his awful misery". (V. 45, see Moses 6:60). Repentance, made possible by the Atonement, can remove all traces of impurity. As John Taylor wrote: "That record is written by the man himself in the tablets of his own mind. It cannot lie and will in that day be unfolded before God and angels" in the absence of repentance. As Paul declared: We are "manifestly declared to be the epistle of Christ ministered by us, written not with ink, but with the Spirit of the living God; not in tables of stone, but in fleshy tables of the heart." (2 Corinthians 3:3).

Contemporary prose illustrates the principle: "My father focuses heart-gripping flashes across the wall screen. Family slides. I am small, my brother is smaller, and my sister is smallest. Days now dead re-open like old storybooks from memory's heaped box. Pulling out pictures of cooking in Grandfather's Dutch oven; playing cheetah in our backyard monkey-jungle; being beautifully Easter-bested with my coat buttoned wrong; hugging a mommy minus grey hair. Soberly, I think of another Father, Who someday shall open my mind, and flash reeling remembering of every day's minute across my soul, across the heavens, and kindly ask me to narrate". (Lora Lyn Stucker, "New Era", 8/1973).

Jacob echoed Isaiah when he implored Israel; "Come, my brethren, everyone that thirsteth, come ye to the waters; and he that hath no money, come buy and eat; yea, come buy wine and milk without money and without price. Wherefore, do not spend money for that which is of no worth, nor your labor for that which cannot satisfy. Hearken diligently unto me, and remember the words which I have spoken; and come unto the Holy One of Israel, and feast upon that which perisheth not, neither can be corrupted, and let your soul delight in fatness". (V. 50-51).

Only a fully committed individual speaking with power and authority could make these remarks. Chapters 2 and 9 of 2 Nephi illustrate why Joseph Smith said: "The Book of Mormon is the most correct of any book on earth, and the keystone of our religion, and a man will get nearer to God by abiding by its precepts than by any other book". (H.C., 4:451).

Second Nephi
Chapter 10

This chapter concerns the righteous branch of the House of Joseph that was preserved by the hand of God. (V. 1, see Commentary Reference to 2 Nephi 3 & 4, & Alma 46:23-24). These scriptures refer to that portion of the story of Joseph that was deleted from The Book of Genesis but that was preserved within The Plates of Brass. It was from these plates that Jacob took the text for this portion of his address to the congregation.

Jacob told his listeners that it had been revealed to him that many of their descendants would come to a knowledge of the Redeemer. (V. 2). This is another indication that the Nephites were not "utterly destroyed" at the time of the last great battles, circa 385 A.D., and also that the descendants of Nephi and his righteous brethren intermingled over the years with the posterity of Laman and Lemuel. (See Commentary Reference to 2 Nephi 3:23, & 2 Nephi 5:9).

Until verse 3, the Savior had generally been referred to by Nephi and Jacob as "the Holy One of Israel". This was a favorite name used by Isaiah, and inasmuch as the brothers were partial to him, it is logical that they would employ the same title. (See Commentary Reference to 2 Nephi 25:28). But here, Jacob stated that it had been revealed by an angel that His name should be "Christ". This is from the Greek and signifies the "Anointed One" or the "Messiah". Later, He is identified as "Jesus", that signifies "Savior". (See 2 Nephi 26:12).

Jacob taught that the Savior would be crucified. (V. 3). Crucifixion was employed by the Egyptians, (Genesis 40:19), and the Persians, (Esther 7:10), and therefore was known among the early Jews well before the rise of the Roman Empire. (See Isaiah 22:21-25). It "behooved" the Savior that he be crucified, or in other words it was required so that the demands of the Law of Justice might be fully met to make possible His intercession for sin through the Atonement.

So wicked were the Jews at Jerusalem that they would even crucify their Lord. In their apostasy, they had "set themselves up for a light unto the world, that they (might) get gain and praise of the world; but they (sought) not the welfare of Zion". (2 Nephi 26:29). A similar situation exists today, when many living in Spiritual Babylon crucify the Lord anew and put Him to open shame. In light of the lukewarm reception the world has given to the restoration of the Gospel, it is interesting to ponder how widespread the acceptance of the Savior will be at The Second Coming.

Because of their iniquities, Jacob warned that the consequences of disobedience, that is to say, "destructions, famines, pestilences, and bloodshed" would be visited upon the people. (V. 6). Iniquity is the bedfellow of weakness, hopelessness, futility, sorrow, and despair. Those who abound in iniquity have no hope of progression, forgiveness, or salvation. "And if ye have no hope, ye must needs be in despair, and despair cometh because of iniquity". (Moroni 10:22).

Nevertheless, in the Last Days, Israel will be gathered "in from their long dispersion, from the isles of the sea, and from the four parts of the earth". (See Commentary References to 1 Nephi 19:10, 15-16, 19, 1 Nephi 22:4-5, 2 Nephi 8:5, 2 Nephi 21:11, 2 Nephi 29:7-8, & Alma 63:5). As we have seen, "from the isles of the sea" means from every land that was only accessible to the Holy Land by sea. As Jacob taught; "We have been driven out of the land of our inheritance; but we have been led to a better land, for the Lord has made the sea our path, and we are upon an isle of the sea". (V. 20). "The four parts of the earth, the four quarters of the earth, and the ends of the earth" mean from every direction and including or covering every conceivable place on the entire earth.

Those who fight against Zion, "both Jew and Gentile, both bond and free, both male and female, shall perish; for they are they who are the whore of all the earth; for they who are not for me are against me, saith our God". (V. 16). They are unfaithful to Gospel principles and have thus prostituted themselves. They are characterized as being "the whore of the earth" in the sense that they are a corrupt or idolatrous community and are idol worshipers. (See Commentary Reference to 1 Nephi 14:10, 2 Nephi 9:37, & Moroni 7:13-17).

God reminded Jacob that He would not break His Covenant with Israel. "For I will fulfil my promises which I have made unto the children of men". (V. 17). As a matter of fact, Jacob taught that God would soften the hearts of the Gentiles, that they should "be like unto a father to (Israel), wherefore, the Gentiles shall be blessed and numbered among the House of Israel". (V. 18). To the extent that they will assist in its gathering, and for these acts of charity, they may be adopted into the House of Israel. (See Abraham 2:10-11). The land of promise would be consecrated to the descendants of Lehi, as well as to the Gentiles who would receive the Covenant of Abraham, by adoption. "Wherefore, I will consecrate this land unto thy seed, and them who shall be numbered among thy seed, forever, for the land of their inheritance; for it is a choice land, saith God unto me, above all other lands, wherefore I will have all men that dwell thereon that they shall worship me, saith God". (V. 19).

Jacob suggested that Lehi's party was not the only one led by the Lord from the Land of Jerusalem to "an isle of the sea". For "great are the promises of the Lord unto them who are upon the isles of the sea; wherefore as it says isles, there must needs be more than this, and they are inhabited also by our brethren. For behold, the Lord God has led away from time to time from the House of Israel, according to his will and pleasure. And now behold, the Lord remembereth all them who have been broken off, wherefore he remembereth us also". (V. 21-22). The Lord later told Nephi: "Know ye not that I, the Lord your God, have created all men, and that I remember those who are upon the isles of the sea? Wherefore, I speak the same words unto one nation like unto another". (2 Nephi 29:7-8).

Jacob urged the congregation to "reconcile" itself to God's will "and not to the will of the devil and the flesh". (V. 24). "Reconciliation" brings opposing parties into friendly relations after an estrangement. 2 Nephi 31:12-21 discusses steps of the reconciliation that would be necessary, because "it is only in and through the grace of God" that we are saved. (V. 24).

Verse 25 explains how grace operates. "Wherefore, may God raise you from death by the power of the resurrection, and also from everlasting death by the power of the Atonement, that ye may be received into the eternal kingdom of God, that ye may praise him through grace divine". The resurrection saves us from physical death, and the Atonement redeems us from spiritual death. We are granted grace proportionately as we conform to the standards of personal righteousness that are part of the Gospel Plan. Thus, the Saints are commanded to "grow in grace" (D&C 50:40), until they are sanctified and justified "thru the grace of our Lord and Savior Jesus Christ". (D&C 20:30-32). Grace is an attribute of perfection possessed by God, and consists of His love, mercy, and condescension toward His children. (See D&C 66:12, 84:102, & 93:6-20). It consists of the gifts and power of God by which His children can be brought to perfection.

When we have a better understanding of grace, the scriptures make more sense to us. For example: "For by grace are ye saved, through faith; and that not of yourselves: it is the gift of God". (Ephesians 2:8). Some Christian denominations distort the true meaning of grace and teach that we are saved by God's good pleasure without any individual effort whatsoever. But as Nephi made clear; "We know that it is by grace that we are saved, after all we can do". (See Commentary Reference to 2 Nephi 25:23). What we can do, Jacob taught in this chapter, is keep all His commandments with exactness, and in particular the injunction to speedily repent of our sins.

"It shall come to pass that they shall be gathered in from their long dispersion, from the isles of the sea and from the four parts of the earth; and the nations of the Gentiles shall be great in the eyes of me, saith God, in carrying them forth to the lands of their inheritance."
(2 Nephi 10:8).

Second Nephi
Chapter 11

This chapter emphasizes the worth of The Book of Isaiah. Christ informed us how he felt about this prophet: "Yea, a commandment I give unto you that ye search these things diligently; for great are the words of Isaiah". (3 Nephi 23:1-3). Nephi likened his words to his own people, as should we. He delighted in Isaiah's ability to clearly teach the importance of the covenants God made with Israel, of the reality of the Savior's mortal ministry, and that save He should come, we all must perish. (V. 2-6). With this appreciation of Isaiah's pre-eminence as a Messianic prophet, it is clear why Nephi quoted so extensively from his writings on The Plates of Brass, and why he transcribed so many of his prophecies on The Small Plates of Nephi

The scriptures teach that in the mouths of two or three witnesses shall every word be established. (V. 3). Nephi testified that he and his brother Jacob had seen the Redeemer, as had Isaiah. The Book of Mormon and the Bible are powerful witnesses of Jesus Christ, and Isaiah was a prolific writer who testified openly of the Lord. More of his writings were preserved than any other biblical prophet, save Moses. He is quoted 57 times in the New Testament, and he had a clear vision of the Lord and His mission. In fact, in his record he referred to Christ as "Savior" 8 times, and as "Redeemer" 12 times. Some of his plain and precious teachings fell between the cracks when the Jews methodically eliminated references to the Savior from within the Old Testament.

Nephi taught that the Law of Moses itself was given to Israel for the purpose of proving to the people that Christ should come. (V. 4). He recognized that the Law of Moses was profoundly symbolic of Christ. (See Mosiah 3:14-15, 13:29-31, Alma 215:15-16, 34:14, & Galatians 32:21-24). This is a principal reason why their possession of The Plates of Brass was so critical to the spiritual welfare of Lehi's family and its righteous descendants.

To bolster their faith, there were many "types" of Christ in the Israelite experience. A "type" has symbolic significance as well as a literal meaning. There are repeated references to types in the Nephite record, for they are very effective teaching tools. An outward observance without any real meaning is only a ceremony. For example, the spontaneous greeting of the bishop, who stands behind the pulpit at the beginning of Sacrament meeting, is a ceremony. His expression of thanks to the Aaronic Priesthood for a job well done after the administration of the Sacrament is a ceremony. The recognition of visitors to Relief Society and other meetings is largely ceremonial. These events pass without any lasting significance.

A rite with a present spiritual meaning is a symbol. No one would dispute the symbolic significance of the bread and water used in the Sacrament. The prayer accompanying the ordinance reminds the participants of Christ's sacrifice and of their covenant relationship with Him. Especially in the temple, the ordinance of baptism is carried out in a font resting on the backs of twelve oxen that is in similitude of the grave and of the twelve tribes of Israel. In the fonts in meetinghouses, the repentant faithful symbolically wash away their sins and emerge clean and pure in the sight of God. Their white clothing is symbolic of purity. The Savior Himself was baptized in Jordan, which is the lowest body of fresh water on earth. This symbolized His willingness to descend beneath us all.

In the font itself, the authority of the priesthood is vested in one who holds his right arm to the square in a symbolic gesture of the power of God. The right hand is used to receive the Sacrament, connoting determination, faithful observance, and obedience. No one who has been the recipient of a priesthood administration when sick can deny the rejuvenating symbolism of pure olive oil that has been consecrated for the healing of the sick in the household of faith. There is symbolic significance in the olive tree itself. It is a living thing that produces good fruit and whose branch has always been associated with peace. But an olive tree cannot become productive by itself. It requires the grafting in of a tame branch by a husbandman. Afterward, careful attention and pruning are required, because whenever the tree is neglected, it will begin to revert to the primitive, wild plant it once was. But once fruitful, it may remain so for centuries. In fact, new shoots from the root of the original tree may continue producing fruit for thousands of years.

It is interesting that, during the siege of Jerusalem (70 A.D.), the Romans symbolically cut down the olive trees, including those in the Garden of Gethsemane beside the Brook Kidron, outside the city walls. Then, three years later, the Romans built a three-foot high wall entirely around the mountain fortress of Masada, (a "line of circumvallation") symbolically demonstrating to the Jewish Zealots within, that there could be no possibility of escape.

If the symbolism associated with a rite also points to a future reality, conveying at the same time by anticipation the blessing that is yet to be received, it is a type. The brazen serpent raised up in the wilderness by Moses pointed Israel to the ministry of Christ and to promised salvation. Much of the symbolism of the temple endowment is a portrayal of the promised blessing of eternal life in the Celestial Kingdom of God. Types have the ability to enlarge our comprehension beyond that which we could ever otherwise gain, and because of our increased capacity to grasp the meaning of the mysteries of the kingdom, there emerges almost miraculously a vital link between the secular and the divine.

An understanding of the symbolism permeating the Gospel and the application of the principles taught therein constitute a stairway to the stars. These symbols can lift us and sustain us as we reach out to embrace expanding circles of knowledge through active and repetitive participation in ordinances and unwavering obedience to their related covenants. With symbolism so subtly interwoven into the fabric of the Gospel, with golden threads our Father has created a tapestry that generates a brilliant sheen capable of stimulating the vitality and the power to change lives.

Those who allow themselves to be thus affected are transformed and their spiritual rebirth is one of generation and not merely one of maturation. As King Benjamin taught his people: "And now, because of the covenant which ye have made ye shall be called the children of Christ, his sons, and his daughters; for behold, this day he hath spiritually begotten you; for ye say that your hearts are changed through faith on his name; therefore, ye are born of him". (Mosiah 5:7).

Introduction to
The Isaiah Chapters
Second Nephi 12 - 24

"The version of Isaiah in the Nephite scriptures hews an independent course for itself, as might be expected of a truly ancient and authentic record. It makes additions to the present text in certain places, omits material in others, transposes, makes grammatical changes, finds support at times for its unusual readings in the ancient Greek, Syriac, and Latin Versions, and at other times finds no support at all. In general, it presents phenomena of great interest to the student of Isaiah". (Sydney B. Sperry, "Book of Mormon Compendium", p. 512).

"The text of Isaiah in The Book of Mormon is not word for word the same as that of the King James Translation. Of 433 verses of Isaiah in the Nephite record, Joseph Smith modified 234, or 53%. Some of the changes were slight, while others were radical. However, 199 verses are word for word the same as the K.J.T.. We, therefore, freely admit that Joseph Smith may have used the K.J.T. when he came to the text of Isaiah on the plates. As long as the K.J.T. agreed substantially with the text on the plates, he let it pass; when it differed too radically, he translated the Nephite version and dictated the necessary changes". (Sydney B. Sperry, "Book of Mormon Compendium", p. 507-508, see C.E.S. Manual, p. 90, & Commentary Reference to 2 Nephi 26:15).

As Hugh Nibley has pointed out: "Resemblances between the Bible and The Book of Mormon are not hard to explain. Far from being evidence of fraud, they are rather confirmation of authenticity. If The Book of Mormon is what it claims to be, we should expect to find a strong biblical influence in it. Its prophets sound like those of the Old Testament because they studied and consciously quoted the words of those prophets, and moreover, all prophets sound alike, being called for the same purpose under much the same conditions". ("Churches in The Wilderness").

Mark E. Petersen wrote: "When the King James translators began their work, they did so with fasting and prayer. For the most part they were pious men who sought the inspiration of the Lord in their work. We believe they received it. The preservation of the Bible thru the ages is itself a miracle. It was accomplished only thru the hand of God. Then why not its translation? The King James translators did everything they knew how to obtain divine inspiration for their task. Knowing the great value of that book to the Gentiles, as Nephi himself said, would God withhold the necessary inspiration?. Those humble translators were instruments in the hands of the Almighty to further His purpose among the Gentiles. ("Those Gold Plates!" p. 52 & 56).

Nephi himself revealed why a comprehension of Isaiah is difficult even for biblical scholars. He wrote: "Now I, Nephi, do speak somewhat concerning the words which I have written, which have been spoken by the mouth of Isaiah. For behold, Isaiah spake many things which were hard for many of my people to understand; for they know not concerning the manner of prophesying among the Jews". (2 Nephi 25:1). That is to say, the prophet Isaiah spoke in figures, using types and shadows to illustrate his points. Thus, the key to an understanding of his scriptural code requires some explanation.

Only Sam and Nephi and perhaps their wives had lived "at Jerusalem". Therefore, they alone had a first-hand understanding of their cultural heritage and the distinctive writing style of the Jews. On the one hand, it would be important that the people of Nephi be familiar with the contents of The Plates of Brass, because the teachings of that body of scripture contained many important doctrinal truths. On the other hand, Nephi abhorred that part of the Jewish mindset which had been responsible for the persecution of his family, its expulsion from their home, their trials in the wilderness, and the hardship of their lives in the promised land.

Nephi expressed his reluctance to teach the people many things concerning the manner of "the Jews", but at the same time, he wrote; "My soul delighteth in the words of Isaiah, for I came out from Jerusalem, and mine eyes hath beheld the things of the Jews, and I know that the Jews do understand the things of the prophets, and there is none other people that understand the things which were spoken unto the Jews like unto them, save it be that they are taught after the manner of the things of the Jews". (2 Nephi 25:6).

Indirectly, Nephi emphasized the importance of Book of Mormon scholarship and of studying his people, their culture, and their world. If we neglect to do that, we cannot understand the manner of prophesying of men like Nephi, Jacob, Abinadi, Alma, Helaman, Mormon, and Moroni, let alone Isaiah. They can be understood, but only if we are willing to first pay the price. Perspiration must precede inspiration, and there can be no revelation where there is no student.

Because Isaiah's writing style employed types and shadows, and because his prophecies were dualistic, meaning that they had application not only for ancient Israel, but also for Israel at the time of the mortal ministry of Christ, and for Latter-day and Millennial Israel as well, it is necessary in many cases to analyze nearly every word of a verse in order to comprehend its true meaning. It will also be necessary to study the chapters against the backdrop of the historical context in which they were written, in order to 'read between the lines' and better understand their meaning. At first, such an exercise might seem a bit cumbersome, but with a deeper understanding, Isaiah's writings will come alive with imagery and metaphor, and loom larger than life, because they were specifically written to transcend the ages.

The Lord declared: "Now behold, a marvelous work is about to come forth among the children of men". (D&C 4:1). "And if thou wilt inquire, thou shalt know mysteries which are great and marvelous". (D&C 6:11). "Now behold, I say unto you, that ye ought to search these things. Yea, a commandment I give unto you that ye search these things diligently; for great are the words of Isaiah". (3 Nephi 23:1).

Only when we have expended soul-sweat will the words of Isaiah flow easily and poetically to our minds. Scriptural fluency will come after practice that is manifested by memorization, recitation, individual and cooperative study, comparison with companion scriptures, expansion of understanding by critical analysis of supportive commentaries, not to mention enduring faith and fervent prayer.

One final thought. The "Isaiah Chapters" may have been strategically placed within the Second Book of Nephi in order to give first-time readers of The Book of Mormon time to acquaint themselves with the "manner of the Jews" (2 Nephi 25:2) through a study of the 22 chapters of the First Book of Nephi, and the first 11 chapters of the Second Book of Nephi, so that they could, when they finally got to 2 Nephi Chapter 12, better appreciate the prophet's style and subject matter. Rather than summarily skipping over these chapters, Nephi may have hoped that, with their placement, latter-day Israel would be in a better position to understand the prophet's messages, for both he and the resurrected Lord felt that the words of Isaiah were of great worth.

"And now, behold, I say unto you, that ye ought to search these things. Yea, a commandment I give unto you that ye search these things diligently; for great are the words of Isaiah. For surely he spake as touching all things concerning my people which are of the house of Israel; therefore, it must needs be that he must speak also to the Gentiles. And all things that he spake have been and shall be, even according to the words which he spake. (3 Nephi 23:1-4).

As Nephi had written: "Wherefore, hearken, O my people, which are of the house of Israel, and give ear unto my words; for because the words of Isaiah are not plain unto you, nevertheless they are plain unto all those that are filled with the spirit of prophecy ... Yea, and my soul delighteth in the words of Isaiah, for I came out from Jerusalem, and mine eyes hath beheld the things of the Jews, and I know that the Jews do understand the things of the prophets, and there is none other people that understand the things which were spoken unto the Jews like unto them, save it be that they are taught after the manner of the things of the Jews." (2 Nephi 25:4-6, see Commentary Reference to 2 Nephi 25:1).

"And it shall come to pass
in the last days when the mountain
of the Lord's house shall be established in
the top of the mountains, and shall be exalted
above the hills, and all nations shall flow unto it.
And many people shall go and say, Come ye, and let
us go up to the mountain of the Lord, to the house of
the God of Jacob; and he will teach us of his ways,
and we will walk in his paths for out of Zion
shall go forth the law, and the word of
the Lord from Jerusalem."
(2 Nephi 12:2-3).

The Second Book of Nephi
About 588 - 570 B.C. to 559 - 545 B.C.
Chapters 12 - 33

Second Nephi
Chapter 12

Isaiah's vision concerned only Judah and Jerusalem, but his words may be likened to all of God's children. (V. 1, see 2 Nephi 11:8). He clearly saw the Last Days, when "the mountain of the Lord's house (should) be established in the tops of the mountains". (V. 2). Latter-day Saints are prone to restrict the geographical setting of this scripture to the intermountain west and specifically to the Valley of the Great Salt Lake. But this interpretation may be too narrow. As the Lord warned Joseph Smith: "And let them who be of Judah flee unto the mountains of the Lord's house". (D&C 133:13). Jerusalem, then, must also be considered in connection to it. The word 'mountain' is used both allegorically and figuratively in the scriptures. In this verse, it refers to a high place of God, a place of revelation, and perhaps to the temple of the Lord. Eerdman's Commentary on The Bible likens 'the mountain of the Lord' to Mount Zion, that is, to Jerusalem. There is certainly ample historical precedent to do so.

Moriah has been a sacred place for over 4 millennia and will yet fulfil its ultimate destiny, as prophesied in the scriptures. Whether or not the mountain of the Lord's house refers to the temple, every house of the Lord stands as a 'type' of the paradise lost in this world, of the contact point between heaven and earth, and of the final temple that the earth will become when it is renewed to receive its paradisiacal glory.

In any event, verses 2 and 3 provide an exalted vision of Israel's future. "He will teach us of his ways, and we will walk in his paths; for out of Zion shall go forth the law, and the word of the Lord from Jerusalem". (V. 3). The stage is set for a description of conditions at or just after the Second Coming of the Lord. Isaiah wrote of a beautiful and idealistic world of peace, as if he were certain of its accomplishment. "And he shall judge among the nations, and shall rebuke many people: and they shall beat their swords into plowshares, and their spears into pruning-hooks – nation shall not lift up sword against nation, neither shall they learn war anymore". (V. 4, see Micah 4:1-4). His faith was magnificent, especially when we consider that over 2,700 years ago, he wrote his prophecy of a millennial world that is still yet to come.

In verse 5, Isaiah contrasted the glory of the millennial Earth with the drab reality of our telestial world, and exhorted Israel to change her ways in order to be worthy of her destiny. "Come ye and let us walk in the light of the Lord". The Book of Mormon addition to K.J.T. Isaiah 2:5 underscores the widespread apostasy then existing in Israel: 'For ye have all gone astray, everyone to his wicked ways".

Isaiah was the last prophet to address assembled Israel. His message, which was a voice of warning to turn away from unrighteousness or face the consequences, has had applications for the Children of the Covenant ever since. During his ministry, the Ten Tribes were taken captive by Assyria; they later fled to the north countries and were lost to history. (See Commentary Reference to 2 Nephi 20:20). But they may have carried the words of Isaiah with them, just as Lehi did upon The Plates of Brass. (See 1 Nephi 22:4 & 2 Nephi 29:13). The Jews also retained his words, and today, Covenant Israel (the Church) treasures them. Secular Christian Churches recognize the prophetic voice of Isaiah even if they do not fully understand it. His is a very diversified audience and his teachings are equally applicable to all who read his words because of the dualistic nature of his prophecies.

Isaiah next identified the reasons why the Almighty had forsaken His people. Since these verses are dualistic, when we read them we should liken them unto ourselves. Israel did not enjoy a close relationship with the Lord because she had been "replenished from the east", that is to say she looked to the religious philosophies of the Assyrians and other heathen countries for power and sustenance. (V. 6). The Lord has assured us that "he that seeketh signs shall see signs, but not unto salvation". (D&C 63:7). The process by which faith is developed is one of testing. The Lord gives certain principles, and by obedience to them, blessings and power follow. But one has no proof of that promise until one acts on the basis of trust or belief. Then comes the confirmation of the reality, but only after one has acted on faith. That is why James taught: "Faith, if it hath not works, is dead, being alone". (James 2:17, see Ether 12:6, & John 7:17).

When we realize that "faith cometh not by signs, but signs follow those that believe", we can see why sign seeking is condemned. (D&C 63:9). Those who demand outward evidence of the power of God as a condition for belief seek to circumvent the process by which faith is developed. They want proof without paying the price. As with the adulterer, they seek the result without accepting the responsibility. They desire only theological titillation.

Israel was drawn to Eastern mysticism as moths are attracted to fire, and she was mesmerized by its worldly manifestations of influence even though they were only illusions and caricatures of the tremendous power symbolized by the Burning Bush at Sinai. Israel was also forsaken because she was drawn to the influences of the world and was superstitious or hearkened "unto soothsayers", and "pleased (herself) in the children of strangers", that is to say, made covenants with foreigners who were not of the true faith. (V. 6). Israel was wealthy and materialistic: Her "land (was) full of silver and gold", wrote Isaiah, and she was running rampant with telestial toys: "Neither (was) there any end of (her) treasure". (V. 7). It was all too easy for her to put her trust in material resources rather than in God.

Isaiah used a symbol of warfare, when he wrote: "Neither is there any end of their chariots". (V. 7). Israel had grown to depend more on her military might than on her spiritual preparedness. Too often, in times of crisis we feel the urge to jump up and grab our weapons rather than drop to our knees and hold tightly to our faith. This is just what Israel did when she worshiped pagan gods. "Their land is full of idols", observed Isaiah. (V. 8). Jeremiah asked: "Shall a man make gods unto himself, and they are no gods?" (Jeremiah 16:20). Ezekiel lamented the fact that Israel had allowed herself to be led into spiritual bondage, until she was "as the heathen, as the families of the countries, to serve wood and stone". (Ezekiel 20:32).

Israel had the opportunity to take advantage of scriptural insight and understanding relative to the doctrines of salvation, but instead she sought after the things of the world. Therefore, even though spiritual treasures were potentially available and could have changed and perfected many lives, they became tarnished and lost the power to do so, because of the pride and vain imaginations of the people.

The whole meaning of K.J.T. Isaiah 2:9 is changed in the corresponding verse in 2 Nephi 12:9, with the inclusion (twice) of the word "not". "And the mean (or common) man boweth not down, and the great man humbleth himself not". Without these corrections, the passage makes no sense, at all.

Isaiah realized that pride was a major problem for the Children of The Covenant, and would be in the Last Days, as well. In both former and latter days, the rebellious "seek not the Lord to establish his righteousness, but every man walketh in his own way, and after the image of his own god, whose image is in the likeness of the world". (D&C 1:16). Even today, men and women fashion gods of wood and stone to assuage their vanities and passions. These idols blind them to the recognition that their faith is flawed and has no power to save.

As a result of their wickedness, God will pass judgment on the people. From verse 10 to the end of the chapter, the orientation of Isaiah's prophecy is toward the Last Days. His message reflects Ezekiel's, who wrote: "As I live, saith the Lord God, surely with a mighty hand, and with a stretched out arm, and with fury poured out, will I rule over you; And I will bring you out from the people, and will gather you out of the countries wherein ye are scattered, with a mighty hand, and with a stretched out arm, and with fury poured out. Note the internal parallelism). And I will bring you into the wilderness of the people, and there will I plead with you face to face ... And I will bring you into the bond of the covenant: and I will purge out from among you the rebels, and them that transgress against me. (Therefore), pollute ye my holy name no more with your gifts, and with your idols. For in mine holy mountain, in the mountain of the height of Israel, saith the Lord God, there shall all the House of Israel, all of them in the land, serve me". (Ezekiel 20:33-40).

In the Last Days, said Isaiah, "the lofty looks of man shall be humbled". (V. 11). The Lord alone, and not the proud, shall be exalted just before, and at the time of, the Second Coming. In a sense, the Lord's exaltation will reach its zenith only after He has established His spiritual kingdom on the earth. The Book of Mormon rendering of Isaiah 2:12 makes clear that the "day of the Lord of Hosts" will soon come upon Israel, and upon all nations, when the proud shall be "brought low" or humbled. (V. 12).

The qualities of the Cedars of Lebanon and the Oaks of Basham mentioned in verse 13 are associated with people. "Yea, and the day of the Lord shall come upon all the cedars of Lebanon, for they are high and lifted up; and upon all the oaks of Basham". (V. 13). The former were evergreen, beautiful, aromatic, wide spreading, long lived and had many uses. The latter were trees that grew to a large size and could reach great age. Basham was an area east of Jordan that was familiar to Israel, so she could not ignore the overt symbolism of the metaphor.

The day of the Lord will be universally recognized by all people, "upon all the high mountains, and upon all the hills, and upon all the nations which are lifted up, and upon every people. And upon every high tower, and upon every fenced wall". (V. 14 & 15). All trade among nations will cease when the great and terrible day of the Lord comes "upon all the ships of the sea, and upon all the ships of Tarshish". (V. 16). This verse is quite remarkable, because the phrase "and upon all the ships of the sea" is found in The Book of Mormon version of Isaiah 2:16, but not in the K.J.T. Book of Isaiah Chapter 2:26. It is, however, found in the ancient Greek, or Septuagint, version of Isaiah, first translated between the third and first century B.C.

Joseph Smith did not know any Greek at the time he translated The Book of Mormon, and there is no record that the Septuagint was available for his study at the Palmyra Lending Library. The only logical conclusion is that The Book of Mormon rendering of this verse from Isaiah is a direct quotation from a text at least as old as the Septuagint. In fact, this Book of Mormon quotation from 2 Nephi 12 may be attributed to The Plates of Brass, a text hundreds of years older than the Septuagint.

Verse 17 reiterates verse 11, that the proud shall be abased while the Lord shall be exalted. "The loftiness of man shall be bowed down, and the haughtiness of men shall be made low; and the Lord alone shall be exalted in that day". Figuratively speaking, man-made idols of silver and gold will be thrown to the moles and bats, that are animals so blind from living for so long in darkness that they cannot appreciate wealth when it is before them.

"And the idols (that) he shall utterly abolish ... shall go into the holes of the rocks, and into the caves of the earth". (v. 18-20).

Finally, Isaiah urged Israel not to trust in man, "whose breath is in his nostrils", but rather to trust in God who has given man "the breath of life", that he might become "a living soul". (v. 22, see Genesis 2:7).

It is easy to see why Jacob would want to teach his family these principles. The imagery with which Isaiah adorned his writing would encourage the faithful of all generations to "increase in beauty, and in holiness", and Zion to "arise and put on her beautiful garments". (D&C 82:14).

Second Nephi
Chapter 13

This chapter, together with Chapter 14, has a dual meaning, with significance for both ancient and Latter-day Israel. The first eight verses were carefully structured as a chiasm in order to create a greater impact upon the reader.

Clearly, Jerusalem and Judah will be punished for their disobedience. They will be left without even the necessities of life: "For behold, the Lord, the Lord of Hosts, doth take away from Jerusalem, and from Judah, the stay and the staff, the whole staff of bread, and the whole stay of water". (V. 1). In Hebrew, "stay and staff" are masculine and feminine forms of the same root and are rendered "masen" and "masenah". Thus, the implication is one of complete physical and spiritual destruction. In addition, the symbols of bread and water often represent Christ, His Gospel, and the Atonement. (See Amos 8:11, Isaiah 48:2 & Psalms 23:4).

There will be no bearers of the priesthood left, neither "the mighty man, (nor) the man of war, the judge ... the prophet ... the prudent ... (nor) the ancient". (V. 2). The leaders of Judah will be deported, as well, "the captain of fifty, and the honorable man, and the counselor, and the cunning artificer, and the eloquent orator". (V. 3). Judah will be ruled by incompetents without ability, by people with a childish understanding, or even by Gentiles. "And I will give children unto them to be their princes, and babes shall rule over them". (V. 4). There will be social chaos as well. "The people shall be oppressed, everyone by another, and everyone by his neighbor; the child shall behave himself proudly against the ancient, and the base against the honorable". (V. 5). Israel will be willing to accept anyone to be their ruler: "When a man shall take hold of his brother of the house of his father, and shall say: Thou hast clothing, be thou our ruler". (V. 6). But no one will be willing to shoulder the responsibility of government. "In that day shall he swear, saying: I will not be a healer; for in my house there is neither bread nor clothing; make me not a ruler of the people". (V. 7).

Isaiah spoke of the coming social, economic, and political disaster as it if had already been accomplished. "For Jerusalem is ruined, and Judah is fallen, because their tongues and their doings have been against the Lord". (V. 8). He began to prophesy to the people about 740 B.C. The Northern Kingdom was defeated in 721 B.C. by the Assyrians, and Judah in 587 B.C. by the Babylonians, and again in 70 A.D. by the Romans.

The faces of Judah shall reveal their sins. "The show of their countenance doth witness against them, and doth declare their sin to be even as Sodom, and they cannot hide it". The Law of Retribution will be operative; the righteous shall prosper, but the wicked shall perish. "Wo unto them, for they have rewarded evil unto themselves! Say unto the righteous that it is well with them; for they shall eat the fruit of their doings. Wo unto the wicked, for they shall perish; for the reward of their hands shall be upon them!" (V. 9-11).

The next few verses complete the intricate chiastic pattern developed in verses 1-8. The repetition that follows emphasizes the abuse of the poor by the rich and powerful, and the oppression the people bring upon themselves. "They who lead thee cause thee to err and destroy the way of thy paths … Ye beat my people to pieces, and grind the faces of the poor, saith the Lord God of Hosts". (V. 12 & 15).

Judah's rulers shall act like children, or worse, like Gentiles, and even corruptible women shall rule over them. "And my people, children are their oppressors, and women rule over them" which was considered an insult in Israel. (V. 12).

The Lord will judge the ancients, or elders, who should have been the primary administrators of justice in Israel. He will also judge the princes or royal appointees, who have abused the vineyard or nation of Israel and have beaten the people to pieces and ground the faces of the poor. (V. 14-15). Of these verses, Joseph Fielding Smith, Jr. declared: "Isaiah saw our day!"

Verses 16-23 stylistically mimic the excessive and vulgar fashions of the day with which Israel was captivated. Isaiah portrayed or symbolized the sad state of the nation to powerful effect by describing the unseemly conduct of women, who took a great deal of pride in themselves and in their appearance, walking about with chains and rings around their ankles. "The daughters of Zion are haughty, and walk with stretched-forth necks and wanton eyes, walking and mincing as they go, and making a tinkling with their feet". (V. 16). Isaiah warned that this evidence of their preoccupation with temporal treasures was only a façade, and that he would smite them, and "discover their secret parts" or put them to shame. (V. 17). He would take away the finery of their anklets or "tinkling ornaments", their headbands or "cauls", and their ornamental jewelry or "round tires like the moon". (V. 18).

Gone would be their pendants or "chains", their bracelets and veils or "mufflers", their head dresses or "bonnets", their ornaments of the legs and sashes or "headbands", and their perfume boxes or "tablets", and their earrings. (V. 19-20). Likewise, their "rings and nose-jewels, their festival clothing or "changeable suits of apparel", and their overcloaks or "mantles", and their cloaks or "wimples", and their purses or "crisping-pins". (V. 21-22). Also, their mirrors of metal or "glasses", and their fine linen and hats or "hoods", and their wraps or "veils". (V. 23).

Verses 24-26 offer a prophetic view of Israelite history. "Instead of sweet smell, there shall be stink, and instead of a girdle, (or normal clothing), a rent, (which was fabric used to bind slaves), and instead of well-set hair, baldness, (which was a sign of degradation in ancient Israel). Instead of a stomacher, (more normal clothing), a girding of sackcloth, (or black goat hair that was the mark of a slave), and burning (or branding, which was also used on slaves), instead of beauty". (V. 24). These verses are eerily reminiscent of conditions within concentration camps during the Holocaust.

In fact, verses 25 and 26 refer to wholesale destruction of a monumental proportion, which, from our perspective, does not seem unrealistic. "Thy men shall fall by the sword, and thy mighty in the war. And her gates shall lament and mourn; and shall be desolate, and shall sit upon the ground".

Second Nephi
Chapter 14

This chapter is a continuation of the previous chapter and concerns the Last Days and the restoration of Zion. In the turmoil before the Second Coming of the Lord, so many men will be killed in battle, that many women will "take hold of one man" and beg to be admitted into his home, rather than remain unmarried. (V. 1). This was unheard of in Isaiah's day, but conventional tactics of courtship would be discarded in favor of a more direct approach reflecting the desperate situation. Abandoning circumspection, they will make unprecedented concessions, saying: "We will eat our own bread, and wear our own apparel; only let us be called by thy name to take away our reproach". (V. 1).

At that time, "the branch of the Lord", a symbolic name of Jesus Christ, "shall be beautiful and glorious, (and) the fruit of the earth", spiritual food, or the blessings of the Restored Gospel, "excellent". (V. 2). John Calvin saw in this verse in Isaiah a promise that "a new Church shall arise" in the Last Days that will be created by Jesus Christ Himself. ("Calvin Commentaries", 1:152-153).

Everyone who remains in Zion or Jerusalem, that is to say, each individual who "is written among the living" or is approved of God, "shall be called holy". (V. 3). The Lord will purge Israel of its moral degradation, while the whole earth will be similarly purged. "The Lord shall have washed away the filth of the daughters of Zion, and shall have purged the blood of Jerusalem from the midst thereof by the spirit of judgment and by the spirit of burning". (V. 4).

In the judgments that precede the Second Coming, all earthly kingdoms will come to an end and the kingdom of God will triumph to become the one political power during the thousand years of peace and righteousness that follow. "And thus, with the sword and by bloodshed the inhabitants of the earth shall mourn; and with famine, and plague, and earthquake, and the thunder of heaven, and the fierce and vivid lightning also, shall the inhabitants of the earth be made to feel the wrath, and indignation, and chastening hand of an Almighty God, until the consumption decreed hath made a full end of all nations". (D&C 87:6).

What are we to do in the face of these judgments that are sure to come?. The answer is given by the Lord Himself: "Wherefore, stand ye in holy places, and be not moved, until the day of the Lord come; for behold, it cometh quickly". (D&C 87:8). Holy places have more to do with how we live than where we live. If we enjoy the companionship of the Holy Ghost, then surely we stand in a holy place. A holy place, then, is anywhere that the Spirit and presence of Divinity is enjoyed.

The Angel Moroni quoted the last two verses of this chapter to Joseph Smith in September 1823, saying they were soon to be fulfilled. (Statement by Oliver Cowdery, in "Messenger & Advocate", p. 110, 4/1835). "The Lord will create upon every dwelling-place of mount Zion, and upon her assemblies, a cloud and smoke by day and the shining of a flaming fire by night". These are symbols of God's Presence. "For upon all, the glory of Zion shall be a defense. And there shall be a tabernacle", or a wedding canopy for the bridegroom, that is another symbol of the Lord's Presence, "for a shadow in the daytime from the heat, and for a place of refuge, and a covert from the storm and from rain". (V. 5-6). For a more revealing description of glorified Zion, read Isaiah Chapter 60.

The Doctrine & Covenants graphically portrays conditions in the Last Days just before the Millennium. The New Jerusalem shall be called "a land of peace, a city of refuge, a place of safety for the saints of the Most High God; and the glory of the Lord shall be there, and the terror of the Lord also shall be there, insomuch that the wicked will not come unto it, and it shall be called Zion. And it shall come to pass among the wicked, that every man that will not take his sword against his neighbor must needs flee unto Zion for safety. And there shall be gathered unto it out of every nation under heaven; and it shall be the only people that shall not be at war one with another. And it shall be said among the wicked; "Let us not go up to battle against Zion, for the inhabitants of Zion are terrible; wherefore we cannot stand. And it shall come to pass that the righteous shall be gathered out from among all nations, and shall come to Zion, singing with songs of everlasting joy". (D&C 45:66-71, see D&C 105:31-33).

Second Nephi
Chapter 15

Verses 1-7 of this chapter are referred to as the "Song of the Vineyard" that has been called the finest example of Isaiah's art and skill. The entire chapter has a chiastic structure that reinforces the message. In the first seven verses, the pattern is A) third person, B) first person, B) first person, A) third person.

Isaiah said that he would relate a story of the Lord of Hosts, whom he characterized as "my well beloved". (V. 1). "His vineyard" is the House of Israel. (V. 7). The master of the vineyard had done everything in his power to insure a bounteous yield. "He fenced it, and gathered out the stones thereof, and planted it with the choicest vine, and built a tower in the midst of it, and also made a winepress therein; and he looked that it should bring forth grapes". (V. 2).

And yet, after all that the master of the vineyard had done, it still "brought forth wild grapes". (V. 2). By shifting to the first-person tense in verse 3, Isaiah reminded his listeners that he was delivering the Lord's message and not just sharing his personal philosophy. He asked them to choose between the Lord and the House of Israel. "And now, O inhabitants of Jerusalem, and men of Judah, judge, I pray you, betwixt me and my vineyard". (V. 3).

"What", he asked, "could have been done more to my vineyard that I have not done in it? Wherefore, when I looked that it should bring forth grapes, it brought forth wild grapes". (V. 4). Because the fruit was not what he had hoped for, the Lord of the vineyard determined to "lay it waste. It shall not be pruned nor digged", he decided, "but there shall come up briers and thorns". (V. 6).

This verse really provides the first clue that this parable does not concern an ordinary landowner, for this individual had such power that he could "command the clouds that they rain no rain" upon the earth. (V. 6). Isaiah then revealed: "The vineyard of the Lord of Hosts is the House of Israel, and the men of Judah his pleasant plant". (V. 7).

Isaiah used striking wordplay in verse 7 to highlight the irony of the situation. In English, the verse is rendered; "And he looketh for judgment, and behold, oppression (or bloodshed); for righteousness, but behold, a cry". In Hebrew, though: "justice" or "judgment" equals "mishpat", and "oppression" or "bloodshed" equals "mispach". "Righteousness" equals "tsed'akah", and "cry" equals "tse'akah". These are examples of similar sounds in words of opposite meaning. The Israelites saw inherent power in words that are mysteriously linked by similarity or contrast. Certainly, Isaiah's choice of words would have had a dramatic effect upon his Hebrew audience.

Verse 7 is a summary of the first verses of this chapter. By concealing the meaning of the parable until the end,

Isaiah manipulated his listeners to pass judgment on the characters before realizing that they were the very ones about whom Isaiah was speaking.

Then, in verse 8 is the beginning of six "woes" that follow in the next 14 verses:

(1). Wo unto those who build up vast estates at the expense of the poor. "Wo unto them that join house to house till there can be no place, that they may be placed alone in the midst of the earth!" (V. 8). In Israel, the Year of Jubilee was supposed to guarantee the return of land to its original owners. But, because of apostasy, that practice had been neglected, and so the land would not be fruitful. "Many houses shall be desolate, and great and fair cities without inhabitant". (V. 9). Ten acres, or the land 10 yokes of oxen were capable of plowing in one day, would yield just one tenth its normal crop; the seed of a homer, or 10 ephahs, should yield just one ephah. "Yea, ten acres of vineyard shall yield one bath, and the seed of a homer shall yield an ephah". (V. 10).

(2). Wo unto those who are enslaved by drunkenness and by selfish indulgence. "Wo unto them that rise up early in the morning, that they may follow strong drink, that continue until night, and wine inflame them!" (V. 11). Such people are blinded to the work of the Lord that is before their very eyes. "They regard not the work of the Lord, neither consider the operation of his hands". (V. 12). Without the knowledge of God, they are captive. "Their honorable men are famished, and their multitude dried up with thirst". (V. 13).

Their condition is contrasted to God's exalted state. "Therefore, hell hath enlarged herself, and opened her mouth without measure; and their glory, and their multitude, and their pomp, and he that rejoiceth, shall descend into it. And the mean (or common) man shall be brought down, and the mighty man shall be humbled, and the eyes of the lofty shall be humbled". (V. 14-15). "But the Lord of Hosts will be exalted in judgment, and God that is holy shall be sanctified in righteousness". (V. 16).

(3). Wo unto those who are yoked to sin as a wagon is yoked to a horse. "Wo unto them that draw iniquity with cords of vanity, and sin as it were with a cart rope. (V. 18). Note the parallelism of this verse. Such people expect God to hasten His work, but at the same time they are skeptical of His power. They toss out the challenge to "let him make speed, hasten his work, that we may see it; and let the counsel of the Holy One of Israel draw nigh and come, that we may know it". (V. 19).

(4). Wo unto those who either willfully pervert standards of right and wrong, or have reached such depths of depravity that they can no longer recognize the moral distinction between the two. "Wo unto them that call evil good, and good evil, that put darkness for light, and light for darkness, that put bitter for sweet, and sweet for bitter!" (V. 20). Again, note the parallelism of this verse.

(5). Wo unto those who, when they are learned, think they are wise, but hearken not unto the counsels of God. "Wo unto the wise in their own eyes and prudent in their own sight!" (V. 21, see 2 Nephi 9:28). An appeal to vanity is the devil's way of turning our minds against The Plan of Salvation. It is an invitation to unfaithfulness. Intellectual apostasy, or the devotion some give to the enticements of Spiritual Babylon, is adultery. The siren call of the great and abominable Church, who is the whore of all the earth, leads the unwary onto forbidden paths and into the depths of hell.

(6). Wo unto those in the military who use strong drink and who take bribes or traffic in privilege and position. "Wo unto the mighty to drink wine, and men of strength to mingle strong drink, who justify the wicked for reward". (V. 22-23). Because they have turned their backs on both the Law and the Savior, their military preparedness will be of no help in avoiding the disaster that will quickly strike the nation. This is symbolized by the burning of stubble and chaff that are quickly consumed in a fire. "Therefore, as the fire devoureth the stubble, and the flame consumeth the chaff, their root shall be rottenness, and their blossoms shall go up as dust; because they have cast away the law of the Lord of Hosts, and despised the word of the Holy One of Israel". (V. 24). Yet, for all the judgments the people deserve, there is still a note of hope. For all this, "his hand is stretched out still" if they will but repent. (V. 25).

Most commentators see in verses 26-30 of the corresponding verses in Isaiah a description of the coming of the Assyrians to carry out the punishment of Israel for her sins. But these verses might also dualistically describe in hyperbole the events of the Last Days. If Nephi had this in mind, he would have felt this prophecy was critically important. When creating his record on The Small Plates, we should remember that, with great difficulty, every word was painstakingly engraved. Remember Moroni's observation: "Thou hast made us that we could write but little, because of the awkwardness of our hands". (Ether 12:24). Later Nephite prophets entrusted with the care and keeping of the records hauled this prophecy around with them for a thousand years, all the while safeguarding it from marauding Lamanites and Lamanite wannabes. All who were privileged to read The Small Plates must have thought these words would be of great value to Latter-day Israel. Truly, The Book of Mormon is a blueprint for survival in the Last Days.

Jacob had reminded the People of Nephi that the Lord "has spoken unto the Jews, by the mouth of his holy prophets, even from the beginning down, from generation to generation, until the time comes that they shall be restored to the true Church and fold of God; when they shall be gathered home to the lands of their inheritance, and shall be established in all their lands of promise". (2 Nephi 9:1-3).

During His post-mortal ministry among the Nephites, the Savior promised the faithful: "Then shall ye, who are a remnant of the house of Jacob, go forth among (the scattered of my people); and ye shall be in the midst of them who shall be many; and ye shall be among them as a lion among the beasts of the forest, and as a young lion among the flocks of sheep, who, if he goeth through both treadeth down and teareth in pieces, and none can deliver". (3 Nephi 20:16, & 21:12).

"And he will lift up an ensign to the nations from far, and will hiss unto them from the end of the earth; and behold, they shall come with speed swiftly; none shall be weary nor stumble among them. None shall slumber nor sleep; neither shall the girdle of their loins be loosed, nor the latchet of their shoes be broken; whose arrows shall be sharp, and all their bows bent, and their horses' hoofs shall be counted like flint, and their wheels like a whirlwind, their roaring like a lion. They shall roar like young lions; yea, they shall roar, and lay hold of the prey, and shall carry away safe, and none shall deliver. And in that day they shall roar against them like the roaring of the sea; and if they look unto the land, behold darkness and sorrow, and the light is darkened in the heavens thereof". (V. 26-30).

These figures of speech describe in contemporary language such Latter-day concepts as radio, the railroad train and air travel. (See Isaiah 60:8). The Lord will "lift up an ensign to the nations from far", or will raise the Gospel standard, which will "hiss unto them from the end of the earth", after the manner of the electronic media, and summon them from afar. They will respond to that call, and "come with speed swiftly; none shall be weary nor stumble among them". They will come to Zion so quickly that before they have had time to be tired they will have arrived at their destination. "None shall slumber nor sleep; neither shall the girdle of their loins be loosed, nor the latchet of their shoes be broken". During their travels, they will have required neither sleep nor even a change of clothing.

Isaiah described the sparking and flashing of "their horses' hoofs", and the great noise the wheeled vehicles make. "Their horses' hoofs shall be counted like flint, and their wheels like a whirlwind, their roaring like a lion." (V. 28). This is the only time the word "wheels" occurs in The Book of Mormon, and is one of only 7 references to horses. (See

Commentary Reference to Alma 18:9, 1 Nephi 18:25, Enos 1:21, Alma 18:12, 20:6, 3 Nephi 4:4. 6:1, & Ether 9:19). It seems that draft animals must have been unavailable for general use and that the cultures of Book of Mormon peoples lacked a sense of "machines". Perhaps, the wheel was never have been popular in Nephite society. (See Alma 18:10, 20:6, & 34:54).

Isaiah wrote that those who would respond to the call would bring many converts to Zion. "They shall roar like young lions ... and lay hold of the prey, and shall carry away safe". (V. 29). In the day of Israel's restoration, the Gospel would go forth amid general conditions of destruction and apostasy raging upon the face of the earth. "And in that day ... behold, darkness and sorrow, and the light is darkened in the heavens thereof". (V. 30).

Second Nephi
Chapter 16

The pathway to personal growth and service is outlined in this chapter and might have been included by Nephi because he wanted the people to know of Isaiah's personal testimony of the Lord. (V. 1, see 2 Nephi 11:2-3). These events took place about 742 B.C., "in the year that king Uzziah died". In these verses, the images of Isaiah's vision may be compared to the symbolism found within the temples of The Church of Jesus Christ of Latter-day Saints.

Verse 1 confirms his vision of the Lord: "I saw also the Lord sitting upon a throne, high and lifted up". He also saw that the train of the Lord "filled the temple" in a manifestation comparable to the veil. This train compares to the veil that separates us from God's direct glory.

A similar vision was manifested to Joseph Smith the Prophet and Oliver Cowdery in the temple at Kirtland, Ohio, April 3, 1836. "The veil was taken from our minds, and the eyes of our understanding were opened. We saw the Lord standing upon the breastwork of the pulpit, before us; and under his feet was a paved work of pure gold, in color like amber. His eyes were as a flame of fire; the hair of his head was white like the pure snow; his countenance shone above the brightness of the sun; and his voice was as the sound of the rushing of great waters, even the voice of Jehovah, saying I am the first and the last; I am he who liveth, I am he who was slain; I am your advocate with the Father." (D&C 110:1-4).

Verses 2-7 describe the activities of creatures called "seraphim". In Hebrew, the plural of words is indicated by "im", as in "seraph / seraphim", "cherub / cherubim", "El / Elohim", and even "Abram / Abraham", or "Ibrahim". Interestingly, in spite of this widely recognized grammatical rule, in the K.J.T. rendering of Isaiah 6:2, we read "seraphims", and D&C 109:79 speaks of "bright shining seraphs". In Hebrew, "seraph" means "burning" and we are reminded that Doctrine & Covenants 45:41 describes "the signs of the coming of the Son of Man" in the following way: "And they shall behold blood and fire, and vapors of smoke".

Isaiah's favorite name-title of the Savior was The Holy One of Israel, and in verse 3 the seraphim describe the Lord of Hosts as "holy, holy, holy". By expressing this quality three times, they give it maximum emphasis. (See Commentary Reference to 2 Nephi 18:9, & Ezekiel 21:27). This action by the seraphim suggests to our mind temple attendants who call to one another in a three-fold petition.

In verse 4, we read that the posts of the door moved, suggesting a stirring of the veil of the temple, and then "the house was filled with smoke", that is symbolic of the presence of the Lord and of the glory of God. Fire and smoke are frequently used to depict the glory of celestial realms. In the language of Joseph Smith: "God Almighty Himself dwells in eternal fire. Flesh and blood cannot go there, for that fire devours all corruption. Immortality dwells in everlasting burnings". ("Teachings", p. 347). "Our God is a consuming fire", taught Paul. (Hebrews 12:29, see Deuteronomy 4:24).

This reminds us of the Church hymn entitled "The Spirit of God Like a Fire is Burning" and of the symbolism associated with the baptism of fire and the Holy Ghost. This second baptism has been described as burning or purging the effects of sin after our water baptism, in the sense that the Spirit ratifies that we are without sin. (See 2 Nephi 31:17). "For by the water ye keep the commandment; by the Spirit ye are justified, and by the blood ye are sanctified". (Moses 6:61). This means that when we submit to baptism by water, we have kept the commandment of God. We are then justified when the validity of the ordinance is ratified, and we are purged of the effects of sin when we submit to the second baptism by the laying on of hands to receive the Holy Ghost. We are sanctified through the atoning sacrifice of Christ and redeemed from the Fall.

Isaiah was distraught in his vision, because he viewed himself as Mosiah had described his "own carnal state, even less than the dust of the earth". (Mosiah 4:2). "Wo is unto me!" wrote Isaiah, with an exclamation point for emphasis. "For I am undone; because I am a man of unclean lips". (V. 5). When the seraphim delivered a live coal to his lips and purged his sins, we think of divine fire, the cleansing power of the Atonement, and of eternal life that has been promised to those who keep the covenants made at temple altars. "Then flew one of the seraphim unto me", declared Isaiah, "having a live coal in his hand, which he had taken with the tongs from off the altar; and he laid it upon my mouth, and said: Lo, this has touched thy lips; and thine iniquity is taken away, and thy sin purged". (V. 6-7, see Jeremiah 1:9)

Having experienced repentance and forgiveness in such a personal and powerful way, these principles became recurring themes for Isaiah. "Here am I; send me", he volunteered. And so, the Lord instructed him: "Go and tell this people ... Make the heart of this people fat, and make their ears heavy, and shut their eyes - lest they see with their eyes, and hear with their ears, and understand with their heart, and be converted and be healed". (V. 8-10). In the Hebrew idiom, result is expressed as if it were purpose: their hearts are fat, their ears heavy, and their eyes shut. That is to say, as a result of their hardness of heart, they have no room for contrition; because they are deaf to the words of their prophets, their ears are heavy, and they may as well shut their eyes if they are going to ignore what is plainly before them, anyway.

It was never the Lord's intention that the people should procrastinate the day of their repentance; He only prophesied that they would not listen to Isaiah. As the Savior explained to His disciples during His mortal ministry: "Therefore I speak to (the people) in parables; because they seeing, see not; and hearing, they hear not, neither do they understand. And in them is fulfilled the prophecy of Esaias, which saith, By hearing ye shall hear, and shall not understand; and seeing ye shall see, and shall not perceive; For this people's heart is waxed gross, and their ears are dull of hearing, and their eyes they have closed; lest at any time they should see with their eyes, and hear with their ears, and should understand with their heart, and should be converted, and I should heal them. But blessed are your eyes, for they see; and your ears, for they hear". (Matthew 13:13-16).

Isaiah needed the sustaining influence of his vision, because as these verses illustrate, God sent him to a nation blind and deaf to his entreaties, a nation that would consequently be destroyed and taken captive. When Isaiah asked the Lord how long his ministry would last, he was told: "Until the cities be wasted without inhabitant, and the houses without man, and the land be utterly desolate". (V. 11). Yet, there was hope, for the germ of a new nation would survive.

Isaiah's prophecy is dualistic in nature. When he asked how long the obstinacy of the people would continue, he was told that it would last until there was a "great forsaking (or solitude) in the midst of the land". (V. 12). Nevertheless, a remnant of Israel would return, either from Babylon, or in the Last Days after two thousand years of dispersion, or "diaspora". In Hebrew, "diaspora" means "a scattering of seeds". (Pronunciation: dai·ass·spor·uh). The escaped remnant would be sown in soil from which Israel would again blossom in a Restoration. "They shall return, and shall be ... as an oak whose substance is in them when they cast their leaves; so, the holy seed shall be the substance thereof". (V. 13, see Commentary Reference to Jacob 5:20).

"Make the heart
of this people fat, and
make their ears heavy, and
shut their eyes – lest they see with
their eyes, and hear with their ears, and
understand with their heart, and be
converted, and be healed."
(2 Nephi 16:10).

Second Nephi
Chapter 17

This chapter is a chiasm in 4 parts. As it is studied, we should carefully consider the dualistic writing style of Isaiah, wherein his prophecies relate not only to his day, but also to Israel at the time of Christ, and to Israel in the Last Days.

The first 9 verses establish a context within which Isaiah delivers his prophecy and consists of an account of the Syro-Ephraimite War of 734 B.C. "It came to pass in the days of Ahaz the son of Jotham, the son of Uzziah, king of Judah, that Rezin, king of Syria, and Pekah the son of Remaliah, king of Israel, went up toward Jerusalem, to war against it". (V. 1). In other words, "the house of David", or the royal household of the Kingdom of Judah, was told that Ephraim and the Ten Tribes were now confederate with Syria. (V. 2). The next 7 verses (3-9) constitute a message to Ahaz, King of Judah, from the Lord.

Isaiah was commanded to take his son Shearjashub, whose name was symbolic, and meant "a remnant shall return", and go to meet with Ahaz. (V. 3). Isaiah was to tell him not to fear Rezin, king of Syria, or his ally, Pekah, king of Israel, or the Northern Kingdom. "And say unto him: take heed, and be quiet; fear not, neither be faint-hearted for the two tails of these smoking firebrands, for the fierce anger of Rezin with Syria, and of the son of Remaliah". (V. 4). For all practical purposes, a civil war had erupted in Israel. Pekah was scorned by Isaiah, who would only refer to him in a derogatory way as "the son of Remaliah".

The objective of Syria and Ephraim was to create a division in Judah and then install a puppet leader on the throne of the Kingdom of Judah who would be more sympathetic to their own anti-Assyrian policies. "Syria, Ephraim, and the son of Remaliah have taken evil counsel against thee, saying: Let us go up against Judah and vex it, and let us make a breach therein for us, and set a king in the midst of it". (V. 5-6, see 2 Chronicles 28:6-15).

But through Isaiah, the Lord predicted that their strategy would not prevail, and Syria and her confederate Ephraim would be confounded. "Thus saith the Lord God: It shall not stand, neither shall it come to pass". Then Isaiah, the prophet of the God of Israel, boldly foretold: "For the head of Syria is Damascus, and the head of Damascus Rezin; and within three score and five years shall Ephraim be broken that it be not a people" anymore. (V. 7-8). The Lord would use Assyria to conquer the Kingdom of Israel or the Northern Kingdom, whose head was Ephraim.

Isaiah stated that the capital city of Ephraim was Samaria, and their king was Pekah. He urged Ahaz to have faith to believe in God's words, that Judah might succeed in defending itself against the Syro-Ephraimite alliance. "And the head of Ephraim is Samaria, and the head of Samaria is Remaliah's son". (V. 9, see v. 16).

In verse 10-11, the Lord offered Ahaz a sign. As D&C 63:10 teaches, signs come "by the will of God". Ahaz could ask for any sign he wished, from "the depths" of sheol or hell, to "the heights" of heaven. But because Ahaz had no faith, he lacked confidence in the Lord, and so "Ahaz said: I will not ask, neither will I tempt the Lord". (V. 12). He refused the offer because he did not want to be bound to take appropriate action, and also because he was afraid of the truth.

Isaiah responded to the king, whom he referred to as "O house of David", with impatience. "Will ye weary my God also?" he asked. (V. 13). He declared that the Lord would give a sign anyway. A "virgin", or young woman, should conceive, and bear a son named Immanuel, or 'God is with us / With us is El.' (V. 14). The name illustrates that God is ultimately on the side of the people. There are three levels of fulfilment to this prophecy: 1) in the time of Ahaz, king of Judah, 2) in the Meridian of Time during the events surrounding the birth of the Savior, which is the one usually stressed by General Authorities and members of The Church of Jesus Christ of Latter-day Saints, and 3) in the Last Days. (See 2 Nephi 18:4 in support of level one, and Matthew 1:23 in support of level two).

Isaiah prophesied that the child should be born into straitened circumstances. "Butter and honey shall he eat". (V. 15). These are symbolic of a desolate land given over to wildflowers. (See v. 22). Ahaz was warned that both the king of Israel and the king of Judah would soon be dethroned. "For before the child shall know to refuse the evil and choose the good, the land that thou abhorest shall be forsaken of both her kings". (V. 16). In fact, this happened within two years after the prophecy had been given. However, there is also a dualistic fulfillment that makes the Lord's infancy a symbolic representation of the short-lived nature of the threat to Israel by worldly governments.

Ahaz was told that the disaster to come would compare only to that brought about by the revolt of Ephraim and the Ten Tribes against the United Kingdom, that had precipitated the creation of the separate kingdoms of Israel and Judah in the first place. "Days that have not come, from the day that Ephraim departed from Judah". (V. 17).

The first level of prophesied disaster was accomplished by the arrival of the conquering armies of Assyria. (V. 17). Like flies and bees, these oppressors settled on the people every time they tried to escape from the invaders. "And it shall come to pass that in that day the Lord shall hiss for the fly that is in the uttermost part of Egypt, and for the bee that is in the land of Assyria. And they shall come, and shall rest all of them in the desolate valleys, and in the holes of the rocks, and upon all thorns, and upon all bushes". (V. 18-19).

"And in that same day shall the Lord shave with a razor that is hired, by them beyond the river, by the king of Assyria, the head, and the hair of the feet, and it shall also consume the beard". (V. 20). Israel's hair would be shaved by the razor that was Assyria. This was a terrible sign of degradation to those who had been defeated in a military conquest. The Assyrians cut the hair from their captives' heads and groins (the hair of the feet) for three reasons actually: 1) humiliation, 2) sanitation, and 3) separation or means of identification. In verse 20 is found the only reference in the entire Book of Mormon to "beards".

After Assyria arrived, primitive conditions would prevail in the ravaged land. "In that day, a man shall nourish a young cow and two sheep". (V. 21). The population would be so diminished that only a few livestock would be present in a land that had been taken over by wildflowers. "For butter and honey shall everyone eat that is left in the land". (V. 22). Their vineyards, previously worth thousands of shekels, would be overgrown with briars and thorns. "Every place shall be, where there were a thousand vines at a thousand silverlings, which shall be for briers and thorns". (V. 23).

Bands of armed men, typifying the lawless conditions that would prevail in these straitened circumstances, would roam the countryside. "With arrows and with bows shall men come thither". (V. 24). Land that had previously been tilled with "the mattock", or the hoe, would remain uncultivated, for men would fear to work because of the desolation. (V. 25).

Second Nephi
Chapter 18

In 2 Nephi Chapter 17, that corresponds to Isaiah Chapter 7, we have read about Isaiah's failure to influence King Ahaz of Judah to trust in the Lord. Therefore, he turned his attention to the people. The prophecies in 2 Nephi Chapter 18 parallel those given in Chapter 17 and should be viewed dualistically.

Isaiah was commanded to take a large tablet, or "a great roll", and write on it in common script, or in the common Aramaic language of the people. "Write it with a man's pen". His subject was to be "Maher-shalal-hash-baz" (V. 1). The message was so important that it was attended by two of Jerusalem's leaders, who served as witnesses. "And I took unto me faithful witnesses to record, Uriah the priest, and Zechariah the son of Jeberechiah". (V. 2).

Isaiah's wife bore a child who had been named by the Lord Himself. "And I went unto the prophetess; and she conceived and bare a son. Then said the Lord to me: Call his name Maher-shalal-hash-baz". (V. 3). The chosen name is the longest in the Bible. Translated from Hebrew, it means "speed spoil, hasten plunder". Assyria was on the move, poised to conquer Damascus, capital of Syria, and Samaria, capital of the Kingdom of Israel. (732 B.C.). "For behold, the child shall not have knowledge to cry my father and my mother, before the riches of Damascus and the spoil of Samaria shall be taken away before the king of Assyria". (V. 4). The name of Isaiah's son, then, is symbolic of the destruction of Syria and the Kingdom of Israel by Assyrian invaders.

Beginning in verse 5, and through verse 15, Isaiah's prophecy parallels 2 Nephi 17:10-25. The people refused "the waters of Shiloah that go softly". (V. 5). In other words, they rejected the silent, unobtrusive, gently flowing power of God. Instead, they rejoiced "in Rezin and Remaliah's son". (V. 5). That is to say, they trusted in the arm of flesh, symbolized by Rezin, King of Syria, and by Pekah, King of Israel.

Therefore, the Lord would allow Assyria to come upon them as the raging floodwaters of the mighty River Euphrates. "Now therefore, behold, the Lord bringeth up upon them the waters of the river, strong and many, even the king of Assyria and all his glory; and he shall come up over all his channels, and go over all his banks". (V. 7). Assyria would be so powerful that it would surge over all of Judah and would "fill the breadth of thy land". (V. 8). Destruction would be so great that it would "reach even to the neck". (V. 8). This verse concludes the warning to Judah.

Next, Isaiah addressed the nations rising against Judah. In Hebrew, to repeat something three times makes it superlative, as in "good", "better", and "best". Isaiah was warning the nations that if they prepared for battle. they would be devastated and if they fought against God, they would be defeated. "Associate yourselves (or take note), O ye people, and ye shall be broken in pieces (or dismayed); and give ear all ye of far countries; gird yourselves, and ye shall be broken in pieces; gird yourselves, and ye shall be broken in pieces". (V. 9, see 2 Nephi 16:3, & 28:15).

Despite Assyria's military success in overrunning the Kingdom of Judah, God would not permit the complete destruction of His people: "Take counsel together, and it shall come to naught; speak the word, and it shall not stand; for God is with us". This is an interesting parallelism, as well as a play on the words "Immanuel / God is with us".

Verses 11-15 provide us with a rare personal glimpse into Isaiah's feelings about his relationship with the people. He had been commanded by the Lord to stand up for principle and not to walk in their way. (V. 11). He was told not to fear the conspiracy between Syria and the Northern Kingdom of Israel, as the people did, but to fear only the Lord in the sense of holding Him in awe and reverence. (V. 12). "Sanctify the Lord of Hosts himself, and let him be your fear, and let him be your dread". (V. 13). For the righteous, the Lord would be a sanctuary; but for the disobedient, He would be a stumbling block. "And he shall be for a sanctuary; but for a stone of stumbling". (V. 14).

Unfortunately, to both Houses of Israel (Ephraim / The Northern Kingdom, and Judah / the inhabitants of Judea and Jerusalem), He would be a gin (or a trap) and a snare. Thus, many among them would "stumble and fall" in the sense that they would falter in faith and commit sin, and "be broken" or suffer the consequences thereof, and "be snared" by Satan, and "be taken" captive. (V. 15).

Isaiah was commanded to record his testimony, and to seal his teachings in the hearts of the people. "Bind up the testimony, seal the law among my disciples". (V. 16). In the Doctrine & Covenants, the Lord warned: "Behold and lo, there are none to deliver you; for ye obeyed not my voice when I called to you out of the heavens; ye believed not my servants, and when they were sent unto you, ye received them not". (D&C 133:71).

President Spencer W. Kimball once remarked that the Gospel did not go from Rome to Galilee, but the other way around. In other words, it is the humble servants of the Lord who bear the responsibility of carrying their testimonies of the truth to all the world. "Wherefore, they sealed up the testimony and bound up the law, and ye were delivered over unto darkness. These shall go away into outer darkness, where there is weeping and wailing, and gnashing of teeth". (D&C 133:71-73). The state of the wicked is truly terrible. "So complete is the darkness prevailing in the minds of these spirits, so wholly has Gospel light been shut out of their consciences, that they know little or nothing of The Plan of Salvation. Hell is literally a place of outer darkness that hates light, buries truth, and revels in iniquity". (Bruce R. McConkie, see 2 Nephi 28:16).

For Isaiah's part, he declared that he would "wait upon the Lord" or trust in His strength. (V. 17). He and his children stand even today as signs and wonders to the faithful in Israel. "Isaiah" means "Jehovah will save", while "Shear-Jashub" means "a remnant shall return", and "Maher-shalal-hash-baz" means "the spoil speedeth, the prey hasteneth" or "speed spoil, hasten plunder". All these names evoke images of disaster to Israel, and yet they provide hope of future restoration, even as they testify of the terrible judgments to come upon the people. (V. 18).

Isaiah contrasted his role as a witness and a symbol with the false messages the people were receiving from evil sources. They were in the habit of consulting with "familiar spirits" or diviners of the occult, and "wizards that peep and mutter" or sorcerers and necromancers who used ventriloquism to call forth "messages" from departed spirits. (V. 19).

Isaiah asked if it were not better for the people to "seek unto their God for the living to hear from the dead". (V. 19). They should look to the Torah, the teachings of "the law", and to the testimony of living witnesses. Those who speak from unauthorized sources do not have the spirit. "If they speak not according to this word, it is because there is no light in them". (V. 20). Such men are "hardly bested" or hard pressed, and "hungry" or spiritually malnourished. In this state, they tend to "fret themselves" or be enraged, and curse God. (V. 21). This is the state of mind described by Bruce R. McConkie, when he declared; "Hell hates light, buries truth, and revels in iniquity". "And they shall look unto the earth and behold trouble, and darkness, dimness of anguish, and shall be driven to darkness". (V. 22).

"Sanctify the Lord of Hosts himself, and let him be your fear, and let him be your dread. And he shall be for a sanctuary." (2 Nephi 18:13-14).

Second Nephi
Chapter 19

In this chapter, Isaiah spoke messianically, but when reading and studying it, one should remember the historical context in which it was written and consider that application as well. This is another example of Isaiah's dual fulfilment prophecies.

The first verse of this chapter serves as a bridge between Isaiah Chapters 7 and 8. In fact, it is included as the last verse of Isaiah Chapter 7 in the Hebrew version of the scriptures. It documents not only the invasion of ancient Israel and Judah by Assyria, but also suggests a more grievous Latter-day invasion by way of the Red Sea.

"Nevertheless, the dimness (or gloom of the people) shall not be such as was in her vexation (or her day of anguish), when at first (or in former times) he lightly afflicted the land of Zebulun (where Nazareth is located) and the land of Naphtali (the first to be crushed by the Assyrians), and afterward (in later times) did more grievously afflict by the way of the Red (added in The Book of Mormon) Sea beyond Jordan in Galilee of the nations". (V. 1). Here we learn which districts were the first to be crushed by the invading armies of the Assyrians, in 732 B.C.

In verse 2, the former times / latter times theme gives way to a darkness / light theme. Possible interpretations include 1) Assyrians verses Hezekiah, 2) a wicked versus a righteous people, and 3) apostasy versus Christ. For obvious reasons, Christian scholars prefer the third interpretation.

One rendering of verse 2 is as follows: "The people that walked in darkness (or wickedness and apostasy) have seen a great light (the Lord Jesus Christ); they that dwell in the land of the shadow of death (in the Galilee), upon them hath the light (Christ) shined". In fact, Christ's ministry was in Galilee, at Capernaum, in the districts of Zebulun and Naphtali.

Matthew 4:12-16 helps us to understand one level of fulfilment of this prophecy: "Now when Jesus had heard that John was cast into prison, he departed into Galilee. And leaving Nazareth, he came and dwelt in Capernaum, which is upon the sea coast, in the borders of   Zabulon and Nephthalim, that it might be fulfilled which was spoken by Esaias the prophet, saying, The land of Zabulon, and the land of Nephthalim, by the way of the sea, beyond Jordan, Galilee of the Gentiles; The people which sat in darkness saw great light; and to them which sat in the region and shadow of death light is sprung up".

The followers of Christ greatly multiplied in the Holy Land, their joy was increased, and the nation prospered because of the coming of the Lord Jesus Christ. The people were joyous as at harvest time, and as after a military victory, for the Lord had broken the oppressive rule of the conqueror, or the temptations of Satan with his yoke of sin. "Thou hast multiplied the nation, and increased the joy - they joy before thee according to the joy in harvest, and as men rejoice when they divide the spoil". (V. 3). "For thou hast broken the yoke of his burden, and the staff of his shoulders, the rod of his oppressor". (V. 4). These represent the unjust and cruel exercise of temporal power and authority.

Verse 5 is symbolic of the Atonement, baptism, and the Holy Ghost. "For every battle of the warrior is with confused noise, and garments rolled in blood; but this shall be with burning and fuel of fire". The point is that all material and equipment needed for war and temporal domination will be destroyed "with burning and fuel of fire" at the Second Coming. "And they that dwell in the cities of Israel shall go forth, and shall set on fire and burn the weapons, both the shields and the bucklers, the bows and the arrows, and the handstaves, and the spears, and they shall burn them with fire seven years". (Ezekiel 39:9).

All the things described in verses 1-5 will take place because of the great event chronicled in verse 6. "For unto us a child is born, unto us a son is given; and the government (or authority of the Priesthood) shall be upon his shoulder, and his name shall be called, Wonderful, Counselor, The Mighty God, The Everlasting Father, The Prince of Peace". (See D&C 25:1, Mosiah 15:18, Hosea 12:10, & 2 Nephi 11:4). According to Joseph Fielding Smith, these are all symbolic name-titles indicative of the service of Jesus Christ to mankind "because of the glory His Father had given Him before He was born, and because at that time He was already God".

The Savior is called The Prince of Peace, but His mission was not to bring peace to the earth. "Think not that I am come to send peace on earth", he warned, "I came not to send peace, but a sword". (Matthew 10:34). John recorded that "there was a division among the people because of him". (John 7:43). J. Reuben Clark, Jr. taught: "The peace He proclaimed was the peace of everlasting righteousness which is the eternal enemy of sin. Righteousness is peace wherever it abides. Sin in itself is war wherever it is found". (C.R., 4/1939).

Verse 7 establishes the role of Christ as Lord and King: "Of the increase of government (or authority of the priesthood) there is no end, upon the throne of David (the prophesied lineage through which the Messiah would come), and upon his kingdom to order (or establish) it with judgment (or justice) and with justice (in Hebrew, this word is rendered "righteousness") from henceforth, even forever. The zeal (or determination) of the Lord of Hosts will perform this". (V. 7).

Verses 8-21 review those judgments upon Israel and Judah both already accomplished and yet to come. The warnings apply to both past and future events. The point is, that Israel could have learned from her mistakes and taken heed so as not to repeat them.

All Israel should have known of these prophecies, "even (the proud and arrogant tribe of) Ephraim", whose capital was Samaria. (V. 9). In spite of Isaiah's warnings, Ephraim expressed in proverbial terms her insistence that she could still improve her circumstances on her own. "The bricks are fallen down", she acknowledged, "but we will build with hewn stones; the sycamores are cut down, but we will change them into cedars". (V. 10). Ephraim was this confident, even in light of the on-going Assyrian onslaught throughout the rest of the Northern Kingdom. Because of Ephraim's arrogance and defiance in the face of impending invasion, the Lord would stir up Rezin, the King of Syria on the east, and the Philistines on the west, to "devour Israel with open mouth". (V. 11).

Isaiah revealed something quite remarkable about God's character in verses 12, 17, 21, and in 2 Nephi 20:4: "For all this his anger is not turned away, but his hand is stretched out still". God still offered rebellious Israel the opportunity to take advantage of His mercy, conditioned only upon repentance.

Even though the wheels had been set in motion and the armies of Syria and Assyria were on the move, all the impending judgments against Israel could have been mitigated by the ability of the Lord to extend mercy. But that was not to be: "For (yet) the people turneth not unto him that smiteth them, neither do they seek the Lord of Hosts". (V. 13). "Therefore, will the Lord cut off from Israel head and tail (or rulers and subjects), branch and rush (the palm branch symbolizing the upper class, and the rush symbolizing the lower class) in one day (or suddenly)". (V. 14).

"The ancient (or elder), he is the head (or ruler); and the (false) prophet that teacheth lies, he is the tail" or the subject of the rulers, publishing only what the rulers wish him to say. (V. 15). "For the leaders of this people (Judah) cause them to err; and they that are led of them are destroyed (or confused)". (V. 16). Of a truth, "When the wicked rule, the people mourn". (D&C 98:9).

Because of widespread apostasy, Isaiah prophesied that the Lord would take no joy in Israel, nor have compassion on her. "Every one of them is a hypocrite and an evildoer, and every mouth speaketh folly". (V. 17). Nevertheless, He was still willing to offer them mercy through repentance and the power of the Atonement. Israel needed to rely on the Author of Salvation more than ever, because of her wickedness wrought by sin. Without repentance, Isaiah said the people would burn "as the fire; it shall devour the briars and thorns (or the common people), and shall kindle in the thickets of the forests (or elders and leaders), and they shall mount up like the lifting up of smoke", that is to say, their moral decay would be as consuming as a forest fire. (V. 18).

There would even be fratricidal conflict: "No man shall spare his brother". (V. 19). There would be grim famine, as well, when those in the land would "snatch on the right hand and be hungry; and ... eat on the left hand and ... not be satisfied. They shall eat every man the flesh of his own arm". (V. 20). Civil strife would replace the rule of law, with "Manasseh, Ephraim; and Ephraim, Manasseh" arrayed together "against Judah". (V. 21). For all this, the Lord would still extend His arm of mercy. (V. 21).

"The people that walked in darkness have seen a great light; they that dwell in the land of the shadow of death, upon them hath the light shined."
(2 Nephi 19:2).

Second Nephi
Chapter 20

Chapter 20 consists of a carefully constructed prophecy, organized as a chiasm in 6 parts in which the destruction of Assyria is a type or a symbol foreshadowing the future reality of the destruction of the wicked at the Second Coming of the Lord. So, this prophecy, as are so many of Isaiah's, is dualistic.

Wo unto the apostate rulers in Israel who make unrighteous laws, pervert justice, and rob the poor of Judah of their legal rights. (V. 1-2). What do these leaders expect to do in the Day of Judgment, when Assyria comes to visit desolation upon the land?. To whom will they turn for help, and what will happen to their wealth? "What will ye do in the day of visitation", asked Isaiah, "and in the day of desolation which shall come from far?. To whom will ye flee for help? And where will ye leave your glory?" (V. 3). Without the Lord's intervention, they will be smitten. "Without me, they shall bow down under the prisoners, and they shall fall under the slain". (V. 4). Yet, if they repent, the Lord will extend His mercy in their behalf.

The wrath of the Lord was as a staff in the hand of the Assyrians. "O Assyrian, the rod of mine anger, and the staff in their hand is their indignation". (V. 5). Assyria was the unconscious agent of the Almighty, sent against Israel, "a hypocritical nation. And against the people of my wrath will I give him a charge to take the spoil, and to take the prey, and to tread them down like the mire of the streets". (V. 6). Maher-shalal-hash-baz / the spoil speedeth, the prey hasteneth. (See 2 Nephi 18:18).

The description in the Cuneiform Text of Pul accurately assesses the extent of Assyria's destruction of the Northern Kingdom: "His noblemen I impaled alive and displayed this exhibition to his land. All his gardens and fruit orchards I destroyed. Towns I laid waste like mounds after the flood". (Avraham Gileadi, "The Book of Isaiah: A New Translation", p. 158).

Assyria's plans were on a grandiose scale. "In his heart, it is to destroy and cut off nations not a few". (V. 7). He was out to conquer "the whole of the Fertile Crescent from the Persian mountains to Asia Minor, and from the Mesopotamian Plain through Lebanon to Palestine. Only Judah and a few other states remained independent, although they had to pay tribute or risk conquest". (Avraham Gileadi, "The Book of Isaiah: A New Translation", p. 159).

The king of Assyria boasted: "Are not my princes altogether kings?" (V. 8). Are not even my field commanders vassal kings? "Is not Calno as Carchemish? Is not Hamath as Arpad? Is not Samaria as Damascus?" (V. 9). Have I not conquered these city-states? "My hand hath founded the kingdoms of the idols, and whose graven images did excel them of Jerusalem and of Samaria". (V. 10). How can the inferior God of Israel save her?. The idols I have established are far more powerful.

In verses 11 and 12, Isaiah gave the first hint that Judah would be attacked by Assyria following its invasion of the Northern Kingdom and Samaria. "Shall I not, as I have done unto Samaria and her idols, so do to Jerusalem and to her idols?" (V. 11). The anticipated seize took place in 701 B.C., although its walls held, and it was spared destruction. (See 2 Nephi 24:25-28).

The fall of Samaria in 722-721 B.C. was the beginning of the exile of the Ten Tribes of Israel, who had inhabited the conquered Northern Kingdom of Israel. (See v. 20). After their deportation, they were lost to history. Assyria then brought in a pagan people to inhabit the land of Samaria. Over time, they intermarried with the few remaining Israelites in the land. Thus, came about the "Samaritans", whom the Jews felt were not entitled to be remembered with the Chosen People, since they were not pure descendants of Abraham.

In verse 12, Isaiah interrupted the blasphemous boasts of Assyria to remind his readers that when God's work of punishment and purification of Israel was completed, He would urn his attention to the Assyrians, and deal with them appropriately. "Wherefore it shall come to pass that when the Lord hath performed his whole work upon Mount Zion and upon Jerusalem, I will punish the fruit of the stout heart of the king of Assyria, and the glory of his high looks". (V. 12). This punishment would be administered because Assyria had boasted: "By the strength of my hand and by my wisdom I have done these things; for I am prudent (or have discernment); and I have moved the borders of the people, and have robbed their treasures, and I have put down the inhabitants like a valiant man". (V. 13).

Moving the borders of the people could refer to the Ten Tribes who later escaped Assyria's grasp and wandered away into oblivion, or it could refer to Assyria's territorial expansion through conquest. Certainly, her hand "hath found as a nest the riches of the people", and "there was none that moved the wing, or opened the mouth, or peeped". (V. 14). In other words, there was a total lack of resistance to the invasion of the Northern Kingdom by Assyria.

Verse 15 reverts from the arrogance of Assyria to Isaiah's commentary on these events. He asked, in effect, "Why should Assyria brag that it was more powerful even than God?" "Shall the ax boast itself against him that heweth therewith? Shall the saw magnify itself against him that shaketh it? As if the rod should shake itself against them that lift it up, or as if the staff should lift up itself as if it were no wood!" (V. 15).

In truth, Assyria was powerless to assert herself in any measure without God's influence. It was He alone who was the Active Agent in these events. Assyria could not swing an ax, pull a saw, or swing a staff on her own. Isaiah was saying that no matter what Assyria did or did not do, it was of no consequence, and she could not thwart God from accomplishing His purposes. "Therefore, shall the Lord, the Lord of Hosts, send among his fat one (Assyria), leanness (or a wasting sickness); and under his glory (or within his internal organs) he shall kindle a burning (or a fever) like the burning of a fire". (V. 16). The Holy One of Israel would use the Babylonians and the Persians or Medes to completely destroy the Assyrian nation. "And the light of Israel shall be for a fire, and his Holy One for a flame, and shall burn and shall devour his thorns and his briers (the Assyrians) in one day". (V. 17).

Note the parallelism of verse 17. The fire represents the Lord Himself; Jehovah is the Holy One. The rank and file of Assyria would be devoured in one day. In fact, the Babylonians and Persians/Medes did later destroy the Assyrian nation. "The glory of his forest" or the upper echelons of Assyrian society, were consumed "both soul and body". (V. 18). Assyria vanished completely from the world stage. "The rest of the trees", or the remnant of the Assyrian nation, could be counted on the fingers of a hand, as it were. (V. 19).

In verse 20, Isaiah returned to his familiar theme: Shear-jashub / a remnant shall return. In the Last Days, the remnant of the House of Israel would no longer lean upon its oppressors, but would rather rely upon the Lord. "And it shall come to pass in that day, that the remnant of Israel, and such as are escaped of the house of Jacob, shall no more again stay upon him that smote them, but shall stay upon the Lord, the Holy One of Israel, in truth". (V. 20). Israel, "even the remnant of Jacob", or the Lost Ten Tribes, would return "unto the mighty God". (V. 21).

Biblical scholars refer to both "historical remnants" and "eschatological remnants". The latter has to do with theological questions of death, judgment, heaven, and hell. The eschatological remnant will emerge from a future action of God and have the qualifications of a Latter-day, millennial society. Covenant Israel is an eschatological remnant.

The apocryphal writer Esdras recorded an intriguing version of the departure of the Ten Tribes from Assyria: "Those are the ten tribes" he wrote, "which were carried away prisoners out of their own land in the time of Hosea the king whom Shalmaneser the king of Assyria led away captive, and he carried them over the waters, and so came they into another land. But they took this counsel among themselves, that they would leave the multitude of the heathen, and go forth unto a further country, where never mankind dwelt, that they might there keep their statutes, which they never kept in their own land. And they entered into Euphrates by the narrow passage of the river. For the Most High then shewed signs for them, and held still the flood, till they were passed over. For through that country there was a great way to go, namely, of a year and a half: and the same region is called Arsareth. Then dwelt they there until the latter times; and now when they shall begin to come, The Highest shall stay the stream again, that they may go through". (Apocrypha, 2 Esdras 13:40-47, quoted in "Doctrine & Covenants Student Manual", p. 341).

Interestingly, Esdras declared that the Ten Tribes determined to keep the statutes of the Lord, even though they had not kept them when they were living in the Northern Kingdom. Other scriptures attest to the fact that these tribes were led away by the Lord, have since been continually preserved by Him, have had their own prophets minister among them, had the Savior Himself visit them after His resurrection, have kept their own scriptures and records, have kept the statutes of God, and will be led out of the North Country by His power to help build the New Jerusalem. (See 1 Nephi 17:36 & 22:3, 2 Nephi 21:15, & D&C 133:28-34).

Verse 22 might refer to the past 2,000 years of persecution of the Jews. Though the numbers of Israelites shall "be as the sand of the sea, yet (only) a remnant shall return", while their decreed destruction during their dispersion will be accomplished, "for the Lord God of Hosts shall make a consumption even (or righteously) determined in all the land", for the people are deserving of punishment. (V. 22-23).

In verse 24-27, Isaiah gave the surviving remnant in the Last Days a message of hope and comfort. "Therefore, thus saith the Lord God of Hosts: O my people that dwellest in Zion, be not afraid of the Assyrian; he shall smite thee with a rod, and shall lift up his staff against thee, after the manner of Egypt. Yet for a very little while, and the indignation shall cease, and mine anger in their destruction. And the Lord of Hosts shall stir up a scourge for him according to the slaughter of Midian at the rock of Oreb; and as his rod was upon the sea so shall he lift it up after the manner of Egypt". (V. 24-26). Twenty-First Century Israelites were told not to be afraid of the "Assyrians" in their lives, though they be "after the manner of Egypt", that anciently was a symbol of all her enemies. Isaiah's Israelite audience was well aware of how God had "delivered Midian, and all the host" into the hands of Israel, and now the "princes of the Midianites" had been slain upon "the rock of Oreb". (Judges 7:14 & 25). Yet a very little while, and the Lord's indignation would cease, and His anger would be directed to the destruction of the wicked, and they will be scourged in the same manner as the Midianites at the rock of Oreb. (V. 25-26).

As David had declared, so should we: "Thou comest to me with a sword, and with a spear, and with a shield: but I come to thee in the name of the Lord of hosts, the God of the armies of Israel, whom thou hast defiled. This day will the Lord deliver thee into mine hand; and I will smite thee, and take thine head from thee; and I will give the carcasses of the host of the Philistines this day unto the fowls of the air, and to the wild beasts of the earth; that all the earth may know that there is a God in Israel. And all this assembly shall know that the Lord saveth not with sword and spear; for the battle is the Lord's and he will give you into our hands". (1 Samuel 17:45-47).

Verses 27-34 may be read in a Latter-day context. Israel's increasing prosperity shall help to relieve her from bondage to her enemies. "And it shall come to pass in that day that his burden shall be taken away from off thy shoulder, and his yoke from off thy neck, and the yoke shall be destroyed because of the anointing". (V. 27). Just as the increasing fatness of an ox breaks the yoke on its neck, so the miraculous invigoration of Israel and the renewal of her prosperity in the Latter-days will help to throw off the oppression of her enemies.

In verse 28, Isaiah ostensibly switched the focus of his attention back to the Assyrian conquest. Assyria had penetrated to Aiath, just nine miles from Jerusalem. She had passed several other cities along the path of the invasion route that had carried her through the Northern Kingdom. "He is come to Aiath, he is passed to Migron; and Michmash he hath laid up his carriages. They are gone over the passage; they have taken up their lodging at Geba; Ramath is afraid; Gibeah of Saul is fled". (V. 28-29). "O poor Anathoth". (V. 30). The invaders had overwhelmed the birthplace of the prophet Jeremiah, just three miles from Jerusalem. The inhabitants of Gebim had fled. (V. 31).

Jerusalem would be besieged by Assyria, who would occupy Nob, or Mt. Scopus, just outside the city walls. "As yet shall he remain at Nob that day; he shall shake his hand against the mount of the daughter of Zion, the hill of Jerusalem". (V. 32). Nevertheless, the Lord is ever in charge, and "the bough", or the Assyrian troops, would be lopped, "the high ones of stature", or the rulers, would be hewn down, and "the thickets of the forests" or the common people of Assyria, would be cut down. (V. 33-34, see V. 11-12).

As Isaiah later prophesied: "I will bring (or break) the Assyrians in my land, and upon my mountains tread him under foot" in a symbol of complete submission. "Then shall his yoke depart from off them, and his burden depart from off their shoulders". (2 Nephi 24:25). The Assyrian fate was sealed. Although her armies reached he gates of Jerusalem, history tells us that a devastating sickness forced her withdrawal before the walls could be breached.

"Thus saith the Lord concerning the king of Assyria, He shall not come into this city, nor shoot an arrow there, nor come before it with shields, nor cast a bank against it. By the way that he came, by the same shall he return, and shall not come into this city, saith the Lord. For I will defend this city to save it for mine own sake, and for my servant David's sake. Then the angel of the Lord went forth, and smote in the camp of the Assyrians" a hundred and eighty-five thousand in all, "and when they arose early in the morning, behold, they were all dead corpses. So, Sennacherib king of Assyria departed, and went and returned, and dwelt at Nineveh". (Isaiah 37:33-37).

Second Nephi
Chapter 21

This chapter, that corresponds to Isaiah Chapter 11, is one of the most important and widely quoted prophecies in all scripture. It is recorded in the Old Testament and The Book of Mormon, and was quoted to Joseph Smith by the Angel Moroni, who said it was about to be fulfilled. (See J.S.H. 1:40). Doctrine & Covenants Section 113 is devoted primarily to an explanation of this chapter.

2 Nephi Chapter 20 ended with a description of old trees being hewn down. "Behold, the Lord, the Lord of Hosts shall lop the bough with terror; and the high ones of stature shall be hewn down; and the haughty shall be humbled. And he shall cut down the thickets of the forests with iron, and Lebanon shall fall by a mighty one". (V. 32-34). This chapter opens with a prophecy of new trees, or leaders, who would come forth out of Israel to rule and bless the earth.

Verse 1 is an example of synonymous parallelism. "There shall come forth a rod out of the stem of Jesse / and a branch shall grow out of his root". The rod = the branch, and the stem = the roots. "Who is the stem of Jesse?" asked Joseph Smith. "It is Christ". (D&C 113:1-2). "What is the rod that should come of the Stem of Jesse? It is a servant in the hands of Christ". (D&C 113:3-4). The rod and branch appear to describe the great Jewish leader of the Last Days who will be called David. He might not be a member of the Church, or even a Christian, but he will respect the Lord and have concern for others.

Verses 2-5 describe some of his characteristics: "And the Spirit of the Lord shall rest upon him, the spirit of wisdom and understanding, the spirit of counsel and might, the spirit of knowledge and of the fear of the Lord". (V. 2). He will not judge by appearances, or by hearsay, "after the sight of his eyes, neither reprove after the hearing of his ears". (V. 3). Rather, "with righteousness shall he judge the poor, and reprove with equity for the meek of the earth; and he shall smite the earth with the rod of his mouth, and with the breath of his lips shall he slay the wicked". (V. 4). That is to say, he will be powerful of speech unto the confounding of the wicked.

"The girdle of his loins" and "the girdle of his reins" described in verse 5 are symbols of strength and denote righteousness. This individual will personify the teaching that authority comes by the laying on of hands, but power comes through righteous living, and that power and violence are mutually exclusive; where one is present, the other is absent.

In poetic metaphor, verses 6-9 describe the Millennium to follow, when "the wolf also shall lie down with the lamb, and the leopard shall lie down with the kid, and the calf and the young lion and fatling together; and a little child shall lead them. And the cow and the bear shall feed; their young ones shall lie down together; and the lion shall eat straw like the ox. And the sucking child shall play on the hole of the asp, and the weaned child shall put his hand on the cockatrice's den". (V. 6-8). However, one should not carry these figures of speech to the extreme when interpreting conditions during the Millennium. (See D&C 49:18-19). At the very least, these verses paint a portrait of a new God-centered earth where righteousness prevails, and "the earth (is) full of the knowledge of the Lord, as the waters cover the sea". (V. 9, see 2 Nephi 30:16 & 18, & Isaiah 65:17). "And because of the righteousness of his people, Satan has no power; wherefore, he cannot be loosed for the space of many years; for he hath no power over the hearts of the people, for they dwell in righteousness, and the Holy One of Israel reigneth". (1 Nephi 22:26).

Verses 10-16 chronologically precede verses 6-9, and deal with the recovery of the remnant of Israel in the Last Days. "And in that day there shall be a root of Jesse, which shall stand for an ensign of the people; to it shall the Gentiles seek; and his rest shall be glorious. And it shall come to pass in that day that the Lord shall set his hand again the second time to recover the remnant of his people which shall be left, from Assyria, and from Egypt, and from Pathros, and from Cush, and from Elam, and from Shinar, and from Hamath, and from the islands of the sea. And he shall set up an ensign for the nations, and shall assemble the outcasts of Israel, and gather together the dispersed of Judah from the four corners of the earth. The envy of Ephraim also shall depart, and the adversaries of Judah shall be cut off; Ephraim shall not envy Judah, and Judah shall not vex Ephraim. But they shall fly upon the shoulders of the Philistines towards the west; they shall spoil them of the east together; they shall lay their hand upon Edom and Moab; and the children of Ammon shall obey them. And the Lord shall utterly destroy the tongue of the Egyptian sea; and with his mighty wind he shall shake his hand over the river, and shall smite it in the seven streams, and make men go over dry shod. And there shall be a highway for the remnant of his people which shall be left, from Assyria, like as it was to Israel in the day that he came up out of the land of Egypt." (V. 10-16).

"What is the root of Jesse spoken of in the 10th verse?" asked Joseph Smith. "It is a descendant of Jesse, as well as of Joseph, unto whom rightly belongs the priesthood, and the keys of the kingdom, for an ensign, and for the gathering of my people in the last days". (D&C 113:5-6).

Joseph Smith could be that descendant of Joseph through his son Ephraim, or a descendant of Judah through Jesse. Remember that in the Kirtland Temple on April 3, 1836, Moses conferred upon Joseph Smith the "keys of the gathering of Israel from the four parts of the earth". (D&C 110:11). Therefore, this verse could refer to him. Certainly, Joseph Smith has been characterized as an "ensign of the people". Since the Restoration of the Gospel, members of the Church have figuratively and literally rallied around him, as they have borne powerful testimony of his mission. Joseph Smith wrote that the Angel Moroni had declared: "God had a work for me to do; and my name should be had for good and evil among all nations, kindreds, and tongues". (J.S.H. 1:33). This was a bold declaration for a young boy living in obscurity on the western frontier of the United States in the 1830s.

Verse 11 speaks of the Last Days, when the Lord would set His Hand a second time to gather His people. The first time was either during the Exodus from Egypt or during Israel's return from the Babylonian captivity, depending upon one's point of view.

When speaking of Israel, most people think of the Jews, and when referring to the Gathering of Israel, they have in mind the return of the Jews to the land of Jerusalem. It should be remembered, however, that the Jews represent but one of the twelve tribes of the House of Israel. "For lo ... I will sift the House of Israel among all nations". (Amos 9:9). As Isaiah saw it, the House of Israel would return from the seven known countries of his day: "From Assyria, and from Egypt, and from Pathros (or upper Egypt), and from Cush (or Ethiopia), and from Elam (east of Babylonia), and from Hamath (Northern Syria), and from the isles of the sea (the rest of the world)". (V. 11, see Commentary References to 1 Nephi 19:10, 15-16, 19, 1 Nephi 22:4-5, 2 Nephi 8:5, 2 Nephi 29:7-8, & Alma 63:5).

"And (the Lord) shall set up an ensign for the nations". (V. 12). This "ensign" is the Church in the Last Days. As the Lord said to Joseph Smith: "I have sent mine everlasting covenant into the world, to be a light to the world, and to be a standard for my people, and for the Gentiles to seek to it, and to be a messenger before my face to prepare the way before me". (D&C 45:9).

There will be two general gatherings. First, there are the "outcasts of Israel" and secondly, "the dispersed of Judah". (V. 12). These gatherings might refer distinctly to the Ten Tribes and to Judah, respectively. (See Commentary Reference to 2 Nephi 20:20). When the gathering takes place, the jealousy of Ephraim and the Ten Tribes of the Northern Kingdom will have dissipated, and they will no longer envy the Kingdom of Judah. In fact, it will be the responsibility of Ephraim to bring to Judah the message of the Restored Gospel. Note once again in this verse the synonymous parallelism that was Isaiah's favorite literary device. "The envy of Ephraim also shall depart, and the adversaries of Judah shall be cut off; Ephraim shall not envy Judah, and Judah shall not vex Ephraim". (V. 13).

Ephraim and Judah will gather to the lands of their inheritance. Verse 14 could be representative of any available means of transportation. "They shall fly upon the shoulders of the Philistines towards the west; they shall spoil them of the east together; they shall lay their hand upon Edom and Moab; and the children of Ammon shall obey them". (See Isaiah 5:28, & D&C 133:26-34).). In other words, they shall settle on the lands of the Gentiles to the west (Gaza), and on the lands of their ancient enemies to the east, that is now modern Jordan. This could also include that land now known as "The West Bank" or "The Occupied Territories", or as the State of Israel prefers to call it, "Judea and Samaria". (See Commentary Reference to 2 Nephi 24:29).

Isaiah declared that Israel would be aided in these endeavors by God's power: "And the Lord shall utterly destroy the tongue of the Egyptian sea". (V. 15). With the construction of the Aswan Dam in Upper Egypt in 1970, the flooding of the Nile Delta each spring was eliminated, and the tongue of the Egyptian Sea was utterly destroyed. "With his mighty wind he shall shake his hand over the river, and shall smite it in the seven streams, and make men go over on dry ground". (V. 15). In other words, the Lord shall divert the River Euphrates so that men might pass over it on dry ground.

Verse 16 then describes a highway "like as it was to Israel in the day that he came up out of the land of Egypt". There was no literal highway for Ancient Israel, but the Lord provided a way for them to reach their destination. We are again reminded of the Apocryphal story in 2 Esdras 13:40-47: "Now when they shall begin to come, The Highest shall stay the stream again, that they may go through". (See Commentary Reference to 2 Nephi 20:21). The Lord revealed to Joseph Smith the following: "And they who are in the north countries shall come in remembrance before the Lord; and their prophets shall hear his voice, and shall no longer stay themselves; and they shall smite the rocks, and the ice shall flow down at their presence. And an highway shall be cast up in the midst of the great deep". (D&C 133:26-27).

"Behold, this is the blessing of the everlasting God upon the tribes of Israel, and the richer blessing upon the head of Ephraim and his fellows. And they also of the tribe of Judah, after their pain, shall be sanctified in holiness before the Lord, to dwell in his presence day and night, forever and ever". (D&C 133:34).

"This is the way;
and there is none other way
nor name given under heaven whereby
man can be saved in the kingdom of God.
And now, behold, this is the doctrine of Christ,
and the only and true doctrine of the Father,
and of the Son, and of the Holy Ghost,
which is one God, without end."
(2 Nephi 21:31).

Second Nephi
Chapter 22

This chapter is the conclusion of 2 Nephi Chapter 21 / Isaiah Chapter 11, and is the capstone of the first 12 chapters of Isaiah. It is a compilation of two Thanksgiving Psalms. First, attention is focused on the person giving thanks and upon the blessing he has received, and secondly, upon the person being extolled. These two psalms reflect a natural pattern of spiritual growth.

"Isaiah yearned for the Millennium, and used short, powerful hymns to give sincere thanks and profound praise to the Lord for the blessings He would give the earth. In a few verses, (he) expressed the gratitude all of us should feel as the Lord's works become manifest among men". (Avraham Gileadi, "The Book of Isaiah: A New Translation", p. 179, see D&C 84:99-102).

"And in that day (in the time of Zion's redemption) thou shalt say: O Lord, I will praise thee". (V. 1). "Behold, God is my salvation". (V. 2). The name "Isaiah" means "Jehovah will save" or "God is my salvation" and typifies God's saving power. Isaiah wrote: "The Lord Jehovah is my strength and my song". (V. 2). "Jehovah" is usually rendered "Lord" in English. In the K.J.T., rather than translating this verse "Lord, Lord", it was rendered "Lord Jehovah", one of only 4 times in the K.J.T. that the name is written out fully as "Jehovah". (See also Exodus 6:4, Psalms 33:18 & Isaiah 12:2).

Isaiah wanted others to share his rapture; "Therefore, with joy shall ye draw water out of the wells of salvation". (V. 3). He publicly exhorted others to make the Lord's deeds known to all. "Declare his doing among the people, make mention that his name is exalted". (V. 4). His deep convictions were manifest in songs of praise and when he bore witness of the truth. "Sing unto the Lord; for he hath done excellent things; this is known in all the earth. Cry out and shout, thou inhabitant of Zion; for great is the Holy One of Israel". (V. 5-6).

"Behold, God is my salvation; I will trust, and not be afraid; for the Lord Jehovah is my strength and my song; he also has become my salvation."
(2 Nephi 22:2).

Second Nephi
Chapter 23

There are two themes in Chapters 23 and 24. First, is the worldwide scope of Jehovah's power and kingdom, and secondly, the end of the foreign oppression of Israel. The concept of the Lord's universal omnipotence was unique to Ancient Israel. Contemporary pagan religions taught that their gods had only limited power within specific restrictive geographical boundaries.

We are reminded of Zadok, who "was a spiritual man whose tired eyes could see beyond the desert to those invisible summits of the imagination where cool air existed and where the one God, El Shaddai, lived. In later generations, people who spoke other languages would translate this old Semitic name, which actually meant 'he of the mountain' as God Almighty, for through change El Shaddai was destined to mature into that god whom much of the world would worship. But in these fateful days, when the little group of Hebrews camped waiting for the signal to march westward, El Shaddai was the God of no one but themselves. They were not even certain that he had continued as the God of those other Hebrews who had moved on to distant areas like Egypt. But of one thing Zadok was sure. El Shaddai personally determined the destiny of this group, for of all the peoples available to him in the teeming area between the Euphrates and the Nile, he had chosen these Hebrews as his predilected people, and they lived within his embrace, enjoying security that others did not know". (James Michener, "The Source" p. 177-178).

Isaiah prophesied dualistically of the city-state of Babylon that fell in 539 B.C., and of Spiritual Babylon that will fall before the beginning of the millennial reign of Christ. "Go ye out from among the nations, even from Babylon, from the midst of wickedness, which is spiritual Babylon". (D&C 133:14, see D&C 1:6). Spiritual Babylon is a symbol of enslavement, and a representation of sin, wickedness, ungodliness, unfaithfulness, and evil.

In verse 1, we learn about "the burden of Babylon, which Isaiah the son of Amos did see" (V. 1). He was told in verse 2 to muster the Host of the Lord by giving it a signal upon the Mountain of the Lord, crying aloud and waving his arms, that they might go into the gates of Spiritual Babylon to do battle against the wicked. "Lift ye up a banner upon the high mountain, exalt the voice unto them, shake the hand, that they may go into the gates of the nobles". (V. 2). The Lord declared that He had consecrated select men to accomplish this task. "I have commanded my sanctified ones, I have also called my mighty ones". (V. 3). In ancient times, warriors were often set apart for a battle or campaign. In much the same way, in latter days, the Saints of the Most High God are set apart to wage war against the wicked.

Verse 4 is a description of the tumult and commotion incident to the gathering of the Lord's Host to do battle in the

Valley of Decision, or the Valley of Jehoshaphat. "The noise of the multitude in the mountains (is) like as of a great people, a tumultuous noise of the kingdoms of nations gathered together". (V. 4, see Joel 3:14).

In verse 5, we learn that the Lord has commanded His forces, comprised of Church leaders, members, and missionaries, to destroy Spiritual Babylon by preaching the Gospel. "They come from a far country, from the end of heaven, yea, the Lord, and the weapons of his indignation, to destroy the whole land". (V. 5, see Helaman 6:37, D&C 29:9-21, & 45:39-59.).

"The day of the Lord is at hand". (V. 6). This descriptive term was first used in the scriptures by Isaiah, Joel, Amos, and Zephaniah. (See Joel 1:15, 2:1-2, Amos 5:18, & Zephaniah 1:7). When that day comes, the wicked shall lose courage, and they shall despair, and their faces shall burn with shame and guilt. "Therefore, shall all hands be faint, every man's heart shall melt". (V. 7). They shall look in astonishment at each other, and their faces shall burn with shame in recognition of their sins. "And they shall be afraid; pangs and sorrows shall take hold of them; they shall be amazed one at another; their faces shall be as flames". (V. 8).

"Blow ye the trumpet in Zion", wrote Joel, "and sound an alarm in my holy mountain: let all the inhabitants of the land tremble: for the day of the Lord cometh". (Joel 2:1-2). It will be a day of thick darkness and gloominess for the wicked, when even the sun and the moon and the stars of heaven obey the voice of the Master. "For the stars of heaven and the constellations thereof shall not give their light; the sun shall be darkened in his going forth, and the moon shall not cause her light to shine". (V. 10, see D&C 88:87 & Matthew 24:29). For the purpose of the day of the Lord is to "destroy the sinners thereof out of (the land)". (V. 9). They will be punished for iniquity, arrogance, pride, and haughtiness, because they have failed to repent. (V. 11).

In that day, a righteous man will be "more precious than fine gold" because they will be few in number, or because the true value of righteousness, when compared to the treasures of the earth, will be obvious. (V. 12). The treasure of the "Golden Wedge of Ophir" (India?) will be insignificant when compared to one righteous man. (V. 12). "The earth shall remove out of her place" or will tremble at the wrath of God, but it will ultimately receive its paradisiacal glory, wherein all life will enjoy continual peace during the Millennium. (V. 13). This is not to be confused with the celestial state that will be its eventual destiny.

From verse 14, this chapter deals with the Babylonian Empire with which Isaiah was familiar. It would yet be as a deer being chased by hunters, or as a sheep without a shepherd. "And it shall be as the chased roe, and as a sheep that no man taketh up". (V. 14). In a parallel style written for emphasis, verse 15 declares; "Every one that is proud shall be thrust through; yea, and every one that is joined to the wicked shall fall by the sword". "Their children also shall be dashed to pieces before their eyes; their houses shall be spoiled, and their wives ravished". (V. 16). This was to be accomplished by the Medes, who would be an instrument in the Lord's hand. For "Behold", said the Lord, "I will stir up the Medes against them". (V. 17). The Medes lived northwest of Persia and conquered Babylon in 539 B.C. Verse 18 is a parallel statement that vividly describes the violent nature of their army. "Their bows shall also dash the young men to pieces; and they shall have no pity on the fruit of the womb; their eyes shall not spare children". They did not care about taking plunder, but were obsessed with the domination of Babylon. They "shall not regard silver and gold, nor shall they delight in it". (V. 17). In a contrasting but similar vein, those who are intent on destroying Spiritual Babylon will be uninterested in plunder, but only in conquering wickedness.

Verse 19 should be read dualistically. Babylon represents both the proud splendor of the Chaldeans, and Satan's worldly kingdom. "And Babylon, the glory of kingdoms, the beauty of the Chaldees' excellency, shall be as when God overthrew Sodom and Gomorrah". (V. 19). Although Babylon did not pose a military threat to Judah during Isaiah's lifetime, her culture and pagan ideology spread rapidly throughout the Middle East. She later became so great an enemy that, in The Book of Revelation, she was represented as the Antichrist, and was called by John "Babylon the Great, the Mother of Harlots and Abominations of the Earth". (Revelation 17:1-5, 18).

In our day, spiritual Babylon has become firmly entrenched in the world and is "the great whore that sitteth upon many waters, with whom the kings of the earth have committed fornication". (Revelation 17:1-2). To some extent, she is in bed with all of the corrupt governments of the earth who associate with harlots and have committed fornication with the whore, for they are a wicked, and an idolatrous community.

One of the terrible consequences of the fascination of the world with Babylon is spiritual insensitivity. Isaiah foresaw the Last Days, when he wrote: "Stay yourselves, and wonder; cry ye out, and cry: they are drunken, but not with wine; they stagger, but not with strong drink. For the Lord hath poured out upon you the spirit of deep sleep, and hath closed your eyes: the prophets, and your rulers, and seers hath he covered". (Isaiah 29:9-11).

Isaiah prophesied that after its destruction, the city of Babylon should never again be inhabited, "neither shall it be dwelt in from generation to generation; neither shall the Arabian pitch tent there; neither shall the shepherds make their fold there". (V. 20). In fact, the site of the great city became a forgotten mound of rubble that soon blended in with the surrounding countryside. It was abandoned in the 4th century B.C. and has remained uninhabited for the last 2,400 years. Only "doleful creatures and owls shall dwell there, and satyrs" or he-goats of folklore "shall dance there". (V. 21). "And the wild beasts of the islands" or hyenas "shall cry in their desolate houses, and dragons" or jackals in their pleasant palaces". (V. 22, see 2 Nephi 24:21-23).

Finally, this significant addition appears in The Book of Mormon version of Isaiah 13:22: "For I will destroy her speedily; yea, for I will be merciful unto my people, but the wicked shall perish". (V. 22).

"I will punish the world
for evil, and the wicked for their
iniquity; I will cause the arrogancy
of the proud to cease, and will lay down
the haughtiness of the terrible."
(2 Nephi 23:11).

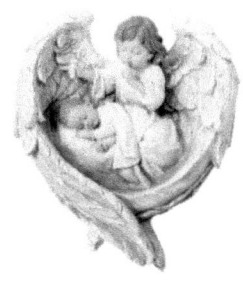

Second Nephi
Chapter 24

Having just predicted the destruction of Babylon, Isaiah now turned his attention to events further in the future. Historically, one level of fulfillment of these verses occurred when Cyrus the Great of Persia allowed all the captives of Babylon to return to their homeland. The first group of Jews to do so arrived in Judea in 538 B.C. But these verses could also refer to The Church of Jesus Christ of Latter-day Saints, whose missionary work spreads to all nations and prepares the world for the Second Coming, or it could refer to the present day gathering of the Jews, and the establishment of the State of Israel, with complete fulfillment when they accept Jesus Christ as their Savior.

Isaiah assured his readers that Israel would return to its own land, and then he said something quite striking: "And the strangers shall be joined with them, and they shall cleave to the house of Jacob". (V. 1). Just who are these "strangers", and what claim could they possibly have on the blessings of Israel through the Covenant?

The Prophet Ezekiel was one of the captives of Judah carried away by Nebuchadnezzar into Babylonia. He began to prophesy to Israel around 498 B.C., just 11 years before the fall of Jerusalem and the Kingdom of Judah to the Babylonians. He wrote: "And it shall come to pass that ye shall divide (the land) by lot for an inheritance unto you, and to the strangers that sojourn among you, which shall beget children among you; and they shall be unto you as born in the country among the children of Israel; they shall have inheritance with you among the tribes of Israel". (Ezekiel 47:22).

Nephi understood this broad concept, when he wrote: "As many of the Gentiles as will repent are the covenant people of the Lord; and as many of the Jews as will not repent shall be cast off; for the Lord covenanteth with none save it be with them that repent and believe in his Son, who is the Holy One of Israel". (2 Nephi 30:2).

In the Last Days, then, Israel must be viewed from three perspectives: Blood Israel, or the ancient covenant people of the Lord; Covenant Israel, or those who accept Christ and His covenants and who are adopted members of the House of Israel and who thus have rights by adoption to the blessings of Abraham; and Land Israel, or those who have inhabited the land since ancient times, and who, as we have read, are included by the Lord among those who will receive the blessings associated with habitation of the Promised Land. (See Commentary References to 1 Nephi 19:19, 2 Nephi 30:2, Jacob 5:3-4 & 9, & Jacob 5:67).

In 2022, there were 464 million people living in the Arab world straddling North Africa and Western Asia. Many of these were children of Abraham through Ishmael. Over 2 million were living in Israel and in its annexed territories. It will be interesting to see in what manner the Lord chooses to remember these of His children. (See Leviticus 19:34).

Verse 2 tells us that foreigners will assist Israel in gathering to her lands of promise. "And the people shall take them and bring them to their place: yea, from far unto the ends of the earth; and they shall return to their lands of promise". Note the plural form of the noun: "lands". Israel shall govern these lands, and she shall preside over those who were her former taskmasters. "And the House of Israel shall possess them, and the land of the Lord shall be for servants and handmaids; and they shall take them captives unto whom they were captives; and they shall rule over their oppressors". In that day, Israel shall rest from millennia of sorrow, fear, and bondage. And it shall come to pass in that day that the Lord shall give thee rest, from thy sorrow, and from thy fear, and from the hard bondage wherein thou wast made to serve". (V. 3).

A five-part chiasm follows in verses 4-21. The context of verses 4-8 is the Earth, wherein is expressed general satisfaction over Babylon's downfall. "And it shall come to pass in that day, that thou shalt take up this proverb against the king of Babylon and say: How hath the oppressor ceased, the golden city ceased!" (V. 4). Here Spiritual Babylon is personified as a king, and the taunting song is given as a symbol of Israel's triumph over her enemies and of the fall of the wicked world in the Last Days. (V. 4-21).

"The Lord hath broken the staff of the wicked, and scepters of the rulers" that are the symbols of their temporal power. (V. 5). "He who smote the people in wrath with a continual stroke, he that ruled the nations in anger, is persecuted, and none hindereth". (V. 6). Spiritual Babylon, who never ceased her persecution of the nations, is now herself persecuted and will ultimately be defeated, which will allow the Earth to enjoy a millennial rest. "The whole earth is at rest, and is quiet; they break forth into singing". (V. 7).

Because of the downfall of spiritual Babylon, the righteous shall sing songs of thanksgiving, and shout praises to God. "Yea, the fir-trees rejoice at thee, and also the cedars of Lebanon, saying: Since thou art laid down no feller is come up against us". (V. 8). Members of the Church, represented as fir trees and cedars of Lebanon, will declare that since the destruction of Babylon, no feller, a person who cuts down trees, has risen against them to smite them.

The location of verses 8-11 is the spirit prison of the unjust where the leaders of Spiritual Babylon will be found following their earthly sojourn. (See D&C 76:73, 138:8 & 28, Isaiah 61:1, 1 Peter 3:19 & Moses 7:57). There, the other disembodied spirits inhabiting hell will ask of them: "Art thou also become weak as we? Art thou become like unto us?" (V. 10). In other words: "You were mere mortals, after all!" "Thy pomp is brought down to the grave; the noise of thy viols is not heard; the worm is spread under thee, and the worms cover thee". (V. 11). As Ezekiel recorded his own vision; "The strong among the mighty shall speak ... out of the midst of hell. ... They are gone down, they lie uncircumcised, slain by the sword". (Ezekiel 32:21). Death, it seems, is the great equalizer.

The setting of verses 12-14 is heaven, where the king of Babylon is personified as Lucifer. This is the only place in the Bible and The Book of Mormon where the name "Lucifer" is found. It means "bright morning star" in Hebrew. Commentators believe it is a reference to the King of Babylon, since it comes in the midst of a prophecy about that city-state, but D&C 76:25-27 confirms that "Lucifer" was also the premortal name of Satan, who is the king, or head, of Spiritual Babylon. Once again, dualistic prophecy is at work.

In a glorious and panoramic vision of the degrees of glory and the events concerning the pre-mortal, mortal, and post-mortal world, Joseph Smith recorded the following: "And this we saw also, and bear record, that an angel of God who was in authority in the presence of God, who rebelled against the Only Begotten Son whom the Father loved and who was in the bosom of the Father, was thrust down from the presence of God and the Son, And was called Perdition for the heavens wept over him - he was Lucifer, a son of the morning. And we behold, and lo, he is fallen! is fallen, even a son of the morning!" (D&C 76:25-27).

It is possible that Isaiah had access to the writings of Moses, restored through Joseph Smith in The Pearl of Great Price, that also concern Lucifer and his role in the pre-earth existence. "Wherefore, because that Satan rebelled against me, and sought to destroy the agency of man, which I, the Lord God, had given him, and also, that I should give unto him mine own power; by the power of mine Only Begotten, I caused that he should be cast down; And he became Satan, yea, even the devil, the father of all lies, to deceive and to blind men, and to lead them captive at his will, even as many as would not hearken unto my voice". (Moses 4:3-4).

Lucifer is called "a son of the morning" who was "cut down to the ground" because he sought personal power and glory. (V. 12). He said: "I will ascend into heaven, I will exalt my throne above the stars of God; I will sit also upon the mount of the congregation", which is also translated "in the assembly of Gods" or "upon the Mount of Assembly, where the Gods meet". (V. 13). "I will ascend above the heights of the clouds; I will be like the Most High". (V. 14). These verses fit very neatly into the L.D.S. doctrine that concerns the pre-mortal role of Lucifer at the Grand Council in Heaven, where God introduced His Plan of Salvation to His assembled spirit children.

The context of verses 15-17 is the spirit world. The scene shifts to Sheol / Hell, or "the pit" where those who behold the fallen King of Babylon will be moved to declare: "Is this the man that made the earth to tremble, that did shake kingdoms?" (V. 16, see 2 Nephi 9:9). They will continue to ask: Is this he who made the world as a wilderness, and destroyed the cities thereof, and opened not the house of his prisoners?" (V. 17). In other words: "Is this he who wreaked such havoc on the earth, who demonstrated such awesome power, and yet is not able to open the doors of the spirit prison of the unjust, to free its captives?" In the end, Satan will abandon those who followed him. As Mormon observed: "And thus we see that the devil will not support his children at the last day, but doth speedily drag them down to hell". (Alma 30:60).

The context of verses 18-21 is the earth. The kings of Babylon and Spiritual Babylon, although once rulers of world-wide empires, today and forever have no monuments or tombs of any kind to memorialize their achievements. "All the kings of the nations, yea, all of them, lie in glory, every one of them in his own house. But thou art cast out of thy grave like an abominable branch, and the remnant of those that are slain, thrust through with a sword, that go down to the stones of the pit, as a carcass trodden under feet". (V. 19).

They are as Ozymandias, of whom Shelley wrote: "I met a traveler from an antique land who said: Two vast and trunkless legs of stone stand in the desert. Near them, on the sand half sunk, a shattered visage lies, whose frown and wrinkled lip and sneer of cold command tell that its sculptor well those passions read, which yet survive. Stamped on these lifeless things, the hand that mocks them and the heart that fed; and on the pedestal these words appear: 'My name is Ozymandias, King of Kings; Look on my works, ye mighty, and despair!' Nothing beside remains. Round the decay of that colossal wreck, boundless and bare, the lone and level sand stretched far away". ("Ozymandias").

Many shades of glory are found within the telestial kingdom. "In my father's house are many mansions", said the Savior, and Isaiah took up where He left off: "All the kings of the nations, yea, all of them, lie in glory, every one of them in his own house". (V. 18). This refers to the family tombs of the nobility as well as to the kingdoms of glory that are tailor made for the wicked who inherit the telestial kingdom. These are they who are cast out of their graves like an unfruitful branch and "go down to the stones of the pit" or to a common grave on the battlefield, that symbolizes spiritual darkness. (V. 19). Because of wickedness, they shall remain unburied in a figurative sense. In ancient times, it was a curse to be denied burial. It was also the curse of the wicked to have no posterity: "The seed of evil doers shall never be renowned". (V. 20).

Verse 21 declares that those who "do not rise" to a kingdom of glory, the Sons of Perdition, will be cast off the celestialized earth. They will be denied eternal increase and will never "possess the land, nor fill the face of the world with cities". In verses 22 and 23, the Lord confirmed His judgment upon temporal, or physical, Babylon. The inhabitants will have no offspring. "For I will ... cut off from Babylon the name, and remnant, and son, and nephew, saith the Lord". (V. 22). The land that might have been their inheritance will instead be the habitation of hedgehogs. "I will also make it a possession for the bittern". (V. 23). The Lord will sweep the land with the broom of destruction. (See 2 Nephi 23:20-22).

In verses 24-27, Isaiah once again turned His attention to Assyria. In parallel prose, he declared in the name of the Lord: "Surely as I have thought, so shall it come to pass; and as I have purposed, so shall it stand". (V. 24). The Assyrians would be swept out of the land of Jerusalem. "I will bring the Assyrian in my land, and upon my mountains tread him under foot; then shall his yoke depart from off them, and his burden depart from off their shoulders". (V. 25).

The Assyrians did, in fact, besiege Jerusalem, but a devastating sickness, characterized as "the Angel of the Lord" in Isaiah 37:33-38, forced their withdraw. (See 2 Nephi 20:11-12, & 32-34). The fate of Assyria was sealed with the fall of Nineveh, and through the combined efforts of the Medes, Scythians, and Babylonians, they were finally destroyed as a nation sometime around 606 B.C. This same fate also awaits Gog and Magog in the Last Days. "This is the purpose that is purposed upon the whole earth; and this is the hand that is stretched out upon all nations". (V. 26).

In Cecil B. DeMille's "The Ten Commandments", when Pharaoh passed judgment, he arrogantly declared: "So let it be written, so let it be done". But the monuments he erected lie crumbling in the desert, silent witnesses to his desperate quest for immortality. How much more powerfully did Isaiah declare: "For the Lord of Hosts hath purposed, and who shall disannul? And his hand is stretched out, and who shall turn it back?" (V. 27).

The prophecy was given "in the year that king Ahaz died", or between 720 and 715 B.C. (V. 28). The Last Days will yet bear witness to the validity of the dual nature and fulfilment of this prophecy: "And thus, with the sword and by bloodshed the inhabitants of the earth shall mourn; and with famine, and plague, and earthquake, and the thunder of heaven, and the fierce lightning also, shall the inhabitants of the earth be made to feel the wrath, and indignation, and chastening hand of an Almighty God, until the consumption decreed hath made a full end of all nations". (D&C 87:6).

Verse 29, and Isaiah 14:29 & 31, use the term "Palestina". (See Exodus 15:44). "Rejoice not thou, whole Palestina, because the rod of him that smote thee is broken; for out of the serpent's root shall come forth a cockatrice, and his fruit shall be a fiery flying serpent". The Philistines inhabited Canaan when Israel entered and conquered the Promised Land. What had been their territory was called "Judea" until the Romans, in turn, conquered it and captured Jerusalem. To indicate to the Jews that they no longer had claim there, the Romans changed the name to "Palestina", which is the Latin form of "Philistine". Modern Israelites, understandably, do not like to use the term "Palestine".

In this verse, Isaiah cautioned Palestina, or the Philistines who where Canaanites, not to rejoice because the power of the Assyrian King Shalmaneser had been broken. Out of Shalmaneser's lineage would come another Assyrian king, Sennacherib, who would shortly destroy the Philistines, anyway. "Howl, O gate (where justice was dispensed in ancient times); cry, O city: thou whole Palestina, art dissolved (or will be destroyed); for there shall come from the north a smoke (the Assyrians), and none shall be alone in his appointed times (or there shall be no stragglers)". (V. 31).

This chapter concludes by declaring that God's people must learn to trust in Him, and the invitation to come to Zion is again offered to all nations. "What shall then answer the messengers of the nations? That the Lord hath founded Zion, and the poor of his people shall trust in it". (V. 32). Implicit in this invitation is the dire warning that the Lord does destroy whole nations because He will not tolerate their existence when they have become morally bankrupt. (See 1 Nephi 17:37).

"For the Lord will have mercy on Jacob, and will yet choose Israel, and set them in their own land; and the strangers shall be joined with them, and they shall cleave to the house of Jacob. (2 Nephi 24:1, see Leviticus 19:34).

Second Nephi
Chapter 25

Chapters 25 through 30 comprise Nephi's inspired commentary on Isaiah. He began by acknowledging that his people found the writings of Isaiah difficult to understand because they were not familiar with the figures, types, and shadows he employed to illustrate his points. (V. 1). The same difficulty exists today among the members of The Church of Jesus Christ of Latter-day Saints. (See Commentary Reference to Introduction to 2 Nephi 11).

Additionally, the Nephites had renounced the way of life and tradition of their forefathers, viewing the lifestyle of "the Jews at Jerusalem" as an abomination. (V. 2). But Nephi wanted his people to understand the scriptures of the Hebrew prophets, and so he was determined "to write, that they (might) know the judgments of God". (V. 3). He explained that he delighted in the words of Isaiah, because he had come "out from Jerusalem" and was familiar with the "things of the Jews". (V. 5). Of all the Nephites, only Sam and Nephi, and perhaps their wives, had actually lived "at Jerusalem", and he was hesitant to teach his family "after the manner of the Jews". (V. 6).

Nephi declared: "There is none other people that understand the things which were spoken unto the Jews like unto them, save it be that they are taught after the manner of the things of the Jews". (V. 5). This is one of the keys to understanding Isaiah, as well as the other prophets. It is necessary to put ourselves into their time and place, walk a kilometer or two in their shoes, and learn of their traditions and of their interrelationships with other contemporary societies. This is why we should comprehensively study the Nephites, their culture, and their world. If we hope to be able to understand the truths expressed in the key doctrine of The Book of Mormon, as well as to identify and heed its warnings, we must know something of those who kept the records and of the society in which they lived.

One day we will meet Nephi, Mormon, Moroni, and Isaiah face to face. When we do, it would be nice to be able to tell them that we have read their words, pondered their counsel, and follow their example. "You and I shall stand face to face before his bar;" Nephi assured us, "and ye shall know that I have been commanded of him to write these things". (2 Nephi 33:11). Moroni wrote in his farewell: "I soon go to rest in the paradise of God, until my spirit and body shall again reunite, and I am brought forth triumphant through the air, to meet you before the pleasing bar of the great Jehovah, the Eternal Judge of both quick and dead. Amen". (Moroni 10:34).

The importance of Isaiah's words is evidenced by Nephi's editorial comment in verse 8: "I know that they shall be of great worth unto them in the last day; for in that day shall they understand them, wherefore for their good have I written them". Apparently, more than any other Old Testament prophet, Isaiah will be the best guide to escort us through the minefields of mortality during the perilous Last Days.

Nephi observed that repeatedly, iniquity had been at the root of the continuing problems of the Jews. (V. 9) As a result, they had been "destroyed from generation to generation". The meaning of the term "destroy" becomes more apparent as Nephite and Lamanite history unfolds. (See V. 15-16 & Commentary Reference to 2 Nephi 3:2).

Nephi declared that, according to his prophecy, the Jews had already "been destroyed, save it be those which are carried away captive into Babylon". (V. 10, see Commentary Reference to 2 Nephi 6:8). Nevertheless, shear-Jashub "a remnant would return", to "possess the land of Jerusalem" and the land of their inheritance. (V. 11). He followed with a prophecy of the Mortal Messiah and His mission that is as specific as any in the Old Testament, for he wrote: "I have seen His day". (V. 13). He stands beside Isaiah as a Messianic Prophet. This portion of his ministry took place around 559-545 B.C., which makes Nephi roughly contemporary with the prophets Habakkuk and Ezra.

As clearly as any of those who later kept The Small Plates, Nephi recognized the pre-eminent position the Savior occupies in the Gospel Plan. When Mormon and Moroni abridged the records of the Nephites and Jaredites, they preserved this focus on the Savior. Of 239 chapters in The Book of Mormon, 233 contain references to Christ. Only Mosiah Chapters 9 and 22, Alma Chapters 51 and 52, and Helaman Chapters 1 and 2 do not.

Nephi told his brethren; "I have spoken plainly that ye cannot err". (V. 20). He would teach in the next 10 verses, that "as the Lord God liveth, there is none other name given under heaven save it be this Jesus Christ, of which I have spoken, whereby man can be saved". (V. 20). We shall see that all of The Book of Mormon prophets understood that the Law of Moses did not contain the fulness of the saving principles and ordinances of the Gospel of Jesus Christ. Nephi taught in verses 20-30 about the relationship of the Law of Moses to the Atonement of Christ because it was the Law that the Nephites understood and by which they were bound to God by virtue of a sacred covenant.

In verse 20, Nephi used a familiar vehicle from The Plates of Brass: "As the Lord liveth that brought up the children of Israel out of the land of Egypt". This was the same language used by Jeremiah, who had been a contemporary of Lehi. (See Jeremiah 16:14-15). The people of The Book of Mormon were apparently using with little deviation the same formulas common in their familiar scriptures. The injunction "As the Lord liveth" was used by many Book of Mormon prophets. (See 1 Nephi 3:15, 4:32, 2 Nephi 9:16, 27:31, Omni 1:26, Alma 44:11, 54:10, Helaman 13:26, 15:17, and Mormon 8:23). As Paul explained to the Hebrews: "Because he could swear by no greater, he sware by himself". (Hebrews 6:13).

Verse 22 contains a potential indictment of each generation that possesses the scriptures. "And the nations who shall possess them shall be judged of them according to the words which are written". This is a very sobering statement, and makes the Church's Book of Mormon Placement Program a missionary activity of eternal significance, for not only will we be judged according to our obedience to the principles contained in this book, but we also have the responsibility to be Saviors on Mt. Zion to those of our fellow men who have not yet embraced the Gospel and The Book of Mormon. (See Obadiah 1:21). As John Taylor declared: "God will hold us responsible for those we might have saved had we done our duty".

To that end, in 2021, The Book of Mormon had been translated into 115 languages, and selections from it into another 25 languages. In 2001, the Church reported that it was available in the native language of 99% of its members, and in 87% of the native languages of the world's population. In 2020, the Church claimed that over 192 million copies of the book had been published since its first edition came off the press in 1830.

In verse 24, Nephi outlined his three-fold mission as a prophet-leader, as a teacher, and as a parent: "For we labor diligently to write, to persuade our children, and also our brethren, to believe in Christ, and to be reconciled to God; for we know that it is by grace that we are saved, after all we can do". (See Commentary Reference to 2 Nephi 10:25).

This last phrase is another example of a Hebrew Hokmah, an aphorism worth remembering. The grace to which Nephi alluded is an attribute of perfection that consists of God's love, mercy, and condescension toward His children. (See D&C 66:12, 84:102, and especially 93:6-20). Its diverse elements include His gifts and power by which the children of God can be brought to perfection.

Jacob explained in 2 Nephi 10:25 how the grace of God operates. We are raised from physical death by the power of the Resurrection and from spiritual death by the power of the Atonement. We are granted grace proportionately as we conform to the standards of personal righteousness that are part of the Gospel Plan. Thus, we are commanded to "grow in grace" (D&C 50:40) until we are sanctified and justified "thru the grace of our Lord and Savior Jesus Christ". (D&C 20:30-32). This is why Nephi declared that we are saved by grace "after all we can do", and it is why repentance is so important, for when the day of repentance is past, so is the day of grace. (See Mormon 2:15).

Nephi continued: "And notwithstanding we believe in Christ, we keep the law of Moses, and look forward with steadfastness unto Christ, until the law shall be fulfilled" at His resurrection. (See 3 Nephi 1:24-25). From the beginning, Book of Mormon prophets placed great emphasis on obedience to the Law of Moses so that it might direct their people toward the Savior. At the same time, they looked forward to the mortal ministry of Christ and saw in His resurrection the fulfillment of the Law. They knew that through obedience to the Law of Moses they might come unto Christ and participate in all of the saving ordinances of the Gospel.

Just so, as scholars examine the Dead Sea Scrolls that predate the mortal ministry of Christ, they consistently find confirming evidence that the community at Qumran was obedient for the same reasons: "For this end was the law given; (to prepare the people to believe in Christ), wherefore the law hath become dead unto us (because we already do believe in Him), and we are made alive in Christ because of our faith; yet we keep the law because of the commandments". (V. 25, see Jacob 4:5).

During his ministry, Jacob described the relationship of the Nephites to the Law of Moses: "Behold, (the prophets) believed in Christ and worshiped the Father in his name, and also we worship the Father in his name. And for this intent we keep the law of Moses, it pointing our souls to him; and for this cause it is sanctified unto us for righteousness". (Jacob 4:5). The Book of Mormon is a vivid example of Old Testament faith in Christ. As Hugh Nibley declared: "It is the Dead Sea Scrolls that have taken away the license of the learned to cut and slash as they pleased, for they have shown that many concepts formerly held to be uniquely Christian were familiar to Jews before the time of Christ". ("Since Cumorah", p. 41-42).

"The one thing that emerges most clearly from all the Dead Sea documents is the picture of a pious community of Israelites who had gone out into the desert in order to live the Law of Moses in its perfection. These people deliberately separated themselves from 'the Jews at Jerusalem' because they were convinced that the nation as a whole under the guidance of ambitious priests and kings had fallen into a state of apostasy. People were behaving in the manner of the Qumran Jews as early as 800 B.C., and there is evidence that such a group was living at Qumran itself as early as the 7th century B.C., that is, during the time Lehi left Jerusalem for the same reasons. There is no question of any of these groups being the true Church; what we are interested in is simply to point out that there were just such Churches before the time of Christ". (Hugh Nibley, "An Approach to The Book of Mormon", p. 149-150, 154).

Nephi was the spokesman for a legitimate "Church of Anticipation" in the wilderness. As a prophet of God and the inspired leader of his people, he declared: "We talk of Christ, we rejoice in Christ, we preach of Christ, we prophesy of Christ, and we write according to our prophecies, that our children may know to what source they may look for a remission of our sins". (V. 25, see 2 Nephi 31:13-20). He had a clear understanding of the principles of the Gospel and knew Who the Author of Salvation was.

Nephi declared in verse 28 that he had spoken plainly to the people to avoid misunderstanding. As one having authority, his words would stand as a testimony against the people should they not hearken to his counsel. The ultimate test when speaking under the influence of the Spirit lies with the listener. The Church and its teachings are not on trial. It is the members who are on trial to see if they will conform their lives to the revealed Gospel standard.

Verse 28 also teaches that The Book of Mormon, standing alone, can be an effective tool of conversion. These words "are sufficient to teach any man the right way". And what is the right way, asked Nephi? "The right way is to believe in Christ". (V. 29).

Nephi frequently called Christ "The Holy One of Israel", an appellation that occurs 25 times in The Book of Isaiah, 29 times in 1 Nephi and 2 Nephi, and only 6 times elsewhere in the entire Old Testament. The name is Isaiah's special title reserved for his God, and may have been first revealed to him, since his is its first recorded application. Nephi may have adopted its use because the writings of Isaiah were so special to him. (See Commentary Reference to 2 Nephi 10:3).

This chapter concludes with Nephi's declaration that it was "expedient", or suitable to the circumstances of the case, to keep the Law of Moses. Nephi was a great leader who emphasized the basic teachings of the Gospel when exhorting his brethren to a higher standard of obedience. After all, his mentor Isaiah had written: "Whom shall he teach doctrine?. Them that are weaned from milk, for precept must be upon precept, line upon line, here a little and there a little". (Isaiah 28:9-10, see D&C 98:12). In this chapter, Nephi did an admirable job of harmonizing obedience to the Law of Moses with a powerful testimony of Christ's divinity and mission. He would have made Isaiah proud.

Second Nephi
Chapter 26

In this chapter, Nephi spoke to future generations as if they were present. "And after Christ shall have risen from the dead he shall show himself unto you ... For behold, I say unto you that I have beheld that many generations shall pass away". (V. 1).

By Ammon's definition, Nephi was a great seer. "A seer can know of things which are past, and also of things which are to come, and by them shall all things be revealed, or, rather, shall secret things be made manifest, and hidden things shall come to light, and things which are not known shall be made known by them, and also things shall be made known by them which otherwise could not be known". (Mosiah 8:17). A seer, quite simply, sees with spiritual eyes and is a perceiver of hidden truth.

Nephi spoke of the coming of the Messiah, together with all the attendant manifestations among his people, as if they were a certainty. "And after the Messiah shall come there shall be signs given unto my people". (V. 2). To view "the slain of (his) people" caused him pain and anguish of soul, but he knew that all the events he saw in vision would be necessary to satisfy the demands of Justice, because the people would not repent. (V. 7).

The righteous, on the other hand, who looked "forward unto Christ with steadfastness" would not perish, but would instead be healed and "have peace with him, until three generations passed away". (V. 8-9). In the long-lived Patriarchal Age, a generation seems to have been 100 years, but 30 - 40 years was later adopted as the reckoning. (See Genesis 15:6, Job 42:16, & "Smith's Bible Dictionary", p. 210).

Through much of The Book of Mormon, we see the shadow of coming Nephite destruction. For example, Nephi wrote that "when these things shall have passed away, a speedy destruction cometh unto my people, for, notwithstanding the pains of my soul, I have seen it; wherefore, I know that it shall come to pass". (V. 10). There is a message here that is applicable to each of us individually: "For the reward of their pride and their foolishness they shall reap destruction; for because they yield unto the devil and choose works of darkness rather than light, therefore they must go down to hell. For the Spirit of the Lord will not always strive with man. Then cometh speedy destruction". (V. 10-11). Such a fate is sometimes temporal, but it is always spiritual. (See 2 Nephi 28:16).

Nephi declared that the Christian world needs to have a testimony of Christ just as much as the Jews do. "It must needs be that the Gentiles be convinced also that Jesus is the Christ, the Eternal God". (V. 12). Therefore, Christ will manifest "himself unto all those who believe in him, by the power of the Holy Ghost". (V. 13). We can see today that this is true, as members and missionaries of The Church of Jesus Christ bear witness of their beliefs to a world that lacks both saving faith in Christ and a testimony of the truths interwoven throughout the Restored Gospel. (See Commentary Reference to 1 Nephi 27:7-10).

What follows is a prophecy concerning the Last Days, "when the Lord God shall bring these things forth unto the children of men". (V. 14). From 2 Nephi 26:15 to 2 Nephi 27:35 is a 54-verse quotation by Nephi of Isaiah 29:2-24 that includes inspired commentary that addresses how these teachings could be applied to his own people and to our day. Interestingly, J.S.T. Isaiah Chapter 29, written four years after the translation of The Book of Mormon, has 32 verses. All 32 are found in both the K.J.T. and The Book of Mormon, but not in just one or the other. (See Commentary Reference to 2 Nephi 11).

Nephi prophesied that the time would come when the descendants of Lehi "shall have dwindled in unbelief, and shall have been smitten by the Gentiles", and there would be "forts" raised against them. (V. 15). This is an interesting choice of words, for the word "fort" occurs just this once in the entire Book of Mormon, only 6 times in the Old Testament, and not once in the New Testament.

Verse 16 parallels Isaiah 29:4: "For those who shall be destroyed shall speak unto them out of the ground, and their speech shall be low out of the dust, and their voice shall be as one that hath a familiar spirit; for the Lord God will give unto him power, that he may whisper concerning them, even as it were out of the ground; and their speech shall whisper out of the dust". (See V. 34, 2 Nephi 3:20, Moroni 10:27 & 34, & Isaiah 29:4). How is it that an ancient people could speak "out of the ground", and how could their speech be "low out of the dust?". These expressions could refer figuratively to the depths of humility, as an example to the world of the consequences of disobedience. But, at the same time, there is an interesting account of the discovery of the Bar Kokhba Documents that were hidden in caves near Ein Gedi on the western shores of the Salt Sea (the Dead Sea), about 3,000 B.C. These records were deliberately buried deeply in the dry earth of the cave floor, and when they came to light there were choking clouds of dust, so that the archaeologists had to wear masks in order to breathe. The Book of Mormon would be a marvelous work and a wonder. (See 2 Nephi 27:26, 3 Nephi 21:9, D&C 4:1, & Isaiah 29:14).

Brigham Young recorded in his journal that when the records from which The Book of Mormon was translated were unearthed, "an angel instructed (Joseph) to carry them back to the Hill Cumorah, which he did. Oliver says that when Joseph and Oliver went there, the hill opened, and they walked into a cave, in which there was a large and spacious room". Miraculous forces were at work here, for the hill literally opened up before them to reveal a depository much larger than the simple stone box normally visualized by Latter-day Saints.

Brigham Young continued: "They laid the plates on the table; it was a large table that stood in the room. Under this table there was a pile of plates as much as two feet high, and there were altogether in this room more plates than probably many wagon loads; they were piled up in the corners and along the walls". (Daniel Ludlow, "A Companion to Your Study of The Book of Mormon", p. 21).

Other records have also come to us "out of the ground". "There is an interesting account in Idrisi (1,226 A.D.) of the opening of the tomb of Mycerinus in the third of the three great Pyramids. The writer reports that all that was found in the tomb was a blue sarcophagus containing the decayed remains of a man, but no treasure, excepting some golden tablets inscribed with characters in a language that nobody could understand. The tablets were used to pay the workmen, and the gold in each of them was worth about two hundred dollars. We leave the reader to speculate on what might have been written on those plates of gold, which one of the mightiest of Pharaohs apparently regarded as the greatest treasure with which he could be buried". (Hugh Nibley, "Lehi in The Desert", p. 120).

From verse 17, until the end of this chapter, Nephi provides us with a commentary on how the prophecy of Isaiah could come to pass. Verse 1 of the next chapter of 2 Nephi picks up Isaiah again with a quotation of Isaiah 29:6. Nephi observed that the mighty powers that rule in the earth should be destroyed speedily. "And the multitude of their terrible ones shall be as chaff that passeth away – yea, thus saith the Lord God: It shall be at an instant, suddenly". (V. 18). Of one such ancient empire, the Israeli archaeologist Yigal Yadin, who excavated Masada, said: "Nothing remains here today of the Romans but a heap of stones in the desert". Just how quickly nations of the earth can be destroyed has become terrifyingly apparent in the Last Days. (See Commentary Reference to 2 Nephi 24:18-21).

Nephi described the pride of the Gentiles, their Churches established to get gain, and the secret combinations of the Last Days. Many of these professors of Christianity have "put down the power and miracles of God, and preach up unto themselves their own wisdom and their own learning, that they may get gain and grind upon the face of the poor. And there are many Churches built up which cause envyings, and strifes, and malice. And there are also secret combinations, even as in times of old, according to the combinations of the devil, for he is the founder of all these things, yea, the founder of murder, and works of darkness". (V. 20-22).

Of these secret societies and their head who is Satan, Nephi had particularly scathing words. In fact, with prophetic foresight, Nephi knew that the devil would be the author of the oaths and covenants that would motivate the Nephites to form secret combinations that would ultimately precipitate their destruction. (See Commentary Reference to 2 Nephi 28:14, Alma 37:27, Helaman 6:26-27, & Ether 8:18-22). Nephi recognized that Satan works very subtly, first leading the unwary with a "flaxen cord" around the neck that actually feels quite comfortable. Once the habit has been set, however, and the person thus involved has sacrificed his agency to act independently, Satan moves in like a black widow spider, and binds him "with his strong cords forever" in a sinewy web of destruction. (V. 22).

In contrast, God does not work in darkness. (V. 23). Verses 23-28 reiterate that salvation is for all mankind. "He doeth not anything save it be for the benefit of the word; for he loveth the world, even that he layeth down his own life that he may draw all men unto him. Wherefore, he commandeth none that they not partake of his salvation". (V. 24). The summation of this doctrine is expressed in verse 28: "All men are privileged the one like unto the other, and none are forbidden". Joseph Fielding Smith taught: "Every soul coming into this world came here with the promise that through obedience, he would receive the blessing of salvation. No person was foreordained to sin or to perform a mission of evil". (Doctrines of Salvation", 1:61).

Interestingly, verse 26 makes a reference to "synagogues" that are compared by Nephi to "houses of worship", or to the congregation of the faithful. Synagogues were a phenomenon of the Babylonian Exile that occurred just after Lehi left Jerusalem; they arose under the leadership of Ezra in the absence of the temple. The oldest synagogue building uncovered by archaeologists is the Delos Synagogue, a possibly Samaritan synagogue that dates from at 150 to 128 BCE, or earlier, and is located on the island of Delos, Greece. There is only one Old Testament reference to synagogues, (Psalms 74:8), but 26 in The Book of Mormon, and 56 in the New Testament. (See Alma 16:13). Why might this be?

The frequent use of the term in The Book of Mormon (it occurs 25 times) can be explained in several ways. First, if synagogue worship predated the exile, then Lehi's party could have brought with it the practice of synagogue worship. However, there is no mention of actual synagogue worship until Alma 16:13. Secondly, another group not identified in The Book of Mormon, (such as the "Mulekites" – 587 B.C.?) arriving in the New World after the Babylonian exile could have brought the concept with them, introducing the practice to the Nephites. Thirdly, by the power of the spirit, Joseph Smith could have translated the Nephite word for "place of assembly" into the English as "synagogue". This explanation is quite intriguing because it makes another powerful statement in support of the authenticity of The Book of Mormon for the following reason.

The Book of Mormon uses both "synagogue", that is a Greek word designating early Jewish assemblies, and "Church", from the Greek "ecclesia", designating such assemblies after they had become Christian. It is hard to think of more appropriate terms, bearing in mind that this is a translation, and the purpose of the words is not to convey what the Nephites called their communities, but only how we are to accurately portray them in our own minds. (See D&C 66:7, Mosiah 25:13, Alma 19:34, 21:16, 23:4, & 32:1-4). In any event, an understanding of their distinction supports the way in which Nephi used the terms "synagogue" and "Church", or "house of worship" in different contexts.

Nephi next defined "priestcraft" as the activity of men who "preach and set themselves up for a light unto the world, that they may get gain and praise of the world; but they seek not the welfare of Zion". (V. 29). Can anyone have Zion's welfare at heart and at the same time set himself up for a light, to get gain and the praise of the world? Verses 30 and 31 emphatically say "No!" and explain that the driving principle by which a righteous priest functions is charity, or a love so centered in righteousness that its possessor has no desire except for the eternal welfare of the souls of those around him. (See Commentary Reference to Moroni 7:47, & 8:25-26).

In these verses, we find that the cure for pride is charity. The Hokmah or aphorism that follows is meant to reinforce the teaching concept that "except they should have charity they were nothing". (V. 30). "But the laborer in Zion shall labor for Zion; for if they labor for money they shall perish". (V. 31). Nephi hoped that those with charity would strive to keep the Law of Moses and the Ten Commandments, 6 of which are identified in verse 32. Their obedience to these commandments would empower them to avoid spiritual death.

Verse 33 is one of the greatest treasures in The Book of Mormon, because in language plain and simple the universality of God's love for all of His children is dramatically expressed: "For none of these iniquities come of the Lord; for he doeth that which is good among the children of men; and he doeth nothing save it be plain unto the children of men; and he inviteth them all to come unto him and partake of his goodness; and he denieth none that come unto him, black and white, bond and free, male and female; and he remembereth the heathen; and all are alike unto God, both Jew and Gentile". (V. 33, see 1 Nephi 26:37, Alma 29:8, D&C 64:22, & Matthew 9:10-12). Considering that Nephi was a "Jew", and understanding how the Jews of his day felt about the Gentiles, this is an amazing statement. It speaks not only to Nephi's understanding of the sum and substance of the Gospel Plan but also says something about his character, as well.

In a similar fashion, the Savior later taught the Pharisees, who had criticized His association with the wrong crowd, consisting of publicans and sinners: "They that be whole need not a physician, but they that are sick ... I am not come to call the righteous, but sinners to repentance". (Matthew 9:11-13). Paul expressed the hope and desire of his brethren, when he wrote to the Thessalonian Saints: "Neither at any time used we flattering words, as ye know, nor a cloak of covetousness ... Nor of men sought we glory, neither of you, nor yet of others, when we might have been burdensome, as the apostles of Christ. But we were gentle among you, even as a nurse cherisheth her children. So being affectionately desirous of you, we were willing to have imparted unto you, not the Gospel of God only, but also our own souls, because ye were dear unto us". (1 Thessalonians 2:5-8). On another occasion, to the Ephesian Saints, he declared: "Ye are no more strangers and foreigners, but fellowcitizens with the saints, and of the household of God." (Ephesians 2:19

Second Nephi
Chapter 27

This chapter parallels Isaiah 29:6-24. Perhaps Nephi was quoting his favorite prophet from The Plates of Brass when delivering this discourse. The focus of the message is the Last Days, and the Days of The Gentiles in particular, when there will be many Churches (2 Nephi 26:20-21), secret combinations (2 Nephi 26:22-23), priestcraft (2 Nephi 26:29-33), divisions because of the Gospel (1 Nephi 14:7), wars and rumors of wars (1 Nephi 14:15), great iniquity (2 Nephi 27:1), and the rejection of new scripture (2 Nephi 29:3). Truly, from the perspective of scriptural prophecy, today is the Time of the Gentiles. (Luke 21:24).

Significant additions in The Book of Mormon quotation of these verses from Isaiah clarify these points. Verses 1-5 refer to a people in apostasy, "drunken with iniquity and all manner of abomination". (V. 1). "And when that day shall come they shall be visited of the Lord of Hosts, with thunder and with earthquake, and with a great noise, and with storm, and with tempest, and with the flame of devouring fire. And all the nations that fight against Zion, and that distress her, shall be as a dream of a night vision; yea, it shall be unto the them, even as unto a hungry man which dreameth, and behold he eateth but he awaketh and his soul is empty; or like unto a thirsty man which dreameth, and behold he drinketh but he awakeneth and behold he is faint, and his soul hath appetite; yea, even so shall the multitude of all the nations be that fight against Mount Zion. For behold, all ye that doeth iniquity, stay yourselves and wonder, for ye shall cry out, and cry; yea, ye shall be drunken but not with wine, ye shall stagger but not with strong drink". (V. 1-4). "For behold", wrote Nephi of the nations that fight against Zion, "the Lord hath poured out upon you the spirit of deep sleep. For behold, ye have closed your eyes, and ye have rejected the prophets; and your rulers and the seers hath he covered because of your iniquity". (V. 5).

Verses 6-14, added in The Book of Mormon and in the J.S.T., concern a book that is brought forth by the power of God. "And it shall come to pass", wrote Isaiah, "that the Lord God shall bring forth unto you the words of a book, and they shall be the words of them which have slumbered". (V. 6). Although a portion of "the book shall be sealed", the book itself shall be a revelation from God "from the beginning of the world to the ending thereof". (V. 7). Not only do these verses foreshadow The Book of Mormon, but they also provide a glimpse into the contents of its sealed portion.

The scriptures also tell us that there are other books that have been sealed, in general because of the iniquity of the people, indicating that the world is not sufficiently spiritually prepared to receive revelation from God. The Lord told His prophet Daniel: "Shut up the words, and seal the book, even unto the time of the end". (Daniel 12:4). John saw God on His holy throne in heaven and described the scene in these words: "And I saw in the right hand of him that sat on the throne a book written within and on the backside, sealed with seven seals. And I saw a strong angel proclaiming with a loud voice, Who is worthy to open the book, and to loose the seals thereof? And no man in heaven, nor in earth, neither under the earth, was able to open the book, neither to look thereon. And I wept much, because no man was found worthy to open and to read the book, neither to look thereon". (Revelation 5:1-4).

The scripture recorded by John the Revelator is itself incomplete, but the Lord has promised: "If you are faithful you shall receive the fulness of the record of John". (D&C 93:18). An angel confirmed to Nephi that many things have been written which are "sealed up to come forth in their purity, according to the truth which is in the Lamb, in the own due time of the Lord, unto the House of Israel". (1 Nephi 14:26).

"For the book shall be sealed by the power of God, and the revelation which was sealed shall be kept in the book until the own due time of the Lord, that they may come forth; for behold, they reveal all things from the foundation of the world unto the end thereof". (V. 10). When the people prove themselves worthy and capable of acceptance, God will reveal to them the contents of these sealed scriptures. Then, "the day cometh that the words of the book which were sealed shall be read upon the house tops; and they shall be read by the power of Christ; and all things shall be revealed unto the children of men which ever have been among the children of men, and which ever will be even unto the end of the earth". (V. 11, see Alma 26:22, D&C 42:61, 88:67, 93:28, 101:32-34, & 121:26-32).

When translating these verses from the plates that were then in his possession, Joseph Smith also learned that there were to be special witnesses of the work he was performing. "The book shall be hid from the eyes of the world, that the eyes of none shall behold it save it be that three witnesses shall behold it, by the power of God, besides him to whom the book shall be delivered; and they shall testify to the truth of the book and the things therein. And there is none other which shall view it, save it be a few according to the will of God, to bear testimony of his word unto the children of men". (V. 12-13, see D&C 17).

Ultimately, there would be eleven Book of Mormon witnesses, in all. To three of these, God Himself declared that the plates were a true record, and an angel showed them the plates, as well. Eight of the eleven witnesses, including all three to whom God had spoken, eventually left the Restored Church and were either disfellowshipped or excommunicated for conduct unbecoming members, but none ever denied his testimony of that which he had heard, and seen, and handled.

One left his sworn statement: "It is recorded in the American Encyclopedia and the Encyclopedia Britannica, that I, David Whitmer, have denied my testimony as one of the three witnesses to the divinity of The Book of Mormon, and that the other two witnesses, Oliver Cowdery and Martin Harris, denied their testimony of that book. I will say once more to mankind, that I have never at any time denied that testimony or any part thereof. I also testify to the world, that neither Oliver Cowdery nor Martin Harris ever at any time denied their testimony. They both died reaffirming the truth of the divine authenticity of The Book of Mormon". (William Berrett and Alma Burton, "Readings in L.D.S. Church History", 1:62).

The Lord always utilizes the Law of Witnesses. "In the mouth of as many witnesses as seemeth him good will he establish his word". (V. 14). Chapter 5 in The Book of Ether serves this purpose as a personal message from Moroni to Joseph Smith concerning the plates and the Three Witnesses. He wrote: "And in the mouth of three witnesses shall these things be established; and the testimony of three, and this work, in the which shall be shown forth the power of God and also his word, of which the Father, and the Son, and the Holy Ghost bear record - and all this shall stand as a testimony against the world at the last day". (Ether 5:4, see v. 14).

It was the opinion of Joseph Fielding Smith that "the Lord does not intend that The Book of Mormon, at least at the present time, shall be proved true by any archaeological findings. The Book of Mormon is itself a witness of its truth". ("Answers to Gospel Questions", 2:196). Archaeological correlation with biblical scriptures has not created faith among Christians. However, for those who already possess faith, pilgrimages to the Holy Land or to the Lands of The Book of Mormon strengthen existing religious conviction.

Verses 15-18 are related to the visit of Martin Harris to Professor Charles Anthon, characterized in these verses as "the learned." (See "Joseph Smith History", 2:63-65). Martin Harris was unacquainted with this prophecy when he embarked upon that mission. Interestingly, he took only a manuscript copy of a number of characters and their translation from The Book of Lehi (The Large Plates of Nephi), and not the book itself, in conformity with the detailed description of the future event provided in verses 10 and 15; "Neither shall he deliver the book (but only) take these words which are not sealed and deliver them to another, that he may show them unto the learned". (V. 10 & 15, see J.S.H. 1:62).

Verses 19 and 20 describe in more detail how Harris hoped to receive a scholarly validation of the authenticity of the records. But, alas, the learned would not read them when he discovered their divine origin, and he rejected them. (See V. 20). The problem with the learned was that his motivation was to enhance his own stature in the eyes of the world. "And now, because of the glory of the world and to get gain will they say this, and not for the glory of God." (V. 16). They fall into the trap of priestcraft that Nephi had earlier warned about: "For, behold, priestcrafts are that men preach and set themselves up for a light unto the world, that they may get gain and praise of the world; but they seek not the welfare of Zion". (2 Nephi 26:29).

Nephi's brother Jacob had taught the same principle; "When (men) are learned they think they are wise, and they hearken not unto the counsel of God, for they set it aside, supposing they know of themselves, wherefore, their wisdom is foolishness and it profiteth them not. And they shall perish. But to be learned is good if they hearken unto the counsels of God". (2 Nephi 9:28-29).

Verse 22 tells us that all the records, including those from which The Book of Mormon was translated, are now in the possession of God. "I (will) preserve the words which thou hast not read, until I shall see fit in mine own wisdom to reveal all things unto the children of men". When He decides that the time is right, God will reveal the sealed portion of the book to us. But He will do it in His own way, very likely through the instrumentality of His Prophet who at that time will stand at the head of His Church. "We believe that (the Lord) will yet reveal many great and important things pertaining to the kingdom of God". (9th Article of Faith).

However, He will not offer up sacred records to be scrutinized, analyzed, criticized, and rationalized by pompous doctors and professors of religion clothed in the robes of the false priesthood who are cloistered in the ivory towers of academia. "You cannot prove the genuineness of any document to one who has previously decided not to accept it. When a man asks for proof, we can be pretty sure that proof is the last thing in the world he really wants. His request is thrown out as a challenge, and the chances are that he has no intention of being shown up. After all these years, the Bible itself is still not proven to those who do not choose to accept it. So, The Book of Mormon as an 'unproven' book finds itself in good company". (Hugh Nibley, "An Approach to The Book of Mormon", p. 2).

Nor will the Lord indulge the prurient interest of those who want only theological titillation to satisfy their twisted and adulterous curiosity. "Critics of The Book of Mormon often remark sarcastically that it is a great pity that the golden plates have disappeared, since they would conveniently prove Joseph Smith's story. They would do nothing of the sort. The presence of the plates would only prove that there were plates, and nothing more. It would not prove that Nephites wrote them, or that an angel brought them, or that they had been translated by the gift and power of God, and we can be sure that scholars would quarrel endlessly about the writing on them without coming to any agreement, exactly as they have done about parts of the Bible. The possession of the plates would have a very disruptive effect and it would prove nothing. On the other hand, a far more impressive claim is put forth when the whole work is given to the world in what is claimed to be a divinely inspired translation. In such a text, any cause or pretext for disagreement and speculation about the text is reduced to an absolute minimum. It is a text which all the world can read and understand, and it is a far more miraculous object than any gold plates would be". (Hugh Nibley, "An Approach to The Book of Mormon", p. 17-18).

Verse 23 clarifies the concept of Gospel "dispensations" with which the Christian world today is unfamiliar, since it rejects the idea of a Great Apostasy: "I will show unto the world that I am the same yesterday, today, and forever; and I work not among the children of men save it be according to their faith". The Lord works with His children only when they have sufficient faith to allow Him to do so. During periods of apostasy from obedience to Gospel principles, the Spirit is withdrawn, the heavens are silent, and miracles cease among the children of men.

However, a Restoration of earth-shaking proportion began with the humble petition of a young boy in a quiet grove. Of that event, Christ said: "Wherefore, I the Lord, knowing the calamity which should come upon the inhabitants of the earth, called my servant Joseph Smith, Jun., and spake unto him from heaven, and gave him commandments ... That faith also might increase in the earth; that mine everlasting covenant might be established". (D&C 1:17, 21-22).

Thus, the Gospel began to be "proclaimed by the weak and the simple unto the ends of the world, and before kings and rulers". (D&C 1:23). Ours is called "the dispensation of the fulness of times" because we have received all the Gospel principles and ordinances that have been taught in all other dispensations. Secondly, it dispenses greater blessings to more people than any other dispensation, for its work includes not only the living but also the dead. "Behold, I will send you Elijah the prophet", Malachi had promised, "before the coming of the great and dreadful day of the Lord. And he shall turn the heart of the father to the children, and the heart of the children to their fathers". (Malachi 4:5-6).

Isaiah foresaw that, in the Last Days, a new dispensation of Gospel knowledge would be necessary. "This people draw near unto me with their mouth, and with their lips do honor me, but have removed their hearts far from me, and their fear towards me is taught by the precepts of men. Therefore, I will proceed to do a marvelous work among this people, yea, a marvelous work and a wonder". (V. 25-26, see 2 Nephi 25:17, 27:26, Helaman 3:13-16, 3 Nephi 5:8, 20:8 & 21:9, Mormon 7:9, Moroni 10:3, D&C 4:1, & Isaiah 29:14).

The marvelous work to which he alluded includes The Book of Mormon, other companion scriptures to the Bible, the Restoration of the Lord's Church with His priesthood power and authority, temples and their ordinances, and prophets, seers, and revelators. It is indeed the restoration of all things, culminating in the establishment of an earthly Zion that "shall flourish, and the glory of the Lord shall be upon her". (D&C 64:41).

Meanwhile, the world will continue "ripening in iniquity". (D&C 18:6). "For the wisdom of their wise and learned shall perish, and the understanding of their prudent shall be hid". (V. 26). A prudent person is adept in following the most politic and profitable course, without rocking the boat or upsetting the status-quo. When we study The Book of Mormon in an attitude of sincere inquiry, however, these qualities of worldly wisdom and learning fade in value.

Instead, Moroni exhorted those who would read The Book of Mormon to simply "Ask God, the Eternal Father, in the name of Christ, if these things are not true; and if ye shall ask with a sincere heart, with real intent, having faith in Christ, he will manifest the truth of it unto you, by the power of the Holy Ghost". (Moroni 10:4). His promise strips away the artifice of the natural man, leaving his spirit prominently vulnerable to the promptings of the Holy Ghost.

But wo unto those who "hide their counsel" from the Lord, whose works have a hidden agenda, a private or secret purpose, design, or opinion. (V. 27). They have not begun to understand that the destiny of the congregations of the faithful is to inherit the celestialized earth. "Yet a very little while and Lebanon shall be turned into a fruitful field;

and the fruitful field shall be esteemed as a forest". (V. 28). In that day, those who are spiritually ignorant through no fault of their own shall have the Gospel preached unto them. "The deaf shall hear the words of the book, and the eyes of the blind shall see out of obscurity and out of darkness". (V. 29). Spiritual Babylon and all those who dwell within her shadow will be overcome. (V. 31-32, see Commentary References to 2 Nephi 23:1 & 17-21, & 24:90-11).

There will be a great outpouring of the Spirit, so that men and women will "come to understanding, and they that murmured shall learn doctrine". (V. 35). Speaking of that day, the prophet Joel wrote: "And it shall come to pass afterward, that I will pour out my spirit upon all flesh, and your sons and your daughters shall prophesy, your old men shall dream dreams, your young men shall see vision". (Joel 2:28).

But those who reject prophecy in our time will find that The Book of Mormon is a sealed book that is beyond the reach of their limited understanding. The subject matter of 2 Nephi 27 / Isaiah 29 is itself a sealed book. As Jacob taught: "The things of the wise and the prudent shall be hid from them forever". (2 Nephi 9:43). Orson Pratt declared: "Every principle of the doctrine of Christ is set forth in such great plainness that it is impossible for any two persons to form different ideas in relation to it, after reading The Book of Mormon". (J.D., 15:189). 2 Nephi chapter 27 attests to the truthfulness of this observation.

"Thus saith the Lord God; I will give unto the children of men line upon line, precept upon precept, here a little and there a little, and blessed are those who hearken unto my precepts, and lend an ear unto my counsel, for they shall learn wisdom; for unto him that receiveth, I will give more."
(2 Nephi 28:30).

Second Nephi
Chapter 28

In Chapters 28-30, Nephi gave passionate counsel to those living in the Last Days. The Spirit had constrained or compelled him to do so. (V. 1). He knew that the counsel of future Nephite prophets, engraven on plates destined to become The Book of Mormon, would some day "be of great worth unto the children of men". (V. 2). As we read them today, we realize that many of the prophecies in these chapters have already been fulfilled.

Verses 3-16 identify practices and attitudes of many of the Churches flourishing at the time The Book of Mormon was published. There would be great pride and vanity among the different denominations professing to be "the Lord's" Church. (V. 3). In fact, many religions of the Last Days lead people away from the truth, in the sense that they discourage inquiry and maintaining an open mind to the message of the Restoration.

The different Churches sometimes "contend one with another", jockeying for position and for market share, while denying the power of the Holy Ghost to change lives. (V. 4). If we teach without the Spirit and use our Church calling as a bully pulpit, even if the scriptures are our text, we are teaching false doctrine at our own peril. "And the Spirit shall be given unto you by the prayer of faith; and if ye receive not the Spirit ye shall not teach". (D&C 42:14). Spencer W. Kimball counseled: "The great objective of all our work is to build character and increase faith in the lives of those whom we serve. If we cannot accept and teach the programs of the Church in an orthodox way, without reservation, we should not teach".

Many Churches contend with each other because they have implicitly denied "the power of God". (V. 5). Myriad organizations have sprung up that have a form of godliness, but on closer scrutiny, actually deny His power. For example, when narrow religious dogma denies God the power to speak to prophets whenever He wishes to do so, it is teaching that God is dead. When professors of religion presume to teach that God cannot provide His children with counsel in addition to that which is contained within the pages of the Bible, they are teaching that God is powerless to speak. When only the trappings of religion are provided, without the mighty works of which the scriptures testify, there is only an empty shell to be found, rather than the true Church and Body of Christ.

The shifting sands of sectarian Christianity deny the fundamental truth that "the holy scriptures are true, and that God does inspire men and call them to his holy work in this age and generation, as well as in generations of old; thereby showing that he is the same God yesterday, today, and forever". (D&C 20:11-12). These Churches take the attitude that "there is no God today, for the Lord and the Redeemer hath done his work, and he hath given his power unto men". (V. 5). When we no longer look to Him to direct our affairs, Satan moves right into the vacuum that has been created and stirs up our hearts to contention. This is one of the reasons why Joseph Smith was told that the

Churches of his day were abominable in the sight of God. They taught "for doctrines the commandments of men, having a form of godliness, but they (denied) the power thereof". (J.S.H. 1:15)

Emerson declared of the clergy of his day that they were "like peas. I cannot tell them apart. It is the old story again. Once we had wooden chalices and golden priests. Now we have golden chalices and wooden priests". (The Works of Ralph Waldo Emerson, V. 10). Those who should have known better had the responsibility to govern the affairs of the Church by the light of the revealed will of Christ. Instead, they transformed it into a caricature of its former self. Four hundred and fifty years ago, Martin Luther defended his actions by declaring: "I have sought nothing beyond reforming the Church in conformity with the Holy Scriptures. The spiritual powers have been not only corrupted by sin, but absolutely destroyed, so that there is now nothing in them but a depraved reason and a will that is the enemy and opponent of God. I simply say that Christianity has ceased to exist among those who should have preserved it". (E.G. Schwiebert, "Luther and His Times", p. 188).

Machiavelli was even more harsh in his condemnation of the prevailing religious authority. He wrote: "Had the religion of Christianity been preserved according to the ordinances of the Founder, the state and commonwealth of Christendom would have been far more united and happier that they are. Nor can there be a greater proof of its decadence than the fact that the nearer people are to the Roman Church, the head of their religion, the less religious are they. And whoever examines the principles on which that religion is founded, and sees how widely different from those principles its present practice and application are, will judge that her ruin or chastisement is near at hand". (Will Durant, "The Reformation", p. 16). Only when the reality of the Restoration is recognized will the consequences of the Apostasy snap into focus and compel us to action.

We need only superficially study the activities of the architects of the Reformation to discover that their common purpose was to strip away layers of tradition and restore Christianity to its historical values. As one united voice, their efforts were directed toward rediscovering the power of God and revitalizing the Church with His authority. As John Wesley declared: "It does not appear that these extraordinary gifts of the Holy Ghost were common in the Church for more than two or three centuries. We seldom hear of them after that fateful period when the Emperor Constantine called himself a Christian. From this time, they almost totally ceased. The Christians had no more of the Spirit of Christ than the other heathens. This was the real cause why the extraordinary gifts of the Holy Ghost were no longer to be found in the Christian Church, because the Christians were turned heathens again, and had only a dead form left". ("Wesley's Works", Volume 7, sermon 89, p. 26-27).

Nephi foretold that in the Last Days professors of religion would "say unto the people: Hearken unto us, and hear ye our precept". (V. 6). Their invitation is itself evidence of the apostasy. "The secular Christians are now providing diagnosis". (Truman Madsen). The Church of Jesus Christ of Latter-day Saints exists to prescribe therapy.

These same people also deny the existence of modern miracles. (V. 6). But as Rufus Jones observed: "Vital religion cannot be maintained and preserved on the theory that God dealt with our human race only in the far past ages, and that the Bible is the only evidence we have that our God is a living, revealing, communicating God. If God ever spoke, he is still speaking. He is the great I Am, not the great He Was".

In the Last Days, there will be many who will deny the reality of the Judgment, and who "will say: Eat, drink, and be merry, for tomorrow we die; and it shall be well with us". (V. 7). Perhaps this is the ultimate rationalization for justification of unrighteous conduct. When there are no consequences, our desire to do right wavers and our anxiety when doing wrong evaporates. Only when we have the capacity to make choices do we have true moral agency, and that, only when the principle of Justice is understood, and an appreciation of the Plan energizes our behavior.

When individuals are all wrapped up in themselves they make very small packages. Selfishness and selflessness are mutually exclusive qualities. The former destroys even the capacity to feel, while the latter builds character and the capacity to love. Nephi said those who deny the Judgment have not learned to trust, to obey, and ultimately to love their Heavenly Father. When they do, they will take great pleasure in the Law of the Lord. "Blessed (are those) that walketh not in the way of sinners, nor sitteth in the seat of the scornful. But (their) delight is in the law of the Lord, and in His law doth (they) meditate day and night". (Psalms 1:1-2).

Merlin the Magician told young Arthur an interesting story about trusting the omniscience of God. "Sometimes", he said, "life does seem to be unfair. Do you know the story of Elijah and the Rabbi?" he asked Arthur. "This rabbi", said Merlin, "went on a journey with the prophet Elijah. They walked all day, and at nightfall, they came to the humble cottage of a poor man, whose only treasure was a cow. The poor man ran out of his cottage, and his wife ran too, to welcome the strangers for the night, and to offer them all the simple hospitality that they were able to give in straitened circumstances. Elijah and the Rabbi were entertained with plenty of the cow's milk, sustained by homemade bread and butter, and they were put to sleep in the best bed, while their kindly hosts lay down on the stone floor before two cakes of coal in the kitchen fire. But in the morning, the poor man's cow lay dead.

Elijah and the Rabbi walked all the next day, and came that evening to the house of a very wealthy merchant, whose hospitality they craved. The merchant was cold and proud and rich, and all that he would do for the prophet and his companion was to lodge them in a cowshed and feed them on bread and water. In morning's cold light, Elijah thanked the miser very much for his hospitality, and sent for a mason to repair one of his walls, which happened to be falling down, as a return for his kindness.

The Rabbi, unable to keep silent any longer, begged the holy man to explain the meaning of his dealings with human beings. In regard to the poor man who received us so hospitably, replied the prophet, it was decreed that his wife was to die that night, but in reward for his goodness, God took the cow instead. I repaired the wall of the rich miser, explained Elijah, because a chest of gold was concealed near the place, and if the miser had repaired the wall himself, he would have discovered the treasure. Say not, therefore, to the Lord, 'What doest thou.' But say in thy heart, 'Must not the Lord of all the earth do right?' (T.H. White, "The Once and Future King").

Verse 8 describes those who teach of a God of Mercy but who at the same time deny His Justice. "If it so be that we are guilty, God will beat us with a few stripes, and at last we shall be saved in the kingdom of God". Sometimes, people incorrectly think that they can escape the negative consequences of their own actions. For example, in the 1970s, the comedian Groucho Marx sued a journalist for $15 million for breach of contract over obscene remarks he had made "off the record" but that were subsequently published. The plaintiff stated that he became ill when he read the final manuscript and needed medical attention because he was so shocked by its contents.

If we could somehow stand back and "read the manuscript" of our own lives, how would we feel about its contents?. The Book of Mormon states that "out of the books which have been written, and which shall be written, shall this people be judged, for by them shall their works be known unto men". (3 Nephi 27:25). We cannot hide our actions from the Lord, and when we attempt to do so it is in vain. "Yea, and there shall be many which shall teach after this manner, false and vain and foolish doctrines ... and shall seek deep to hide their counsels from the Lord". (V. 9).

Nephi and Amulek both described what happens to those who die without repentance. "Wo unto him that has the law given, yea, that has all the commandments of God, like unto us, and that transgresseth them, and that wasteth the days of his probation, for awful is his state ... They must be damned; for the Lord God, the Holy One of Israel, has spoken it". (2 Nephi 9:27 & 24). "If we do not improve our time while in this life, then cometh the night of darkness wherein there can be no labor performed". (Alma 34:33). Of these verses, Joseph Fielding Smith, Jr. declared: "Do not think that this was said of the world. It is said of members of the Church". (C.R., 4/1969).

In the Last Days, virtually all on the earth will have deserted righteousness: "Yea, they have all gone out of the way; they have become corrupted". (V. 11. See Helaman 6:31 & J.S.H. 219). They will have fallen prey to the three great shortcomings that are found within many of the denominations of Christianity in the Last Days. These are "pride ... and false teachers, and false doctrines". (V. 12). Righteousness, on the other hand, will be defined by the principles of the Restored Gospel found in The Book of Mormon, that "contains a record of a fallen people, and the fulness of the Gospel of Jesus Christ to the Gentiles, and to the Jews also". (D&C 20:9).

Verse 14 addresses the widespread apostasy of the Last Days that even extends to "the humble followers of Christ". Many have committed "whoredoms", typified by idolatry and other forms of unfaithfulness to the true God. (See Commentary Reference to 1 Nephi 14:10). Uninspired leaders have also led some astray. "The ravening wolves are amongst us from our own membership", declared J. Reuben Clark, Jr., "and they, more than any others, are in sheep's clothing, because they wear the habiliments of the priesthood. We should be careful of them". ("Improvement Era", May 1949). Ezra Taft Benson said: "There are some in our midst who are not so much concerned about taking the Gospel into the world, as they are about bringing worldliness into the Gospel". (C.R., 4/1969). On another occasion, he said: "It would be impossible for us to be popular with the world, because then all hell would want to join us".

Four danger signals in The Book of Mormon are identified that should have chastened the Nephites and initiated individual repentance and redemptive course correction. The one external threat, the Lamanites, was used repeatedly by the Lord to chasten the Nephites and to encourage them to repent. Three of the signals, though, were internal. First, was the accumulation of wealth accompanied by the deterioration of basic moral values. Secondly, was the rise of ambitious men to positions of power and influence, in spite of the Lord's counsel that "when the wicked rule, the people mourn". (D&C 98:9). Lastly was the rise of secret societies or combinations. "Whatsoever nation shall uphold such secret combinations, to get power and gain, until they shall spread over the nation, behold, they shall be destroyed". (Ether 8:22). In our day, it is equally important to be alerted to these same signs of danger. (See Commentary Reference to 2 Nephi 26:20-22).

To emphasize the need to repent, in verse 15 we are given one of the few "wo, wo, wo" phrases in scripture. (See 3 Nephi 9:2 & D&C 38:6). In Hebrew, it is impossible to express a statement more strongly than to repeat it three times. "O the wise, and the learned, and the rich, that are puffed up in the pride of their hearts, and all those who preach false doctrines, and all those who commit whoredoms, and pervert the right way of the Lord, wo, wo, wo be unto them". Nephi then left no room to speculate Whom he was quoting here. It was "the Lord God Almighty" who declared that the unrepentant wicked must "be thrust down to hell". (See Commentary Reference to 2 Nephi 18:9).

But because He is also the Redeemer of the world, the Messenger of the Covenant, the Author of Salvation, the Judge of both the quick and the dead, and our Advocate with the Father, his servants Nephi and Isaiah devoted the rest of this chapter to the process by which repentance is made possible. Verse 16 speaks of a people who are "fully ripe in iniquity" and no longer have the capacity or desire for repentance. Fullness and ripeness signify that the process has reached its inevitable conclusion. (See Mormon 2:13-15, & Moroni 9:3-4, 18-22, & Commentary Reference to 2 Nephi 18:16). When we strip ourselves of the protective influence of our Heavenly Father, we leave ourselves vulnerable to the lethal storms sweeping the face of the earth, that have been initiated by the destroyer, and whose suffocating winds threaten to suck the very life sustaining marrow from our bones. (See Proverbs 3:8).

"The great principle of repentance is always available, but for the wicked and rebellious there are serious reservations to this statement. For instance, sin is intensely habit forming, and sometimes moves us to the tragic point of no return. Without repentance, there can be no forgiveness, and without forgiveness all the blessings of eternity hang in jeopardy. As transgressors moves deeper and deeper in their sins ... and the will to change is weakened, it becomes increasingly near hopeless, and they skid down and down until either they do not want to climb back, or they have lost the power to do so". (Spencer W. Kimball, "The Miracle of Forgiveness", p. 117).

In spite of "wickedness and abominations" in the Last Days, the Lord still offers the world unconditional forgiveness if it repents. "If the inhabitants of the earth shall repent of their wickedness and abominations they shall not be destroyed, saith the Lord of Hosts". (V. 17). Because of the Atonement and the sacrifices of repentant souls that consist of broken hearts and contrite spirits, He can extend Mercy without, at the same time, denying the harsh demands of Justice. Those who take advantage of His offer satisfy His ultimate and selfless purpose, which is to bring about our immortality and eternal life. (See 2 Nephi Chapter 9, & Moses 1:39).

Regarding those sins for which we have repented, it is true that we might retain a remembrance of them insofar as they increase our testimonies and make us more stalwart soldiers in the Army of Christ. But we will no longer feel the guilt or suffer the consequences of disobedience that include withdrawal of the Spirit. Repentance, then, can satisfy a two-fold purpose. First, it allows us to be justified by the Spirit, become holy or sanctified, and qualifies us to enter the Presence of the Lord. Secondly, by strengthening our testimonies it is less likely that we will later yield to the temptations of the devil.

The foundation of Nephi's teachings was that when we fall short of obedience to any of God's laws, the Atonement stipulates that we travel the Royal Road of Repentance. This Requires that we act with Responsibility, as we Recognize the Reality of our transgression and view it with Revulsion, and experience Remorse that drives us to our knees. In our heart-felt prayers, we Relate to our Heavenly Father how we feel, in a process of confession that is the most painful example of Revelation. This demands that we Renounce our self-defeating behaviors, make Restitution to injured parties where possible, and then do whatever is necessary, as the Spirit directs us, to submit ourselves to a Refiner's fire that will help us to Re-establish a Reconciliation with heaven and Regain the Rapport with Jesus Christ that had formerly been our hope and our joy. As we Renew our Resolve to Recommit ourselves to walk the covenant path, it will be through the miracle of the grace of Him Who is our Redeemer, that we will Receive a Remission of our sin. Only then, will it become possible to move forward with purpose toward our Reward in heaven.

For the third time, Nephi taught that the world as we know it, or Spiritual Babylon, must crumble. "That great and abominable Church, the whore of all the earth, must tumble to the earth, and great must be the fall thereof". (V. 18, see 1 Nephi 14:15-17, & 1 Nephi 22:13-15, 23). "And the end shall come, and the heaven and the earth shall be consumed and pass away, and there shall be a new heaven and a new earth". (D&C 29:23).

The next few verses confirm that the author of disobedience is a personal being. We are better equipped to deal with his tactics when we are fortified with an understanding of his nature. Satan has always raged "in the hearts of men, and stir(ed) them up to anger against that which is good". (V. 20). But sometimes he pacifies us and lulls us into a false sense of worldly security, that we "will say: All is well in Zion, yea, Zion prospereth, all is well, and thus the devil cheateth (our) souls, and leadeth (us) away carefully down to hell". (V. 21). Very subtly, so as not to alarm us or awaken our senses to the reality of what is really happening, he makes us believe that we are gaining something when we are really losing.

He seems to move us from brilliant, dazzling white, through every shade of grey, to a fathomless black that, by subtraction, is the absence of every good thought, word, deed, or worthy principle. He tells us that "there is no hell; and he saith unto (us) I am no devil, for there is none – and thus he whispereth in (our) ears, until he grasps (us) with his awful chains, from whence there is no deliverance". (V. 22). He flatters us, and makes us believe that he does not exist, that leads us think we are deserving of peace and plenty without earning the reward. But, as C.S. Lewis wrote: "Little people, like you and me, if our prayers are sometimes granted beyond all hope and probability, had better not draw hasty conclusions to our own advantage. If we were stronger, we might be less tenderly treated. If we were braver, we might be sent, with far less help, to defend far more desperate posts in the great battle". ("The World's Last Night", p. 10-11). If we are not careful, we will be "grasped with death, and hell". (V. 23).

The seven woes in verses 24 - 32 recap verses 1 - 23. These correspond to the woes in 2 Nephi 15 / Isaiah 5. When we read them, we should perk up our ears and listen. It is not often in scripture that we are given such specific instruction, especially when the counsel is punctuated by exclamation points! We are especially fortunate to have these scriptures, for they provide us with the tactical and strategic advantage to understand the devil's battle plan in the Last Days. They bless us with clearly defined goals and a plan of action to counter his offensives and meet our objectives.

1). Wo unto those who are "at ease in Zion!" (V. 24). Those who are gliding smoothly and effortlessly through life can be pretty sure that they are going downhill, because progress takes effort as we climb to new heights of achievement.

2). Wo unto those who cry "All is well!" and who are led into a false sense of carnal security and complacency. (V. 25). "The first principle that is the mainspring of all action is the principle of improvement". (Brigham Young, D.B.Y., p. 87). We must constantly strive to do more, to be better, to seek knowledge and wisdom. The Lord has promised: "If thou shalt ask, thou shalt receive revelation upon revelation, knowledge upon knowledge, that thou mayest know the mysteries and peaceable things - that which bringeth joy, that which bringeth life eternal". (D&C 42:61). "For he will give unto the faithful line upon line, precept upon precept". (D&C 98:12).

3). "Wo be unto him that hearkeneth unto the precepts of men, and denieth the power of God, and the gift of the Holy Ghost!" (V. 26). In doing so, we turn our backs on our greatest ally. When we reject the doctrine of revelation, we throw away the key to the storehouse of God's hidden treasure of knowledge, which, in comparison to that of men in the world, is as a mighty ocean compared to a mud puddle. His knowledge gives us the opportunity to enjoy spiritual and priesthood power through the endowment in the temple, which is one of the crowning ordinances of mortality, for it puts us squarely on the covenant path.

4). "Wo be unto him that saith: we have received, and we need no more!" (V. 27). How sorry is the state of those who do not feel the need to receive any more instruction from God! For as the Savior taught: "He that receiveth my law, and doeth it, the same is my disciple". (D&C 41:5). Blessings that follow true discipleship have a performance cost. "Blessed are those which hunger and thirst after righteousness, for they shall be filled. (Matthew 5:6). Receiving the Law of Christ is an ongoing process, and we can never get enough. Without yielding to overindulgence or gluttony, the Lord has nevertheless prepared for us a table overflowing with a delicious and nutritious spiritual feast, and even in the presence of our enemies our heads are anointed with oil and our cups run over. (See Psalms 23:5).

As a society, our challenge is not that we receive too much revelation, but that we receive too little. We also look in all the wrong places. Throughout the Bible, the prophets repeatedly warned Israel against dalliances with magicians, sorcerers, witches, familiar spirits, soothsayers, astrologers, exorcists, and in participating in divinations, enchantments, and other activities that solicit the intervention of evil spirits. Isaiah foresaw our day when he wrote: "Thou art wearied in the multitude of thy counsels. Let now the astrologers, the stargazers, the monthly prognosticators, stand up, and save thee from these things that shall come upon thee. Behold, they shall be as stubble; the fire shall burn them; they shall not deliver themselves from the power of the flame; there shall not be a coal to warm at, nor fire to sit before it". (Isaiah 47:13-14).

On one occasion the Prophet Joseph Smith asked: "Does it remain for a people who never had faith enough to call down one scrap of revelation from heaven, and for all they have now are indebted to the faith of another people who lived hundreds and thousands of years before them, does it remain for them to say how much God has spoken and how much he has not spoken?" (H.C, 11:17-18). Another time, he declared: "We shall at last have to come to this conclusion, whatever we may think of revelation, that without it we can neither know nor understand anything of God, or the devil". The Book of Mormon attests to that fact. By the Spirit, Nephi taught truths about both God and the devil that are vital to our understanding, enabling us to successfully negotiate the minefields of mortality.

Joseph Smith said: "I thank God that I have got this old book (as he held up the Bible) but I thank him more for the gift of the Holy Ghost. I have got the oldest book in the world, but I (also) have the oldest book in my heart, even the gift of the Holy Ghost". ("Teachings", p. 349). The Lord explained the process when He asked: "He that is ordained of me and sent forth to preach the word of truth by the Comforter, in the Spirit of truth, doth he preach it by the Spirit of truth or some other way? And if it be by some other way, it is not of God. And again, he that receiveth the word of truth, doth he receive it by the Spirit of truth or some other way? If it be some other way, it is not of God". (D&C 50:17-20). As Paul taught, the key to Gospel knowledge is personal revelation, and "let him be accursed who preaches any other Gospel". (Galatians 1:8-12). "That which is of God is light; and he that receiveth light, and continueth in God, receiveth more light: and that light groweth brighter and brighter until the perfect day". (D&C 50:24).

5). "Wo unto all those who tremble, and are angry because of the truth of God!" (V. 28). The rebellious "take the truth to be hard". (1 Nephi 16:2). Those whose conduct reflects the values of spiritual Babylon most vigorously resist the principles of the Gospel. On the other hand, Brigham Young, who was a true and faithful disciple, once said: "I never count the cost of anything. I just find out what the Lord wants me to do, and I do it".

6). "Wo unto him that shall say: We have received the word of God, and we need no more of the word of God, for we have enough! For behold, thus saith the Lord God: I will give unto the children of men line upon line, precept upon precept, here a little and there a little; and blessed are those who hearken unto my precepts, and lend an ear unto my counsel, for they shall learn wisdom; for unto him that receiveth I will give more; and from them that shall say, We have enough, from them shall be taken away even that which they have". (V. 29-30). Proverbs counsels us: "Trust in the Lord with all thy heart, and lean not unto thine own understanding". (Proverbs 3:5). But we must also remember that there is no revelation where there is no student, and that perspiration precedes inspiration. With this in mind, Emerson wrote: "Truth comes only to the prepared mind".

We are cursed if we put our trust in man or make flesh our arm or hearken to the precepts of men, because to do so leads us away from the saving principles of the Gospel Plan. (V. 31). The first issue of "The Times and Seasons" contained an editorial to the Elders: "Be careful that you teach not for the word of God the commandments of men, nor the doctrine of men, nor the ordinances of men, for no man's opinion is worth a straw". At the conclusion of a General Conference of the Church, Harold B. Lee counseled the Saints: "If you want to know what the Lord has for this people at the present time, I would admonish you to get and read the discourses that have been delivered at this conference, for what these brethren have spoken by the power of the Holy Ghost is the mind of the Lord, the will of the Lord, the word of the Lord, and the power of God unto salvation". (C.R., 4/1973, see D&C 68:4).

We can emulate the example of the Sons of Mosiah, of whom Alma wrote: "And they had waxed strong in the knowledge of the truth; for they were men of a sound understanding and they had searched the scriptures diligently, that they might know the word of God. But this is not all; they had given themselves to much prayer, and fasting; therefore, they had the spirit of prophecy, and the spirit of revelation, and when they taught, they taught with power and authority of God". (Alma 17:2-3).

In contrast to those who are prepared to receive additional blessings, are those who say: "We have enough", for "from them shall be taken away even that which they have". (V. 30). For example, testimony that the Bible is the word of God has largely been taken away from the Christian world. So has the testimony that Christ is the Son of God. (See 1 Nephi 13:24, & Commentary Reference to 2 Nephi 29:3). In the face of the further light and knowledge manifest in The Book of Mormon and reflected in the testimonies of countless Latter-day Saints, many Christians still deny the power or ability of God to speak to mankind.

7). "Wo unto the Gentiles, saith the Lord God of Hosts!" (V. 32). The sad reality is that although the Lord stretches forth His arm unto them from day to day, they still deny His power to save and instead put their trust in man. In the scriptures, the "arm" is a symbol of power. The "arm of flesh" is the antithesis of the arm of the Lord, and will be a curse to those who rely on it. At the last day, they will find the support of the devil and his angels is in reality a millstone around their necks, and they will be abandoned and left alone to be dragged kicking and screaming "down to hell". (Alma 30:60).

One thing the devil and his followers do not understand is that power and violence are mutually exclusive. Where one is present the other is absent. This is why the arm of the Lord will be a sure source of strength and support, while the arm of flesh will remain unstable, volatile, and subject to senseless outbursts of self-defeating behaviors. (V. 32). God's power stems from love, in contrast to the elusive and transient power that is driven by greed, avarice, lust, and the unrighteous desire for dominion. It is not too difficult to see the fingerprints of Satan, smeared all over the policies, pronouncements, and parties that promote petty, provincial, and personal programs.

The Lord operates according to different guidelines because He knows that we will lose power whenever our priorities are out of order. This is why it has been necessary for Him to clarify His Gospel in dispensations. He wants all His children to have an equally clear perspective so they may focus on the unchanging principles of perfection.

Second Nephi
Chapter 29

This chapter addresses the question: "Why do we need more scripture than the Bible?" God, Who is speaking through His prophet, gives the three-fold answer.

First, His concern is not only for the Jews, but also for all nations. Therefore, He speaks to whomever He will, and in the process of canonization His recorded words become scripture, or Holy Writ. In a more general sense, when His prophets "speak when moved upon by the Holy Ghost", their words also assume "the power of God unto salvation". (D&C 68:4). The Savior taught: "These words are not of men nor of man, but of me; wherefore, ye shall testify they are of me and not of man; For it is my voice which speaketh them unto you; for they are given by my Spirit unto you, and by my power you can read them one to another; and save it were by my power you could not have them; Wherefore, you can testify that you have heard my voice, and know my words". (D&C 18:34-36).

Secondly, additional scriptures satisfy the requirements of the Law of Witnesses, wherein by two or three independent sources shall every word of God be established. The Book of Mormon, Another Testament of Jesus Christ, is an additional and necessary second witness. (V. 8). The Lord told the Pharisees: "It is also written in your law, that the testimony of two men is true". (John 8:17). Whenever Christ or His ordained messengers have ministered on the earth, He has "left not himself without witness". (Acts 14:17). Jeremiah implored the spiritually blind and deaf inhabitants of Jerusalem: "Hear now this, O foolish people, and without understanding; which have eyes, and see not; which have ears, and hear not". (Jeremiah 5:21). "For this people's heart is waxed gross", said the Savior, "and their ears are dull of hearing, and their eyes they have closed; lest at any time they should see with their eyes, and hear with their ears, and should understand with their heart, and should be converted, and I should heal them". (Matthew 13:15).

Most importantly, the scriptures are the foundation on which God will judge the world. "Therefore, having so great witnesses, by them shall the world be judged, even as many as shall hereafter come to a knowledge of this work. And those who receive it in faith, and work righteousness, shall receive a crown of eternal life. But those who harden their hearts in unbelief, and reject it, it shall turn to their own condemnation". (D&C 20:13-14). Of The Book of Mormon, Ezra Taft Benson taught; "Every Latter-day Saint should make the study of (this text) a lifetime pursuit. Otherwise, he is placing his soul in jeopardy and neglecting that which could give spiritual and intellectual unity to his whole life". (C.R,. 4/1975).

In the Last Days, God is performing a work of unprecedented substance, significance, scale, and scope among the people, and He will remember the Abrahamic Covenant made to their forefathers. "I shall proceed to do a marvelous work among them, that I may remember my covenants which I have made unto the children of men, that I may set my hand again the second time to recover my people, which are of the House of Israel". (V. 1). All who qualify by the Lord's standard will once again receive the blessings and ordinances specific to the Covenant. These include baptism, that is a covenant of salvation, the companionship of the Holy Ghost, that is a covenant of justification, the Sacrament, that is a covenant of sanctification, and celestial marriage, that is a covenant of exaltation. These blessings also include an inheritance in the various lands of the Covenant.

Through the power of the Abrahamic Covenant, scattered Israel will be gathered the second time. When this happens, God will also remember the promises made to the Nephites of old, as His words "hiss forth unto the ends of the earth". (V. 2). But at the same time, many will deny the very reality of the Covenant and its necessity, even though Paul taught: "if ye be Christ's, then are ye Abraham's seed, and heirs according to the promise". (Galatians 3:29). Some lack faith in the universal application of the Covenant, while others do not understand how true believers may become Israelites through adoption. Many with closed minds do not realize that God has always had an interest in His scattered people. In response to the bold declaration that The Book of Mormon is another testament of Jesus Christ, some will cry: "A Bible! A Bible! We have got a Bible and there cannot be any more Bible". (V. 3). These are the same people who deny the power of God (2 Nephi 28:26), who do not feel the need to receive more instruction from Him (2 Nephi 28:27), and who recoil from light and truth. (2 Nephi 28:28). As Neal Maxwell observed, such individuals stare with slit-eyed skepticism at the sudden sunburst of spiritual sensitivity that lies before them.

In verse 3 is found the first of only four direct references to the Bible in The Book of Mormon. All are in this chapter, in verses 3, 4, 6, & 10. Understandably, the word "Bible" is not found in the Old Testament or the New Testament, since the scriptures as we know them were not gathered into one book or "Byblos" until hundreds of years after the close of the Apostolic Ministry. We do not know what the Nephite word for "Bible" was, but without explanation Joseph Smith used this familiar term in his translation.

Nephi taught that, in the Last Days, Satan will "rage in the hearts of men, and stir them up to anger against that which is good". (2 Nephi 28:20). For example, in the early nineteenth century, he fought a desperate battle to prevent the receipt, translation, publication, and distribution of The Book of Mormon. Having failed in that, he now attempts to discredit the content of the work. But, as Hugh Nibley has pointed out: "The whole corpus of literature devoted to exposing The Book of Mormon succeeds only in exposing the confusion of its authors". ("Since Cumorah", p. 160). Verse 3 is really an indictment of the spiritual state into which Christianity had fallen by the time of the Restoration, and is an indication that just as the first war waged against Satan was ideological, so too will be the last one.

In verses 4 and 5, the Lord expressed His displeasure with those who have the Bible but fail to give thanks to "the Jews, (His) ancient covenant people", for their role in providing it to the Gentiles. "Do they (not) remember the travails, and the labors, and the pains of the Jews, and their diligence in bringing forth salvation unto the Gentiles?" (V. 4). He made a terrifying statement to those who have "cursed (the Jews), and have hated them, and have not sought to recover them. "Behold", He said, "I will return all these things upon your own heads". (V. 5, see Commentary Reference to 1 Nephi 19:14).

"Thou fool!" exclaimed Nephi, "that shall say: A Bible, we have got a Bible, and we need no more Bible". (V. 6). "Raca" is translated from the Chaldean as "Fool", that means "worthless" or "a wicked and reprobate person". (See Matthew 5:22). Those who believe they need no more Bible, and who hold that ancient and imperfect text as their ultimate authority, deny themselves refreshment from the fountain of living water that flows freely from the Source of all truth. (See Commentary Reference to 2 Nephi 28:30, & the 8th Article of Faith). The Book of Mormon provides "a wealth of doctrine imbedded in a historical matrix that touches on reality in a thousand different ways. On all these points, The Book of Mormon can be tested. Joseph Smith placed it before the world without a single reservation". (Hugh

Nibley, "The World and The Prophets", p. 192-193). Those who summarily dismiss The Book of Mormon and pass judgment on its value without having paid the price to discover its merits and treasures, do so foolishly.

The encouragement to find wisdom and great treasures of knowledge, even hidden treasures, empowers us to find pearls that may not be readily discernible after only a cursory glance. We are putting our security in jeopardy when we summarily dismiss as a thing of no consequence a book that so boldly declares itself to be the word of God. "And all they who receive the oracles of God, let them beware how they hold them lest they are accounted as a light thing, and are brought under condemnation thereby, and stumble and fall when the storms descend, and the winds blow, and the rains descend, and beat upon their houses". (D&C 90:5). Those who have access to the revelations through the prophets, but who do not take them seriously, will not be able to successfully withstand the trials of this life or grow from their experiences.

In verse 7, we find what could be a reference to the party of Hagoth, who around 56 B.C. led a group of Nephites into the "west sea", and who was never heard from again. (See Alma 63:6-8). "I remember those who are upon the isles of the sea". Of course, "the isles of the sea" could also refer to any number of locations where are found expatriate Israelite settlements that were only accessible to the Holy Land when traveling over the sea. (See Commentary References to 1 Nephi 19:10, 15-16, 19, 1 Nephi 22:4-5, 2 Nephi 8:5, & Alma 63:5). In any event, the assurance is given here that God "rules in the heavens above and in the earth beneath" or wherever His children might be. (See Commentary Reference to 1 Nephi 22:4).

The Law of Witnesses establishes God's word, proving that He is I Am, "the same yesterday, today, and forever". (V. 8-9). He speaks according to His "own pleasure". "Wherefore, murmur ye, because that ye shall receive more of my word?" asked the Lord. "Know ye not that the testimony of two nations is a witness unto you that I am God, that I remember one nation like unto another?" (V. 8). God has caused much to be written, in order to prove that He "is the same yesterday, today, and forever". (V. 9). Just because He has spoken to one people, we need not suppose that He cannot speak to others if His work among them has not been completed.

"If you will bring together all the written records of man's past, you will find that the overwhelming mass of materials is religious in nature, and that the primary purpose to which writing has been put through the ages has been for keeping in remembrance God's dealing with His children", wrote Hugh Nibley. "The striking exception to this rule has been the profusion of profane material that has cascaded from the press in the past 200 years like an avalanche. The secular humanists have finally found a forum to present their case in the print media". ("The World and The Prophets", p. 189). It is no wonder that Jacob cautioned that it is good to be learned, but only if we hearken unto the counsels of God. (2 Nephi 9:29).

God commands everyone, wherever they might live, to write the words that He speaks to them. "Because that I have spoken one word, ye need not suppose that I cannot speak another; for my work is not yet finished ... Wherefore, because that ye have a Bible ye need not suppose that it contains all my words; neither need ye suppose that I have not cause more to be written. For I command all men, both in the east and in the west, and in the north, and in the south, and in the islands of the sea, that they shall write the words which I speak unto them; for out of the books which shall be written I will judge the world, every man according to their works, according to that which is written". (V. 9-11).

"The scriptures overcome time, and are the common meeting ground of all the prophets. Here they all speak a common tongue, and all bear witness to each other. The prophets constantly and characteristically quote each other. The Book of Mormon was meant as a sign and a wonder to an unbelieving world. It was meant to give instruction to those who should believe in the Last Days. It is a book for hard times and for great times". (Hugh Nibley, "The World and The Prophets", p. 190 & 195). It is a book that has the power to focus the thoughts of its readers on the issues of real substance that should occupy our attention, but that often do not because worldly concerns get in the way.

The language of The Book of Mormon is simple, yet lofty, and can carry us to new heights and solid plateaus of understanding. It is unpretentious, yet momentous, as it grapples with the significant issues of our time. It is clear and concise, yet expansive, and far-reaching in its content. The English language translation of The Book of Mormon sometimes quotes the Bible, and when it does so, it is in the vernacular of the English of the King James Translation that would be familiar to Joseph Smith's contemporaries.

Verse 12 clearly teaches that The Book of Mormon is a second witness of Jesus Christ, and the record of the Lost Ten Tribes is a third witness, not to mention the Doctrine & Covenants and the Pearl of Great Price. There may yet be additional scripture of which we are unaware that also testifies of Christ. "For behold, I shall speak unto the Jews, and they shall write it; and I shall also speak unto the Nephites, and they shall write it; and I shall also speak unto the other tribes of the House of Israel, which I have led away, and they shall write it; and I shall also speak unto all nations of the earth, and they shall write it". (See Commentary Reference to 2 Nephi 20:20).

Verse 13 is structured as a chiasm that emphasizes the promise that the Covenant Children of Israel, no matter where they are, will ultimately share their sacred scriptures with each other. "And it shall come to pass that the Jews shall have the words of the Nephites, and the Nephites shall have the words of the Jews; and the Nephites and the Jews shall have the words of the lost tribes of Israel; and the lost tribes of Israel shall have the words of the Nephites and the Jews". (See 1 Nephi 17:28).

This chapter begins and ends with God's declared commitment to Israel, whom He specifically addressed as His Covenant "people" in five of its 14 verses. Ultimately, as His people are gathered into one unified congregation of the faithful, His words will be incorporated into one body of scripture. "And I will show unto them that fight against my word and against my people, who are of the House of Israel, that I am God, and that I covenanted with Abraham that I would remember his seed forever". (V. 14). Just how God will show the rebellious that He is Almighty will be, for them, a terrible demonstration of His awesome power.

Second Nephi
Chapter 30

Chapter 30 opens with the declaration that righteousness is more important than lineage: "As many of the Gentiles as will repent are the covenant people of the Lord; and as many of the Jews as will not repent shall be cast off; for the Lord covenanteth with none save it be with them that repent and believe in his Son, who is the Holy One of Israel". (V. 2, see Commentary References to 1 Nephi 19:19, 1 Nephi 21:10 & 23, Jacob 5:3-4 & 9, & Jacob 5:67). Nephi wanted to emphasize to his people that the converted Gentiles would be numbered among the Covenant People of the Lord. This may have been as difficult for Nephi to teach his people as it was for Paul to teach the Jewish Christians of his day. Sometimes, it even seems difficult for members of The Church of Jesus Christ of Latter-day Saints to understand that the Gospel of Jesus Christ is to be shared with the world, and that sinners in particular are welcome in the congregations of the Saints.

The Covenant did not originate with Father Abraham. He received the Covenant of Salvation, or baptism, and then the Higher Priesthood and the Covenant of Exaltation, or Celestial Marriage, as had Adam and his righteous posterity. As Abraham wrote: "And, finding there was greater happiness and peace and rest for me, I sought for the blessings of the fathers, and the right whereunto I should be ordained to administer the same; having been myself a follower of righteousness, desiring also to be one who possessed great knowledge, and to be a greater follower of righteousness, and to possess a greater knowledge, and to be a father of many nations, a prince of peace, and desiring to receive instructions, and to keep the commandments of God, I became a rightful heir, and High Priest, holding the right belonging to the fathers. It was conferred upon me from the fathers; it came down from the fathers, from the beginning of time, yea, even from the beginning, or before the foundation of the earth, down to the present time". (Abraham 1:1-2).

Abraham was given the unique promise, however, that through his seed, all the nations of the earth should be blessed. "Blood Israel", or those of the lineage of Abraham, was thus able to bless others by offering them the priesthood ordinances of salvation, that they might also become "Covenant Israel", or those who, by adoption, enjoy the blessings promised to Abraham. Because of the Restoration, in the Last Days it is the Gentiles, or Covenant Israel, who shall be empowered to carry the Gospel to the remnant of Lehi. (See Commentary References to 1 Nephi 19:19, 2 Nephi 30:2, Jacob 5:3-4 & 9, & Jacob 5:67).

One might conclude that Nephi was suggesting in verse 4 that the descendants of Lehi were of the tribe of Judah: "And then shall the remnant of our seed know concerning us, how that we came out from Jerusalem, and that they are descendants of the Jews". But when he wrote this, he was speaking in a cultural and not a literal sense. In 2 Nephi 33:8, he used the term "Jew" in the same generic way, meaning "them from whence I came". We know that Lehi was of the tribe of Manasseh through the lineage of Joseph, and was not of the tribe of Judah. (See 1 Nephi 5:14). He was only a "Jew" in the societal sense that he was a citizen of the Kingdom of Judah.

On the other hand, we also know that later in Book of Mormon history, a minority of the Nephites under Mosiah joined with the people of Zarahemla, who had left Jerusalem with Mulek, who was a son of King Zedekiah. These people, commonly referred to as "Mulekites" by students of The Book of Mormon (although that term does not appear in the text), were of Judah. Therefore, the blood of Judah ran prominently in the veins of the Nephites after this merger, sometime between 279 B.C. and 130 B.C. (See Omni 1:19 & Commentary Reference to Jacob 3:4).

In verse 5, Nephi used the term "the Gospel of Jesus Christ" for the first time. This expression is found 40 more times in The Book of Mormon and 101 times in the New Testament. Consequently, this type of word usage tricks the casual reader into thinking that The Book of Mormon is a text contemporary with the New Testament, when actually much of it predates the ministry of Christ by hundreds or thousands of years.

One of the signs of the times in the Last Days is that the Gospel will be preached to the remnant of the seed of Lehi, who are commonly identified as "Lamanites". Some Native American peoples may have "Lamanite" blood, but certainly not all do. As Hugh Nibley wrote: "The Book of Mormon is not a history of the Lost Ten Tribes. It is not a history of the Indians. It does not describe or designate any known ancient people, civilization, or individual in the Western Hemisphere, nor does it designate any recognized place, city, or territory in the New World. Even Cumorah receives only limited recognition and (then) only by Latter-day Saints". ("Since Cumorah", p. 161).

It is likely that there are influences of many cultures among the peoples of the New World. Today, whoever the remnant of the seed of Lehi actually is, the scriptures tell us that they will be taught the Gospel "and they shall be restored to the knowledge of Jesus Christ, which was had among their fathers". (V. 5). In October 1960 General Conference, Spencer W. Kimball confirmed: "The day of the Lamanites is here!" As the curtain rises in the Last Days and the children of Israel find themselves on center stage, the signs of the times will be revealed, unfolding a drama of all-encompassing proportion.

Then shall "their scales of darkness begin to fall from their eyes", and "they shall be a pure and a delightsome people". (V. 6). Before the 1978 revision of the English language scriptures, this verse was rendered "white" as opposed to "pure", to emphasize, by contrast, the concept of "spiritual blackness". (See Commentary Reference to 2 Nephi 5:21). In any event, the quality of darkness seems to apply more to the spiritual condition of the Lamanites than to any physical characteristic they may have had.

In verse 7, we learn that, in the Last Days, the Jews shall also "begin to believe in Christ" and shall "begin to gather" in the land of Israel. Bruce R. McConkie felt that "the great conversion of the Jews will follow the Second Coming", when they shall join His Church in significant numbers. But the harvest has already begun. Missionaries have commenced the work of gathering the Covenant People of the Lord "among all nations, kindreds, tongues, and people". (V. 8). In 2021, The Book of Mormon had been translated into 115 languages, and there were over 62,000 missionaries serving in 410 missions in over 160 countries throughout the world. By most accounts, there are 195 nations on earth, so the Church has a way to go, although great progress is being made. It is unlikely, however, that the Gospel will be preached any time soon in at least one of those independent countries, namely The Vatican City! Still, miracles never cease.

The Lord's work among all nations includes technological development as well, that will aid in the process of teaching the Gospel and in administering the ordinances of salvation throughout the world. As these remarkable innovations in science and industry invoke wonder and amazement, we should remember from Whom they have come and for what purpose they have been given.

Verse 9 is a quotation of 2 Nephi 21:4. "And with righteousness shall the Lord God judge the poor, and reprove with equity for the meek of the earth. And he shall smite the earth with the rod of his mouth; and with the breath of his lips shall he slay the wicked". The "rod" is a symbol of the power by which He will engage the forces of spiritual Babylon in mortal combat. During the war in heaven, the battle lines were drawn according to contrasting ideologies and the weapons used were words that articulated opposing positions. It is much the same today, when a priesthood army of missionaries will smite the earth with the power of the word and figuratively slay the wicked. They will follow the example of Alma, of whom Mormon reported that his "preaching of the word had a great tendency to lead the people to do that which was just - yea, it had more powerful effect upon the minds of the people than the sword, or anything else". (Alma 31:5).

In the Last Days, the combatants are once again forming into diametrically opposed camps with increasingly polarized ideologies. "For the time speedily cometh that the Lord God shall cause a great division among the people". (V. 10, see Commentary Reference to 1 Nephi 22:19). We should remember how enticingly Satan beckons us with his soothing words. With deceit and deception, he will try to ensnare us. But the word of God is "quick" or living in a biblical sense. It is "powerful" or a source of life and energy, and "sharper than a two-edged sword, to the dividing asunder of both joints and marrow" or penetrating to the innermost parts of man. "Therefore, give heed unto (his) words". (D&C 6:2)

As he launched into an extensive recitation of the words of his favorite prophet, Nephi undoubtedly quoted verses 11-15 from The Plates of Brass. (See Isaiah 11:4-9). Isaiah described the millennial Earth, when Satan will be bound for a thousand years, Israel will be gathered, the Ten Tribes will return, Zion will be established, and Christ will come to reign personally upon the earth, when it will be renewed to receive its paradisiacal glory. (10th Article of Faith).

Verses 16-18 suggest a great outpouring of the Spirit, when "there is nothing which is secret, save it shall be revealed; there is no work of darkness save it shall be made manifest in the light; and there is nothing which is sealed upon the earth save it shall be loosed. (V. 17). In that millennial day, "Satan shall have power over the hearts of the children of men no more, for a long time". (V. 18). Of these verses, Spencer W. Kimball declared: "Through our faithfulness, all that God has promised will be fulfilled". (C.R., 4/1980).

"As many of the Gentiles as will
repent (shall become) the covenant people of the Lord; and
as many of the Jews as will not repent shall be cast off; for the
Lord covenanteth with none save it be with them that repent and
believe in his Son, who is the Holy One of Israel." "For the Lord will
have mercy on Jacob, and will yet choose Israel, and set them in
their own land: and the strangers shall be joined with them,
and they shall cleave to the house of Jacob. And the people
shall take them and bring them to their place; yea,
from far unto the ends of the earth; and they
shall return to their lands of promise."
(2 Nephi 30:2 & 24:1-2; see
Isaiah 14:1-2).

Second Nephi
Chapter 31

Chapters 31-33 represent the fulfilment of Nephi's desire to write only those things that were pleasing to God and to those who were not of the world. "For the fulness of mine intent", he wrote, "is that I may persuade men to come unto the God of Abraham, and the God of Isaac, and the God of Jacob, and be saved". (1 Nephi 6:4). We wonder, here, about the significance of the thrice-repeated name of God. In any event, these final three chapters that comprise Nephi's last recorded sermon appropriately concern what he called "the doctrine of Christ". (V. 2).

He wrote that he could record "but a few things". (V. 1). In fact, the prophecies in Chapters 25-33 span a time of approximately 14 years. (V. 1). But, as Nephi had explained early in his record: "It mattereth not to me that I am particular to give a full account of all the things of my father, for they cannot be written upon these plates, for I desire the room that I may write of the things of God". (1 Nephi 6:3).

It is likely that their straitened circumstances made it even more difficult to engrave upon plates. Even in the best of times, the process would have been frustrating for the Nephite record keepers. Jacob wrote somewhat characteristically: "And I cannot write but a little of my words, because of the difficulty of engraving our words upon plates". (Jacob 4:1, see Ether 12:24-25, & 40). What few things Nephi did write concerned the doctrine of Christ. Verses 2 & 3 suggests that we are in for a very special treat: "Wherefore, I shall speak unto you plainly, according to the plainness of my prophesying. For my soul delighteth in plainness; for after this manner doth the Lord God work among the children of men. For the Lord God giveth light unto the understanding; for he speaketh unto men according to their language, unto their understanding". (V. 2). Rarely in scripture do we find an explanation describing such clarity or focus.

Simply stated, the doctrine taught by Nephi was that if we have faith in Jesus Christ, and truly repent of our sins and enter into a baptismal covenant with the Lord, we will receive the Holy Ghost Who will then direct our path, showing us the things we must do to achieve salvation. (See 3 Nephi 11:31-40, 27:8-22, & Moses 6:48-68). To facilitate our spiritual transformation, the capabilities of all three members of the Godhead are energized in our behalf. Once again, the scriptures impress us with the metaphysical power of "three".

The doctrine of Christ speaks to our spirits, for every Gospel principle carries its own witness that it is true. "The Lord giveth light unto the understanding," taught Nephi, "for he speaketh unto men according to their language, unto their understanding". (V. 3). The language of the spirit is universal, and illuminates our minds with spiritual fluency and familiarity that open up vistas of eternal proportion.

It had been fifty years since Nephi had delivered a sermon about the mission of John the Baptist, and so it is interesting that he would now say: "I would that ye should remember that I have spoken unto you concerning the prophet which the Lord showed unto me, that should baptize the Lamb of God, which should take away the sins of the world". (V. 4, see 1 Nephi 10:9). Either Nephi had a razor-sharp memory and expected his people to have the same mental faculties, or he had returned to that same theme over the years, keeping the anticipation of the mission of John the Baptist fresh in their memories.

After a lifetime of reflection, he now emphasized that the Lord would "be baptized by water to fulfil all righteousness", which is to obey every commandment and to perform every ordinance necessary for us to attain eternal life. (V. 5). Nephi did not make any special mention regarding the manner of baptism among his people, but they clearly understood that baptism had always been the standard for the Children of the Covenant. Five hundred years later, when John the Baptist went into the wilderness of Judea preaching repentance and baptism, his actions didn't arouse any curiosity among the people, as would have been the case if He had been introducing some new doctrine or strange practice. The Jews of that day understood it as an essential Gospel ordinance, and so it was. Even the Jewish Encyclopedia states: "John stood forth in the spirit of the prophets of old to preach his baptism of repentance symbolized by cleansing with water". (2:499).

"The fact that baptism was practiced in ancient Israel might help to explain why the Savior was not criticized by the orthodox Jews when He was baptized. The Pharisees, who were quick to (rebuke) Him whenever He did anything contrary to their law, did not raise a single word of criticism concerning the baptism of Jesus Christ." (Robert L. Millet, et. al., "Commentary on The Book of Mormon", p. 155). Interestingly, the traditional place of baptism on the River Jordan is even today called "El Maghtas", which is Arabic, meaning "the place of immersion". It is the lowest place on earth that has fresh, running water, symbolizing the Savior's desire to descend beneath us all, that He might lift us up to greater heights by obedience to His doctrine.

As early as 914 B.C., during the prophet Elijah's ministry in Israel, there was biblical evidence of baptism. Can it be that "John's baptism was the counterpart of Elijah's novel rite on Mt. Carmel? (See 1 Kings 18:19-40). It may be recalled that when Elijah was testing the gods of Baal against the power of Jehovah, he covered the sacrifice on the altar with water and then called down fire from heaven to consume it. (Is there) a similarity between this rite and the Gospel's ordinances of baptism by water and by the Spirit? (Is it possible) that Elijah was familiar with baptism?" ("Christ's Eternal Gospel", p. 118, see Commentary Reference to 2 Nephi Chapter 11).

There is also evidence of pre-Christian baptism at Qumran. In the "Manual of Discipline" from the "Serek Scroll" that was their equivalent of our "General Handbook of Instructions", we read: "His sin is forgiven him, and in the humility of his soul he is for all the laws of God; his flesh is cleansed, shining bright in the waters of purification, even in the waters of baptism, and he shall be given a new name in due time to walk perfect in all the ways of God".

It is obvious, then, that baptism is an ordinance of great antiquity, and one requiring humility and obedience before God the Father. (V. 7). "The Lamb of God ... fulfil(ed) all righteousness in being baptized by water". (V. 6). Howard W. Hunter declared that "Jesus entered into all the saving ordinances of the Melchizedek Priesthood", and baptism is the gate through which we all must pass in order to qualify for participation. (Los Angeles Area Conference Address, 1980).

Following baptism by water, the next of these ordinances is receipt of the Holy Ghost through the baptism of fire and of the Spirit. (See v. 17, & Moses 6:56). Water baptism is only half a baptism if not followed by laying on of hands to receive the Holy Ghost by those holding the appropriate priesthood authority. In this, the Savior also showed the way, for "after he was baptized with water, the Holy Ghost descended upon him in the form of a dove". (V. 8). Joseph Smith taught: "The sign of the dove is an emblem or token of truth and innocence". ("Teachings", p. 276).

The Savior's example demonstrated that entrance into the Church and Kingdom is strait, or narrowly defined. There need be no discussion or variance of opinion regarding the prescribed way, for He set the pattern when He "said unto the children of men: Follow thou me". (V. 10). Among the Nephites, it is possible that these teachings were a retrenchment or reestablishment of ordinances that had not been recently practiced by them. If this were the case, the focus of this particular aspect of the ministry of Nephi would be similar to that of the Latter-day prophets who have specifically invited less active members of the Church to return to the fold in full fellowship.

To a later Nephite society, the Savior taught these principles with unmistakable clarity. "And he said unto them: On this wise shall ye baptize". (3 Nephi 11:22). There followed explicit instruction to the priesthood leaders of the Nephite Church regarding the manner of baptism that underscored the vital importance of His doctrine being clearly understood. "Neither shall there be disputations among you concerning the points of my doctrine", He cautioned. (3 Nephi 11:28). As Nephi asked: "Wherefore, my beloved brethren, can we follow Jesus save we shall be willing to keep the commandments of the Father? And the Father said: Repent ye, repent ye, and be baptized in the name of my Beloved Son". (V. 10 & 11). Then Nephi taught the principle of the second baptism or receipt of the Holy Ghost. For the voice of the Son had come unto him, saying: "He that is baptized in my name, to him will the Father give the Holy Ghost". (V. 12, see Mosiah 27:4-26, 3 Nephi 12:1, & 27:19-21).

Baptism, then, serves a number of purposes. Among them are the following: 1) It allows us to follow the example of the Savior, 2) It gives us the opportunity to be born again so that we may experience a new life in Jesus Christ, 3) It allows us to receive a remission of sins, 4) It enables us to gain admission to the Lord's Church, 5) It gives us access to personal sanctification through the Holy Ghost, and 6) It is outwardly symbolic as the gateway to the Celestial Kingdom of God. (See also "One Hundred and One Reasons Why We Are Baptized – The First Principles and Ordinances Series: Volume 3: Baptism").

While teaching the simple truths concerning baptism and the Holy Ghost, verses 7-12 also clearly differentiate the Father, the Son, and the Holy Ghost. "He humbleth himself before the Father, and witnesseth unto the Father that he would be obedient unto him in keeping his commandments. Wherefore, after he was baptized with water the Holy Ghost descended upon him in the form of a dove". (V. 7-8). "And the Father said: Repent ye, repent ye, and be baptized in the name of my Beloved Son. And also, the voice of the Son came unto me, saying: He that is baptized in my name, to him will the Father give the Holy Ghost, like unto me". (V. 11-12). Jesus Christ reiterated the same truths to the Nephite Church during his brief ministry in the Americas, when He said: "And after this manner shall ye baptize in my name; for behold, verily I say unto you, that the Father, and the Son, and the Holy Ghost are one; and I am in the Father, and the Father in me and the Father and I are one". (3 Nephi 11:27, see Mosiah 15:4, & Alma 11:44).

The members of the Godhead are one in purpose, and are completely unified. (See 3 Nephi 11:27). They are "One Eternal God." (See Mosiah 15:4 & Alma 11:44). There is a physical and spiritual rapport between the Father and the Son, and between them and true believers. Through this rapport, that is for us effected by the Holy Ghost, we become "one" in the spiritual sense. The unity of the Godhead expressed by Nephi is a type of completeness. The mind of any one member is the mind of the others. "Seeing, as each of Them does with the eye of perfection, they see and understand alike, guided by the same principles of unerring justice and equity. (See James E. Talmage, "Articles of Faith," p. 41).

This principle, so beautifully illustrated in many different teaching moments throughout the scriptures, stands in bold contrast to the incomprehensible doctrine of the Trinity that was formulated by a Church council hundreds of years after the inspired Apostolic Ministry ended. Of that doctrine, Thomas Jefferson wrote: "Three are one and one is three, and yet the one is not three, and the three are not one. This constitutes the craft, the power and profit of the priests. Sweep away their gossamer fabric of factious religion, and they would catch no more flies." (Milton Backman, "American Religions and The Rise of Mormonism," p. 202).

Verse 13 tells why we should be baptized and summarizes verses 4-12. "Wherefore, my beloved brethren, I know that if ye shall follow the Son, with full purpose of heart, acting no hypocrisy and no deception before God, but with real intent, repenting of your sins, witnessing unto the Father that ye are willing to take upon you the name of Christ, by baptism - yea, by following your Lord and your Savior down into the water, according to his word, behold, then shall ye receive the Holy Ghost; yea, then cometh the baptism of fire and of the Holy Ghost; and then can ye speak with the tongue of angels, and shout praises unto the Holy One of Israel".

The next few verses outline The Plan of Salvation, culminating in verse 20 that explains how we can gain eternal life. We cannot be hypocritical when we follow the Savior. The word "hypocrite" is from the Greek, where it describes the mask used by actors. A hypocrite, then, is someone who professes to be one thing, when actually it is a charade. There is an entirely different person behind the mask. (See D&C 121:37, & 41-42).

Verse 14 reiterates the concept of the two baptisms previously discussed. "After ye have repented of your sins, and witnessed unto the Father that ye are willing to keep my commandments, by the baptism of water (ye shall receive) the baptism of fire and of the Holy Ghost". (See Mosiah 18:9, & Alma 5:14 & 26). Joseph Smith said: "You might as well baptize a bag of sand as a man, if not done in view of the remission of sins and getting the Holy Ghost. Baptism by water is but half a baptism, and is good for nothing without the other half, that is, baptism of the Holy Ghost". ("Teachings", p. 314).

In verse 15, Nephi added the testimony of the Father to his words: "And I heard a voice from the Father, saying: Yea, the words of my Beloved are true and faithful. He that endureth to the end, the same shall be saved". It is not often in the scriptures that the solemn testimony of the Father is recorded, but baptism is such an important ordinance of the Gospel and is so central to the doctrine of Christ that it merits such attention. Just so, the same holy witness attended the baptism of Jesus at Jordan. (See Matthew 3:17).

The atoning blood of Jesus Christ cleanses, while the presence of the Holy Ghost purges the effects of sin. (See Moses 6:60). "For the gate by which ye should enter is repentance and baptism by water; and then cometh a remission of your sins by fire and by the Holy Ghost". (V. 17). This puts us on the "strait and narrow path which leads to eternal life". (V. 18).

Once on the path, we must "press forward" with complete dedication and "steadfastness" or confidence and a firm determination in Christ, "having a perfect brightness of hope" or perfect faith, and "a love of God and of all men" or charity. If we do this, "feasting upon the word of Christ" or receiving strength and nourishment from the scriptures, and endures to the end in righteousness, we "shall have eternal life" which is the greatest gift that God can bestow. (V. 20). This is our on-going opportunity and responsibility.

This doctrine is properly the Gospel of the Father as well as of the Son and the Holy Ghost because these three distinct members of the Godhead are One in complete unity, love, and purpose. Nephi taught in this chapter how all Three work together to craft the opportunity for us to have immortality and eternal life. "For by the water ye keep the commandment; by the Spirit ye are justified, and by the blood ye are sanctified". (Moses 6:60).

Christ is the Author of Salvation (Hebrews 5:9), but it was Heavenly Father Who first introduced His Plan to His spirit children. (2 Nephi 9:13). By the spirit of revelation, the Holy Ghost reconfirms both the divinity of Jesus Christ and the majesty of the Father's Plan. (D&C 8:2-3). In perfect harmony, the three members of The Godhead work to promote the doctrine of Christ among men with one shared goal: to bring the children of God to the waters of baptism. In this way, the wheels are set in motion to bring to pass our immortality and eternal life.

As that gate leading to the Celestial Kingdom swings open to admit the penitent, the words of King Benjamin ring in our ears: "And now, because of the covenant which ye have made ye shall be called the children of Christ, his sons, and his daughters; for behold, this day he hath spiritually begotten you; for ye say that your hearts are changed through faith in his name; Therefore, ye are born of him and have become his sons and his daughters". (Mosiah 5:7).

So critically important to our eternal welfare is the decision to enter the waters of baptism, that Benjamin further counseled: "And under this head ye are made free, and there is no other head whereby ye can be made free. There is no other name given whereby salvation cometh; therefore, I would that ye should take upon you the name of Christ, all you that have entered into the covenant with God that ye should be obedient unto the end of your lives". (Mosiah 5:8).

Nephi stated this doctrine in simple language that makes misinterpretation difficult. "This is the way, and there is none other way nor name given under heaven whereby man can be saved in the kingdom of God. And now, behold, this is the doctrine of Christ, and the only and true doctrine of the Father, and of the Son, and of the Holy Ghost, which is one God, without end". (V. 21, see D&C 20:28). The power of three cannot be over-emphasized.

"Then are ye in this strait
and narrow path which leads to
eternal life; yea, ye have entered in
by the gate; ye have done according to
the commandments of the Father and the
Son, and ye have received the Holy Ghost,
which witnesses of the Father and the Son,
unto the fulfilling of the promise which
he hath made, that if ye entered in
by the way, ye should receive."
(2 Nephi 31:17-18).

Second Nephi
Chapter 32

The nine verses in this chapter are a guide to help us to live in the world without being tainted by it, by relating the doctrine of Christ both symbolically and literally to baptism and receiving the Holy Ghost. In doing this, Nephi illustrated that these ordinances are not only essential to salvation, but they also have the power to create a celestial environment within a telestial world. As the Savior revealed: "Abundance is multiplied unto (the Saints) through the manifestations of the Spirit". (D&C 70:13). "'Happiness is the object and design of our existence and will be the end thereof, if we follow the path that leads to it. And this path is virtue, uprightness, faithfulness, holiness, and keeping all the commandments of God. In obedience there is joy and peace ... and as God has designed our happiness ... He never has, He never will, give a commandment to His people that is not calculated in its nature to promote that happiness which He has designed." (History of the Church, 5:134-135, see Commentary Reference to 2 Nephi 2:13).

Nephi asked his brethren if there was any question in their minds regarding what they should do following baptism. "I suppose that ye ponder somewhat in your hearts concerning that which ye should do after ye have entered in by the way". (V. 1). King Benjamin also anticipated the need of his brethren for Gospel instruction following their own token of commitment represented by baptism. Consequently, he "appointed priests to teach the people, that thereby they might hear and know the commandments of God, and to stir them up in remembrance of the oath which they had made". (Mosiah 6:3).

In our own day, it is the duty of the priest to "preach, teach, expound, exhort, and baptize, and administer the sacrament. And visit the house of each member, and exhort them to pray vocally and in secret and attend to all family duties". (D&C 20:46-47). The teachers are to "watch over the Church always, and be with and strengthen them; And see that there is no iniquity in the Church, neither hardness with each other, neither lying, backbiting, nor evil speaking; And see that the Church meet together often, and also see that all the members do their duty". (D&C 20:53-55). "And (the teacher) is to be assisted always, in all his duties in the Church, by the deacons, if occasion requires". (D&C 20:57). The welfare of the Church is always in the capable hands of the priesthood.

Today, the example of Jesus Christ stands out above all others. When our lives are patterned after His, we are on a solid footing. He told the Nephite Saints in Zarahemla: "Ye know the things that ye must do in my Church; for the works which ye have seen me do that shall ye also do". (3 Nephi 27:21). The New Testament Gospels and 3 Nephi in The Book of Mormon are guides of inestimable value because they vividly record the teachings of the Savior and document His example as they testify of His divinity. As He declared to His Nephite disciples: "Therefore, I would that ye should be perfect even as I, or your Father who is in heaven is perfect". (3 Nephi 12:48). In his abridgment, Mormon did not capriciously dangle that brass ring before us. He did it deliberately and thoughtfully, because he understood the implications should we reach for it. In fact, Moroni may have had in mind the Savior's confidence in our potential when he wrote at the end of his own record: "Come unto Christ, and be perfected in him, and deny yourselves of all ungodliness; and if ye shall deny yourselves of all ungodliness, and love God with all your might, mind and strength, then is his grace sufficient for you, that by his grace ye may be perfect in Christ". (Moroni 10:32).

Whether we receive the doctrine of Christ in biblical teachings, Book of Mormon instruction, commandments in the Doctrine & Covenants, exhortation from the pages of The Pearl of Great Price, from pulpits aflame with faith, or from any combination of the above, it is the same. The Savior "expounded all the scriptures in one" when He taught the Nephite Saints. (3 Nephi 23:14). It is the practice of the Church in the Latter-days to do the same.

It always comes down to key doctrine that is accompanied by an invitation to action and a description of anticipated blessings that flow from obedience. As his descendant Nephi wrote in the closing verse of 3 Nephi: "Turn, all ye Gentiles, from your wicked ways; and repent of your evil doings, of your lyings and deceivings, and of your whoredoms, and of your secret abominations, and your idolatries, and of your murders, and your priestcrafts, and your envyings, and your strifes, and from all your wickedness and abominations, and come unto me, and be baptized in my name, that ye may receive a remission of your sins, and be filled with the Holy Ghost, that ye may be numbered with my people who are of the House of Israel". (3 Nephi 30:2, see 3 Nephi 27:33).

If we ponder the mysteries of life, feast upon the word of Christ, and ask in faith, the promised blessing is spiritual guidance. (V. 1, 3, & 4). Nephi had taught his brethren this doctrine concerning the Holy Ghost, and declared that the Spirit would reveal to them all things necessary for their salvation. (V. 5).

Following his own baptism, Lorenzo Snow described his endowment of the Spirit: "It was a tangible immersion in the heavenly principle or element, the Holy Ghost", he said, "and even more real and physical in its effects upon every part of my system than the immersion by water; dispelling forever, so long as reason and memory last, all possibility of doubt or fear in relation to the fact ... that the Babe of Bethlehem is truly the Son of God; also the fact that He is now being revealed to the children of men, and communicating knowledge, the same as in the Apostolic times". ("Biographical and Family Records of Lorenzo R. Snow").

One who is filled with the Holy Ghost can speak with the "tongue of angels". (V. 2). The scriptures teach that angels may be any of the following: 1) pre-earth existent spirits (Revelation 12:7, D&C 130:5), 2) translated beings (J.S.T. Genesis 14:26-36, "Teachings", p. 170), 3) spirits of just men made perfect, awaiting the resurrection (D&C 76:66-69), 4) resurrected beings (D&C 129), or 5) righteous mortal men (Genesis 19, J.S.T. Genesis 19). All of the above speak by the power of the Holy Ghost. (V. 3). Faithful members of The Church of Jesus Christ of Latter-day Saints often speak "with the tongue of angels" as they teach, preach, expound, and exhort one another, sharing their feelings about Gospel principles. (See D&C 20:46).

Nephi then declared: "This is the doctrine of Christ" concerning baptism and the Holy Ghost, "and there will be no more doctrine given until after he shall manifest himself unto you in the flesh". (V. 6). Nephi had clearly explained these doctrines to his people, and there would be no need for additional doctrine on the subject until the post-mortal ministry of Christ, when He would teach by personal example, restore the authority of the Aaronic Priesthood, and institute the Sacrament as an ordinance of the Gospel to be performed in remembrance of Him. (See 3 Nephi 11:22 & 28, & 27:13-14). Even in the Holy Land, the Sacrament was not introduced until the close of Christ's mortal ministry, just before Calvary; nor was it practiced among the Nephites until after He had taught them many other important basic principles as a foundation for their faith.

The Spirit constrained Nephi from saying more, because of "the unbelief, and the wickedness, and the ignorance, and the stiffneckedness of men, (who would) not search knowledge" even when it was spelled out for them as clearly as it could be. (V. 7). When the power of the Gospel is neutralized by unbelief and faithlessness, or when the Law of the Lord is not written in the hearts of men, it cannot transform lives, nor can it transcend the telestial tendencies of profane existence. Whether Nephi was constrained because of the self-defeating behaviors of his own people or because he foresaw these traits in the character of those living in the Last Days is unclear.

From his confinement in Liberty Jail, Joseph Smith pleaded with the Saints to embrace the doctrine of Christ: "Let thy bowels also be full of charity towards all men, and to the household of faith", he urged them, "and let virtue garnish thy thoughts unceasingly; then shall thy confidence wax strong in the presence of God; and the doctrine of the priesthood shall distill upon thy soul as the dews from heaven. The Holy Ghost shall be thy constant companion, and thy scepter an unchanging scepter of righteousness and truth; and thy dominion shall be an everlasting dominion and without compulsory means it shall flow unto thee forever and ever". (D&C 121:45-46).

Nephi had similar concerns about his own brethren. He perceived that they were having difficulty with the doctrine of Christ because they were not exercising faith sufficient to pray. He equated the qualities necessary for salvation with our ability and willingness to pray. Verses 8 and 9 contain especially meaningful and inspired counsel on prayer. "If ye would hearken unto the Spirit which teacheth a man to pray", he wrote, "ye would know that ye must pray; for the evil spirit teacheth not a man to pray, but teacheth him that he must not pray. But behold, I say unto you that ye must pray always, and not faint; that ye must not perform any thing unto the Lord save in the first place ye shall pray unto the Father in the name of Christ, that he will consecrate thy performance unto thee, that thy performance may be for the welfare of thy soul".

Long ago, the Psalmist wrote: "Evening, and morning, and at noon, will I pray, and cry aloud: and he shall hear my voice". (Psalms 55:17). In the Garden of Gethsemane, the Savior counseled Peter: "Watch and pray, that ye enter not into temptation: the spirit indeed is willing, but the flesh is weak". (Matthew 26:41). To his brethren, Nephi provided the additional insight that it is the evil one who teaches that we must not pray. With this knowledge, we better understand the practice of the Church to consistently pray, since its members need regular reinforcement against encroachments by Satan and the natural tendency to be carnal, sensual, and devilish. Brigham Young once observed that it does not matter if we feel like praying or not; we should nevertheless pray. He said if we waited until we felt like praying, there would not be much prayer in this world.

"The builder who first bridged Niagara's gorge, before he swung his cable, shore to shore, sent out across the gulf his venturing kite, bearing a slender cord for unseen hands to grasp upon the further cliff and draw a greater cord, and then a greater yet; 'til at last across the chasm swung The Cable - then the mighty bridge in air! So may we send our little timid thoughts, across the void, out to God's reaching hands. Send our love, and faith, to thread the deep, thought after thought, until the little cord, and we, are anchored to the Infinite!" (Edward Markham, "Anchored to The Infinite", cited by David O. McKay, C.R, 4/1946).

"If ye will enter in by the way, and receive the Holy Ghost, it will show unto you all things what ye should do. Behold, this is the doctrine of Christ."
(2 Nephi 32:5-6).

Second Nephi
Chapter 33

As a retrospective, Nephi made brief closing remarks in his record that are incorporated into this chapter. He admitted that he was not mighty in writing, but he must have been a great orator. The Holy Ghost carried his message into the hearts of his listeners. (V. 1). In truth, the power of his words is validated each time his books are read, his sermons quoted, and his counsel followed by those with inquiring minds in the Last Days. As Another Testament of Jesus Christ, the First and Second Books of Nephi are tremendous tools of conversion.

In his teaching, Nephi gave three frameworks within which we may develop saving faith in the doctrine of Christ: first, the scriptures, secondly, the inspired words of the prophets and teachers, and thirdly, the promptings of the Holy Ghost. Speaking of the scriptures, the Lord told Joseph Smith that "these words are not of men nor of man, but of me ... For it is my voice which speaketh them unto you; for they are given by my Spirit unto you, and by my power you can read them one to another ... Wherefore, you can testify that you have heard my voice, and know my words". (D&C 18:34-36). Elsewhere, He counseled: "Learn of me, and listen to my words; walk in the meekness of my Spirit, and you shall have peace in me". (D&C 19:23).

It is a terrible thing when men and women throw up barriers to the Spirit and value the revealed word of God as nothing. "But behold, there are many that harden their hearts against the Holy Spirit, that it hath no place in them; wherefore, they cast many things away which are written and esteem them as things of naught". (V. 2). "For the things which some men esteem to be of great worth, both to the body and soul, others set at naught and trample under their feet. Yea, even the very God of Israel do men trample under their feet; I say, trample under their feet but I would speak in other words - they set him at naught, and hearken not to the voice of his counsels". (1 Nephi 19:7).

It is evident that Nephi agonized over the temporal and spiritual welfare of his people, for he wrote: "Mine eyes water my pillow by night, because of them; and I cry unto my God in faith". (V. 3). His prayers were consecrated solely "for the gain of (his) people". (V. 4). In other words, his prayers were dedicated to a sacred purpose and were made fit for holy use as the quality of his personal righteousness benefited those with less than perfect faith.

Taking comfort in his efforts to record his history and that of his father on the plates, Nephi wrote: "The words which I have written in weakness will be made strong unto (my people)". (V. 4). In other words, The Book of Mormon would have the power to speak harshly against sin, persuade men and women to do good, reveal to the descendants of Lehi a knowledge of their fathers, boldly testify of the divinity of the Savior, persuasively teach men and women to believe in Christ, and encourage them to endure to the end in righteousness with eternal life the reward for their obedience. (V. 5).

The Book of Mormon would be a blueprint for our temporal and spiritual survival in the Last Days. "The events and situations that not many years ago seemed wildly improbably to some, and greatly overdrawn, have suddenly become the story of our times, and we see and shall see the words of the prophets who speak to us from the dust fearfully and wonderfully vindicated". (Hugh Nibley, "The World and The Prophets", p. 196).

It is exactly because The Book of Mormon speaks harshly against sin that the wicked revile against it. Only those who have the spirit of the devil, said Nephi, would be angry at the words he spoke. (V. 5). This is a visible yardstick by which we may measure our own attitudes, not to mention the inclinations and loyalties of others.

Nephi reiterated that he had written only those things he esteemed to be of great worth, and he declared that because his own soul had been redeemed from hell he took particular satisfaction in speaking and writing in unambiguous language when declaring the truth. (V. 6). No-one is exempt from the requirements of The Plan of Salvation. God hands out no free passes, and dispenses no golden tickets. All have to "Pass Go" to receive $200.00, or they will surely go to jail.

Jesus was Nephi's rock, his foundation, and his salvation. He was drinking from the saucer because his cup had run over. His calling and election were made sure. He declared: "I have beheld his glory, and I am encircled about eternally in the arms of his love". (2 Nephi 1:15). He was assured of eternal life because of his unequivocal commitment to the Lord. He had received the Second Comforter. His perfect faith now equaled perfect knowledge. He would forever be undeviating.

"There is a crowning event for the faithful. Perhaps, it will not come until you have endured to the end of this life. Generally, at that time, but sometimes earlier, your calling and election may be made sure, when the Lord or one of his servants speaks that assurance to you". ("Book of Mormon C.E.S. Manual", p. 223). For example, the voice of the Lord came to Alma, speaking peace to his soul, saying: "Thou art my servant; and I covenant with thee that thou shalt have eternal life; and thou shalt serve me and go forth in my name, and shalt gather together my sheep". Alma's subsequent ministry testifies that the Lord's confidence in him was well-founded. Because of Nephi's faith, those who read his words may also be carried to an understanding that the power of the Redemption transcends time and reaches out to the faithful and obedient of all ages.

The love typified by the Savior was a part of Nephi's character, as well. He was sure of many things, and confidently wrote; "I have charity for my people, and great faith in Christ that I shall meet many souls spotless at his judgment-seat". (V. 7). He qualifies to stand with the Savior in our joyful reunion at the Judgment Bar. "You and I shall stand face to face before his bar; and ye shall know that I have been commanded of him to write these things". (V. 11). Moroni will be there, as well, for as he bid farewell to his brethren he promised that he would "meet (them) before the pleasing bar of the great Jehovah, the Eternal Judge of both quick and dead". (Moroni 10:34, see Ether 12:38).

It would be nice to be able to stand at that Bar and tell Nephi, Moroni, and the other prophets of The Book of Mormon that we have studied their words and followed their counsel. As Moroni wrote: "I exhort you to remember these things; for the time speedily cometh that ye shall know that I lie not, for ye shall see me at the bar of God; and the Lord God will say unto you: Did I not declare my words unto you, which were written by this man?" (Moroni 10:27).

The next two verses exemplify Nephi's expanding circle of concern. First, he expressed charity for the Jews, and then for the Gentiles. (V. 8 &9). He reiterated that righteousness, and not lineage, is important to the Lord. Salvation and exaltation are available to all who are "reconciled unto Christ, and enter into the narrow gate, and walk in the strait path which leads to life, and continue in the path until the end of the day of probation". (V. 9).

"Hearken unto these words!" urged Nephi. (V. 10). "The Book of Mormon is the keystone of our religion", taught Joseph Smith. (H.C, 4:46). "Take away The Book of Mormon and the revelations", he said, "and where is our religion? We have none". ("Teachings", p. 71). Nephi understood how powerful a witness The Book of Mormon would be in the Last Days. He wrote: "If ye believe not in these words believe in Christ. And if ye shall believe in Christ ye will believe in these words, for they are the words of Christ, and he hath given them unto me". (V. 10).

Nephi knew that Christ would show us "with power and great glory, that they are his words, at the last day". (V. 11). He has the power to dispense knowledge. (See D&C 121:33 & 45). Indeed, He has power over all things. (See Mosiah 4:9). In a breathtaking manifestation of wonder, He will reveal to every serious disciple The Book of Mormon as a divinely inspired work. His gift to the righteous of all ages is an expression of might, majesty, power, and dominion; it is grace, equity, truth, patience, and mercy. (See Commentary Reference to Alma 5:50, & 9:26).

Nephi pragmatically prayed that "many of us, if not all, may be saved" in the Lord's kingdom at the last day. (V. 12). Then, he evoked the imagery of his mentor Isaiah one last time and declared that he spoke "as the voice of one crying from the dust. Farewell", he wrote, "until the day of judgment". (V. 13, see Isaiah 19:4).

To those who would not heed "the words of the Jews" or the Old Testament, "and also (Nephi's) words" or The Book of Mormon, and also "the words which shall proceed forth out of the mouth of the Lamb of God" or the New Testament, he bid "an everlasting farewell, for these words" would condemn the heart-hearted "at the last day". (V. 14). The witness of The Book of Mormon cannot be conveniently ignored or expediently expunged by a world too preoccupied with telestial trivia to acknowledge its worth or heed its message.

"Nephi was an extraordinary man. He was firm and as unflinching as a rock in standing up for the right. He was full of faith, and uncomplaining in the face of adversity, and yet was as humble and tender as a child. The Holy Ghost seems constantly to have attended him and instructed him. He is one of the very greatest spiritual characters of The Book of Mormon". (Sydney B. Sperry, "Compendium", p. 253).

He set a tremendous example and raised the bar to dizzying heights. He was self-effacing, and would be embarrassed if he knew he were being held up as a role model. His Exemplar was Jesus Christ, and he would count his ministry a failure if he thought he had been unable to deepen our commitment to the Savior, strengthen our insight relating to the holy scriptures, and fortify our testimony of Gospel principles. The Tree of Life was very real to Nephi, and his constant prayer must have been to be sensitive to the whisperings of the Spirit so that he might know how to shepherd as many as possible along the path to reach the fruit that was most precious and "desirable above all other fruits". (1 Nephi 15:36).

"I pray the Father
in the name of Christ that
many of us, if not all, may
be saved in his kingdom at
that great and last day."
(2 Nephi 33:12).

The Book of Jacob
The Brother of Nephi
About 544 B.C. to 421 B.C.

Jacob
Chapter 1

The Book of Jacob reintroduces us to Nephi's younger brother, whose sermons and instructions were also recorded by Nephi in The Second Book of Nephi. It is in The Book of Jacob, however, that the full expression of his personality and writing style emerges. Jacob's character had been refined in the fires of adversity and he was well-seasoned and prepared to assume the responsibilities associated with the spiritual leadership of his people.

Jacob lived about 599 to 505 B.C., and his son Enos about 520-510 B.C. to 420 B.C. (Enos 1:25). The Book of Jacob was written somewhere between 544 B.C. and 505 B.C., but does not comprehensively span these dates. The superscript at the beginning of The Book of Jacob is part of the original text of The Book of Mormon, and was likely written by Jacob.

Interestingly, responsibility for recording the religious history of the Nephites on The Small Plates of Nephi passed from Nephi to his younger brother Jacob, and then to a succession of Jacob's, rather than Nephi's, direct line descendants. (See Commentary Reference to The Book of Omni). Nowhere does the text provide a clue to the relative prominence of any descendants of Nephi in Book of Mormon history.

We can only speculate if the Nephite kings, who receive scant mention in The Small Plates, were descendants of Nephi. We simply do not know. Perhaps The Large Plates of Nephi would have given us this information. Joseph Smith, who translated those plates, and his scribes, remained silent on the matter. It is clear, however, that the kings guarded the emblems of authority such as the Liahona, the Sword of Laban, and The Plates of Brass. In ancient times, such relics and genealogies were the only tangible evidence of legitimate rule. The Nephite kings also kept the record of the secular activities of the people of Nephi on The Large Plates of Nephi. (See Commentary Reference to Mosiah 1:16).

Mayan codices might have provided additional insight, at least into late or post-Book of Mormon history. "There were many such books in existence at the time of the Spanish conquest of Yucatán, and Alonso de Zorita wrote that in 1540 he saw numerous such books in the Guatemalan highlands, but they were ordered destroyed by Bishop Diego de Landa in July of 1562. With their destruction, the opportunity for insight into some key areas of Mayan life was greatly diminished". ("Wikipedia").

Around 544 B.C., when Nephi was in his seventies and near death, he gave Jacob the commission to care for The

Small Plates of Nephi. "For behold, it came to pass that fifty and five years had passed away from the time that Lehi left Jerusalem". (V. 1). Jacob was about 50 years old, and he had already received many personal spiritual manifestations that had prepared him to serve as the custodian of the record.

Nephi had given Jacob the charge to write the things of a religious nature upon "these plates", while the history of the people was to be engraven upon the "other plates", or those plates. (V. 2-3). Throughout The Book of Mormon, whenever there is a reference to The Plates of Nephi, "these" refers to The Small Plates, while "those" always refers to The Large Plates. The First Book of Nephi through The Words of Mormon, translated from The Small Plates of Nephi, focus primarily on the religious history of the descendants of Lehi, and deal only summarily with the secular affairs of his people.

Hugh Nibley wrote: "One of the most important discoveries of The Book of Mormon was the process and technique of recording, transmitting, concealing, editing, translating, and duplicating ancient writings". ("Of All Things", p. 78, see Enos 1:1). The world got its first good glimpse of this after the publication of The Book of Mormon, and its example has been vindicated by the 1947 discovery and subsequent study of the Dead Sea Scrolls from Qumran.

Jacob took very seriously the admonition of his brother, that "if there were preaching which was sacred, or revelation which was great, or prophesying, that (he) should engraven the heads of them upon these plates, and touch upon them as much as it were possible, for Christ's sake, and for the sake of (his) people". (V. 4). In other words, Jacob's task was to record the important highlights of the spiritual experiences of his people, that they might be strengthened in testimony, that the mission of Christ might not be in vain, and that his people might enjoy blessings of eternal worth.

This accurately describes the content of The Book of Jacob. The Nephites were led by inspired leaders who received revelation and who taught with power and authority. The spirit had revealed to them the fate of their descendants, and so they were naturally concerned and wanted to fortify their people as much as possible with the nourishment that only the word of God could provide. It was "because of faith and great anxiety" or concern that these things "had been made manifest unto (the Nephites. They) "had many revelations, and the spirit of much prophecy; wherefore, (they) knew of Christ and his kingdom, which should come". (V. 5-6).

The testimony of Jesus is the spirit of prophecy. (See Revelation 19:10). Jacob and his younger brother Joseph had received personal witnesses of the divinity of the Savior, just as every member of the Church may today. The spirit of prophecy is the revealed word of God that is ratified by the Holy Ghost. Every member of the Church who bears testimony of the principles of the Gospel has experienced personal revelation and the spirit of prophecy. Therefore, our testimonies may stand independently, without qualification or corroboration by external proof. We never need to apologize for our testimonies.

Jacob and his younger brother Joseph ministered to the people so that they might enjoy the same sure witness. Jacob wrote: "Wherefore we labored diligently among our people, that we might persuade them to come unto Christ, and partake of the goodness of God, that they might enter into his rest". (V. 7, see Enos 1:25-26).

During these years, there was a subtle change coming over the people of Nephi. They engaged more frequently in apostate practices that made it more difficult for them to enjoy the guidance of the Spirit, and their prophet-leaders had to preach more forthrightly among them. In particular, they "began to grow hard in their hearts, and indulge themselves somewhat in wicked practices ... and began to be lifted up somewhat in pride". (V. 15 & 16, see Commentary Reference to Jacob 2:14-16).

The ministry of Jacob, therefore, addressed a number of concerns. First, was rebellion by the people against God, manifested by their preoccupation with worldly pursuits. He wrote: "Would to God that we could persuade all men not to rebel against God". (V. 8). Rebellion is the crime committed by Lucifer that precipitated the ideological War in Heaven. The English word "apostasy" derives from the Greek, meaning "defection" or revolt", or "to cause to stand away from". Thus, an apostasy can be a falling away, manifest as a collective act of rebellion.

Secondly, Jacob was concerned that the people might provoke God to anger by neglecting the invitation to enjoy His grace manifest in the Atonement of Christ. It must be very frustrating for God to watch us when we ignore our opportunities for repentance, reject salvation, and forsake the invitation to obtain mercy through the merits of Christ. Sometimes, we look beyond the mark, and "lose sight of the central core of the Gospel; (we) believe in Jesus Christ as the great Coach, as the eternal Advisor, but not as the Savior". (Stephen Robinson, "Believing Christ", Flyleaf).

Jacob wished that all "would believe in Christ, and view his death, and suffer his cross, and bear the shame of the world". (V. 8). He visualized a righteous society that would actively and consciously take up the Cross of Christ, and "deny (itself) all ungodliness, and every worldly lust, and keep (His) commandments". (J.S.T. Matthew 16:25-26, see Commentary Reference to 2 Nephi 9:18).

Jacob exhorted his people to remember that when the day of repentance is past, so too is the day of forgiveness, when Justice must be squarely addressed and undeviatingly served. (V. 7). The Savior reminded Joseph Smith: "For behold, I, God, have suffered these things for all, that they might not suffer if they would repent. But if they would not repent they must suffer, even as I". (D&C 19:16-17).

Jacob's next focus of concern was the absolute necessity of developing a testimony of the Gospel and belief in Christ, together with the witness that He is our Advocate and Intercessor with the Father. After all, we cannot be saved in ignorance of the saving principles and ordinances of the Gospel. (See D&C 131:6). As Jacob later explained: "For this intent have we written these things, that they may know that we knew of Christ, and we had a hope of his glory many hundreds of years before His coming". (Jacob 4:4). Likewise, today we might declare: "For this intent have we read these things, that we might know of Christ, and have a hope of his glory many hundreds of years after His coming".

Jacob's desire that the people "view the Savior's death" was based on his realization that our hope is founded on His Atonement and Resurrection. (V. 8). With their relationship with Him secured, the people would be prepared to suffer His cross, or bear the burdens of service, consecration, devotion, and obedience.

Their "view" was based on faith in a Savior Who was yet to come to Earth. While this may seem strange, it is no more so than it is for us to focus our faith on a Savior whose mortal ministry was 2,000 years in the largely forgotten past. In either case, the most important thing is to enjoy a covenant relationship with God, consecrate ourselves to His service, and bear the shame of the world. That is to say, it has always been the lot of the Saints to be responsible for the continuing concern with which God views the wicked world, and at the same time to suffer humiliation for the conduct of our friends and neighbors who brazenly violate the commandments. We seek the favor of God, but we also add flavor to His efforts to influence all of His children. It has something to do with being "the salt of the earth".

In verse 9, Jacob reported that when Nephi's physical strength began to diminish, he anointed "a man" to be a king and a ruler over his people. We do not know who this individual was, but verse 15 suggests that it was not Jacob. If Jacob witnessed the reign of "second Nephi, third Nephi, and so forth", then perhaps he lived to a great age. (V. 11). Nephi did not. Verse 12 simply states: "Nephi died". What more needed to be said?

A distinction is made in verse 13 regarding the divisions based on religion among the children of Lehi. "The people which were not Lamanites were Nephites". But within this group of Nephites were "Jacobites, Josephites, Zoramites, Lamanites, Lemuelites, and Ishmaelites". This is a startling declaration, because it leads us to conclude that Lehi's and Nephi's ministries that had focused on the elder sons and their posterity and on the posterity of Ishmael had not been entirely in vain. Likewise, among the Lamanites were counted those who "were a compound of Laman and Lemuel, and the sons of Ishmael, and all who had dissented from the Nephites". (Alma 43:13). In other words, the ministry that had been oriented toward solidifying the faith and testimony of the balance of Lehi's descendants had not been entirely successful, either. (See Alma 24:29, 43:13, 55:4 & 56:3).

Inasmuch as 2 Nephi 5:5-6 reports that "all those who would go" went with Nephi when he departed into the wilderness from the Land of Their First Inheritance during the Great Separation, it is plausible to assume that this group included descendants of Laman, Lemuel, and Ishmael, who are called "Lamanites, Lemuelites, and Ishmaelites" in verse 13. Parenthetically, note the absence of a reference in this verse to "Samites", consistent with the patriarchal blessing given to Sam by Lehi, wherein he was told that his posterity would be included with Nephi's. For Lehi "spake unto Sam, saying ...Thy seed shall be numbered with his seed; and thou shalt be even like unto thy brother". (2 Nephi 4:11, see D&C 3:17).

Then, verse 14 makes a cultural distinction between the Lamanites and Nephites. "I, Jacob, shall not hereafter distinguish them by these names, but I shall call them Lamanites that seek to destroy the people of Nephi, and those who are friendly to Nephi I shall call Nephites, or the people of Nephi". (See Commentary Reference to Alma 3:4-12).

Jacob must have been proud of his lineage, and of the righteous tradition established by both his father and his older brother Nephi. Likewise, he took very seriously his stewardship over his people. The 5th Article of Faith and D&C 11:15 clearly state; "A man must be called of God, by prophecy and by the laying on of hands by those who are in authority, to preach the Gospel and administer in the ordinances thereof". The Nephite record confirms that before Jacob undertook to teach the people, he too "obtained (his) errand from the Lord". (V. 17). As the Savior explained to Hyrum Smith: "Behold, I command you that you need not suppose that you are called to preach until you are called". (D&C 11:15).

"No man is authorized to act in the name of the Lord, or to officiate in any ordinance unless he has been properly called. For this reason, the priesthood was restored, and the Church organized". (Joseph Fielding Smith, Jr.). Paul taught: "No man taketh this honour unto himself, but he that is called of God". (Hebrews 5:12). Jacob held the Melchizedek Priesthood, but equally importantly, he was also consecrated by Nephi as a priest and a teacher of the people. (V. 18, see 2 Nephi 5:26, & Jarom 1:11). He was set apart under the hand of Nephi to minister to his people.

When we are set apart to do a particular work in the Church, the position becomes ours. It doesn't belong to anyone else, and no one else has a right to it. If we do not do the job, it will not be done. Therefore, we should accept positions with the intention to carry out the associated responsibilities as though our lives depended on it, as indeed they do.

It is amazing what can happen when we set our minds to a task. The secret of success is to accept an assignment without reservation and to carry out our responsibilities with a strong heart. When we become Church members, great benefits accrue to us, but when we get the spirit of the Gospel coursing through our veins, we are truly "quickened". This burning zeal to serve God gives us authority over both our weaknesses and the defeats of life. But our efforts are strangely impotent when our hearts are not in our work.

John Taylor said: "If you do not magnify your calling, God will hold you responsible for those whom you might have saved had you done your duty". (Quoted by Hugh B. Brown, C.R., 10/1962). Who among us can afford to be responsible for the loss of the eternal life of a human soul? If great joy is the reward for saving one soul, then how terrible must be the remorse of those whose timid efforts have allowed a child of God to be lost? We must raise our voices to be heard over the din of noise caused by the confusion of the world. As Abraham Lincoln declared: "To sin by silence when words should be spoken makes cowards of men". Certainly, we who hold positions in the Church should pledge our best efforts, and this might include going out on a limb now and then. Not only other lives, but our own depend on it, for those who are "not valiant in the testimony of Jesus" cannot hope to enter the Celestial Kingdom of God. (D&C 76:79).

We have within us the seeds of greatness, for we have been endowed with the personality and character traits of our Father. We call forth power through faithful activity when we fight to sustain the greatest truths and highest standards. We are "set apart" because ours is a work of eternal significance that is carried out in partnership with our Creator. (See Moses 1:39). We are "set apart" by our convictions, our enthusiasm, our righteousness, and our faith. "What a piece of work is a man!" wrote the Bard of Avon. "How noble in reason, how infinite in faculty, in form and moving how express and admirable, in action how like an angel, in apprehension how like a god - the beauty of the world, the paragon of animals! (Hamlet, Act 2, scene 2). Our constant prayer should be that after we have been "set apart", everyone within the sphere of our influence will be enriched because His work was given into our hands.

Therefore, said the Lord, "Let every man stand in his own office, and labor in his own calling, that the system may be kept perfect". (D&C 84:109-110). "The way to magnify our callings is to do the work designed to be performed by those who hold the particular office involved". (Joseph Fielding Smith, Jr.).

So seriously did Jacob take his calling to be a priest and a teacher, that he even accepted the responsibility for the sins of his flock should he be found to have failed in his assignment to "teach them the word of God with all diligence". (V. 19). He lived among members who were far from perfect in their commitment to the principles of the Gospel and to the government of the Church. Nevertheless, he labored unceasingly in their service, and was moved to declare: "We did magnify our office unto the Lord". (V. 19).

In our day, Christ has promised the Saints: "I will bless all those who labor in my vineyard with a mighty blessing". (D&C 21:9). Joseph Smith taught that we magnify our calling by "performing the service that pertains to it". Latter-day scripture reaffirms the importance of commitment to the covenants of baptism, including dedication to our callings in Church. In other words, when we respond to an inspired call from our priesthood leaders and are set apart to carry out specific assignments in the Church, when we earnestly seek the gifts necessary to succeed in the tasks at hand, and when we support and sustain others in their callings, as well, the system will be perfect in the sight of the Lord, Who heads the Church, and to Whom we are ultimately responsible. Jacob's ministry is a classic illustration of this principle in action.

"Now the people
which were not Lamanites were
Nephites; nevertheless, they were called
Nephites, Jacobites, Josephites, Zoramites,
Lamanites, Lemuelites, and Ishmaelites.
But I, Jacob, shall not hereafter distinguish
them by these names, but I shall call them
Lamanites that seek to destroy the people
of Nephi, and those who are friendly
to Nephi, I shall call Nephites,
or the people of Nephi."
(Jacob 1:13-14).

Jacob
Chapter 2

God had instructed Jacob to address what was, for him, a very difficult subject. Nevertheless, he declared: "Notwithstanding the greatness of the task, I must do according to the strict commands of God, and tell you concerning your wickedness and abominations, in the presence of the pure in heart, and the broken in heart, and under the glance of the piercing eye of the Almighty God". (V. 10). He was required to do so because he had accepted both the privileges and the liabilities associated with the calling that had come to him by inspiration and the laying on of hands. As he explained to his people: "I, Jacob, according to the responsibility which I am under to God, to magnify mine office with soberness, and that I might rid my garments of your sins, I come up into the temple this day that I might declare unto you the word of God". (V. 1, see Jacob 1:19).

He first stated his authority, describing himself simply and yet eloquently as "the brother of Nephi". (V. 1). Appropriately, the setting of his discourse was the temple, a house of learning and of revelation that the Church has always been commanded to build to the Holy Name of God. (D&C 89:119, & 124:39-40). The fact that there were unrighteous Church members in the House of the Lord, though, is indicative of the apostasy of the people of Nephi, and perhaps even of carelessness by Church leaders when administering their ecclesiastical responsibilities and interviewing members regarding temple attendance worthiness.

Spencer W. Kimball once likened himself to an old shoe, to be worn out in the service of the Lord. So, too, Jacob observed that he had been "diligent in the office of (his) calling". This day, however, the burdens of leadership were particularly heavy. Jacob wrote that he was "weighed down with much more desire and anxiety for the welfare" of the souls of his people than he had ever been before. (V. 3).

By the power of discernment vested in him by virtue of his priesthood office, Jacob knew the thoughts of the people, who had heretofore "been obedient unto the word of the Lord". (V. 4). Now, however, they were "beginning to labor in sin". (V. 5). Nephi had recognized the insidiously dangerous practice of flirting with sin when he wrote that the devil leads the people "with a flaxen cord, until he bindeth them with his strong cords forever". (2 Nephi 26:22). The feel of a flaxen cord around our necks can actually be quite comfortable, at least initially, but once habit patterns have been set, if we have been unwary and lulled into a false sense of carnal security, we will be surprised to find that we have sacrificed our agency to act independently as we are bound under the yoke of sin in habit patterns that are very difficult to break.

Contrast the symbolism of the weight of sin with the invitation of the Savior, Who said: "My yoke is easy, and my burden is light". (Matthew 11:30). Though the sins of the world were upon His shoulders, His life was unencumbered by unresolved transgression. His life was the perfect expression of the Law of Liberty. His Gospel, and in particular the Atonement, is the key to making us free in every liberating sense of the word.

Jacob wished that the feelings of his brethren had been as "tender and chaste and delicate" as those of their women and children. (V. 7). These innocents had come to the temple expecting to be comforted by the "pleasing word of God (that) heals the wounded soul". (V. 8). But when, instead, the prophet was compelled to expose the sins of their loved ones, their souls were pierced with daggers and their delicate sensitivities were seared by salt in their wounds. (V. 9).

Jacob's chastisement was necessary because when the people lost their humility a number of character flaws moved into the void thus created. (V. 16). They became haughty and arrogant, exercised undue self-assertiveness, and were aggressive in their interactions with others. They failed to submit to proper authority, and lacked modesty and meekness. They also sought after riches, and "that for which all virtue now was sold, and almost every vice – almighty gold!" (Ben Johnson). However, they were soon to learn the real value of these things. Hundreds of years later, the Spanish Conquistadors were amazed to find that the Aztecs of Meso-America did not really place a high value on gold for the simple reason that it was so plentiful. They appreciated it only in an artistic sense. The Nephite and Lamanite understanding of the worth of "precious metals" was also limited due to their frame of reference; they only indirectly comprehended Old World standards that put a high priority on the accumulation of "rare" metals. Yet, they seem to have gotten so caught up in the lust for temporal wealth that they forgot that "the hand of providence (had) smiled upon (them) most pleasingly" in a land overflowing with milk and honey. (V. 13).

Had they not abandoned their core values, surely they would have understood that God could not justify their obsessive quest for telestial trivia. In unequivocal language punctuated by exclamation marks, Jacob declared; "He condemneth you, and if ye persist in these things his judgments must speedily come upon you. O that he would show you that he can pierce you, and with one glance of his eye he can smite you to the dust! O that he would rid you from this iniquity and abomination. And O that ye would listen unto the word of his commands, and let not this pride of your hearts destroy your souls!" (V. 14-16).

Ezra Taft Benson made the condemnation of pride the centerpiece of several of his last sermons. Drawing on Book of Mormon teachings, he called it "the universal sin, the great vice" and identified its central feature as "enmity toward God and enmity toward our fellowmen". The insidiously evil and destructive quality of pride is that it is "essentially competitive in nature, arising when individuals pit their will against God's, or their intellects, opinions, works, wealth, and talents against those of other people". President Benson warned that "pride is a damning sin" for "it adversely affects all our relationships" and "limits or stops progression". He also warned that pride can infect those who are otherwise active, participating members in full fellowship in the Church, for it includes "faultfinding, gossiping, living beyond our means, envying, coveting, withholding gratitude, and being unforgiving and jealous".

Jacob gave his Nephite brethren the antidote for pride, that also addressed all of the attendant negative qualities that ride on its coattails. The formula consists of the Nephite version of the Golden Rule: "Think of your brethren like unto yourselves", and "before seeking for riches", seek the kingdom of God. (V. 17). This is our number one priority. When we have shed ourselves of pride and other character crippling personality traits, God will grant us the temporal blessings necessary to "clothe the naked, and to feed the hungry, and to liberate the captive, and administer relief to the sick and the afflicted". (V. 19).

These verses are reminiscent of another scripture from a distant time and place: "Righteousness is not that ye turn your faces to the East or to the West, but righteousness is this: whosoever believeth in God, and the Last Day, and the angels, and the Book and the Prophets; and whosoever, for the love of God, giveth of his wealth unto his kindred, unto orphans, and the poor, and the wayfarer, and to the beggar, and for the release of captives; and whoso observeth prayer ... and when they have covenanted, fulfill their covenant; and who are patient in adversity and hardship and in the time of violence; these are the righteous, these are they who believe in the Lord!" It might be surprising to learn that this counsel comes from the Muslim Koran. (ii, 177). The Church, it would seem, does not have a monopoly on inspiration.

After his chastisement of the people for their pride, Jacob challenged them to reply. He asked: "What say ye of it?" (V. 20). We do not know how they responded, but we do have Jacob's benevolent reflection: "The one being is as precious in his sight as the other. And all flesh is of the dust; and for the selfsame end hath he created them, that they should keep his commandments and glorify him forever". (V. 21).

N. Eldon Tanner observed: "The craving for praise and popularity too often controls actions, and as a people succumb, they find themselves bending their character, when they think they are only taking a bow". But Jacob's people had a worse problem as their pride carried them to greater sin. They had forgotten that with every gift of power comes the temptation to abuse it, and so they found themselves guilty of "grosser crimes". (V. 23). They had gotten themselves into this situation because of a lack of understanding, and because they had wrested the scriptures or had twisted their meaning, in particular because they failed to liken the scriptures to their own circumstances. (V. 23).

It is critical to our spirituality to study the scriptures. The Nephite prophets labored diligently to preserve their records for the Last Days, but the Nephites must have also had their own personal copies of the scriptures. For example, only a few years later, when Jacob had once again restored peace and the love of God among the people, "they searched the scriptures, and hearkened no more" to the voices of wicked men. (Jacob 7:23, see Alma 13:20, 14,:2, 8, & 3 Nephi 20:11). Jacob knew that God's ways can only be understood by the spirit of revelation and by prayerful study of His word. (See Jacob 4:3, 6 & 8). The scriptures provide an excellent pathway to a testimony of Jesus, and the love of God and scripture study go hand in hand. (See Jacob 7:10-11, & 28).

But in their present circumstances, the people of Nephi had not yet determined to make a habit of careful and prayerful scripture study. Their scriptural illiteracy invited misunderstanding and misapplication of the conditional doctrine of plural marriage. For reasons known only to God, Israel had rarely been instructed to emulate her righteous forefathers such as Abraham, Isaac, and Jacob, whose plural families had been approved of Him. Instead, she followed the examples of David and Solomon, who, in their intimate lives, had violated sacred trusts with rash, impulsive, and profligate behavior. (V. 23-24).

The Latter-day Saint understanding of the doctrine of plural marriage has been explained by Steven Robinson: "The Latter-day Saints do not maintain that the practice of plural marriage is a requirement for entrance into the kingdom of God, nor do they argue that plural marriage is taught in the New Testament. While Latter-day Saints do believe that whenever God commands, the Saints must obey, they do not insist that plural marriage is an essential element of the Gospel of Jesus Christ, or that plural marriage is intrinsically preferable to monogamy. (Also), because plural marriage is neither a universal nor an essential principle of the Gospel, the Lord may command, tolerate, or forbid the practice among his people as their circumstances warrant. For example, in The Book of Mormon itself, the Lord forbade plural marriage to the Nephites, though apparently the practice had been allowed to Israelites generally under the Law of Moses. Conversely, in the Nineteenth Century, the Lord commanded that plural marriage be practiced among the Latter-day Saints; thus L.D.S. plural marriage was not the result of some scriptural discovery or a doctrinal preference for polygamy, but was due to the direct command of God in revelation to the Prophet Joseph Smith. For Latter-day Saints, plural marriage of itself has nothing to commend it, and only the command of the Lord makes the practice right or wrong. What the Lord requires is right; what he forbids is wrong". ("Are Mormons Christians?" p. 91-92).

Jacob's Nephite brethren were ignorant of these fundamental doctrinal principles. In verse 24, in reference to all the plural marriages of the Old Testament patriarchs, Jacob condemned only two: David and Solomon. Specifically, it was only the unauthorized wives and concubines of these men that were an abomination in the sight of God. (V. 24, see D&C 132:38). Nevertheless, speaking as the Lord's prophet, Jacob taught his people that they were not to engage in plural marriage. (V. 26-27).

Verse 29 then teaches that the people must be given permission by the Lord before they may enter into plural marriage: "Wherefore, this people shall keep my commandments, saith the Lord of Hosts". Verse 30 more directly addresses the doctrine. "For if I will, saith the Lord of Hosts, raise up seed unto me, I will command my people; otherwise, they shall hearken unto these things". This verse suggests that one objective of the practice of plural marriage is to increase the population of the children of the Covenant.

Next, we are given to believe that infidelity is a universal problem. "For behold, I, the Lord, have seen the sorrow, and heard the mournings of the daughters of my people in the land of Jerusalem, yea, and in all the lands of my people, because of the wickedness and abominations of their husbands". (V. 3). The situation is even worse today, inasmuch as both men and women widely participate in lascivious behavior.

The disastrous effects of adultery on the family include broken hearts, lost confidences, and the destruction of faith and testimony. The consequent despair of those who have been betrayed stands as a witness to God against the guilty. (V. 35). Jacob's denunciation of immorality in this chapter is a powerful defense of home and family in all ages, and foreshadowed the latter-day Proclamation on The Family (1995) with prescience.

Jacob
Chapter 3

Jacob opened this chapter by speaking to those who were "pure in heart". He encouraged them, exhorting them to "look unto God with firmness of mind, and pray unto him with exceeding faith ... Lift up your heads and receive the pleasing word of God, and feast upon his love; for ye may (do so) if your minds are firm, forever". (V. 1-2).

Then he turned his attention to the wicked, and warned that unless they repented, the righteous among them would be led away, and the Lamanites would be allowed to overrun and possess the land of their inheritance. (V. 4). Immorality, it would seem, is responsible for the destruction, not only of individuals, but also of nations.

Jacob's dire warning was realized in the days of the Elder Mosiah, when the Lord commanded him to leave the main body of Nephites and flee into the wilderness with any and all who would go with him. The rest of the Nephites were destroyed soon thereafter by the Lamanites. Mosiah united with "Mulekites" in the Land of Zarahemla. (Omni 1:4-19, see Commentary Reference to 2 Nephi 30:4). Nephite history from that point on became the history of the united body of Nephites and "Mulekites", with "Mulekites" predominating in numbers.

Of those who were wicked among the Nephites, Jacob declared that even the Lamanites were more righteous, because they did not violate the law of chastity. (V. 5). In fact, the Lamanites escaped destruction, and were promised by the Lord that one day they would "become a blessed people" precisely because they kept that law. (V. 6).

The reference to white and dark skin in verses 8 and 9 should be read in the context of spiritual darkness versus purity. "Revile no more against (the Lamanites) because of the darkness of their skins", cautioned Jacob, "neither shall ye revile against them because of their filthiness; but ye shall remember your own filthiness, and remember that their filthiness came because of their fathers. (V. 9). In just the same metaphorical way, Nephi wrote of the Lamanites in the Last Days: "And then shall they rejoice ... and their scales of darkness shall begin to fall from their eyes; and ... they shall be a pure and a delightsome people". (2 Nephi 30:6). Before the 1978 revision of the English language scriptures, this verse was rendered "white" as opposed to "pure", to illustrate the concept of spiritual blackness.

Nevertheless, on at least one other occasion, The Book of Mormon taught that the skin of the Lamanites was darker than that of the Nephites. Nephi wrote: "That they might not be enticing unto my people, the Lord God did cause a skin of blackness to come upon them". (2 Nephi 5:21). When they entered into the Lord's covenants, the curse was taken from them, and "their skin became white like unto the Nephites". (3 Nephi 2:15).

Jacob clearly taught that righteousness is more important to the Lord than is lineage or racial stereotype. "A commandment I give unto you, which is the word of God, that ye revile no more against them because of the darkness of their skins; neither shall ye revile against them because of their filthiness; but ye shall remember your own filthiness, and remember that their filthiness came because of their fathers". (V. 9). Nephi had taught the same principle. The Lord, he had said, "denieth none that come unto him, black and white, bond and free, male and female; and he remembereth the heathen; and all are alike unto God, both Jew and Gentile". (2 Nephi 26:33). In The Book of Mormon, the "filthiness" of both Lamanites and Nephites is equated with apostasy, while the righteous are characterized as being "pure in heart". "I, the Lord, require (only) the hearts of the children of men", said Jesus Christ, speaking metaphorically to emphasize powerful symbolism and drive His point home. (D&C 64:22).

Jacob taught the sobering truth that parents are responsible for bringing up their children in light and truth, and that if they fail to do so, the sins of the children will be upon the heads of the parents. "Wherefore, ye shall remember your children, how that ye have grieved their hearts because of the example that ye have set before them; and also, remember that ye may, because of your filthiness, bring your children unto destruction, and their sins be heaped upon your heads at the last day". (V. 10). The Lord declared to Latter-day Israel: "Inasmuch as parents have children in Zion, or in any of her stakes which are organized, that teach them not to understand the doctrine of repentance, faith in Christ the Son of the living God, and of baptism and the gift of the Holy Ghost by the laying on of the hands, when eight years old, the sin be upon the heads of the parents. And they shall also teach their children to pray, and to walk uprightly before the Lord". (D&C 68:25 & 28).

Spencer W. Kimball assured the Saints that "righteous parents who strive to develop wholesome influences for their children will be held blameless at the last day, and they will succeed in saving most of their children, if not all" from the harsh realities of mortality and the school of hard knocks. (C. R. 10/1974). Nephi had said something similar in his farewell; "And I pray the Father in the name of Christ that many of us, if not all, may be saved in his kingdom at that great and last day". (2 Nephi 33:12).

Jacob begged his audience to "awake(n) from the slumber of death". (V. 11). Those who suffer the second or spiritual death are they who "have had the testimony of the Holy Ghost, and who have known the truth, and then have rejected it and put Christ to open shame". (Joseph F. Smith). These are they who suffer "the pains of hell" and become "angels to the devil, to be cast into that lake of fire and brimstone, which is the second death". (V. 11). Earlier, Jacob had characterized the torment of the wicked "as a lake of fire and brimstone, whose flame ascendeth up forever and ever and has no end". (2 Nephi 9:16). This is a symbolical representation of the fate of the wicked, but should not be taken literally.

The Small Plates of Nephi were beginning to fill up. The Words of Mormon illustrate that Mormon was able to fit in just a page or two of historical information on plates that were already essentially full. We receive some insight, not only into the quantity of information, but also on the quality of Nephite religious history, when we read that not one percent could be contained on The Small Plates. (See The Words of Mormon 1:5, Helaman 3:14, 3 Nephi 5:8, 26:6, & Ether 15:33). "But many of their proceedings are written upon the larger plates, and their wars, and their contentions, and the reigns of their kings". (V. 13).

Jacob called these plates The "Plates of Jacob". That portion upon which he wrote was properly his record, but in a larger sense all the early prophets wrote upon The Small Plates of Nephi, "made by the hand of Nephi". (V. 14).

Jacob
Chapter 4

It is obvious that the Nephites struggled with the manner of engraving upon plates of ore. Even in the best of times, the process must have been tedious. Jacob recorded: "I cannot write but a little of my words, because of the difficulty of engraving our words upon plates". (Jacob 4:1). In straitened circumstances, it would have been even more difficult. "We could write but little", explained Moroni, "because of the awkwardness of our hands. Wherefore, when we write we behold our weakness, and stumble because of the placing of our words; and I fear lest the Gentiles shall mock at our words". (Ether 12:25, see Commentary Reference to 2 Nephi 31:1).

Mormon's perceived inability to communicate in writing as fluidly as he would have liked is expressed with both an acknowledgement of his responsibility and with just a hint of frustration: "And if there be faults they be the faults of a man". (Mormon 8:17). On the Title Page of The Book of Mormon, he reiterated: "And now, if there are faults they are the mistakes of men; wherefore, condemn not the things of God". How The Book of Mormon is received in literary circles though, is of no concern to the Lord: "Fools mock, but they shall mourn". (Ether 12:26).

Mormon's abridgment was written, he said, in "the characters which are called among us the reformed Egyptian, being handed down and altered by us, according to our manner of speech. And if our plates (The Plates of Mormon, and not necessarily The Small Plates of Nephi) had been sufficiently large we should have written in Hebrew; but the Hebrew hath been altered by us also; and if we could have written in Hebrew, behold, ye would have had no imperfection in our record". (Mormon 9:32-33, see 1 Nephi 1:2, & Mosiah 1:4).

Nephite writing only gradually evolved into "reformed Egyptian". The details of the characters of the written language have long been of interest to students of The Book of Mormon. The Prophet Joseph Smith, who translated The Small Plates of Nephi, The Large Plates of Nephi, and The Plates of Mormon, was inclined to allow The Book of Mormon to speak for itself on this matter.

We know from a careful reading that the language of the Egyptians spoken of by King Benjamin referred to the characters on The Plates of Brass; "For it were not possible", he said to his sons, "that our father, Lehi, could have remembered all these things, to have taught them to his children, except it were for the help of these plates; for he having been taught in the language of the Egyptians therefore he could read these engravings, and teach them to his children". (Mosiah 1:4).

Of this language, Hugh Nibley wrote: "Demotic is that peculiar and remarkably abbreviated style of writing developed out of the Hieratic by systematic abbreviation from the 8th to the 4th centuries, which enjoyed its heyday of popularity in Lehi's own time". ("Since Cumorah", p. 167-168). Demotic could have been the shorthand adopted by the Nephites, or at least by those who kept the record, for it would have allowed a great deal of information to be engraven on metal plates with minimal effort. (See Commentary Reference to Mosiah 1:3).

Enos wrote that he was taught in the language of his father. (Enos 1:1). This probably meant that he was comfortable writing in the language of the plates and not that he learned an oral language other than Hebrew. (See 1 Nephi 1:2, & Mosiah 1:2). "Reformed Egyptian" is as good a term as any to describe that language.

There are at least 60 passages in The Book of Mormon that clearly illustrate the difficulty of writing upon plates and of correcting that which had already been engraven. (See Essay: "Writing on Metal Plates Was a Pain"). Mormon, realizing that he had not written exactly what he had intended to in the abridged record, added many such clarifications.

There is another interesting insight into the awkwardness of working with metal plates. Mormon knew that his abridgment of The Book of Lehi, that ended when King Benjamin was an old man ready to die, would be lost. (See Words of Mormon 1:7). Consequently, Book of Mormon readers would not have access to the account of Benjamin's life. The Book of Omni, which is a part of The Small Plates of Nephi, deals with King Benjamin in only three of its verses, and what Mormon had written about him in The Book of Mosiah was confined to the last three years of the king's life. The Words of Mormon, tacked on to the end of The Small Plates, serves as a bridge between The Small Plates and Mormon's abridgment. Words of Mormon verses 15 - 18 flow as if Mormon, knowing that there was so little room left on The Small Plates of Nephi, hastily finished the record in uncharacteristically awkward style. Perhaps the straitened circumstances under which he labored also help to account for the fact that one sentence of 172 words makes up these four verses:

"And it came to pass that after there had been false Christs, and their mouths had been shut, and they punished according to their crimes; and after there had been false prophets, and false preachers and teachers among the people, and all these having been punished according to their crimes; and after there having been much contention and many dissensions away unto the Lamanites, behold, it came to pass that king Benjamin, with the assistance of the holy prophets who were among his people - for behold, king Benjamin was a holy man, and he did reign over his people in righteousness; and there were many holy men in the land, and they did speak the word of God with power and with authority; and they did use much sharpness because of the stiffneckedness of the people - wherefore - with the help of these, king Benjamin, by laboring with all the might of his body and the faculty of his whole soul, and also the prophets, did once more establish peace in the land". (Words of Mormon, 1:15-18).

This passage and many others give us subtle insight into the human weaknesses of The Book of Mormon prophets, and they are powerful witnesses to the validity of the record and to Joseph Smith's testimony that The Book of Mormon was translated by the gift and power of God, warts and all.

Moroni exhorted those who would receive The Book of Mormon to: "Ask God, the Eternal Father, in the name of Christ, if these things are not true; and if ye shall ask with a sincere heart, with real intent, having faith in Christ, he will manifest the truth of it unto you, by the power of the Holy Ghost. And by the power of the Holy Ghost ye may know the truth of all things". (Moroni 10:4-5). To the Three Witnesses, the Lord said: "Wherefore, you can testify that you have heard my voice, and know my words". (D&C 18:36). Truly, any of us who have read the words of the Lord in The Book of Mormon and have heard His voice by the power of the Spirit can testify, as did Oliver Cowdery, David Whitmer, and Martin Harris. When the plates were shown to these Three Witnesses, the angel who delivered them said: "These plates have been revealed by the power of God. The translation which you have seen of them is correct, and

I command you to bear record of what you now see and hear". (H.C., 1:54-55). Since the Restoration of the Gospel, millions of God's children have received the same sure witness of the Spirit that The Book of Mormon is true. Jacob next made a dramatic statement of declaration, revealing the specific intent for which the Nephite record was kept: "That (our beloved brethren and children - our descendants) may know that we knew of Christ, and we had a hope of his glory many hundred years before his coming; and not only we ourselves had a hope of his glory, but also all the holy prophets which were before us". (V. 4). They "believed in Christ and worshipped the Father in his name". (V. 5). Herein is revealed the inherent power of The Book of Mormon. It is a Another Witness of Jesus Christ and stands independent of the Bible as a Messianic text.

The Jewish scribes and Pharisees determined to eradicate every reference to Jesus Christ from the scriptures, for, as Jacob taught, every prophet of the Old Testament had a sure testimony of His divinity. (See v. 4 & Alma 30:44). Because the writings of the prophets of The Book of Mormon suffered no such excoriation, its spirit is unrestrained and bears a powerful witness when its pages are read.

Evidently, "all the holy prophets which were before" the Nephites taught the same basic principles of the Gospel as did Lehi, Nephi, and Jacob. (V. 4). If they seem to repeat themselves, often using language that is reminiscent of theatrical encore, it is because their message is essentially unchanged, inasmuch as they have received their inspiration from the same Source.

They are somewhat like the captain of a ship who was seen to carefully examine a certain desk drawer in his cabin, shortly before the commencement of each voyage. This elicited much curiosity on the part of the officers and crew, but they were never so bold as to inquire as to the significance of his ritual. One day, the captain reached the age of retirement, and he was piped ashore for the last time. As soon as he was gone, the crew rushed to his former quarters and threw open the drawer. There, taped to a 3 x 5 card on the bottom of the drawer was this message: "Starboard is right, port is left". The point is that we should all stick to the basics and pay attention to fundamental principles.

Jacob did just that as he taught his people to "worship the Father" and to reverence His name. (V. 5). "Reverence embraces regard, deference, honor, and esteem. Without some degree of it, therefore, there would be no courtesy, no gentility, no consideration of others' feelings, or of others' rights. It is the fundamental virtue in religion. If there were more reverence in human hearts, there would be less room for sin and sorrow, and increased capacity for joy and gladness. Reverence for God and sacred things is the chief characteristic of a great soul". (David O. McKay).

We can see why, in a world with less reverence, there is more selfishness. With less reverence, there is a greater desire for power, les respect, more rudeness, less honor, more contempt, vulgarity, and superficiality. With less reverence, contention dominates, and spiritual power is sapped. With less reverence, human sophistry is substituted for the counsel of the Almighty God. With less reverence, "freedom weeps, wrong rules the land, and justice sleeps". (Josiah Gilbert Holland).

There is a perpetual battle raging in the hearts of men, and thus, "two ways lie open before us - one leading to an ever lower and lower plane, where are heard the cries of despair and the curses of the poor, where manhood shrivels and possessions wear down the possessor; and the other leading to the highlands of the morning where are heard the glad shouts of humanity, and where honest effort is rewarded with immortality". (John P. Altgeld).

Ancient Israel was bound to Jehovah by the Law, and its outward observances were as phylacteries to them. The Nephite branch of Israel kept the Law of Moses, even though they had a steadfast hope in Christ, many revelations, the spirit of prophecy, and power in the priesthood. (V. 5-7). For them, the Law was truly a schoolmaster orienting their souls to Christ. As Jacob explained: "For this cause (the Law) is sanctified unto us for righteousness". (V. 5).

During His post-mortal ministry among the Nephites in the New World, the Savior taught: "The Law is fulfilled that was given unto Moses". (3 Nephi 15:4). Abinadi had said that the Law of Moses was given to point the attention of the people to Christ, and that its elements were types of things to come. (See Mosiah 13:27-32, Galatians 3:24, & D&C 84:27). Now the Savior confirmed: "I am he that gave the law, and I am he who covenanted with my people Israel; therefore, the law in me is fulfilled ... therefore, it hath an end". (3 Nephi 15:5). It is clear from this verse that Christ is the God of the Old Testament. (See Mosiah 15:1). By that authority, He set aside the Law of Moses.

To the Nephite Saints, the resurrected Christ declared: "The covenant which I have made with my people is not all fulfilled; but the law which was given unto Moses hath an end in me". (3 Nephi 15:8). Salvation is in Christ, and not in the Law. The Covenant was between Christ and His people, and not between the Law and His people. (See Mosiah 13:27-28, & 2 Nephi 11:4). We sometimes observe of the ancient Jews that because they were caught up in the mechanics of the Law, they forgot to whom it pointed. Our challenge today is to see that we are converted to the Gospel, rather than just to the Church. We can get caught up in the machinery of the Church without making contact with the Savior, and without being spiritually begotten of Him. If we have done so, life can become a treadmill. Gospel ordinances were designed to be a springboard that launches us to greater spiritual heights.

Jacob understood this, when he wrote: "We search the prophets, and we have many revelations and the spirit of prophecy; and having all these witnesses we obtain a hope, and our faith becometh unshaken, insomuch that we truly can command in the name of Jesus and the very trees obey us, or the mountains, or the waves of the sea". (V. 6). It is Jesus who delegates the power. But Jacob was not deceived by these marvelous manifestations of spiritual and priesthood power. He knew the source from whence they came. Jacob wrote: "Nevertheless, the Lord God showeth us our weakness that we may know that it is by his grace, and his great condescensions unto the children of men, that we have power to do these things". (V. 7).

"There is no doctrine, ritual, principle, ordinance, law, performance, Church, belief, program, angel, or prophet that can save us in the absence of the personal intervention in our lives of the Lord and Savior Jesus Christ. This is the teaching of The Book of Mormon, as well as of the Bible". (Stephen Robinson, "Are Mormons Christians?" p. 106). Everything we do in the Church, every priesthood action, every ordinance, every covenant, every prayer offered in the name of Christ, has meaning and purpose only because of God's love. "We are saved by (His) grace, and condemned without it, no matter what else we might have or do. Grace is a sine qua non, an essential condition for salvation". (Stephen Robinson, "Are Mormons Christians?" p. 107). Jacob was awed by the incomprehensible power of God to lift us to sublime heights. "Great and marvelous are the works of the Lord", he wrote. "How unsearchable are the depths of the mysteries of him; and it is impossible that (we) should find out all his ways". (V. 8).

He explained; "No man knoweth of (God's) ways, save it be revealed unto him". (V. 8). This verse presaged the teaching of John Taylor, who said: "No matter what ability and talent we may possess, we must come under this rule if we wish to know the Father and the Son. If knowledge of them is not obtained through revelation it cannot be obtained at all". ("The Gospel Kingdom", p. 112). This process of "revelation" is the power that drives the light and knowledge we receive of God, and is a principle so basic that it almost requires no definition, because it speaks to our very souls.

Because God addresses His children "according to his will and pleasure", Jacob advised his people not to counsel the Lord, or to tell Him what He could or could not do, but to take counsel from Him, and to have confidence that His instruction would be given with a complete understanding of their circumstances and with total impartiality. (V. 9-10).

We must not be as the Priests of Baal, who, after confronting the Prophet Elijah on Mount Carmel "cried aloud, and cut themselves after their manner with knives and lancets, till the blood gushed out upon them". Then, Elijah said: "Hear me O Lord ... that this people may know that thou art the Lord God". Then "the fire of the Lord fell, and consumed the burnt sacrifice, and the wood, and the stones, and the dust, and licked up the water that was in the trench. And when all the people saw it, they fell on their faces, and they said, The Lord, he is God". (1 Kings 18:17-40).

The Savior Himself said: "Except ye are one, ye are not mine". (D&C 38:27). In our day, we give our attention and our loyalty to the First Presidency and to the united voice of the brethren. We turn our attention to the Head of the Church, who is Jesus Christ. J. Reuben Clark, Jr. observed: "We do not lack a prophet. What we lack is a listening ear by the people and a determination to live as God has commanded". The real questions are these: Do we listen to the counsel of the brethren at General Conference? Do we read what they have written? Do we live in conformity to the principles of the Gospel so that we are entitled to the guidance of the Spirit and recognize the truth?

A pillar of light that was above the brightness of the sun stood exactly over the head of young Joseph Smith in the Sacred Grove before it gradually descended and rested upon him. He and every subsequent President of the Church have enjoyed this mantle, "for surely the Lord God will do nothing but he revealeth his secret to his servants the prophets". (Amos 3:7).

Our reconciliation with Christ comes through the Atonement, the Resurrection, and the Power that is intrinsic to His nature. (V. 11). Jacob asked his listeners not to marvel at what he was teaching, in spite of the fact that the Atonement and Resurrection would not take place for another four or five hundred years! Nevertheless, the people were told to "attain a perfect knowledge" of Christ, or in other words, to develop perfect faith. (V. 12). The Nephite Saints could realistically expect to develop faith unto salvation centered on a future Messiah, just as it is a reasonable expectation for us to have faith in Christ nearly two millennia after His mortal ministry.

Once again, Jacob explained that the knowledge necessary for perfect faith is given by the Spirit, that "speaketh of things as they really are, and of things as they really will be", and that were manifest in plainness to his brethren, for the salvation of their souls. (V. 13). In addition, God provides witnesses, for the prophets of old taught these things as well. Beginning in this verse, and continuing through the balance of this chapter, Jacob led his audience to "the unfolding of this mystery" that is found in the "Parable of Zenos" in the chapter that follows. (V. 18).

The Jews of antiquity did not understand the Parable of Zenos, or The Allegory of The Tame and Wild Olive Tree, because they looked "beyond the mark" that was Jesus Christ. (V. 14). "Intellectual embroidery seems to have been preferred to the whole clothing of the Gospel - the frills to the fabric. There is more realism in the revelations than in reams of secular research, for secularism is congenitally short sighted. Revelation (provides) absolute anchors". (Neal Maxwell).

Because the Jews were "a stiffnecked people ... they despised the words of plainness, and killed the prophets, and sought for things that they could not understand". (V. 14, see Commentary Reference to 1 Nephi 1:19). Many Gentiles have fallen victim to the same spiritual insensitivity in the Last Days, attacking the Church of Jesus Christ with a blind vengeance and irrational zeal.

Jacob foresaw, by the spirit of prophecy, that the Jews would reject "the stone upon which they might build and have safe foundation". (V. 15). This stone was Jesus Christ. The mystery in the minds of the Nephites was this: How could the Jews "ever build upon it, that it might become the head of their corner?" (V. 16). In other words, having first rejected Christ, how could the Jews ever again, even at the millennial day, accept Him as their Savior? Jacob would utilize The Parable of Zenos to address this question.

"Great and marvelous are the works of the Lord. How unsearchable are the depths of the mysteries of him; and it is impossible that man should find out all his ways. And no man knoweth of his ways save it be revealed unto him; wherefore, brethren, despise not the revelations of God."
(Jacob 4:8).

Jacob
Chapter 5

A study of Jacob's writing reveals that he foresaw, by the spirit of prophecy, that the Jews would reject "the stone upon which they might build and have safe foundation". (Jacob 4:15). This stone was Jesus Christ. The mystery in the minds of the Nephites was this: How could the Jews "ever build upon it, that it might become the head of their corner?" (Jacob 4:16). In other words, having first rejected Christ, how could the Jews ever again, even at the millennial day, accept Him as their Savior?

To answer this question, Jacob related The Allegory of The Tame and Wild Olive Tree that comprises this chapter. There are 77 verses in the Allegory, which makes this the longest chapter in The Book of Mormon. Given the difficulty of engraving upon plates, this must have been considered an extremely important prophecy. It certainly was well known to Nephite prophets subsequent to Jacob. (See Jacob 4:1). Lehi had used the same profound symbolism in 1 Nephi 10:12, and Alma would refer to Zenos in his sermons, as well. (See Alma 5:35-36, & 33:3).

There are also significant parallels between The Allegory of Zenos and the Thanksgiving Hymns that are part of the Dead Sea Scrolls from Qumran, suggesting that the Dead Sea Covenantors were familiar with this prophet as well. Furthermore, Paul used identical symbols, indicating that he too might have been acquainted with the Allegory. (See Romans 11:17-24).

The reasons for the allegorical format of the prophecy were not only so that only the spiritually literate would understand its meaning, but also that the impact upon the listener would be more penetrating than if ordinary language were used. Even then, understanding could only be derived from pondering, searching, and praying. Yet, after all is said and done, "caution should be taken to keep the interpretations within reasonable bounds". ("Introduction to The Book of Mormon", Instructor's Guide, p. 304).

"The words of the prophet Zenos" were found in the Nephite scriptures but are to us a lost prophecy. Both he and his Allegory " could be a type and an image, rather than a unique historical event and personality, (since) ancient religious texts operate with interchangeable parts, characters, and names, which makes it hard for analytical minded Westerners to figure out what is going on". (V. 1, & Hugh Nibley, "Since Cumorah", p. 327).

There is symbolic significance in the olive tree. It is a living thing that produces good fruit and whose branches have always been associated with peace. But an olive tree cannot become productive by itself; it requires the grafting of a tame branch by the husbandman. Afterward, careful attention and pruning are required, because whenever the tree is neglected, it will begin to revert to the primitive, wild plant it once was. But once fruitful, it may remain so for centuries. In fact, new shoots from the root of the original tree may continue producing fruit for thousands of years. With this in mind, we begin to see how this allegory is going to play out.

In the prophecy, Israel is likened "unto a tame olive-tree". (V. 3). The Allegory immediately becomes significant to those who are of the lineage of Abraham, Isaac, and Jacob (Blood Israel), to those who have, by adoption, become partakers of the covenant that God first made with Father Abraham (Covenant Israel), and to those who live in the land promised to Abraham for an inheritance (Land Israel). (See Commentary References to 1 Nephi 19:19, 1 Nephi 21:10 & 23, 2 Nephi 24:1, 2 Nephi 30:2, & Jacob 5:67).

The vineyard is a world that has begun "to decay" into apostasy. (V. 4). Verses 1-4 concern the first visit of the master, who is Jesus Christ, to His vineyard. Seeing that His olive tree, Blood Israel, had begun to apostatize, He pruned it, or called it to repentance. "I will prune it, and dig about it, and nourish it", He said, "that perhaps it may shoot forth young and tender branches, and it perish not". (V. 4). This therapy improved the health of the tree somewhat, but it was obvious that, by-and-large, it was still dying. "Behold", observed Zenos, "the main top thereof began to perish". (V. 6).

In consequence of this, the Master called His servants the prophets, and commanded them to go and find branches from a wild olive tree, that is symbolic of the Gentiles, or Covenant Israel, and bring them to Him. (See 2 Nephi 30:2). At the same time, the withering branches of apostate Israel were to be plucked off and cast into a fire and burned. "It grieveth me that I should lose this tree;" said the Lord, "wherefore, go and pluck the branches from a wild olive-tree, and bring them hither unto me; and we will pluck off those main branches which are beginning to wither away, and we will cast them into the fire that they may be burned". (V. 7).

The young shoots from the tame tree that were still healthy were to be taken from the tree and grafted into other trees elsewhere in the vineyard. "And behold, saith the Lord of the vineyard, I take away many of these young and tender branches, and I will graft them in whithersoever I will". (V. 8). These represent various groups of Israelites led by the Lord to different parts of the world. They were "planted" in order to preserve some of the natural branches and fruit of Israel, the tame olive tree. Of course, Lehi's party was such a group, although clearly not the only one.

In addition, the wild olive-tree, representing the Gentiles, was to be grafted into the tame olive-tree, representing Blood Israel or the Jewish nation. "Take thou the branches of the wild olive-tree, and graft them in", that they might partake of the Covenant through Adoption. (V. 9). This is another powerful illustration that righteousness, and not lineage, is important to the Lord. (See 1 Nephi 17:33-35, & 2 Nephi 26:28-33). We are also taught here that when one is bound to the Covenant, there is a spiritual rebirth and awakening. "That I might preserve the roots thereof that they perish not", explained the Lord, "I have done this thing". (V. 11). In other words, the Lord of the vineyard accomplished the graft so that the Gentiles might be joined to Israel by Gospel covenants symbolized by the roots of the tree, and endure.

As Creator of the earth, the Lord of the vineyard is concerned about its welfare. In order to preserve the fruit of the tree, or the good works of Blood Israel, He determined to scatter the young and tender branches of the tame olive tree to "the nethermost part" of the vineyard that is the earth. (V. 8). This He did, as the Allegory reports that "it came to pass that the Lord of the vineyard went his way, and hid the natural branches of the tame olive-tree in the nethermost parts of the vineyard, some in one (place) and some in another". (V. 14).

Verses 15-28 concern a second visit of the Lord to the vineyard, "after a long time passed away". (V. 15). Upon inspection of the trees into which the wild branches, or the Gentiles, had been grafted, He found that "the tree in which the wild olive branches had been grafted ... had sprung forth and begun to bear fruit. And he beheld that it was good; and the fruit thereof was like unto the natural fruit". (V. 17). Furthermore, "because of the much strength of the root thereof the wild branches have brought forth tame fruit". (V. 18). In other words, in the Old World part of the vineyard, the Gentiles had helped to save Israel. Under the care of watchful husbandmen, the graft was successfully incorporated into the tame olive tree.

The Lord also inspected the "nethermost part of the vineyard". (V. 19 See 3 Nephi 15 & 16, that concern His "other sheep"). "And it came to pass that they went forth whither the master had hid the natural branches of the tree". (V. 20). We know that the blood of Israel is scattered throughout the world. This is called "the Diaspora". (See Commentary Reference to 2 Nephi 16:13). In these verses, four specific groups of people are identified. Although the soil in which these different groups had been planted was of varying quality, each had still brought forth much good fruit. (V. 21-25).

The last group, however, had been planted in a particularly "good spot of ground", representing the Promised Land of Lehi. (V. 25). This verse and verse 45 tell what happened to the descendants of Lehi, who were represented by this branch. "I have nourished it this long time, and only a part of the tree hath brought forth tame fruit, and the other part of the tree hath brought forth wild fruit". (V. 25). Some good fruit, or the Nephites, and some wild fruit, or the Lamanites, had been produced. Because the Lord had not plucked the wild branches that had grown up, and cast them into the fire, they had "overcome the good branch that it hath withered away". (V. 45). The Book of Mormon testifies that the Lamanites did overwhelm their brethren the Nephites just as the Allegory predicted they would.

Eighty-three years before the birth of Christ, Alma urged the members of the Nephite Church to repent, that they might "not be hewn down and cast into the fire. For behold, the time is at hand that whosoever bringeth forth not good fruit, or whosoever doeth not the works of righteousness, the same have cause to wail and mourn". (Alma 5:35-36).

In the Allegory, the Lord of the vineyard saw what was happening to this branch in the nethermost part of His vineyard, and declared His intention to "pluck off the branches that have not brought forth good fruit, and cast them into the fire". (V. 26). But His servant, the prophet, begged Him to forebear. "Let us prune it", he implored, "and dig about it, and nourish it a little longer, that perhaps it may bring forth good fruit". (V. 27). So, the Lord did forebear, and instead of destroying it, He "did nourish all the fruit of the vineyard". (V. 27-28).

By the time Christ visited the Americas, the designations of "Nephite" and "Lamanite" had essentially lost their hereditary distinctions. The cultural, political, social, economic, military, and religious differentiations had become far more significant. As a matter of fact, it is likely that by 33 A.D., the majority of the righteous "Nephites" were actually Lamanites who had renounced their apostasy, repented of their sins, been converted to the Gospel, and joined the Church of Christ. Thus, we can see that there was wisdom in the Lord's decision to wait, and to nourish all the fruit of the vineyard.

Verses 29-60 concern a third visit of the Lord and His servant to His vineyard after "a long time had passed away". (V. 29). The setting is the earth just before the end of the world. On this visit, "they came to the tree whose natural branches had been broken off, and the wild branches had been grafted in; and behold all sorts of fruit did cumber the tree". (V. 30). These wild branches represent the many Churches of Christendom, who, unfortunately, were in universal apostasy. Of all the fruit that had been produced, the Lord declared: "There is none of it which is good, and behold, there are all kinds of bad fruit; and it profiteth me nothing". (V. 32).

In the Sacred Grove, Joseph Smith was given a description of contemporary Christian Churches: "I was answered that I must join none of (the Churches), for they were all wrong. All their creeds were an abomination in his sight. They draw near to me with their lips", said the Personage, "but their hearts are far from me, they teach for doctrines the commandments of men, having a form of godliness, but they deny the power thereof". (Joseph Smith 1:19).

The abomination of the Churches of his day was that they pretended to have the power of the priesthood and the saving principles and ordinances of the Gospel, when in reality, they had neither. It is blasphemous to God when those without authority to do so invoke His name. It is taking the name of the Lord in vain. Roger Williams once declared: "There is no regularly constituted Church on earth, nor any person authorized to administer any Church ordinance; nor can there be until new apostles are sent by the Great Head of the Church, for whose coming I am seeking". ("Picturesque America," p. 502). Creeds are an abomination in the sight of God and are corrupt when they lead people away from the truth, and insult is added to injury when hypocrisy further perverts humanized, spiritually impotent creeds, and when people do not really believe in but are only professors of religion. (See Essay: "Professors").

Nevertheless, the Gentiles, or branches of the wild olive tree, had nourished Israel, or the roots, insomuch that the roots were yet alive. "(Behold), the servant said unto his master ... Because thou didst graft in the branches of the wild olive-tree they have nourished the roots, that they are alive, and they have not perished; wherefore thou beholdest that they are yet good". (V. 34). The Lord of the vineyard had preserved them for His own purpose, for in His omniscience, He knew that the House of Israel would yet recognize the Messiah.

In the Last Days the condition in which the Lord found the wild branches, or the Gentiles, was pitiable. "But behold, the wild branches have grown and have overrun the roots thereof;" therefore "it hath brought forth much evil fruit (and) it beginneth to perish. And it will soon become ripened, that it may be cast into the fire, except we should do something for it to preserve it". (V. 37).

In His allegorical inspection, the Lord of the vineyard found that even the natural branches that had been planted in the best soil of the nethermost part of the vineyard "had all become corrupt. And the wild fruit of the last had overcome that part of the tree which brought forth good fruit, even that the branch had withered away and died". (V. 39). By the time of the battles at Cumorah, the Nephite nation was in a self-destruct mode, and the Lamanites were sinking further and further into a long, dark night of apostasy. In the Fifth Century A.D., (400 - 421 A.D.) Moroni reported: "The whole face of this land is one continual round of murder and bloodshed; and no one knoweth the end of the war. And now, behold, I say no more concerning them, for there are none save it be the Lamanites and robbers that do exist upon the face of the land. And there are none that do know the true God". (Mormon 8:8-10). This state of affairs continued unabated for more than a thousand years.

Therefore, "the Lord of the vineyard wept". (V. 41). Three times He asked Himself: "What more could I have done for my vineyard?" (V. 41, 47, & 49). Before this question was answered, the Lord philosophized on the state of affairs in the Last Days. (V. 42-46). He reasoned that the world would sink into a universal state of apostasy, and that according to the justice of God, it must therefore be destroyed. "And now, all the trees of my vineyard are good for nothing save it be to be hewn down and cast into the fire". (V. 42).

The Lord of the Vineyard had led Lehi's party to a land of promise where they had been given every opportunity to flourish. "And behold this last, whose branch hath withered away, I did plant in a good spot of ground; yea, even that which was choice unto me above all other parts of the land of my vineyard". (V. 43). The Jaredites, who had occupied the land previous to the Nephites and Lamanites, had been removed to make way for them. "And thou beheldest that I also cut down that which cumbered this spot of ground, that I might plant this tree in the stead thereof". (V. 44, see Ether 2:8). Some have wondered how the tail-end of the Jaredite civilization could have lived contemporaneously with Lehi's people, and yet remained undetected in a relatively small geographical area. Evidently, the Lord never intended that they intermingle or that the Jaredites compromise in any way the opportunities created by the Lord for the Nephites and Lamanites to prosper in the land without interference from outside influences.

Over a period of time, the Lamanites had overpowered the Nephites, and nearly all had apostatized. The Lord of the vineyard beheld "that a part thereof brought forth good fruit, and a part thereof brought forth wild fruit; and because I plucked not the branches thereof and cast them into the fire, behold, they have overcome the good branch that it hath withered away". (V. 45). All the branches of the House of Israel, as well as the Gentiles who were grafted in, had become corrupted by the time the Gospel was restored to the earth in 1830. "And now, behold, notwithstanding all the care with which we have taken of my vineyard, the trees thereof have become corrupted, that they bring forth no good fruit; and these I had hoped to preserve, to have laid up fruit thereof against the season, unto mine own self. But, behold, they have become like unto the wild olive-tree, and they are of no worth but to be hewn down and cast into the fire". (V. 46).

"But what could I have done more in my vineyard?" He asked again. (V. 47). Throughout history, the Lord has attempted to redeem His people through the ministry of His prophets. "Have I slacked mine hand?" He asked. "Nay, I have nourished it, and I have digged about it, and I have pruned it, and I have dunged it; and I have stretched forth mine hand almost all the day long". (V. 47).

After all is said and done, just what is it that has corrupted the vineyard in the Last Days? Is it "the loftiness of (the) vineyard", or the haughtiness and pride of the world? Is it because people tend to raise themselves above the word of the Lord, and "look beyond the mark" which is Jesus Christ? Is it because some members of the Church pay no heed to the teachings of the Gospel, but instead follow their own agenda and make their own rules according to the shifting sands of expediency? Is it because even Church members sometimes exercise unrighteous dominion, or take "strength unto themselves?" Is it because we sometimes try to bring the world into the Gospel, rather than the Gospel into the world? (V. 48, see Jacob 4:8, 10, & 14-15, & D&C 121:39). As Spencer W. Kimball once observed: "The Gospel went from Palmyra to Paris, and not the other way around".

A third time, the Lord of the vineyard asked: "What could I have done more for my vineyard?" (V. 49). This rhetorical question of the Master is more penetrating when we realize that He is ever in control, is wise, benevolent, and knows our individual and collective weakness, and that "His grace is sufficient for all men that (simply) humble themselves" before Him. (Ether 12:27, see v. 75).

With an eye on the tinder-dry kindling prepared for the anticipated bonfire, the servant of the Lord begged: "Spare it a little longer", and so the Lord relented. "Yea, I will spare it a little longer". (V. 50). Just why He chose to do so becomes obvious in the last 25 verses of this chapter. From here on in the Allegory, the focus of attention is our own generation.

Verse 52 concerns the Gathering of Israel. The Lord had enjoined His Apostles: "Go ye into all the world and preach the Gospel to every creature". (Mark 16:15, see D&C 84:62, & Moroni 9:22). As the missionaries of The Church of Jesus Christ of Latter-day Saints carry the Gospel to the world, their task will be made easier because of the scattering of Israel. With her blood flowing in the veins of Gentile nations, the foundation covenants may find nourishment and take root. David B. Haight once said that we do not preach the Gospel so that people can enjoy a better life. We do it so that they can be saved in the Celestial Kingdom of God. "And this will I do that the tree may not perish", said the Lord, "that, perhaps, I may preserve unto myself the roots thereof". (V. 53).

The remnant of the House of Israel that includes the Lamanites will be taught the Gospel by the Gentiles and will be provided the opportunity to enter into covenants with the Lord. "I will graft in unto them the branches of their mother tree, that I may preserve the roots also unto mine own self, that when they shall be sufficiently strong perhaps they may bring forth good fruit unto me, that I may yet have glory in the fruit of my vineyard". (V. 54). "And we will nourish again the trees of the vineyard" with the message of the Gospel, "and we will trim up the branches thereof", with problem-focused teaching, said the Lord, so they may mend their ways, become spiritually mature, and develop fluency in the language of the Spirit. (V. 58). "For this is my work and my glory", He declared, "to bring to pass the immortality and eternal life of man". (Moses 1:39).

Nevertheless, those branches that are ripened in iniquity will, of necessity, be cast into the fire. (V. 58). As Isaiah foretold, "When the boughs are withered, they shall be broken off; the women come, and set them on fire; it is a people of no understanding; therefore, he that made them will not have mercy on them, and he that formed them will show them no favour". (Isaiah 27:11). As we can see, understanding The Allegory of Zenos makes even the prophecies of Isaiah much more understandable and relevant to our day.

There are three qualifying reasons, outlined in verses 59 and 60, why the Lord of the vineyard chose to nourish the trees in the Last Days. Perhaps, Israel will seize upon this as an opportunity for her redemption. "And this I do that, perhaps, the roots thereof may take strength because of their goodness; and because of the change of the branches, that the good may overcome the evil". (V. 59). Perhaps, with the restoration of Israel to her lands of promise, she will finally acknowledge the Master and Lord of the Vineyard. (V. 60). Perhaps, when Israel again bows her knee, the Lord will once more take joy in the Children of the Covenant. (V. 60).

These conditional reasons for nourishing the trees of the vineyard one final time in the Last Days laid the foundation for verses 61-67, that concern a fourth visit of the Lord and His missionary army to His vineyard. "Wherefore, go to, and call servants", He commanded His prophet, "that we may labor diligently with our might in the vineyard, that we may prepare the way, that I may bring forth again the natural fruit, which fruit is good and the most precious above all other fruit". (V. 61). "For thou art called to prune my vineyard for the last time". (V. 62, see D&C 24:19).

To be a literal or adopted child of the Abrahamic Covenant and to receive the ordinances of the Priesthood, is to receive the fruit of the tree of life, which is "desirable above all other fruit". (1 Nephi 8:12). When Lehi tasted this fruit in his Vision of the Tree of Life, he described it as "the most sweet, above all that (he) ever before tasted. Yea, and (he) beheld that the fruit thereof was white, to exceed all the whiteness that (he) had ever seen". (1 Nephi 8:11). Those who attain eternal life in the Celestial Kingdom of God enjoy undistorted spiritual clarity as they partake of that fruit that is "good and the most precious above all other fruit". (V. 61).

The final gathering of Israel in the Last Days will prepare her for a celestial destiny. Verse 63 chiastically sets the pattern. In the Last Days, the Gentiles are to have the Gospel preached to them first, and then the Jews will have their turn. "Graft in the branches; begin at the last that they may be first, and that the first may be last, and dig about the trees, both old and young, the first and the last; and the last and the first, that all may be nourished once again for the last time". (See 1 Nephi 13:42, D&C 88:51-62, Matthew 11:25-26, & 20:16).

The imagery in verse 64 is graphic: "Wherefore, dig about them, and prune them, and dung them once more, for the last time". To "dung" a plant is to spread manure around its base, that is symbolic of the nourishment of gathered Israel with the restored Gospel. This will cause it to grow or to increase in righteousness. Verse 65 is reminiscent of the Parable of The Wheat and The Tares related by the Savior. The bad fruit should not be cleared "away all at once, lest the roots thereof should be too strong for the graft, and the graft thereof shall perish, and I lose the trees of my vineyard". (See D&C 86:7).

The roots and the top branches grafted into the tree should be "equal in strength". (V. 66). As such, they shall be nourished with the word of the Lord, as they receive "line upon line, precept upon precept". (D&C 98:12). The Gentiles and gathered Israel will grow together in the knowledge of the Lord. It will not be as it was formerly, when the branches grew faster than the strength of the roots could bear. (See V. 48). The natural branches or Blood Israel that had grown wild, will be grafted back into the natural tree, in a spiritual rebirth. (V. 67, see Commentary References to 1 Nephi 19:19, 1 Nephi 21:10 & 23, 2 Nephi 24:1, 2 Nephi 30:2, & Jacob 5:4).

For one last time, the servants of the Lord are to labor in the vineyard, taking, as He put it to Joseph Smith, "all the strength of mine house, which are my warriors, my young men, and they that are of middle age". (D&C 101:55). Because of the wickedness and abominations wrought by the great and abominable Church in the Last Days, the numbers in the army of the Lord will be relatively few. (V. 70, see 1 Nephi 14:12). But they will take great joy in the harvest of souls. (V. 71). The Savior gave them the comforting reassurance that "if it so be that (they) should labor all (their) days in crying repentance unto this people, and bring, save it be one soul unto me, how great shall be (their) joy with him in the kingdom of my Father". (D&C 18:15).

Thus, the missionaries will go forth, full of the Spirit of God like a burning fire, to preach the Gospel. "And it came to pass that the servants did go and labor with their mights, (note the plural form of the passive verb, that is so characteristic of Semitic grammar), and the Lord of the vineyard labored also with them; and they did obey the commandments of the Lord of the Vineyard in all things". (V. 72). "Send forth the elders of my Church unto the nations which are afar off;" declared the Lord, "Unto the islands of the sea; send forth unto foreign lands; call upon all nations, first upon the Gentiles, and then upon the Jews". (D&C 133:8).

The Times of the Gentiles will be over when the Jews have been gathered and when Jerusalem is no longer trodden down. This will occur at a time when there is great social turmoil on the Earth and when the Gentiles for the most part have begun to reject the Gospel. (See D&C 45:25-29). Prophets in our day have declared that the Times of the Gentiles has been fulfilled. This is an ominous sign indicating that the end is near. "And the natural branches began to grow and thrive exceedingly; and the wild branches began to be plucked off and to be cast away". (V. 73).

In the Allegory of Zenos, many who had lived outside the sphere of influence of the Church and Gospel have become, by adoption, "the natural fruit", or the Covenant Children of Israel. "And they became like unto one body; and the fruits were equal". (V. 74). As Ezekiel foresaw: "They shall become one in thine hand". (Ezekiel 37:17).

It is under these unique circumstances that the Lord calls his people "Zion, because they (are) of one heart and one mind, and (dwell) in righteousness; and there (are) no poor among them". (Moses 7:18). Verses 74 and 75 indicate that the great missionary harvest will have preserved from apostasy "the natural fruit", or the Children of Israel. These were "most precious unto the Lord from the beginning", for they were Children of the Covenant and heirs of the blessings first promised to Abraham. One of the purposes of this Allegory is to teach us that the Lord is in control, He knows the end from the beginning, and we should not counsel Him but rather should take counsel from Him. As the Lord told Moses: "Remember the days of old ... when the Most High divided the nations their inheritance ... he set the bounds of the people according to the number of the children of Israel". (Deuteronomy 32:7-8).

Israel and the Church will be profitable servants in the Last Days and will be rewarded for their efforts. "I will bless all those who labor in my vineyard with a mighty blessing". (V. 75, see D&C 21:9). They will be aided by the intervention of the Lord Himself, Who will personally usher in the millennial era, and only at the end of a thousand years of peace will "evil fruit again come into (the) vineyard". (V. 76). At this time, Satan will be loosed again "for a little season, and then cometh the end ... and the earth shall pass away so as by fire". (D&C 43:31-32). "The good will (the Lord) preserve unto (Himself), and the bad will (He) cast away into its own place". (V. 76).

"And my vineyard will I cause to be burned with fire" or refined, said the Lord. (V. 77). To the Nephites, the Resurrected Savior prophesied: "For behold, the day cometh that shall burn as an oven; and all the proud, yea, and all that do wickedly, shall be stubble, and the day that cometh shall burn them up, saith the Lord of Hosts, that it shall leave them neither root nor branch". (3 Nephi 25:1).

Of the Allegory of Zenos, Joseph Fielding Smith, Jr. declared: "When you read thru that chapter, if you cannot say in your soul 'This is absolutely a revelation from God,' then there is something wrong with you".

Jacob
Chapter 6

Zenos evidently recorded his Allegory without any explanation whatsoever. After The Book of Mormon acccunt, however, Jacob offered a very tight, compact mini-sermon that he began by enlarging upon the Allegory, and ended with his final testimony and farewell.

In verse 1, he confirmed the validity of the Allegory of Zenos, declaring that "the things which this prophet Zenos spake, concerning the House of Israel, in the which he likened them unto a tame olive-tree, must surely come to pass". (V. 1). All the prophets repeat each other and teach the same things. (See Commentary Reference to Jarom 1:2, Jacob 4:4, & 7:11). In the scriptures, we have a history of "characteristic and repeating events recounted in a formulaic language of set terms and expressions that cannot be limited to any time or place". (Hugh Nibley, "Since Cumorah", p. 149).

Therefore, Jacob reiterated Nephi's prophetic description of conditions in the Last Days, when "the Saints (would be) scattered upon all the face of the earth, and they (would be) armed with righteousness, and with the power of God in great glory". (1 Nephi 14:14). Ours is the day when "the servants of the Lord shall go forth in his power, to nourish and prune the vineyard". (V. 2). It is also a time when the Gospel will be taught to every nation, kindred, tongue, and people. (See D&C 45:53, & 133:37). After this great missionary work takes place, the end of the world "soon cometh". This is one of the most important messages of the ancient Allegory of Zenos.

Verse 3 utilizes the Hebraic style of contrasting thought patterns, which is a literary device called antithetical parallelism: "How blessed are they who have labored diligently in his vineyard; and how cursed are they who shall be cast out into their own place"! The idea in one stanza is contrasted with an opposite or antithetical idea in a parallel stanza. There are many examples of this style throughout The Book of Mormon, for example, in Alma 5:40, 9:28, & 36:21. (See Essay: "Parallelism in Hebrew Poetry").

Those who are "cast out" of the vineyard are telestial individuals who will be consumed by fire at the Second Coming. (V. 3). The glory of God cleanses and purges out all impurity. Following its refining process, metal has no value if imperfections remain. Good for nothing, it must be cast upon the scrap heap. Only if it is clean, can it be transformed into a thing of beauty, will it stand up under punishing use, and with proper care will it give many years of reliable service.

Jacob said God was "merciful", because in spite of Israel being "stiff-necked" or rigid, and "gainsaying" or contradictory, His hand is stretched forth unto them "all the day long". (V. 4). He would yet save them in His kingdom if only the people would not harden their hearts. When we harden our hearts, we are not teachable. (See Commentary Reference to the Introduction to 2 Nephi 31-33). Verses 4-6 illustrate that when we have "full purpose of heart", however, we rely completely on the merits of Christ's Atonement, and repent.

Thus, verses 4-6 urge those in Israel to "repent with full purpose of heart", and not "harden (their) hearts". The clear message is that sclerosis and calcification of our spiritual arteries are symptoms of a self-defeating illness that, left untreated, will create a stagnation that numbs our feelings. We can be saved only if the signs of heart disease are recognized "in the light of day" before the darkness of apostasy falls. Then, spiritual surgery can quicken the life-force within clogged arteries, restoring circulation with the stent of spirituality, allowing vitalizing energy to flow freely.

Verse 7 refers directly to The Allegory of Zenos. Pointed questions loaded with powerful action verbs were intended by Jacob to hold the attention of his listeners. "Will ye reject Christ", he asked, "and deny (His words), and the power of God, and the gift of the Holy Ghost, and quench the Holy Spirit, and make a mockery of the great plan of redemption?"

In the context of our weaknesses, The Plan of Salvation is The Plan of Redemption, and so, Jacob's message was a call to repentance. (See 2 Nephi 25:26). If we do not repent, the Holy Spirit that burns like a fire will be quenched, and the priesthood keys of redemption and resurrection held by Christ will be ineffectual. Without repentance and forgiveness, we will stand before the Bar of God with "shame and awful guilt". (V. 9). Without the Atonement, the Law of Mercy is out of options. It must of necessity yield to the exacting demands of the Law of Justice. If the Law of Mercy, energized through the Redemption, does not intervene in our behalf, the Law of Justice cannot be denied, and we must suffer endless punishment, that is God's punishment. "And according to the power of justice", Jacob explained, "ye must go away into that lake of fire and brimstone, whose flames are unquenchable, and whose smoke ascendeth up forever and ever, which lake of fire and brimstone is endless torment". (V. 10, see D&C 19:12). Clearly, the intelligent choice is to "repent and enter in at the strait gate, and continue in the way which is narrow, until ye shall obtain eternal life". (V. 11). This verse recapitulates the line of thought begun in verse 5, when Jacob asked: "I beseech of you in words of soberness that ye would repent, and come with full purpose of heart, and cleave unto God as he cleaveth unto you".

Faith and repentance lead us to the strait and narrow gate of baptism. On the far side of this portal, we will walk in the light of a new day, enjoy a remission of our sins, gain membership in the Church, commune with the Saints in full fellowship, entertain new vistas leading to our sanctification through repentance and receipt of the Holy Ghost, and find ourselves on the path of eternal progress leading to the Celestial Kingdom. But the Gospel standard is undeviating, with no room for rationalization or compromise. There is no latitude in God's declaration that He "cannot look upon sin with the least degree of allowance". (D&C 1:31).

"This seems a harsh scripture", taught Steven Robinson, "for it clearly states that God cannot tolerate sin or sinfulness in any degree. He can't wink at it, or ignore it, or turn and look the other way. He won't sweep it under the rug or say, 'Well, it's just a little sin. It'll be all right.' God's standard, the celestial standard, is absolute, and it allows no exceptions. There is no wiggle room. Many people seem to have the idea that the Judgment will somehow involve weighing or balancing, with their good deeds on one side of the scales and their bad deeds on the other. If their good deeds outweigh their bad, or if their hearts are basically good and outweigh their sins, then they can be admitted into the presence of God. This notion is false. God cannot, and will not, allow moral or ethical imperfection in any degree whatsoever to dwell in his presence. He cannot tolerate sin 'with the least degree of allowance.' It is not a question of whether our good deeds outweigh our sins. If there is even one sin on our record, we are finished. The celestial standard is complete innocence, pure and simple, and nothing less will be tolerated in the kingdom of God". ("Believing Christ", p. 1-2).

After explaining the great Plan of Redemption that solved the dilemma created by God's demand for perfection coupled with our inability to live sinless lives, Jacob simply stated: "O be wise; what can I say more?" Moroni similarly urged: "Be wise in the days of your probation; strip yourselves of all uncleanness ... ask with a firmness unshaken, that ye will yield to no temptation, but that ye will serve the true and living God". (Mormon 9:28). One way we can do this is to read this chapter in conjunction with Alma Chapter 41, that illustrates how our agency and accountability influence the nature of our personal judgment.

It is likely that Jacob intended to end his book at this point, because he bid us farewell and declared that he would meet us "before the pleasing bar of God". along with Nephi, Moroni, Joseph Smith, Christ, and others. (See 2 Nephi 33:7).

"And the day that he
shall set his hand again the
second time to recover his people, is
the day, yea, even the last time, that
the servants of the Lord shall go forth
in his power, to nourish and prune
the vineyard; and after that
the end soon cometh."
(Jacob 6:2).

Jacob
Chapter 7

"Some years had passed away" before Jacob continued his narrative on The Small Plates of Nephi. (v. 1). Evidently, he felt that he should report the events surrounding the appearance in the Land of Nephi of a man called Sherem, possibly because his actions were characteristic of so many misguided evangelists in the Last Days. This man was the first Book of Mormon "anti-Christ", who is one who opposes Christ, or sets himself up as a savior, or establishes any other person or system as a substitute for the Savior, and who then seeks to promulgate this substitute in the hearts and minds of the people. Sherem was adept at what he did. He was flattering (v. 2), labored diligently (v. 3), was learned (v. 4), had the power of speech (v. 4), was assisted by the power of the devil (v. 18), and called light darkness (v. 7).

He was beguiling and by false representation raised the hopes of the people. He likely taught that it is okay to sin a little, to lie a little, and to procrastinate the initiation of the process of repentance. Perhaps he condoned cheating one's neighbor, or said that the Word of Wisdom was outdated. He might have condoned immorality. Maybe he even rationalized sexually deviant lifestyles. Surely he would have praised the people for the efforts they were making, and assured them that their good works guaranteed their salvation. He might have taught that good works are unnecessary as a token of obedience to covenants made with God, or that by a declaration of faith one is saved. Perhaps he believed that Sabbath day worship was unnecessary. He might have helped the people to justify gambling and other vices that violate Gospel principles. Perhaps he endorsed the consecration of the clergy by popular demand.

He may have rationalized away dishonesty by describing it as "misleading others," and transgression as "misbehavior". He might have justified sin by characterizing it as "poor judgment", looting as "undocumented shopping" or the "redistribution of wealth to the underprivileged". Lying might have been excused as "hyper-exaggeration".

Sherem might have taught all these things, in order to "overthrow the doctrine of Christ" for some perverted, twisted reason. (v. 2). Perhaps he did this in order to wrest the power vested in the priesthood. Surely he sought unrighteous dominion over his brethren. He seemed so sure of his position that he relished the opportunity to contend with the Prophet Jacob. Flushed with confidence because of his popularity, he may have felt as Cain, who had exulted: Truly, I am Mahan!" (Moses 5:31).

He certainly had formidable skills in his arsenal and felt prepared to debate Jacob. Within his cache of weapons was "a perfect knowledge of the language of the people". (v. 4). This could mean that he spoke the same language as the people, or more likely, that he had a golden tongue. (See 1 Nephi 1:2). He had "power of speech, according to the power of the devil". (V. 2). We can only imagine the persuasiveness of his oratory skills and his rhetoric, which must have been polished with a flair for the dramatic.

But like the Sophists of old, he was an intellectual guerilla, insisting on fighting his battles on his own turf. Because his back had never been against the wall, his tactics had been aggressive and his actions swift and decisive. Yet, he had never had to defend himself against one such as Jacob, who had received the Second Comforter while still in his youth. Jacob's credentials were more than adequate to shake the logic of a troublesome man such as Sherem, and knock away the bulwark of his fortifications, for they were built on faulty reasoning, so even though he stood his ground against the prophet of God, it was shaky.

Priestcraft should not be confused with the behavior of the "anti-Christ" Sherem. These two are not one and the same. An "anti-Christ" openly rebels against Christ, while the user of priestcraft claims a belief in Christ, but perverts His teachings. (See Commentary Reference to 2 Nephi 26:29).

Jacob had no self-doubts about his approaching encounter with Sherem, for he had enjoyed many manifestations of the Spirit, and "could not be shaken". (V. 5). He had powerfully taught the people the same principles that his elder brother Nephi had rehearsed for the people many years before, namely, "the Gospel, or the doctrine of Christ". (V. 6).

With the forked tongue of a serpent, Sherem opened the dialogue by addressing the prophet with the velvety smooth and syrupy salutation: "Brother Jacob". (V. 6). Devils such as he often put on the manners of angels, but they are wolves in sheep's clothing. In verse 7, he commenced to call black white and white black, even accusing Jacob of blasphemy for the crime of false prophecy and "after this manner did (he) contend against" Jacob, fighting him in strident but increasingly anxious opposition. (See Deuteronomy 18:20).

But Jacob, being filled with the Holy Ghost, confounded, or utterly defeated, the nefarious plans of his antagonist. When we have made deposits to our spiritual bank accounts over many years' time, it is not likely that they will be overdrawn in our times of need. The Lord "poured in his Spirit into (Jacob's) soul". (V. 8). With David, Jacob could exclaim, "Thou anointest my head with oil; my cup runneth over". (Psalms 23:5).

Because Sherem's spiritual perceptions had shut down, and since he would only accept evidence that he could feel through his physical senses, he asked for a sign. (V. 13). But he really only wanted theological titillation, since he confused the illusion of reality for the flowing cornucopia of life itself. The charade that had sustained him was falling apart. There were no reserves of substance upon which he could fall back.

The process by which real faith, or power, is developed is one of testing. The Lord gives us certain principles, and by obedience to them, blessings and power follow. But we have no proof of that promise until we act on the basis of trust or belief. Then comes the confirmation of the reality. That is why James taught: "Faith if it hath not works, is dead, being alone". (James 2:17, see John 17:7, & Ether 12:6). "Faith cometh not by signs, but signs follow those that believe". (D&C 63:9). When we understand this process, we can see why sign seeking is condemned. Someone like Sherem who demands outward evidence of the power of God as a condition for his belief is really seeking to circumvent the process by which faith is developed. He wants proof without paying the price. As with the adulterer, he seeks the result without accepting the responsibility. Without the moral element of responsibility that we call faith, belief is dangerously vulnerable to a host of influences that can erode it into a stammering babble of contradictory nonsense.

Jacob declared that Sherem was "of the devil" and a slanderer, for he was maliciously misrepresenting the word of God. (V. 14). In spite of this, he granted his adversary his wish for a sign, and said that God would smite him, which occurred immediately. (V. 15). Thus, Sherem was punished for the crime of his own false prophecy, and also for his failure to follow Jacob, who was the true Prophet of God.

Only after many days, when Sherem regained his senses, did he ask to speak one last time to the people. (V. 15-17). He knew he was dying, and desired to speak plainly, in contrast to the vain and flattering speeches he had previously made. He confessed "Christ, and the power of the Holy Ghost, and the ministering of angels". (V. 17). Perhaps, due to the unconditional love of a benevolent God, he had directly experienced such things.

He said that he had been deceived by the power of the devil. He felt the uncomfortably close proximity of hell, eternity, and God's punishment, and he feared "the second death", or remaining eternally dead to things of the Spirit. (V. 18-19). He had good cause to fear. "Those in this life who gain a perfect knowledge of the divinity of the Gospel cause, that comes only by revelation from the Holy Ghost, and who then link themselves with Lucifer and come out in open rebellion, become Sons of Perdition". (Bruce R. McConkie, "Mormon Doctrine", p. 746, see D&C 76:31-37). But, it is not for us to say whether Sherem was doomed to outer darkness.

Having expressed his fears, Sherem quickly "gave up the ghost". (V. 20). Properly speaking, a ghost is a spirit. Sherem's spirit left his body and went to the spirit prison of the unjust, where it would be given over to the buffetings of Satan, to await resurrection and redemption after he had personally paid the uttermost farthing for his gross sins. (See 2 Nephi 9:13, D&C 76:73, 138:8 & 28, Isaiah 61:1, 1 Peter 3:19 & Moses 7:57).

The death of Sherem had eliminated an immediate threat to the spirituality of the Nephites. "Peace and the love of God was restored again among the people, and they searched the scriptures". (V. 23). This verse implies that the people had personal copies of the scriptures and suggests that they turned to them for fortification, in an attitude of recommitment and rededication to the principles of the Gospel.

Having done so, they then unsuccessfully turned their energies to reclaiming their lost brethren, the Lamanites. "And it came to pass that many means were devised to reclaim and restore the Lamanites to the knowledge of the truth; but it all was in vain, for they delighted in wars and bloodshed, and they had an eternal hatred against us, their brethren. And they sought by the power of their arms to destroy us continually. (V. 24). In this verse, Jacob provided the most vivid description yet of the widening gulf that was emerging between the Nephites and the Lamanites. We would know more about their wars and contentions if we had the record of The Large Plates of Nephi. It is probable that their kings had kept this secular history of his people, while their prophets preserved their religious history on The Small Plates of Nephi, from which was translated The Book of Jacob. (V. 26).

It is with real melancholy that we read Jacob's farewell, wherein he declared: "The time passed away with us, and also our lives passed away like as it were unto us a dream, we being a lonesome and a solemn people, wanderers, cast out from Jerusalem, born in tribulation, in a wilderness, and hated of our brethren, which caused wars and contentions; wherefore, we did mourn out our days". (V. 26, see Omni 1:12).

Jacob entrusted the plates and the other tokens and emblems of authority to the care of his son, Enos, bid farewell to those who would someday read his words, and closed his record as his pragmatist brother Nephi had, declaring: "I make an end of my writing upon these plates, which writing has been small; and to the reader I bid farewell, hoping that many of my brethren may read my words". Then, he simply wrote: "Brethren, adieu". (V. 27). This expression might seem strange for a Hebrew prophet, but actually the Hebrew "Lehitra ot" has essentially the same meaning as the French "adieu". Both are much more than a simple farewell or an expression of kind wishes. Rather, they include the idea of a blessing as well, commending one to the care of God at parting. Joseph Smith's inspired translation seems appropriate to the circumstances.

"I conclude this record
declaring that I have written
according to the best of my knowledge,
by saying that the time passed away with
us, and also our lives passed away like as it
were unto us a dream, we being a lonesome and
a solemn people, wanderers, cast out from Jerusalem,
born in tribulation, in a wilderness, and hated of our
brethren … And I make an end of my writing upon
these plates … and to the reader, I bid farewell,
hoping that many of my brethren may read
my words. Brethren, adieu."
(Jacob 7:26-27).

The Book of Enos
About 420 B.C.

Enos
Chapter 1

The short books of Enos, Jarom, and Omni, comprising only 7 pages in total in the current edition of The Book of Mormon, span 414 years from 544 B.C. to 130 B.C., which is almost one-third of Nephite history.

Enos was the son of Jacob, and the grandson of Lehi. In Hebrew, his name means "Mortal man" or "Son of Seth". His father taught him "in his language". (V. 1). Enos would not have required tutoring from his father to learn the spoken language of the Nephites, so this reference might refer to the written language specifically used by the guardians of the plates. Moroni later called this language "the reformed Egyptian". "And now, behold, we have written this record according to our knowledge, in the characters which are called among us the reformed Egyptian, being handed down and altered by us, according to our manner of speech. (Mormon 9:32, see 1 Nephi 1:2, Mosiah 1:2, & Commentary Reference to Jacob 4:1). Whatever "language" the Nephite prophets used when engraving upon the plates, it would likely have been a form of shorthand, in order to facilitate the process.

The Book of Enos opens at a time in his life when he wrestled before the Lord; that is to say, he struggled with the recognition of his sins and shortcomings, as part of the process of receiving forgiveness. (V. 2). President Kimball once observed: "To those of us who would pay pennies toward our unfathomable debt, we remember Enos, who. like many of us, had great need". Truman Madsen wrote: "At one level, we all indulge in daily clichés and more or less mean them. 'Forgive us, help us to overcome our weaknesses.' At a deeper level, we voice actual present feelings, even when they are raw, ugly, miserable ones. 'Father, I feel awful!' 'I am racked with anxiety!' But there is yet a deeper level, the innermost of which often defies words, even feeling words. This level may be likened to what the scriptures call 'groanings which cannot be uttered.' (Romans 8:26). Turned upward, they become the most powerful prayer thrust of all. There is a wordless center in each of us!" ("Christ and The Inner Life", p. 17-18, see Ether 1:34-43).

During his quest, Enos went into the forest and traveled a path he had never walked before. The words of his father that he had doubtless heard many times in Church meetings, family home evenings, family councils, and personal exchanges, "sank deep" into his heart. (V. 3). Memory can be both cruel and kind and so his soul "hungered" and he "cried" unto God in "prayer and supplication". (V. 4). All the day long, he raised his voice to heaven. At eventide, the answer finally came: "Enos, thy sins are forgiven thee, and thou shalt be blessed". (V. 5).

Christ is "the Lamb slain from the foundation of the world". (Moses 7:47). In other words, in the ages before His mortal ministry, the details of the Atonement had already been worked out, and so all those who lived and died before the Meridian of Time could be assured of forgiveness for their sins as was Enos, following the steps of repentance and through continuing obedience to the principles and commandments of the everlasting Gospel.

For them, Christ was a present reality, although He would not manifest Himself in the flesh for another 400 years. It has now been nigh unto 2,000 years since His ministry, yet the Atonement is still a certain reality in our lives. Not retrospectively, but in the present tense, we look to Christ. "Now, after the many testimonies which have been given of him, this is the testimony, last of all, which we give of him: that he lives!" (D&C 76:22). We think of Him as the Great I Am in both a spiritually figurative and temporally literal sense. He is our Friend, our Advocate, our Intercessor, and the Mediator of the Covenant, and we enjoy a continuing and close personal relationship with our Savior.

The story of Enos is inspirational because it illustrates the personal concern of Jesus Christ. Enos is a great example, as well, because in his account we recognize an expanding circle of concern for his "brethren the Nephites", and for his "brethren the Lamanites". (V. 9 & 11). The natural reaction of committed converts is a selfless desire and anxiety to share the truth with others, that they might also be partakers of the Divine Gift and enjoy God's Rest. (See Commentary Reference to 2 Nephi 33:8-9).

Verse 10 is a classic expression of personal revelation: "And while I was thus struggling in the spirit", wrote Enos, "behold, the voice of the Lord came into my mind". When this voice comes, wrote Truman Madsen, "as a flow of pure intelligence attended by a burning in the center self, it is of God. Our search for external warrant is really the confirmation and application of what is already, and more certainly, known". ("Eternal Man", p. 73, see "Teachings", p. 151 & D&C 9:8-9).

The guilt Enos had felt "was swept away", and his "faith began to be unshaken in the Lord". (V. 6 & 11). We withhold ourselves from the Lord when we express our faithlessness by failing to repent, and our disobedience mandates a withdrawal of the Spirit that cripples God's Plan for our improvement.

After the martyrdom of Joseph Smith, Brigham Young led the Church through difficult times. As he was guiding a company of the Saints across the Plains toward the Valley of The Great Salt Lake, the Prophet Joseph appeared to him in a dream. Of all the counsel he could have given, his message to Brother Brigham was simple: "Tell the brethren to be humble and faithful, and be sure to keep the Spirit of the Lord, that it will lead them aright. Be careful and not turn away the still small voice; it will teach them what to do and where to go". (H.C., 1:316, see Brigham Young, vision, Feb. 17, 1847, in Brigham Young Office Files, 1832-1878, Archives of The Church of Jesus Christ of Latter-day Saints, Salt Lake City, Utah). It almost sounds too simple. Keep the commandments and listen to the whisperings of the Spirit. The heavens are open, and God speaks to us. But there is no revelation if there is not a listening ear.

His father had entrusted Enos with the records, and his concern was that they now be preserved for the benefit of the Lamanites. "This was (my) desire" he wrote", that if it should so be, that my people, the Nephites, should fall into transgression, and by any means be destroyed, and the Lamanites should not be destroyed, that the Lord God would preserve a record of my people, the Nephites; even if it so be by the power of his holy arm, that it might be brought forth at some future day unto the Lamanites, that, perhaps, they might be brought unto salvation". (V. 13).

The preservation of the records was a miracle, and the power of the holy arm of God is evident in the story of their receipt by Joseph Smith and their subsequent translation, publication, and distribution. (See Commentary Reference to 2 Nephi 25:22). As the Angel Moroni explained to Joseph: "Wherever the sound (of the marvelous work) shall go, it shall cause the ears of men to tingle, and wherever it shall be proclaimed, the pure in heart shall rejoice, while those who draw near to God with their mouths, and honor him with their lips, while their hearts are far from him, will seek its overthrow, and the destruction of those by whose hands it is carried. Therefore, marvel not if your name is made a derision, and had as a by-word among such, if you are the instrument in bringing it, by the gift of God, to the knowledge of the people". ("Joseph Smith & The Restoration", p. 14).

The Lamanite contemporaries of Enos would have destroyed the oracles of God had they been given the chance. "And they swore in their wrath that, if it were possible, they would destroy our records and us, and also all the traditions of our fathers". (V. 14). The situation is no different today. There are "Lamanite" enemies of truth whose mission is to destroy the faith they recognize in others but that is so alien to their own nature.

In spite of opposition by the Lamanites, the Nephites, under the direction of Enos, sought to restore them to "the true faith in God". (V. 20). But their hatred was fixed. We know that if a parent will "train up a child in the way he should go ... when he is old, he will not depart from it". (Proverbs 22:6). Unfortunately, the converse is also true. For many years, Lamanite children had listened to their parents speak of the Nephites in unflattering terms. But we cannot sling mud for long without getting dirty ourselves. The filthiness of the Lamanites was that they had become "wild, and ferocious, and a blood-thirsty people, (and) full of idolatry". (V. 20). Contrast this description with that of the Nephites in the next verse, where they are described as gentle farmers: "And it came to pass that the people of Nephi did till the land, and raise all manner of grain, and of fruit, and flocks of herds, and flocks of all manner of cattle of every kind, and goats, and wild goats, and also many horses". (V. 21).

Many Nephites had the testimony of Jesus, for Enos recorded that "there were exceedingly many prophets among (them)". (V. 22, see Revelation 19:10). However, their prosperity created problems, for they began to be "a stiffnecked people, hard to understand". (V. 22). Four hundred and sixty years later, there was a similar attitude among them when "there began to be men inspired from heaven and sent forth, standing among the people in all the land, preaching and testifying boldly of the sins and iniquities of the people, and testifying unto them concerning the redemption which the Lord would make for his people". 3 Nephi 6:20).

It was difficult for Enos to deal with his brethren, for "there was nothing save it was exceeding harshness, preaching and prophesying of wars, and contentions, and destructions, and continually reminding them of death, and the duration of eternity, and the judgments and the power of God, and all these things - stirring them up continually to keep them in the fear of the Lord. I say there was nothing short of these things, and exceedingly great plainness of speech, would keep them from going down speedily to destruction". (V. 23).

It may be that stiffneckedness creates a skin so thick and rigid that extraordinary means become necessary to penetrate it, create pliancy, and touch the Spirit. After his own marvelous experiences in the forest, Enos was on such a high spiritual plane that he described the stubborn behavior of his brethren as "stiffnecked and hard to understand". (V. 22).

Only 3 generations after Lehi's party had left Jerusalem, Enos reported that there were already wars between the Nephite and Lamanite branches of the family. (V. 24). One wonders if the Nephites ever paused to consider that the Lord might have been extending His chastening hand to them, offering them the opportunity to repent, and that He used the Lamanites to intervene in their lives for their benefit. Since Nephi had emphasized that this was to be a religious history, perhaps the number and quality of spiritual experiences of the Nephites might have already been shrinking during the ministry of Enos. Possibly, growing apostasy contributed to the brevity of his book due to a scarcity of positive experiences about which he could report. As Thumper was counseled by his mother: "If you can't say nuttin' nice about someone, don't say nuttin' at all". (Bambi).

Still, Enos had "declared the word of God in all (his) days, and (had) rejoiced in it above that of the world". (V. 26). Whatever pleasures spiritual Babylon could offer him in enticement were no equal to the matchless power of God that had brought soul-satisfying perspective to him at an early and impressionable age. He knew that drinking from the sewage of the world could not quench his thirst. Eating garbage from a pigsty could not satisfy his spiritual hunger. He had experienced the more sure word of prophecy after all, and knew that he was sealed up unto eternal life. (See D&C 131:5). "For I know that in him I shall rest", he declared: "And I rejoice in the day when my mortal shall put on immortality, and (I) shall stand before him; then shall I see his face with pleasure". V. 27).

The Church of Jesus Christ of Latter-day Saints emphasizes that we may literally find God in revelatory experiences. The story of the struggle of Enos to find Him is therefore of great religious significance, as it stirs our hearts with renewed confidence in the mercies of God, in His personal concern, and in His unconditional love.

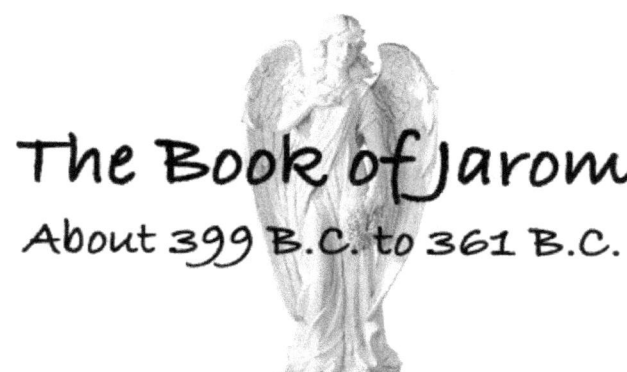

The Book of Jarom
About 399 B.C. to 361 B.C.

Jarom
Chapter 1

The 15 verses in this, the shortest book within The Book of Mormon, cover about 60 years of Nephite history. They were written by Jarom, who was the great grandson of Lehi, the grandson of Jacob, and the son of Enos. It is curious that the descendants of Jacob, and not of Nephi, were the record keepers among the Nephites until the reign of King Mosiah. It would be interesting to know more about the descendants of Nephi, but the text is silent on the subject. (See Commentary Reference to Jacob Chapter 1).

Jarom was entrusted by his father with the care of the records and was commissioned to keep a genealogy of his people. (V. 1). The Plates of Brass contained "the genealogy of the fathers" (1 Nephi 3:12), but the continuing Nephite family history was kept on The Small Plates. By Jarom's account, although there was not much room left on the plates, there was still enough to satisfy his meager needs. (See V. 2, & 14).

Jarom clearly understood that his writings would benefit the Lamanites and their descendants more than his own people. (V. 2). To his great credit, though, he continued with his recording efforts even during a period of intense persecution when the Lamanites were his bitter enemies.

On the plates, Jarom could have recorded his prophesying and revelations, but all the prophets repeat themselves, after all. "None of the prophets", declared Jacob, "have written, nor prophesied, save they have spoken concerning Christ". (Jacob 7:11, see Commentary References to 2 Nephi 25:20 & 26, & Jacob 4:4). This has always been their central message. He said: "For what could I write more than my fathers have written? For have they not revealed The Plan of Salvation? I say unto you, Yea; and this sufficeth me". (V. 2). Then he continued: "It is expedient that much should be done among this people". (V. 3). In other words, perhaps Jarom felt that others had written enough to satisfy the spiritual needs of the descendants of the Lamanites who would be the recipients of his message. What he may have perceived to be a more pressing need was the initiation of a religious reformation among his own people, who were in imminent danger of slipping away into wholesale apostasy.

Certainly, Jarom was familiar with the Vision of The Tree of Life that had been carefully recorded by his great uncle Nephi many years before. In that vision, Father Lehi had seen "numberless concourses of people, many of whom were pressing forward, that they might obtain the path which led unto the tree by which (he) stood … And it came to pass that there arose a mist of darkness; yea, even an exceedingly great mist of darkness, insomuch that they who had commenced in the path did lose their way, that they wandered off and were lost". (1 Nephi 8:21, & 23). We do not know if Jarom specifically applied this dream to the state of affairs in the Nephite society of his own day, but the parallels seem obvious.

Apostasy had become rooted among the Nephites by the time Jarom was entrusted with the record. His people were contaminated with the stain of four Satan-inspired influences: "Hardness of their hearts, deafness of their ears, blindness of their minds, and stiffness of their necks". (V. 4). Because it had not yet been determined if the infection would prove to be terminal, Jarom persevered. One thing was certain, though. He took his priesthood responsibilities seriously enough to want to be the vessel through whom the Lord might pour a healing balm over the spiritual wounds infecting the Nephites. Lehi's vision, after all, had also held out the promise of redemption of his own people, and he had described a hopeful scene as it passed before his eyes: "And it came to pass that I beheld others pressing forward, and they came forth and caught hold of the end of the rod of iron; and they did press forward through the mist of darkness, clinging to the rod of iron, even until they did come forth and partake of the fruit of the tree". (1 Nephi 8:24).

Nephi later reported that his father had seen "other multitudes pressing forward; and they came and caught hold of the end of the rod of iron; and they did press their way forward, continually holding fast to the rod of iron, until they came forth and fell down and partook of the fruit of the tree". (1 Nephi 8:30). This is a description of disciples who are actively, passionately, and even desperately, fighting their way toward the tree of life and the fruit thereon, that represent the love of God and eternal life. In Nephi's account, when they arrived at the tree, they fell down exhausted by their efforts. New meaning is given to the scriptural admonition to work out our salvation with fear and trembling. (See Philippians 2:12).

Jarom drew a contrast between those who are stiff-necked, and those who have faith. (V. 4). The former cannot look up to Heavenly Father for guidance, over to priesthood leaders for counsel, around to seek out those in need, or down in an attitude of humility. The latter have access to the Holy Spirit or Holy Ghost, "which maketh manifest unto the children of men, according to their faith". (V. 4).

The Nephites "observed to keep the law of Moses and the sabbath day holy unto the Lord", and "they profaned not; neither did they blaspheme". (V. 5). Perhaps it was "the laws of the land" that were exceedingly strict that kept them in the strait and narrow way. In any event, Jarom may have been saying in a subtle way that their outward observances were not accurate reflections of their innermost feelings.

These circumstances among the Nephites may have been a precursor to the state of affairs in their society just a few years later. (See Omni 1:11). In another 120 years, the more wicked part of the nation would be destroyed because, through unrighteousness, they would lose the protection of the Lord. (Omni 1:5). With their veneer of righteousness stripped away by the acids of indiscretion, they would be fully exposed to the corrosive influences of Satan.

The course of Nephite history paints a portrait with a recurring theme of righteousness, followed by prosperity, that leads to self-indulgence and neglect of spiritual responsibilities. This, in turn, causes the spirit to withdraw, and results in a loss of divine protection. God chastens His people in the hope that they will repent, which they sometimes do, but more often do not. When finally, they are destroyed by whatever means are convenient at the time, the conditions re-set, and the cycle repeats itself. In our society, because we see things so close at hand, it is difficult to recognize that the same patterns are at work. We cannot see the Cedars of Lebanon or the Oaks of Bashan (the forest) for the trees. (2 Nephi 12:13).

Long ago, Alexis de Tocqueville wrote: "I sought for the greatness and genius of America in her commodious harbors and her ample rivers, and it was not there; in her fertile fields and boundless prairies, and it was not there; in her rich mines and her vast world commerce, and it was not there. Not until I went to the Churches of America and heard her pulpits aflame with righteousness did I understand the secret of her genius and her power. America is great because she is good, and if America ever ceases to be good, America will cease to be great". ("Democracy in America")

During Jarom's lifetime, the lynchpin of the Nephite battle plan embraced by the government was still obedience to Gospel principles. As Jarom wrote: "Our kings and our leaders were mighty men in the faith of the Lord; and they taught the people the ways of the Lord". (V. 7). They believed, as John Taylor taught, that "we will be held accountable for those we might have saved, had we done our duty". Lord Acton felt that "it was from America that the plain ideas came that the nation is responsible to Heaven for the acts of the State". And it was from America, he said, "that the principle gained ground, that a nation can never abandon its fate to an authority it cannot control". ("The History of Freedom in Antiquity").

Jarom repeated the basic principle guaranteeing prosperity among the Nephites: "Inasmuch as ye will keep my commandments, ye shall prosper in the land". (V. 9). "God, give us men and women!" wrote Josiah Gilbert Holland. "A time like this demands strong minds, great hearts, true faith, and ready hands; those whom the lust of office does not kill; those whom the spoils of office cannot buy; those who possess opinions and a will; those who have honor; those who will not lie; those who can stand before a demagogue and damn his treacherous flatteries without winking!. Tall men and women, sun-crowned, who live above the fog in public duty and in private thinking. For while the rabble, with their thumb-worn creeds, their large professions and their little deeds, mingle in selfish strife, lo, Freedom weeps, Wrong rules the land, and Justice sleeps". (Bartlett's Familiar Quotations, 10th ed.).

The Nephites "multiplied exceedingly", and as we look on their efforts to build a new home in the promised land, we are reminded of the Welfare Plan promoted by the L.D.S. Church in 1935: "The aim of the Church is to help people to help themselves. Work is to be re-enthroned as a ruling principle in the lives of our Church membership". (Heber J. Grant, C.R., 10/1936, V. 8). If Nephi and his three righteous brothers (not to mention his sisters, Zoram, and whatever sons of Ishmael remained with the Nephites) married and had large families, a population numbering in the thousands within a few generations would be reasonable.

It was necessary, however, that the prophets in Jarom's day continually stir the people "up unto repentance", just as it had been necessary during his father's ministry. (V. 12, see Enos 1:23, & Moroni 9:4). They had to "threaten the people of Nephi, according to the word of God", and exhort them to diligence. (V. 11). What a sorry state of affairs, that the pleasing word of God should be viewed by a society of critics as a threat to their worldly ways and their free-wheeling, no-holds-barred, lifestyle.

The Gospel is as much the sum of "Thou shalt" commandments, as it is "Thou shalt not" commandments. Its composite principles are the consummate compilation of affirmative actions. When we are converted, the relationship between commandments and blessings becomes blurred. Since you can't have one without the other, the Savior's invitation to follow Him with the assurance that His yoke is easy, and his burden is light, makes more sense. We see the wisdom in Alma's invitation to the Zoramites: "Plant the word in your hearts ... and then may God grant unto you that your burdens may be light, through the joy of his Son. And even all this can ye do, if ye will". (Alma 33:23).

Through their strenuous efforts, the leaders of the Nephites kept their people "from being destroyed upon the face of the land; for they did prick their hearts with the word, continually stirring them up unto repentance". (V. 12). The exercise of free will in the process of repentance is preferable to external pressure, but let us remember that the Nephite prophets, priests, and teachers took their responsibilities very seriously, "answering the sins of the people upon (their) own heads if (they) did not teach them the word of God with all diligence". (Jacob 1:19). Their goal, of course, was to penetrate the hearts of the people, heal their deafness and blindness, and ease the tension and stiffness that characterized their attitudes. They only wanted the Nephites to "believe in (Christ) to come, as though he already was".

(V. 11). These prophets understood that our mortal curriculum is principally involved in restoration, restitution, and recommitment leading to renewal, and that reconciliation comes only when we allow Jesus Christ into our lives.

Jarom did not want to write about the "wars, and contentions, and dissensions" of the Nephites, not only because there was no room to do so on The Small Plates of Nephi, but also because these plates had been designated for the recording of religious history, even though such experiences were not common among the Nephites at this time. The secular history of the people was written instead on The Large Plates of Nephi, perhaps by scribes of the kings, but this record is not currently available to us. (See Omni 1:11). Mormon may have included these details in his abridgment of The Book of Lehi (taken from the Large Plates of Nephi), but we may never know. This abridgment was part of the 116 pages of manuscript lost by Martin Harris. (See Commentary Reference to Words of Mormon 1:1).

After safekeeping the records for about 60 years, Jarom delivered them into the hands of his son Omni, who was charged with the responsibility to protect them and add to them, as the Spirit moved him to do so.

The Book of Omni
About 323 B.C. to 130 B.C.

Omni
Chapter 1

For whom was The Book of Mormon written? It was not written for the Nephite and Lamanite people in general, the majority of whom did not have access to the plates. It was written for us, specifically to prepare us for the Second Coming of The Lord. "Wherefore it is an abridgment of the record of the people of Nephi, and also of the Lamanites ... Which is to show unto the remnant of the House of Israel what great things the Lord hath done for their fathers; and that they may know the covenants of the Lord, that they are not cast off forever - And also to the convincing of the Jew and Gentile that Jesus is the Christ, the Eternal God, manifesting himself unto all nations". ("Title Page to The Book of Mormon"). This book contains a blueprint that prepared the Nephite Saints for the First Coming of The Lord. If the past truly is prologue, we may profit from their experiences as we prepare for the millennial reign of Christ.

Omitting quotations from Isaiah, out of the 600-year Book of Mormon history that precedes the Coming of the Lord, over two-thirds of the text (68%) is devoted to the 175 years immediately before His ministry. This is a period roughly equivalent to the span of time between the Restoration of The Gospel and our present day. About half of the book is devoted to a single 100-year period immediately preceding His Coming. In other words, 50% of the text is devoted to 10% of the time span of The Book of Mormon. "He that hath ears to hear, let him hear". (Matthew 11:15).

The principal problems facing the ancient Saints during that period were unprecedented prosperity, apathy, apostasy of members of the Church, secret combinations desiring to wrest control of the government, and the collapse of government resulting in war. Hmmm.

The Book of Omni was written during these pivotal times with a number of individuals responsible for the record. These were Omni, the son of Jarom, grandson of Enos, and great grandson of Jacob, and then Omni's sons Ammaron and Chemish, who were followed by Abinadom, the son of Chemish. Finally, Abinadom's son Amaleki was entrusted with the records. These individuals also safeguarded the Liahona and the Sword of Laban that were emblems of authority. The Plates of Brass continued to be safeguarded by the Nephite kings.

With so many involved in the process of record keeping, it would be logical if their individual writing styles stood out in a book that claims to be an inspired translation. In fact, this is just the case. Researchers have identified at least 24 distinct and different "word prints", or authors, in The Book of Mormon. (See "Who Wrote The Book of Mormon?" An Analysis of Wordprints", BYU Studies, Spring 1980). In a sense, our challenge is to be so intimately familiar with The Book of Mormon that we can easily recognize the writing styles of favorite authors such as Nephi, Jacob, Benjamin, Alma, Abinadi, Mormon and Moroni, to name just a few.

The first five books in The Book of Mormon concern a time span of 239 years and consume 140 pages of text. The Book of Omni spans 231 years of Nephite history in just 30 verses of text. Inasmuch as The Small Plates of Nephi concerned the religious history of the Nephites, this suggests a period of great apostasy among the people.

The first four individuals to write on the plates at this time had no new prophecies or revelations to report. They wrote only in order to preserve their genealogy. (V. 1). Omni characterized himself as "a wicked man" who had not kept the statutes of God. (V. 2). Therefore, he might have been unaware of revelation that may have come to other Nephites during his lifetime.

To his credit, Omni "fought much with the sword to preserve (his) people, the Nephites, from falling into the hands of their enemies, the Lamanites". (V. 2). The Nephite battle plan, however, had changed significantly. No longer was righteousness the keystone of their defense. No longer would a righteous nation rely upon the power of God as a shield of safety. Now, the arm of flesh would be central to their strategy for survival. The terrible price for "seasons of peace" was gunboat diplomacy, an escalating arms race, saber-rattling, and the perpetual threat of the use of brute force. Even these, however, could not prevent "many seasons of serious war and bloodshed". (V. 3).

Omni was so preoccupied with self-preservation that he did not even begin his record for 38 years after his father Jarom had entrusted the plates to his care. (V. 3). Verse 3 alone spanned 6 years of time. "And it came to pass that two hundred and seventy-six years had passed away, and we had many seasons of peace; and we had many seasons of serious war and bloodshed. Yea, and in fine, two hundred and eighty and two years had passed away, and I had kept these plates according to the commandments of my father". (V. 3). Then, the record was abruptly given to his son. "And I conferred them upon my son Amaron. And I make an end". (V. 3). In marked contrast to the previous custodians of The Small Plates of Nephi, Omni closed his account with no expression of personal testimony, and without the typical exhortation to keep the commandments. (See V. 25-26).

Amaron followed in his father's footsteps, only initiating his meager contribution to the record 38 years after receiving it from Omni. "And now I, Amaron, write the things whatsoever I write, which are few, in The Book of my father. Behold, it came to pass that three hundred and twenty years had passed away". (V. 4 & 5). The apostasy of the Nephites was firmly established, for as Amaron reported: "The more wicked part of the Nephites were destroyed". (V. 5). A deterioration of the fortification of their spiritual symmetry and an erosion of the foundation of their faith had preceded their physical destruction. In any case, the recurring warning of the Nephite prophets began to be fearfully vindicated: "Inasmuch as ye will not keep my commandments, ye shall not prosper in the land". (V. 6).

Chemish, the brother of Amaron, made a staggering disclosure when he revealed that Amaron had, in fact, written his entire record "in the day that he delivered them unto (him). And after this manner we keep the records". (V. 9). However, Chemish did not do much better than his brother, since his entire contribution to The Book of Omni was only this one verse that was undoubtedly also written in just one day.

Quite candidly, Chemish wrote: "After this manner we keep the record". (V. 9). His was a frank expression of the reality that as the Nephite nation sank into apostasy, their record keeping reflected the quality of their lives. Only a few would escape destruction, for the Lord would "spare the righteous that they should not perish, but (would) deliver them out of the hands of their enemies". (V. 7).

Abinadom's contribution followed that of Chemish, and focused on his defense of his brethren as he wielded his sword against the Lamanites. (V. 10). Perhaps this was the Sword of Laban or a copy of that lethal weapon. Certainly, the two verses in The Book of Omni attributed to Abinadom contain no startling revelation or doctrinal information. He admitted that he knew "of no revelation save that which has been written, neither prophecy". (V. 11). The fact that Abinadom was unaware of revelation or prophecy confirms that this was a time of great apostasy among the Nephites.

In fact, Abinadom acknowledged that the record of his people was a secular history, engraven upon the Large Plates of Nephi that were kept by the kings, rather than a sacred history, that would have been engraven upon The Small Plates of Nephi. "The record of this people is engraven upon plates which is had by the kings … and I know of no revelation save that which has been written, neither prophecy". (V. 11).

Omni 1:12 records that Amaleki, the son of Abinadom, next received the record. The name Abinadom, in Hebrew, means, "My father is a wanderer". The feeling of being wanderers was strongly felt among the Nephites. Jacob had written: "The time passed away with us, and also our lives passed away like as it were unto us a dream, we being a lonesome and a solemn people, wanderers, cast out from Jerusalem, born in tribulation, in a wilderness, and hated of our brethren, which caused wars and contentions; wherefore we did mourn out our days". (Jacob 7:26, see Alma 13:23, & Helaman 7:7). Now, Amaleki would record the story of a man named Mosiah, another such wanderer.

Amaleki was born in the days of Mosiah and lived to see Mosiah's son Benjamin assume leadership of the Nephites. (See V. 23). Mosiah was warned by the Lord to flee from the Land of Nephi, and to take with him all those who "would hearken unto the voice of the Lord". (V. 12). This was the Nephites' first migration in several hundred years, and was accomplished in fulfilment of the prophecy made by Jacob, who said: "The time speedily cometh, that except ye repent (the Lamanites) shall possess the land of your inheritance, and the Lord God will lead away the righteous out from among you". (Jacob 3:4). The exodus of Mosiah from the Land of Nephi, foretold by Jacob, took place about 225 B.C.

The main body of Nephites chose to stay behind in the Land of Nephi, and The Book of Mormon never again makes mention of them. They were in all probability destroyed or assimilated by the Lamanites, who then took over their land and cities. Chapter 9 of The Book of Mosiah recounts the story of Zeniff, who returned after many years to the land of their forefathers, but found no one but Lamanites living there among the desolate remains of ruined Nephite cities. (See Commentary Reference to Words of Mormon 1:13).

Mosiah and his followers were those Nephites who did not trust in the arm of flesh, but who instead "were admonished continually by the word of God; and they were led by the power of his arm". (V. 13). They journeyed through the wilderness for approximately 40 days (See Mosiah 7:4), until they came down into the land of Zarahemla. It is possible that they traveled from the Guatemalan Highlands, down into the lower elevations to the north, into what is now the Mexican state of Chiapas. (See Helaman 6:10).

Joseph Smith once made a statement about Palenque, a Mayan ruin in Chiapas that dates from 300 B.C. but was only rediscovered in 1773. He said it was within the Nephite region of the land southward and went on to describe the geography of an isthmus as it might apply to the narrow neck of land. In the October 1, 1842 issue of "Times and Seasons", he explicitly outlined Central America in general, and Guatemala in particular, between the Isthmus of Tehuantepec and the Isthmus of Panama, as the land southward of The Book of Mormon. (See Essay: "Were There Two Cumorahs?").

Actually, as it has turned out, all of Joseph Smith's observations about the archaeological discoveries in Central America relate to Mayan ruins that fall within a post Book of Mormon timeline. No one in his day knew the antiquity of these cities, but now we realize that they were built on top of earlier ruins that do, in fact, date from Book of Mormon times. Joseph Smith made only one unequivocal statement on this subject, and that was that "the city of

Zarahemla stood upon this land" of Guatemala in Central America. ("Times & Seasons", V. 8, N. 22-23, p. 927). It remains to be seen whether this statement was prophetic or anecdotal. (See "San Lorenzo as The Jaredite City of Lib", FARMS, 6/1983).

In the land to the north of Nephi, Mosiah and his followers "discovered a people who were called the people of Zarahemla", but who are typically described as "Mulekites" by Latter-day Saints, although that name does not occur in The Book of Mormon. (V. 14, see Mosiah 25:2, & Helaman 6:10). The people of Zarahemla were of Jewish ancestry, and rejoiced that Mosiah had the Hebrew scriptures, or The Plates of Brass, with him. (V. 14-15).

It had undoubtedly been no small feat for Mosiah to smuggle The Plates of Brass and the Large Plates of Nephi out of the Land of Nephi, since those records had been in the care of the apostate Nephite king, who would naturally have been reluctant to surrender them to his departing brethren, in the tradition of Laban. As for The Small Plates of Nephi, the Sword of Laban, and the Liahona, Amaleki had been entrusted with their care by his father Abinadom, and surely brought them with him when he left Nephi with Mosiah's party. (V. 12 & 23).

The people of Zarahemla were descendants of Mulek, who was a son of King Zedekiah. (See Helaman 6:10, & 8:21). Mulek is not named in the Old Testament, but we know from The Book of Mormon that he left Jerusalem at the time that "Zedekiah, king of Judah, was carried away captive into Babylon" in 589 B.C. (V. 15). His group was one of many, perhaps, who had been guided "by the hand of the Lord" to the New World. (V. 16, see Commentary Reference to Jacob 5:8). The people of Zarahemla provided the first independent confirmation of Lehi's prophecy that Jerusalem had been destroyed.

A FARMS report explains: "Helaman 6:10 records that Zedekiah had a son named Mulek, who escaped execution by the Babylonians, despite the statement in 2 Kings 25:4-7 that the king's sons were slain before his very eyes. While the name Mulek is not mentioned directly in the Bible, scholars have recently drawn some interesting conclusions about a person named Malchiah, mentioned in Jeremiah 38:6. Could he have been Mulek? Malchiah was 'the son of Hammelech' according to Jeremiah. But, clearly, this should have been translated 'the son of the king' since '-melech' in Hebrew means the same as '-melek' or 'king.' Several factors now indicate that Malchiah was, in fact, not just the son of an anonymous king, but also the son of Zedekiah. Thus concluded Yohanan Ahareoni, the late head of the Department of Archaeology at Tel Aviv University. Furthermore, it is known that names like Malchiah took a shortened form in the 6th century B.C. An abbreviation would reduce Malchiah to something very much like the name 'Mulek' that is found in The Book of Mormon. A prominent non-member and Old Testament scholar visiting B.Y.U. was impressed to learn that The Book of Mormon names Mulek as a son of Zedekiah. He remarked: 'If Joseph Smith came up with that one, he did pretty well!'" (John Welch, "Re-exploring The Book of Mormon", p. 142-144).

The escape of Mulek from Jerusalem is also indirectly confirmed by other oblique scriptural references. In the Allegory of The Tame and Wild Olive Trees recorded in Jacob Chapter 5, we read: "And behold, saith the Lord of the vineyard, I take away many of these young and tender branches, and I will graft them whithersoever I will; and it mattereth not that if it so be that the root of this tree will perish. I may preserve the fruit thereof unto myself; wherefore, I will take these young and tender branches, and I will graft them whithersoever I will". (Jacob 5:8, see Helaman 8:21). The young sprouts represent various groups of Israelites, led by the Lord to different parts of the world. They were 'planted' in order to preserve some of the natural branches of the tame olive tree.

"Thus saith the Lord God;" wrote the prophet Ezekiel, "I will also take of the highest branch of the high cedar and will set it. I will crop off from the top of his young twigs a tender one, and will plant it upon an high mountain and eminent ... and it shall bring forth boughs, and bear fruit and be a goodly cedar, and under it shall dwell all fowl of every wing, in the shadow of the branches thereof shall they dwell. And all the trees of the field shall know that I the

Lord have brought down the high tree, have exalted the low tree, have dried up the green tree, and have made the dry tree to flourish". (Ezekiel 17:22-24).

The meaning is clear. A child of Zedekiah, the 31-year-old king, was to be cropped off from the family tree and planted in another land. The name "Muleq" (Hebrew variant = "to break or nip off") reminded his followers that he was both their king and the plucked off twig of Ezekiel's prophecy, fulfilled in the grim fall of Jerusalem and in the transplanting of Judah's ruling house to another land. This land was the South Wilderness, in the land of The Book of Mormon. (See Alma 22:31). In spite of their close proximity to the Land of Nephi, the people of Zarahemla had lived independently of contact with the Nephites and Lamanites for about 400 years. During that time, they had "become exceedingly numerous". (V. 17). In fact, there were more "Mulekites" than Nephites. Mosiah 25:2 reports that "there were not so many of the children of Nephi, or so many of those who were descendants of Nephi, as there were of the people of Zarahemla, who was a descendant of Mulek, and those who came out with him into the wilderness".

However, because they had not brought any written records with them at the time of their hurried escape from Jerusalem, not only had their language "become corrupted", but they had lost the knowledge of "their Creator". (V. 17). The wisdom of the Spirit that had spoken to Nephi in the dark streets of Jerusalem hundreds of years earlier had been validated: "It is better that one man should perish than that a nation should dwindle and perish in unbelief" (1 Nephi 4:13).

The people of Zarahemla had experienced "many wars and serious contentions, and had fallen by the sword from time to time". (V. 17). It is unclear just who fought in these wars, but it was not Lamanites. Evidently, there were other indigenous groups occupying the land and vying for territorial control, who remain unidentified in The Book of Mormon.

Because they were not grounded on the sure footing of the knowledge of God, the people of Zarahemla were in a self-destruct mode. Fortunately, the timely intervention of Mosiah prevented the implosion of their infrastructure, their complete cultural collapse, and their societal suicide.

When they had been taught the language of the Nephites, their leader Zarahemla gave "a genealogy of his fathers, according to his memory", in the manner of South Pacific Islanders, whose oral traditions are handed down from father to son. This genealogy was then recorded, "but not in these plates". (V. 18).

The people of Zarahemla united with the Nephites, and perhaps in a demonstration of gratitude for their timely assistance, they adopted Nephite leadership, language, and culture. Interestingly, because they were numerically superior to the Nephites, from this point on, Nephite history is more properly the history of the people of Zarahemla. (V. 17, see Mosiah 25:2). With the addition of this new ethnic group, those who called themselves Nephites now included members of the tribes of Manasseh through Lehi, Ephraim through Ishmael, and Judah through Mulek. There were still no Levites among the Nephites. The priesthood authority by which the ordinances of the Gospel were administered (before the ministry of the Savior among the Nephites) continued to be Melchizedek.

Some time after Mosiah had become king in the land of Zarahemla, a large stone with engravings thereon was brought to him. He translated these writings by "the gift and power of God". (V. 20). The engravings, found by the People of Limhi and not to be confused with the 24 gold plates of Ether, gave an account of a Jaredite named Coriantumr, that provided a much more comprehensive account of that people. (V. 21 See Mosiah Chapter 8).

Mosiah may have received the Urim and Thummim at this time from the people of Zarahemla, who might have received it, in turn, from Coriantumr, the last survivor of the Jaredite nation. In the Doctrine & Covenants, when the

Lord spoke through Joseph Smith to the Three Witnesses, He revealed that the Jaredites had possessed a Urim and Thummim: "Behold, I say unto you, that you must rely upon my word, which if you do with full purpose of heart, you shall have a view of the plates, and also of the breastplate, the sword of Laban, and the Urim and Thummim, which were given to the brother of Jared upon the mount, when he talked with the Lord face to face". (D&C 17:1).

Many years later, Mosiah's grandson used "the interpreters", which were most likely this same Urim and Thummim. (See Mosiah 28:13). There is no indication that Lehi had possession of a Urim and Thummim, or that Amaleki brought one with him when he left the Land of Nephi. Lehi had used a different device called the Liahona, that served the same general purpose. (See Mosiah 8:13-18, & 28:13).

Coriantumr was the last king of the Jaredites. He died of battle wounds in Zarahemla just 9 months after the "Mulekites" had found him wandering in the wilderness. (V. 21). He had seen the terrible prophecies of Ether fulfilled concerning his people. (See Ether 13:21). The events and circumstances surrounding Coriantumr place the last great battles of the Jaredites as late as 400 B.C. - 300 B.C., which makes these events contemporary with the rise of the Nephite, Lamanite, and "Mulekite" cultures.

The destruction of the Jaredite civilization took place in a geographical area not far to the north of the Land of Zarahemla that the people later named "The Land of Desolation". (V. 22, see Alma 22:30-31). This was also the general location of the first landfall of the People of Mulek when they arrived in the new world. (See Alma 22:30). Sydney Sperry observed: "Finding Coriantumr near the Land of Zarahemla strongly suggests that the last great battles of the Jaredites took place (nearby). A wounded man is not likely to have wandered thousands of miles from the site of his last great battle". The significance of this likelihood will become apparent when this Commentary addresses the question: "Were there two Cumorahs?" (See Commentary Reference to Mosiah 8:9, and the Essay: "Were There Two Cumorahs?"). Here, then, the "Mulekites" are the connection between the Jaredites, the Nephites, and even the Lamanites, where these four Book of Mormon peoples briefly unite.

The stone that Mosiah translated also chronicled the ancestry of the Jaredites from the time of the tower of Babel, about 2,200 B.C. (V. 22). The confounding of the languages of the people coincident with the destruction of that ziggurat is mentioned here and is discussed in greater detail in "Journey to Cumorah: A Book of Mormon Commentary, Volume Three.

Verse 22 makes mention of a land just to the north, where the bones of the Jaredites lay scattered upon the ground. Alma referred to this land as "Desolation". (Alma 22:30). It was "a land which was covered with bones of men, and of beasts, and was also covered with ruins of buildings of every kind". (Mosiah 8:8). That the Nephites would call it "Desolation" is understandable, because to the ancients, to remain unburied was one of the worst forms of degradation. Nephite scouts had discovered the remains of not just one individual, but of thousands whose flesh had been torn from their bodies by wild beasts, or who had rotted in the hot sun until nothing was left but bleached bones. The evidence suggested unspeakable horror, and understandably the Nephites never colonized there.

Amaleki had been born "in the days of Mosiah, and (he had) lived to see his death; and Benjamin, his son, reign(ed) in his stead". (V. 23). Amaleki was probably the one responsible for safely carrying the records out of the Land of Nephi. (V. 23, see V. 12). Even though the people of Zarahemla had lived for over 400 years in the land without ever having had any documented interaction with either Nephites or Lamanites, not long after the people of Mosiah joined them, the Lamanites discovered their whereabouts. In all likelihood, the Nephites who had fled the Land of Nephi had not covered their tracks very well, and Lamanites scouts had been able to follow them to Zarahemla. Not long thereafter, "there commenced a serious war and much bloodshed between the Nephites and the Lamanites". (V. 24).

Mosiah's son, Benjamin, served as the second Nephite king in the land of Zarahemla and he was able to drive the Lamanites out of the land". (V. 23 & 24). Amaleki was evidently more righteous than the previous four guardians of the records, since he had heard the word of the Lord and had joined those Nephites who fled apostate conditions in the Land of Nephi. His closing testimony in verses 25 and 26 stands in sharp contrast to the anemic efforts of Omni, Amaron, Chemish, and Abinadom". And it came to pass that I began to be old; and, having no seed, and knowing king Benjamin to be a just man before the Lord, wherefore, I shall deliver up these plates unto him, exhorting all men to come unto God, the Holy One of Israel, and believe in prophesying, and in revelations, and in the ministering of angels, and in the gift of speaking with tongues, and in the gift of interpreting languages, and in all things which are good; for there is nothing which is good save it comes from the Lord; and that which is evil cometh from the devil. And now, my beloved brethren, I would that ye should come unto Christ, who is the Holy One of Israel, and partake of his salvation, and the power of his redemption. Yea, come unto him, and offer your whole souls as an offering unto him, and continue in fasting and praying, and endure to the end; and as the Lord liveth ye will be saved". (See 2 Nephi 25:20).

Amaleki closed his record with a brief reference to Zeniff, "who went up into the wilderness to return to the land of Nephi; for there was a large number who were desirous to posses the land of their inheritance". (V. 27). For a complete account of Zeniff and his people, read Mosiah Chapters 9-22. Evidently, Zeniff and others of like mind were homesick and probably missed the temperate climate of their former home in the highlands to the south. In this verse, and in the next, Amaleki makes a direct reference to the direction in which they traveled. He wrote that they went "up" into the wilderness. Although they were probably headed in a southern direction, they were nevertheless climbing in elevation. Throughout The Book of Mormon, the references to the Land of Nephi being higher in elevation relative to the Land of Zarahemla are undeviating. (See Mosiah 7:1, 8:2, 20:7, 28:1 & 5, 29:3, Alma 17:8, 20:2, 24:20, 29:14, 47:1 & 12, & Helaman 4:4).

It is likely that Zeniff's party did not go into high mountains. At least, snow and winter conditions are never mentioned or even hinted at in this or any other section of The Book of Mormon. Therefore, we might logically conclude that the events recorded in the book were played out entirely in tropical and subtropical theaters. If the book truly had a Meso-American setting, this would be the case, because there are no mountains high enough to have snowfall or winter conditions, even in the rainy season. Arenal, in Costa Rica, is one of the most active volcanoes in the world and is the tallest mountain in Central America. (5,480 feet / 1,670 meters). Daily volcanic eruptions add to its height, but it may be years before its altitude at the summit will support snowfall.

Amaleki "had a brother, who also went with" Zeniff, but the jungle swallowed them up and they were never heard from again. (V. 30). Soberly, Amaleki wrote: "I am about to lie down in my grave; and these plates are full. And I make an end of my speaking". (V. 30). He had "no seed, and knowing king Benjamin to be a just man before the Lord", he entrusted him with the care and keeping of the plates. Thus, is completed the chronological record on The Small Plates of Nephi, which is the "second" set of records that were kept for a wise purpose. (See 1 Nephi 9:5, & Words of Mormon 7). These plates comprise slightly less than half of the chronological history of the Nephites, or 470 years out of 1,021.

This is also the end of the record made by the early Nephite prophets upon The Small Plates of Nephi, from which the first six books of The Book of Mormon were translated. These are the first-person account of Nephi, Jacob, Enos, Jarom, Omni, Amaron, Chemish, Abinadom, and finally Amaleki, who gave King Benjamin possession of all the plates, as well as the other emblems of authority. (V. 25). What follows upon The Small Plates are the transitional Words of Mormon.

"After I had made an abridgement
from the plates of Nephi, down to the reign
of this king Benjamin, of whom Amaleki spake,
I searched among the records which had been delivered
into my hands, and I found these plates which contained
this small account of the prophets from Jacob down to the reign
of this king Benjamin, and also many of the words of Nephi."
(Words of Mormon 1:3).

The Words of Mormon
About 385 A.D.

The Words of Mormon
Chapter 1

The Words of Mormon were written by Mormon on The Small Plates of Nephi about 385 A.D. (V. 1). It was intended to serve as a bridge between the body of The Small Plates comprising The First Book of Nephi through The Book of Omni, and Mormon's own abridgment of The Large Plates of Nephi that starts with The Book of Mosiah.

Even though Mormon's abridgment of The Book of Lehi, originally transcribed on The Large Plates of Nephi, was included with all the other records, he must have known that Joseph Smith's manuscript translation of The Large Plates up to The Book of Mosiah would in some way become corrupted. Therefore, he went to great pains to include this transitional book on the last leaf of the original records comprising The Small Plates of Nephi so there would be an uninterrupted flow from "these plates" to his abridgment of "those plates".

It was Joseph Smith's 116-page manuscript translation of Mormon's abridgment of The Large Plates (down to the reign of King Benjamin) that was lost by Martin Harris. This required the translation of the entire record of The Small Plates of Nephi, which was a record of the same period of Nephite history (albeit "a small account of the prophets") as that which had been lost. (V. 3).

Referring to the loss of the manuscript translation of The Book of Lehi, the Lord declared to Joseph Smith that "the works, and the designs, and the purposes of God cannot be frustrated, neither can they come to naught". (D&C 3:1). He prepares for every eventuality, inasmuch as He knows all things. (2 Nephi 9:20). He knows the end from the beginning. (1 Nephi 9:6). He is the same yesterday, today, and forever. (1 Nephi 10:18). Past, present, and future are ever before His eyes. (D&C 130:7). "With (Him), all things are possible". (Matthew 19:26).

God the Father is "from everlasting to everlasting". (Moroni 7:22). From our perspective, eternity spans the time from uncreated intelligence, through our spiritual development in our pre-mortal existence, on into mortality, and finally to our reunion with Him in the resurrection. As far as we are concerned, God is in every sense perfect with faith, hope and charity defining His attributes. If we are to model our behavior after anyone, it should be Christ, Who in every sense is One with the Father. This is why Mormon taught: "In Christ, there should come every good thing". (Moroni 7:22)

We are completely helpless to alter the progress or affect the outcome of any of God's activities. It was when Moses realized his utter dependence upon Him that he exclaimed: "Now, for this cause I know that man is nothing, which thing I never had supposed". (Moses 1:10). Our debt to God is total and complete, which is why King Benjamin asked his people: "Can ye say aught of yourselves? I answer you, nay. Ye cannot say that ye are even as much as the dust of the earth; yet ye were created of the dust of the earth; but behold, it belongeth to him who created you". (Mosiah 2:25).

Jesus Christ counseled: "Remember, remember that it is not the work of God that is frustrated, but the work of men". (D&C 3:3). "No power on earth or hell can overthrow or defeat that which God has decreed. Every plan of the Adversary will fail; for the Lord knows the secret thoughts of men and sees the future with a vision clear and perfect, even as though it were in the past". (Joseph Fielding Smith, Jr.). Jacob clearly understood this, when he wrote: "Oh, how great the holiness of our God. For he knoweth all things, and there is not anything save he knows it". (2 Nephi 9:20). Else He would cease to be God, and we could not have faith in Him.

Joseph Smith explained to John Wentworth: "No unhallowed hand can stop the work from progressing. Persecutions may rage, mobs may combine, armies may assemble, calumny may defame, but the truth of God will go forth boldly, nobly, and independent, until it has penetrated every continent, visited every clime, swept every country, and sounded in every ear; till the purposes of God shall be accomplished, and the Great Jehovah shall say 'The work is done.'" (H.C., 4:540). "After the thousands of attacks, and scores of books that have been published, not one criticism has survived, and millions have borne witness that the Lord has revealed to them the truth of this marvelous work". (Joseph Fielding Smith, Jr.).

At the opening of every Dispensation, Satan has made a frontal attack against the truth. He deceived the sons and daughters of Adam and Eve in the First Gospel Dispensation. At the beginning of the Mosaic Dispensation, "Satan came tempting him saying: Moses, son of man, worship me". (Moses 1:12). In the Meridian of Times, Satan attacked the Master Himself. (Luke 4:1-13). We learn from the Prophet Joseph Smith that Satan was present and actively contested the opening of the Dispensation of The Fulness of Times, as well. (J.S.H. 1:15).

Certainly, he tried very hard to frustrate the work of translation of the plates that had been delivered into the hands of Joseph Smith. He knew that The Church of Jesus Christ could not be organized before the publication of The Book of Mormon. "The loss of 116 pages of manuscript translated from the first part of The Book of Mormon, which was called The Book of Lehi", must have seemed a serious blow to Joseph Smith, at first. "The Prophet had reluctantly allowed these pages to pass from his custody to that of Martin Harris, who had served for a brief period as scribe in the translation of The Book of Mormon". (Superscript to D&C 3). But the Lord had already proactively initiated damage control by providing a duplicate record, in the form of The Small Plates of Nephi. Mormon had witnessed the last great battles between the Nephites and the Lamanites, and the record of his people had been completed. He had finalized his abridgment of The Large Plates of Nephi from The Book of Lehi through The Book of Mormon Chapter 7, and he was about to deliver The Plates of Mormon to his son Moroni. His exhaustive and comprehensive effort had chronicled almost 1,000 years of Nephite history. "And it came to pass that when we had gathered in all our people in one to the land of Cumorah ... I made this record out of The Plates of Nephi, and hid up in the hill Cumorah all the records which had been entrusted to me by the hand of the Lord, save it were these few plates which I gave unto my son Moroni". (Mormon 6:6).

Mormon hoped that Moroni would at least be able to continue the documentation of the outcome of the final conflict between the Nephites and Lamanites. "And it is many hundred years after the coming of Christ that I deliver these records into the hands of my son", Mormon wrote, "and it supposeth me that he will witness the entire destruction of my people. But may God grant that he may survive them, that he may write somewhat concerning them, and somewhat concerning Christ, that perhaps some day it may profit them". (V. 2).

On The Plates of Mormon, he wrote: "And it came to pass that my people, with their wives and their children, did now behold the armies of the Lamanites marching towards them; and with that awful fear of death which fills the breasts of all the wicked, did they await to receive them". (Mormon 6:7). What a contrast this was to a description of the death experiences of the righteous, provided by the Savior: "And it shall come to pass that those that die in me shall not taste of death, for it shall be sweet unto them". (D&C 42:46). "They shall never die the second death and feel the torment of the wicked, when they come face to face with eternity", said Joseph Fielding Smith, Jr.. "Death hath passed upon all men", as a matter of fact, "to fulfil the Merciful Plan of the Great Creator". (2 Nephi 9:6).

When the work of death at Cumorah had been completed, Mormon confirmed: "All my people, save it were . . twenty and four who were with me, and also a few who had escaped into the south countries, and a few who had deserted over unto the Lamanites, had fallen". (Mormon 6:15). "And they that die not in me," said the Lord, "wo unto them, for their death is bitter". (D&C 42:47). Such are unprepared to meet God. (See Alma 48:23). "Do not (then) procrastinate the day of your repentance until the end", pleaded Alma, "for after this day of life, which is given us to prepare for eternity, behold, if we do not improve our time while in this life, then cometh the night of darkness wherein there can be no labor performed". (Alma 34:33).

Mormon's wish that his son Moroni might survive the conflict to record the destruction of the Nephites was granted, and his writing has been preserved on The Plates of Mormon and comprise Mormon Chapters 8 and 9, as well as The Book of Moroni. The Doctrine & Covenants consecrated the efforts of both Mormon and Moroni: "And for this very purpose are these plates preserved, which contain these records - that the promises of the Lord might be fulfilled, which he made to his people". (D&C 3:19).

In The Words of Mormon, he explained his intention to write an appendage to The Small Plates of Nephi that he had only recently discovered among all the other plates in the library of the Nephite prophets. "After I had made an abridgment from The (Large) Plates of Nephi, down to the reign of this king Benjamin, of whom Amaleki spake, I searched among the records which had been delivered into my hands, and I found these plates". Mormon also wanted to add a few historical notes, in order to bring the narrative of The Small Plates of Nephi to the precise point at which The Book of Mosiah, abridged from The Large Plates, began on The Plates of Mormon.

The portion of The Large Plates of Nephi concerning Nephite history to the reign of Benjamin was called The Book of Lehi. This book covered the same time period as the whole of The Small Plates of Nephi, but was probably much more detailed, for Mormon observed that The Small Plates "contained (only a) small account of the prophets, from Jacob down to the reign of this king Benjamin". (V. 3). Just how small this account was is evident when we consider the meager efforts of Enos, Jarom, Omni, Amaron, Chemish, Abinadom, and Amaleki that concern a time span of 290 years but comprise only 72 verses of text. The Book of Omni alone spans 193 of those years in just 30 verses.

The Book of Mosiah, that followed The Book of Lehi on The Large Plates of Nephi, inaugurated a combined religious and secular history that continued until the time of Mormon. The entire record of The Large Plates of Nephi was then abridged onto The Plates of Mormon and was deposited with the other records in the sanctuary at the Hill Cumorah.

When Mormon was yet a child, the body of plates of all the Nephite prophets had been deposited for safekeeping by Amaron, who, "being constrained by the Holy Ghost, did hide up ... all the sacred records which had been handed down from generation to generation". (4 Nephi 1:48).

Mormon was of such spiritual stature that he was charged with the responsibility to care for these plates when only 10 years of age. "And Amaron said unto (Mormon): I perceive that thou art a sober child, and art quick to observe. Therefore, when ye are about twenty and four years old I would that ye should ... go to the land Antum, unto a hill which shall be called Shim; and there have I deposited unto the Lord all the sacred engravings concerning this people". (Mormon 1:3).

Fourteen years later, Mormon "did go to the hill Shim, and did take up all the records which Amaron had hid up unto the Lord". (Mormon 4:23). At this time, "wickedness did prevail upon the face of the whole land". (Mormon 1:13). By that time, the entire fabric of Nephite society was unraveling, and it must have taken extraordinary powers of concentration for Mormon to focus on his responsibilities as prophet-historian, and editor of The Large Plates of Nephi.

Mormon wrote of his experience at the hill Shim: "I searched among the records which had been delivered into my hands, and I found these plates, which contained this small account of the prophets, from Jacob down to the reign of this king Benjamin, and also many of the words of Nephi". (V. 3). He related that after he had made an abridgment from The (Large) Plates of Nephi, he discovered within The Small Plates of Nephi much that was pleasing to him, "because of the prophecies of the coming of Christ". (V. 4). Therefore, he chose them as the vehicle to finish his record. (V. 5). Following the engravings Amaleki had made at the end of The Book of Omni, Mormon wrote his last few words (The Words of Mormon) in the little space that remained on The Small Plates of Nephi.

When Mormon wrote that the "remainder of my record I shall take from The (Large) Plates of Nephi", he meant that, in order to write an understandable transitional narrative that would maintain continuity from The Small Plates to his abridgment of The Large Plates (which was already completed), he would need to make a brief account on The Small Plates of the life of King Benjamin, using as his reference text The Large Plates of Nephi. (V. 5).

Mormon's statement that he could not "write the hundredth part of the things of (his) people" is tantalizing to the mind and whets our appetite, making us hungry for more scripture. (V. 5). Jacob had said the same thing, and both Mormon and Moroni repeated this observation in various places in their abridgments. (V. 5, see Jacob 3:13, Helaman 3:14, 3 Nephi 5:8 & 26:6, & Ether 15:33).

"For a wise purpose", Mormon took The Small Plates of Nephi and put them with the remainder of his own abridgment, called the Plates of Mormon. (V. 7). A thousand years earlier, Nephi had been commanded by the Lord to make a duplicate record for the same reason. (1 Nephi 9:5). That purpose would only become apparent when the translation by Joseph Smith of the abridgment of The Large Plates of Nephi, concerning Nephite history from Lehi down to the reign of King Benjamin, and comprising the 116 pages of handwritten manuscript, would be lost by Martin Harris, to whom it had been temporarily entrusted. (See D&C 3 & 10).

In verse 8, we once again encounter the expanding circle of concern by the prophets, as faith, hope, and charity are manifested in Mormon's thoughts, words, and deeds. Remember that he had just witnessed "almost all the destruction of (his) people". (V. 1). Nevertheless, he wrote: "My prayer to God is concerning my brethren (the Lamanites), that they may once again come to the knowledge of God, yea, the redemption of Christ; that they once again be a delightsome people". (V. 8, see Moroni 7:44-48). One is reminded of Spencer W. Kimball's observation that in our mind's eye we should visualize signs above the entrances to every one of our Church buildings that include the invitation: "Sinners welcome!"

Mormon's feelings toward the Lamanites become a powerful witness to his total commitment to the teachings of Jesus Christ. (See Moroni 7:25-48). His summary statement made in Moroni 7:48 is all the more meaningful when it is understood in the context of the turmoil existing in Zarahemla around the year 385 A.D. Written at about the same time he engraved The Words of Mormon, he said: "Wherefore, my beloved brethren, pray unto the Father with all the energy of heart, that ye may be filled with this love, which he hath bestowed upon all who are true followers of his Son,

Jesus Christ; that ye may become the sons of God; that when he shall appear we shall be like him, for we shall see him as he is; that we may have this hope; that we may be purified even as he is pure. Amen".

"And Now I ... proceed to finish out my record, which I take from The (Large) plates of Nephi; and I make it according to the knowledge and the understanding which God has given me". (V. 9). When Mormon wrote these words, he had already completed his abridgment of The Large Plates of Nephi and had also recorded his testimony in The Book of Mormon inclusive of Chapter 7. His knowledge, understanding, and ability came by the Spirit. "And now come, saith the Lord, by the Spirit, unto the elders of his Church, and let us reason together, that ye may understand". (D&C 50:10).

With the completion of The Words of Mormon, the records of the Nephite people were reconciled. After King Benjamin had received The Small Plates from Amaleki, he put them with The Large Plates, and from that point on, they were kept together by the Nephite kings and by the prophets who wrote exclusively upon The Large Plates of Nephi. But it was left to Mormon to fashion the bridge connecting The Small Plates of Nephi with his abridgement The Large Plates of Nephi.

From verse 12 to the end of The Words of Mormon, we are provided with a brief summary of the reign of King Benjamin: "And now concerning this king Benjamin", wrote Mormon. (V. 12). He knew that we would not have access to the account of the whole life of King Benjamin that was contained in The Book of Lehi, for this was part of the infamous 116 pages of lost manuscript translation.

Mormon also knew that only 3 verses had been devoted to King Benjamin in The Book of Omni, and what Mormon had written about him in his abridgment of The Book of Mosiah was confined to the last 3 years of the king's life. Nevertheless, what we do know of Benjamin because of Mormon's abridgment of The Book of Mosiah is invaluable. The recorded discourse of King Benjamin is one of the greatest sermons in the scriptures and is a practical statement of religious conduct applicable to all times. It is The Book of Mormon equivalent to the Sermon on the Mount.

Verse 13 of The Words of Mormon suggests that the Lamanites had overrun the wicked Nephites who had stayed behind in the Land of Nephi. The Lamanites had come down out of that land (the very land from which Mosiah's band of refugees had fled many years before) to battle the Nephites in the Land of Zarahemla. (See Omni 1:12). At this time, the young and vigorous Benjamin fought "with the strength of his own arm" wielding the Sword of Laban, which was kept by the Nephite kings throughout their history. Fortunately, the battle plan and strategy of these Nephites under the leadership of King Benjamin was once again founded in the Lord, and in His strength "they did contend against their enemies" until the Lamanites were driven from the "land of their inheritance", which was now Zarahemla.

The construction of verses 15-18 suggest that Mormon, anxious because there was so little room left on The Small Plates of Nephi, hastily finished his record in an uncharacteristically awkward style. One cumbersome sentence of 174 words makes up these verses. (See Commentary Reference to Jacob 4:1, & Ether 12:24).

"And it came to pass that after there had been false Christs, and their mouths had been shut, and they punished according to their crimes; And after there had been false prophets, and false preachers and teachers among the people, and all these having been punished according to their crimes; and after there having been much contention and many dissensions away unto the Lamanites, behold, it came to pass that king Benjamin, with the assistance of the holy prophets who were among his people - For behold, king Benjamin was a holy man, and he did reign over his people in righteousness; and there were many holy men in the land, and they did speak the word of God with power and with authority; and they did use much sharpness because of the stiffneckedness of the people - Wherefore, with the help of these, king Benjamin, by laboring with all the might of his body and the faculty of his whole soul, and also the prophets, did once more establish peace in the land". (V. 15-18).

These verses might be condensed down to the following 16 words: "And it came to pass that ... king Benjamin ... did once more establish peace in the land". In effect, Mormon wanted to say (in just 41 words) that after the Nephites in Zarahemla had dealt with false Christs, prophets, and teachers, and after desertions and defections to the Lamanites by those weak in testimony, with the help of holy men, Benjamin was able to establish peace in the land.

Mormon was an amazing individual. He could see beyond the terrible suffering caused by the apostasy of his own people, and he could differentiate their behavior from the intrinsic nature of both the Nephites and the Lamanites. He truly believed that his people were "numbered among the people of the first covenant", or the magnificent Abrahamic Covenant, which had first been made between the Father of The Faithful and God Himself. (Mormon 7:10). His perceptions were clear and accurate, allowing him to see his people's autobiographical thread leading back to Deity. He understood that even the most hardened soul has "the acorn of a potential oak, the unsculptured image of a glorified personality". (Truman Madsen, "Eternal Man", p. 17). To the very last, perhaps just hours before he was slain by the Lamanites, he wrote: "If it so be that ye believe in Christ, and are baptized, first with water, then with fire and with the Holy Ghost, following the example of our Savior, according to that which he hath commanded us, it shall be well with you in the day of judgment. Amen". (Mormon 7:10).

"It is a serious thing to live in a society of possible Gods and Goddesses", wrote C.S. Lewis, "to remember that the dullest and most uninteresting person you talk to may one day be a creature which if you saw it now, you would be strongly tempted to worship ... There are no ordinary people. You have never talked to a mere mortal. It is immortals with whom we joke, work, marry, snub and exploit. ... Our charity must be a real and costly love ... Next to the blessed sacrament itself, your neighbor is the holiest object presented to your senses. If he is your Christian neighbor, he is holy in almost the same way, for in him also Christ is truly hidden and glorified". Mormon believed that both the Nephites and Lamanites were "no ordinary people".

Perhaps this is the hidden meaning in the scripture that enjoins Christ's disciples to "love the Lord thy God with all thy heart, and with all thy soul, and with all thy strength, and with all thy mind; and thy neighbour as thyself". (Luke 10:27). Mormon had a great capacity to love his people. The essence of his message on faith, hope, and charity (see Moroni 7) is reflected in these lines penned by Edwin Markham: "He drew a circle that shut me out, Heretic, rebel, a thing to flout. But Love and I had the will to win. We drew a circle that took him in".

Mormon felt genuine love as the Savior had, Who, on the Cross besought His Father, and prayed: "Father, forgive them; for they know not what they do". (Luke 23:34). He surely would have agreed with the following sentiment, articulated on a smaller scale, but nevertheless relevant; "Wouldn't it be nice if, as we tuck our child into bed after a particularly stressful day, we could say something like this: 'I've been watching you, and you are about the most special human being I've ever met. I'm proud to wear your name. I know we had an argument today, but that was behavior. It's the person I love. It's behavior I got bothered with, but not you. I love you unconditionally, not based on achievement, but based on you, and your potential. I love you very much.' (Anonymous). This is charity, the pure love of Christ, and the quality that Mormon personified throughout his writings. We will find its full expression throughout his abridgment of The Large Plates of Nephi and within The Plates of Mormon that follow, in volumes two and three of this commentary.

Observations

When the
weaknesses of the
Nephites were linked to
repentance, it was actually
quite motivating, since they
responded positively to the
invitation to do better,
and to be merciful,
forgiving, and
kind.

It is by grace that
our burdens are lightened
if we've found them too heavy
to bear alone. Then it stands
ready to pluck us out of the
gaping jaws of hell, and
whisk us out of harm's
way, right into the
embrace of
God.

When we
allow it to do so,
the principles that are
illuminated by The Book of
of Mormon completely envelop
us in a shower of divinely directed
diamond dust. They glow and glitter with
thousands of points of pulsating light that
peacefully settles down upon us. These are
reflections from heaven that could only flow
from above. When they come together, they
work tirelessly on our sense of duty, our
conscience, and our scruples, and they
slowly nurture our faith to believe. In
these ways and more, the myriad
elements of the book stimulate
our soul sweat.

Our
faith that
is nurtured
by The Book of
Mormon asks us to
forge a spiritual bond
with our fellow travelers
by obedience that is more
expansive than a law of
carnal commandments.
It requires the inter-
dependency of
the greater
law.

The prophets of
The Book of Mormon are the
embodiment of honesty, chastity,
truth, benevolence, and virtuosity.
As we adhere to our faith in God's
divine design, and we see our
neighbors thru the softening
lens of charity, our hopes
and dreams are more
comprehensive, and
our love is more
inclusive.

The Book of
Mormon prepares us
to move onward along
a steady course of progress
without encumbering ourselves
with the wobbly constraints of
uncertainty that always lie in
wait to mislead those who
manifest a timid and
hesitant spiritual
constitution.

Surely, we need the wise counsel of prophets now, as much as we ever have, because we have exponentially increased the odds that we will destroy ourselves if we are careless; if we do not both carefully and prayerfully adhere to the principles of the Book of Mormon, in all we undertake to do.

The Book
of Mormon asks
that we give ourselves
completely and without
reservation, that we might
enjoy a state of harmony with
God and synchronization with the
eternities. He asks us to search
without ceasing, that we might
discover the divine center
of our faith.

If we fail to embrace
The Book of Mormon, but
allow ourselves to be habitually
distracted by trifling concerns, we
will be at risk of becoming mired in
the marshland of mediocrity, to be
trapped in the quicksand of
sin, from which there is
no easy escape.

Our faith may as well be dead, without the accompanying work of repentance that is made possible by the Atonement and continually fortified as we partake of the Sacrament. Our faith notwithstanding, we do not have the power to save ourselves from the unalterable demands of Justice. So Mercy might abound, our Heavenly Father created covenants that are linked to the features of The Book of Mormon.

Those who
profess to believe
The Book of Mormon
recognize its positive and
pleasant aspects. It carries a
performance requirement that
will motivate us to maintain
spiritually aerobic fitness,
that we might meet the
unwavering demands
of our discipleship,
but not fatigue
our faith.

The Book
of Mormon
will cares our
spirits and massage
our minds with images
of a religious recognition
confirming the nobility of
our birthright. It blesses us
with a spiritual sixth sense,
allowing us to create order
out of chaos and make
sense of creation.

The great Plan that is so clearly described in The Book of Mormon envisions a utopian society, but it is also pragmatic, anticipating our weaknesses and our inability to live in obedience to every commandment of God, by providing the Atonement as a practical solution for those of us whose agency would lead us away from the Rod of Iron.

The Plan
grounds us,
not on telestial
turf that is soiled
with the stain of sin,
but on broad celestial
boulevards that have been
paved with shining bricks of
24 carat gold. As we look into
the distance thru the shimmer
of everlasting burnings, we
can just make out the
dwelling place of
God.

The Book of Mormon will introduce us to one pleasant surprise after another, during a spiritual metamorphosis that will prove to be as challenging as it will be rewarding. If we want to embrace its delights, we must 'let go, and let God.' Only then, will we catch a religious fever that spikes the temperature of our testimonies, and gets our juices flowing.

We are much more
than just the sum of our
somatic senses. The Book of
Mormon will trigger the activation
of our spiritual sixth sense. When
it does, we will have discovered
a key that unlocks the door
to undreamed of vistas of
otherwise inaccessible
experience.

Faith
is impotent
when it does not
lead to purposeful
performance. It is the
sizzle without the steak.
Real faith involves a vital,
personal self-commitment to
The Book of Mormon. But in
the end, even our belief will
ring hollow if it lacks the
confirming witness of
faith that we receive
from the Spirit.

The
reach of the
Plan of Salvation
and of the Atonement
that are described in The
Book of Mormon has power
to extend so far that the sins
of the best of us and the worst
of us can be neutralized. There
is no end to their temporal or
eternal influence. They only
wait upon our initiative to
manifest their energy and
to transport us into a
state of harmony
with heaven.

Choice lies at the heart of the Gospel of Jesus Christ, and The Book of Mormon nudges us off our comfortable cushions of complacency, setting us squarely on the hot seat of our personal accountability.

When
the descendants
of Lehi and Sariah
were born again through
faith, repentance, baptism,
and the gift of the Holy Ghost,
their orientation was more toward
the expansive laws of the eternal
world than to the restrictive
confines of their physical
surroundings. This is
why our spirits are
always nurtured
by obedience.

Obedience
to gospel principles had
the power to bring the Nephites and
Lamanites into harmony with eternity,
allowing them to overcome the world, with a
freedom from confinement to the inexorable
immutability of the destructive laws
of disproportion that so often
govern our temporal
affairs.

For the descendants of Lehi and Sariah,
repentance was just the prescription the Doctor
ordered, to deal with the religious fever that
elevated their testimony temperatures
enough to get their juices flowing
with an appreciation of the
Savior's sacrifice.

It was
the Lamanites'
faith, which just so
happens to be the traveling
companion of repentance, that
motivated them to action, and to
the waters of baptism, by jarring
them out of their complacency
regarding their standing
before God.

When
the Nephites and
Lamanites repented,
they enjoyed serenity
and harmony in ways
that were thoughtfully
programmed by our
Heavenly Father to
touch their heart
strings.

Repentance endowed the people of Ammon with power to reach out and touch the face of God with an incorruptible and unassailable spiritual sixth sense that found its expression deep inside them, within their hearts.

When we are
first introduced to The Book of
Mormon, but we are assaulted on all
sides by sounding brass and tinkling
cymbals, if we hearken to the Spirit and
we believe the promise of Moroni, we will
find the power within ourselves to sift
thru the discordant cacophony of
confusing voices to find
revealed truth.

Diligent study of
The Book of Mormon
teaches us to suppress the
natural inclinations of the
telestial world that surround
us, continually encroaching
upon our spiritual stability,
and threatening to dilute
our faith and testimony
of the principles of
the Gospel.

If we neglect to devour The Book of Mormon by feasting upon the words of Christ (see 2 Nephi 32:3), we must at least admit to ourselves that when we kill time, we damage our eternal selves, for the Lord warned, "in an hour when ye think not, the summer (is) past, and the harvest ended, and your souls not saved." (D&C 45:2). We must realize that each second of every day, as Hamlet observed, we are one tick of the clock closer to that "undiscovered country from whose bourne no traveler returns."

As
we read
The Book
of Mormon,
we discover that
we have come home
to a more comfortable
and expansive dominion,
where power and authority
take on new meanings that
beforehand had only been
dimly perceived.

Without
immersing ourselves
in The Book of Mormon,
we may find that we can only
indirectly appreciate the eternities.
As we seek learning by study and by
faith, "we can make our lives sublime, and
departing, leave behind us footprints on the
sands of time." (Longfellow). If scripture
study has been neglected, however, those
footprints may be washed away by the
incessant action of the waves that
beat relentlessly upon our
shores.

Our love
of the scriptures,
and in particular of
The Book of Mormon, was
nurtured within our spiritual
kindergarten, is heightened in
our mortal classroom, and will
be established in eternity, when
heaven will smile upon us and
we will be clothed in the
glory of God.

We can better
relate to the other
participants in life's
Three Act Play, and they
to us, if we view each other
against the milieu of the First,
Second, and Third Acts, namely,
our pre-earth life, mortality, and our
life after death. Familiarity with this
sweeping panorama, of the intricacy,
complexity, and sophistication of the
Play itself, is alluded to by the
prophets of The Book of
Mormon.

The
Book of
Mormon
can become
the locomotive
during our ride
thru mortality. We
board a train that is
bound for glory with a
first-class ticket, so that
the dust, delays, sidetracks,
smoke, cinders and jolts will
be a lot more comfortable. The
conductor of that train is Jesus
Christ, Who punches our ticket
and provides significant relief
from the inconveniences of
the journey, with His
Atonement.

If we
stubbornly refuse to
acknowledge the reality
of eternity by neglecting to
embrace The Book of Mormon,
where will our sanctuary be if the
wind blows and the rain beats down?
To what safe harbors will we flee when
the ocean of life is in turmoil? If we are
tossed about as flotsam and jetsam, and
never come to a knowledge of what is true,
to what source will we look for the stability
we so desperately seek, or for the answers
to the greatest questions in life that
trouble our spirits?

When we make the effort to define ourselves from the eternal perspective of The Book of Mormon, we raise our sights to the possibility of an expanded view of life. We are up and moving on the pathway to our personal rediscovery and self actualization.

It is because of
The Book of Mormon that
we cast ourselves off from the
self limiting conditions and
self defeating behaviors that
would otherwise have blinded
us to a larger view of life. We
enjoy a settled conviction of
the truth. That peace follows
our observance of celestial
principles that are taught
in the scriptures, that
brings the Rest of God
within the reach of
our uplifted
hands.

Our
embryonic study
of The Book of Mormon
won't give us a second wind
in the first mile of the race, when
we have only just begun our journey.
If we have previously been caught up in the
trauma of temporal traps, if our timid faith still
blinds us to the impotence of our false gods, sooner
or later, the darkness that we are trying so desperately to
cast off can overwhelm us. Without an infusion of Book of
Mormon stories that are aflame with faith to give us renewed
bursts of energy, and without relying upon the miraculous
fulfilment of Moroni's promise (see Moroni 10:4) those who
are studying the Book of Mormon for the first time may
experience feelings of confusion, disillusionment, or
abandonment, and they risk wandering off
into mists of darkness and perishing
in Babylon.

Our introduction to, and our study of, The Book of Mormon creates a scenario that gives our Father in Heaven a pretty good idea of just how we would behave if were left to our own devices, after having received instruction regarding what we ought to do. Our Savior is the Architect of the Cosmos, and those with the mighty faith to believe The Book of Mormon, Another Testament of Jesus Christ, add strength to His pillars of creation.

At the
conclusion of
our initial forays into
The Book of Mormon, we are
spiritually sensitive and prepared
to move. Our experience, as we act upon
Moroni's promise (Moroni 10:4), is almost
transparent. We sense the expansion of God's
powers, as the glittering facets of the life of
the Spirit wash over us. As quiet spiritual
stirrings propel us into the presence of
beings from the unseen world, they
confirm our faith with barely
audible hallelujahs.

We may
passionately
pursue happiness,
and yet never be able to
find it. Some don't seem to
realize that happiness is really
like a butterfly. If we chase it, we
will never catch it. But if we quietly
contemplate the harmony within The
Book of Mormon and its symmetry
with its companion scriptures, the
joy of the Lord and a peace that
surpasses our understanding
will come and gently rest
on our shoulders.

We
pay dearly for
our secular education,
and we expect a return on
investment. Our introduction to
The Book of Mormon is equivalent
to engaging in an independent study
fine arts program. Its requirements for
enrollment are simply a ready heart and
a willing mind, and there is no temporal
tuition. Its design and its purpose is to
teach us what we need to know and
do, so God may guide us back to
His heavenly home, to live with
Him in His kingdom.

The Book of
Mormon reveals hints of
what it must have been like in
our pre-mortal existence, and then
it explains the purpose of life on earth.
Lastly, it opens our hearts and our minds
to soul-expanding eternal opportunities.
When we conform to its overall strategy
for success, we become better friends,
neighbors, and witnesses of Christ,
and we are also better prepared
to find the elusive equations
that relate to lasting
happiness.

We
cannot
hope to find
life's meaning
if we treat our study
of The Book of Mormon
superficially or carelessly.
Our conscious appreciation of
its value must be earned. When
we take it for granted, or if we've
abandoned the core principles that
are taught by Book of Mormon
prophets, their power to bless
our lives may slip away
and be lost for time,
if not for all of
eternity.

The Lord selects the humble and worthy, and then He tutors them through the power of the Holy Ghost with the guidance of the scriptures and counsel from His servants, revealing to them His will. Those whom He selects are "the weak things of the world." (D&C 1:19. As President Kimball declared: "Christianity did not go from Rome to Galilee. It was the other way around. In our day, the route is from Palmyra to Paris, and not the reverse."

A tenet of
faith of the members of
The Church of Jesus Christ of
Latter-day Saints is that they
believe that The Plan of God provides
for us, with institutional and personal
continuing revelation that comes through
the medium of the Holy Ghost. This power is
intimately related to our acceptance of The
Book of Mormon as holy writ. However,
"looking for the spectacular, we often
miss the constant flow of revealed
communication that comes."
(Spencer W. Kimball).

Blind opposition,
enmity, hatred, hostility,
obstinacy, and intolerance are
the raw manifestations of pride,
but these are overwhelmed by the
accommodation, benevolence,
approachability, faith, hope,
and sociality of those
who rely upon The
Book of Mormon
as a primer on
charity.

The Book of
Mormon can purify us
from caustic influences,
and decontaminate us from
the toxicity that is so prevalent
in the world. It neutralizes the
homogenization process that
occurs when we are tossed
about by the vagaries of
men, let alone the
vicissitudes
of life.

The Book
of Mormon illustrates the
principle that darkness simply
can't abide the illumination of faith.
We who embrace its teachings relish the
opportunity to be enveloped within the light,
and we've learned to anticipate the sunshine of
revelation that is a gift from God. The shadows
may still exist, but they will remain behind
us. The traveling companion of iniquity is
despair, but it is because of the Savior's
intervention in our behalf that the
fog of fear will be dissipated, so
that it cannot harm us.

We are
anchored by The
Book of Mormon into
gospel topsoil and we tap
into limpid pools of living
water. Our testimonies of the
truth of the Restoration of the
Gospel are evidences of our
honesty with ourselves,
with our Father, with
the Savior, and
with the Holy
Ghost.

The Book of Mormon is the great equalizer. It matters little in what exclusionary ecclesiastical country club we might have held membership, or on what constricted theological terrace we may have paused to catch our breath. All we need to do, to come unto Christ, is to be moving along on a path that leads to the truth.

In between
the sights and
sounds, rides and
attractions, and thrills
and spills of our earthly
theme-park experience upon
the carousel of life, The Book
of Mormon illustrates how to
use spiritual hygiene practice
to remove the grit and grime
that always threaten to foul
our inner workings. These
are the carnival barkers
and flim-flam artists,
whose sole mission on
earth seems to be to
slow our progress
on the pathway
to perfection.

The
Book of
Mormon shows
us how to overcome
our selfishness and
our indefensible desire
to be shown Mercy without
satisfying the unavoidable
demands of Justice, which
is nothing more than a
doctrine of the
Devil.

The Savior is our Advocate with the Father, and is the Bread of Life, the Foundation of Faith beneath our existence, and the Cornerstone of our Belief. He is the Deliverer of the Everlasting Covenant, and in The Book of Mormon, He is clearly identified as "the Rock of (our) Salvation." (2 Nephi 9:45).

If it is our
wish to be saved in
the Celestial Kingdom
of God, we must keep our
eyes fixed on the prize, as we
reach out beyond our comfort
zones to snatch the golden
ring that hangs beside
The Book of Mormon
on the carousel
of life.

The Book of Mormon can help us catalyze our feeling, capture our emotion, contour our attitude, crystallize thought, congeal passion, compartmentalize action, and convey sentiment, that lead to spiritual revitalization.

The
only
payment
necessary
for the gift
of salvation is
the heart and a
willing mind. It
is in The Book of
Mormon that we are
reminded that sin is
the only thing that
we must give up, to
inherit eternal
life.

If we
snub the
teachings
of The Book
of Mormon, we
cannot suppose
to superficially
whitewash our
sins to cover
them up, no
matter how
hard we
try.

The Book of Mormon has purpose and meaning only for those who are prepared to sacrifice their broken heart and contrite spirit to the Savior of the world.

At times,
a testimony
of The Book of
Mormon must be
felt thru suffering.
As Paul wrote: "For
unto you it is given
in behalf of Christ,
not only to believe
on him, but also
to suffer for
his sake."

The invitation to forgive and to be forgiven is juxtaposed against the sense of despair, despondency, gloom, and desperation that often accompanies our mortal schooling. The Book of Mormon is a beacon of hope in a bewildering world where opposition is our constant companion.

Lucifer
fell from
heaven with
a deafening
thud. We feel
its after-shock
even now, when
our knees shake
under the weight
of sin. It's in The
Book of Mormon
that we can find
the strength to
stand tall and
not topple
over.

The Spirit extends to us the promise of a wonderful opportunity to enjoy the bliss of our abode in heaven. Thru the Book of Mormon, we anticipate the warm embrace of Heavenly Father, His Son Jesus Christ, and the Holy Ghost.

The
virtues of
accord with
the exigencies
of the Law as it is
defined in The Book
of Mormon are first,
a well-trained mind, a
body to match, a love of
achievement, and finally,
focused faith. Without these,
life may seem to be nothing
but smoke and mirrors, a
cruel deception, and we
grow old before our
time.

There is no revelation where there is no student, and so if we do not ask the right questions that relate to the truth that is found within The Book of Mormon, we will remain at odds with our faith and we will be condemned to receive the wrong answers. Sadly, rational minds will never be able to bridge the gap that must exist between the profane character of the worldly-wise and the divine nature.

Blessed
are they who,
when they face
temptation, have
the faith to turn to
the right. It is by the
Holy Ghost that they
will be taught how to
find a route around
the doctrinal detours
and telestial traffic
that block the way
to The Book of
Mormon.

Our
faith is
impotent if it
does not lead us
to our testimony of
The Book of Mormon,
where we can make the
connection between it and
God's divine design that
exists for each one
of us.

The
Book
of Mormon
can catalyze
our relationship
with God when it
unshackles us from
the icy grasp of our
captivity to Satan.
This is because of
the Atonement
of Christ.

Some may ask: "What do I want out of life?" but those who have faithfully read The Book of Mormon are instead motivated to softly ask: "What is it, dear Lord, that Thou wouldst have me do?"

The Book of Mormon
clearly teaches that when
we stand before God on the
Day of Judgment, we may be
uncompromised by corruption.
Repentance is one of the things
in life that seems just too good
to be true, but what makes it
believable is our faith in
the miracle of the
Atonement.

The Book of
Mormon anchors us
to practical belief, even
as its elements commit
us to an upward thrust.
The Spirit whispers that
we are known to God,
and to the angels in
heaven who, even as
we speak, silently
are writing down
everything we
think, say
and do.

The
Book of Mormon
is a dowry from Deity
that has been designed to
compound our faith in the
financial stability of His
treasury, and facilitate
unwavering fidelity to
Him who serves as
Chief Financial
Officer of
Heaven.

Knowledge that we gain thru the exercise of our faith is as a mortar that fastens together the building blocks of our testimonies and our conversion. It is by the truth that we are bound to The Book of Mormon. (See John 8:32).

The Devil urges
us to follow his detours
from the strait and narrow
path that will lead us through
conceptual cul-de-sacs, telestial
traffic, religious roundabouts, and
doctrinal dead ends, from which our
escape is possible only if we link our
fortunes to the teachings found
within the pages of The Book
of Mormon.

The Book of Mormon nurtures our relationship with God and the Spirit, freeing us to become the fashioners of our fortunes, while teaching us how to take maximum advantage of intangible resources that are greater than ourselves.

The
Book
of Mormon
is a catalyst
that propels us
upward toward the
discovery of personal
levels of experience with
Jesus Christ. Its doctrine
can only be tested if we've
nurtured a companionship
with the Spirit. When we
fall under its spell, we
will be at-one with
the Savior of the
world.

The
Book
of Mormon
will catalyze
our relationship
with God when it
shatters the icy grip
of our captivity to
Satan; and all is
because of the
Atonement
of Christ.

Whenever we are spiritually neglectful in our Book of Mormon study, drastic action is required. The plastic surgery of the Atonement is indicated if we want to experience a reversal of our fortunes and if we hope to restore the likeness and image of our Father to countenances that have been blemished by our sins of omission.

Without our
resolute repentance
that is founded upon
an understanding of
the Atonement of Christ
that results from Book of
Mormon study, we cannot
reasonably expect to inherit
the glory of celestial realms;
especially if we have aforetime
been agreeable to abide by only
telestial or terrestrial principles
that may put fewer demands on
discipleship, or may be found
to be the tenets of faith of
secular Christianity.

If we
do not beg for
our own forgiveness,
and if we do not forgive
those who have purportedly
trespassed against us, The Book
of Mormon illustrates that we will
find ourselves trapped within the
spiritual vacuum of souls bound
by sin. We will gasp for air
while we were only inches
away from the rescue of
the Atonement of
Jesus Christ.

The Book
of Mormon
admonishes us
to constantly strive to
do more and to be better, to
seek understanding, and to
become empowered by wisdom.
It emulates the Olympic motto:
"Citius, Altius, Fortius," that
is to say, "Faster, Higher,
Stronger."

The Book of
Mormon is a primer on
midwifery, with the Savior
our labor coach, as we begin
the arduous birthing process
of our reunion with God
that He characterizes
as being born
again.

As we begin
our study of The Book
of Mormon, we experience
feelings of harmony and the
stirrings of serenity, in ways
that have been delightfully
designed by our Father in
Heaven to give us pause
and touch our heart
strings.

The Book of Mormon teaches powerful doctrine. It gives us the means to suppress the natural inclinations of the telestial world that surrounds us, continually encroaching upon our spiritual stability, and threatening to erode our testimony of gospel principles that relate to discipleship.

We are on the
path that leads to
celestial glory if we
accept inspired direction
with dedicated purpose. Our
discipleship is actively linked
to faithful consistency in our
study of The Book of Mormon.
Thereby, we will be blessed with
the revelatory guidance we
need to find our way
back to our home
in heaven.

The Book of Mormon
forthrightly demands that we
pass through the portal of baptism,
because our lives will open up in an
expansion of eternal opportunities as
we obtain the remission of our sins
through the Atonement of Christ,
gain membership in the Church,
and are personally sanctified
by receiving the gift of the
Holy Ghost. We will have
the Spirit of God to
be with us.

The authors of
The Book of Mormon
knew that powerful forces
would constantly refine us by
pushing and pulling at us within
the crucible of experience. During the
process, we would not be able to eliminate
the consequences of our actions that would
be less than perfect. For that to happen, our
Heavenly Father would provide us with
the Atonement of Christ; He Who
was the Lamb slain from
before the foundation
of the world.

Weakness can seed the atmosphere of our inspiration, (see Ether 12:27), to moisten and nurture our tender testimonies as well as to germinate our budding desires to repent from our wicked ways by taking full advantage of every blessing of the Gospel.

The Book of Mormon can become the initiator of a constructive process designed to build us up, even if it has to first tear us down. It is involved with recovery, to be sure. But its primary focus is on discovery.

In historical context, the milieu
of The Book of Mormon is nurtured
within a rich culture medium of faith,
testimony, and conversion, validated by
baptism, and a metaphysical reunion
with God. It is witness to the fiery
cauldron of the Spirit, and we
follow its glowing path in
the hope that we might
experience that same
fire in our own
bones.

In matters of faith, altitude is all about attitude. If we stay focused on The Book of Mormon, we'll raise our sights, so that we are always looking up, in the direction of our dreams.

The
Book of
Mormon
emboldens
us with hope,
and blesses us
with the fortitude
to be able to endure,
motivating us to seek
after everything that is
lovely, of good report,
or praiseworthy.

The Book
of Mormon very
forcefully teaches us
that even when the raw
feelings of pride taint and
twist our character, salvation
lies in the Atonement. When
we look about and argue who
is right, repentance stands
ready to look up to God,
and ask what is
right.

No
matter how
ponderous the
burdens are that we
have created due to our
inattention to our spiritual
well-being, The Book of Mormon
stands at attention and reminds us
that Jesus Christ, Who is the Savior of
the world and is the Mediator of the
Covenant, will lift us up at the
last day, especially if we
are carrying dead
weight.

In the last days, our
society, which is by most
standards "good", nevertheless
has failed miserably to cultivate
faith within the rising generation. If
a culture really believes that the merits
of faith are arbitrarily determined, that
truth is relative, that there's no coherent
Plan of God or divine design, or that
The Book of Mormon is nothing but
a delusion and a snare, or is the
fabrication of a frenzied mind,
the stage is set for temporal
and spiritual disasters
that will be of biblical
proportion.

In our obedience
to the principles within
The Book of Mormon, we try
to be perfect in our repentance,
that God might give unto us the
spirit of wisdom and of revelation,
to enlighten our understanding,
that we might embrace the hope
of the high calling of Jesus
Christ, and that the riches
of glory might abide as
our inheritance.

Life's
purpose can
be quantified; it
is to grow in stature,
until we have developed
the image and likeness
of our Heavenly Father.
(See 2 Peter 3:1, &
Alma 5:14).

The Lord recognizes that the righteous cannot expect to become perfect in a day. Therefore, He has promised: "As often as my people repent will I forgive them their trespasses." (Mosiah 26:30).

We are
fully repentant
only if we have charity,
or the pure love of Christ (see
Moroni 7:47), and are strictly
obedient to the principle of
forgiveness, and that
door swings both
ways.

Our Lord Jesus Christ taught that we must be perfect, for otherwise we cannot hope to inherit the Kingdom of God. (See 3 Nephi 12:48). Perhaps, He meant that we must be quick to repent of all of our sins.

The Book of Mormon teaches us to be patient, even in the face of challenges when our portion seems unfair, when our difficulties seem unreasonable, and when the proportions of the problems looming before us seem daunting.

The Book of Mormon teaches that we will receive the strength to endure the suffering that is part of life, and especially that which is not of our own making. (See Alma 32:43).

The Book
of Mormon is
like a stethoscope that
gauges the vital capacity of
our prideful hearts, which must
be broken in contrition in order to
exhibit the steady sinus rhythm that
confirms perfect harmony with
its proven principles
of perfection.

The
Book of
Mormon is a
pacemaker doling
out therapeutic pulses
of doctrinal energy to
those who need it the
most, when they
need it the
most.

The
Bard of
Avon mused:
"All the world's
a stage," and life is a
3 Act Play (See Mosiah
2:23-24). We become the
willing participants within
a drama whose script was set
in stone even before the earth
upon which we live fell
into existence.

If we examine
it closely, woven into
the fabric of our Book of
Mormon tapestry, there are
quite often "dark threads
that are as needful in the
Weaver's skillful hand as
the threads of gold and
silver, in the pattern
He has planned."
(B. Franklin).

Legions of angels stand at attention before the golden gate of heaven, patiently waiting for us to recognize the power of The Book of Mormon to transform our lives.

The examples of Laman
and Lemuel illustrate that those
of weak will who voluntarily give up their
agency in exchange for whatever provocative
pleasures their poor choices may provide, are
snared by Satan and bound by his strong
chains. Too late, they realize that their
misguided loyalties have fettered
their self expression, limited
their options, and have
restricted their
actions.

The first step in the process of repentance, that is well defined in The Book of Mormon, is a tipping point at which we consciously recognize our sins. The second step is our clear understanding of Justice, Mercy, and the grace of God, and our appreciation of the relationship between them because of The Plan of Deliverance From Death.

The habitual sins of
the wicked Lamanites became a quicksand that
mired the unwary in a monotonously repetitive and
underwhelming convention, and in a mind-numbing
conformity. These were the polar opposites of the
imaginative spontaneity and refreshingly
distinctive artistic individuality
of those Nephites who counted
themselves among the
disciples of
Christ.

God
glories in
the possibility
that we may become
like Him, which may be
the ultimate expression of
His matchless grace. When we
are sanctified unto the remission
of our sins, we are perfect in Christ,
in the sense that we have "become
holy, without spot." (Moroni
10:33).

The Holy Ghost testifies of the truthfulness of The Book of Mormon, and stands ready to guide us unerringly, until we reach a point that we know the truth of all things. It does this by molding us into revelatory reservoirs. As long as we have become new creatures in Christ, pure intelligence will flow unto us as the dews of Carmel.

The Book of Mormon
teaches that baptism by water
will qualify us for membership in
the church, but it cannot guarantee
the total spiritual transformation of
our nature that is envisioned by the
Plan. But that is exactly what will
be required if we hope to regain
the presence and glory of God,
and that is only possible
through the baptism of
fire and the Holy
Ghost.

The Plan, described in The Book of Mormon, elevates our level of worship to something that is more dynamic than the mechanical observance of a multiplicity of ceremonial rules and regulations. Its eternal scope generates power, "for a mind that is once stretched by a new idea can never again return to its original dimension." (Oliver Wendell Holmes).

Father
Lehi clearly taught
that when we choose not
to travel the path that leads
to the Tree of Life, or if we do
not work diligently to harvest
the delicious fruit of that tree,
we cannot receive the things
of the Spirit of God, for
to our eyes, they will
seem foolish.

We cannot hope to comprehend with
fluency the language that is spoken by the
Spirit, that touches our heartstrings and bears
solemn witness of the truthfulness of The Book of
Mormon, until we have paid the price of admission.
We may dismiss its whisperings as nothing but a
gentle breeze that passes by. The quiet counsel of
the Holy Ghost may sound pleasant to our ears,
but its message of hope may remain elusive,
until we actually invite its companionship.
At the end of the day, we are saved by the
grace of God, but only after we have
done all that we can while the
sun is still shining.

Those who embrace The Book of Mormon will have the image of God engraven upon their countenances. They shall ascend onto the hill of the Lord. They shall stand in His holy place to partake of His divine nature, because they have clean hands and their hearts are pure, and they have not lifted up their souls to vanity, nor have they sworn deceitfully.

The resources of The
Church of Jesus Christ are largely
focused upon programs that nurture
our familiarity with the Holy Ghost, Who
introduces us to the Plan of Salvation and to
The Book of Mormon. His bestowal of spiritual
gifts is the antidote we all need for poisonous
telestial tendencies. Like noxious weeds that
may be overlooked in a flower garden, our
tolerance of worldliness can crowd out
His expression of celestial sureties
that are found in both the
Plan and the book.

We
can be fully
committed to he
Plan of God and still
have very special moments
of reconfirmation. The Spirit
sometimes works so powerfully
upon us that we can say, as did
the people of Zarahemla, that our
hearts have been changed through
faith on the name of Christ, that
we have been born of Him, and
that we have become His sons
and daughters who no longer
have the disposition to do
evil, but to do good
continually.

We are intertwined
with Heavenly Father, Jesus
Christ, and with the Holy Ghost,
in palpable connections. They notice
when sparrows fall from trees, and on
clear winter nights, they help us notice
the explosion of supernovas in distant
galaxies. They do not play dice with
Their creations. We also remember
that we can be at-one with Them
when we are studying The
Book of Mormon.

What we call "coincidence" is often simply our Heavenly Father Who is working behind the scenes. Every moment of our lives is influenced by His divine design and His Plan. This is important to remember when we read The Book of Mormon. We just need to be in tune with His Spirit in order to recognize that, and act upon it.

When our minds
are locked on telestial
targets, and we even attempt
so-called higher-level thinking,
without the influence of the Spirit
and the perspective of God's Plan that
is outlined in The Book of Mormon, we
will always remain at risk of becoming as
sounding brass and tinkling cymbals.
When we do not merit His guidance,
our existence will have a hollow
ring, and the echo of silence
when He does speak will be
deafening to our
ears.

The Plan provides
the loom upon which we
weave the complex tapestry of
our lives, as we create our own
coats of many colors. But central
to the vitalization and execution of
our efforts is detailed instruction that
comes from The Book of Mormon, to be
sure, but more importantly from above,
in the form of personalized guidance
from the Master Tailor Himself, as
well as from His equal and not
so silent partner, the
Holy Ghost.

Revelation may be
recognized only when we
have allowed ourselves to fall
under the spell of the Holy Ghost.
That will happen only if we are in
a state of harmony with the Plan.
This is particularly important when
we are reading The Book of Mormon.
Our acceptance of communication
from the heavens waits upon our
initiative. It is not subject to
amendment, to our private
interpretation, or to the
scrutiny of others.

It is one thing when ignorant people live in opposition to the laws of God. But it is quite another when those who have walked in the light and who have enjoyed familiarity with The Book of Mormon will turn from it, willfully dissent, and intentionally seek darkness. To do so is an abomination, because their behavior is an expression of the rebellion that first occurred in the Council, and remains one of the worst forms of infidelity to the Bridegroom.

The intuitive spiritual
sixth sense that drives both a
witness of God's Plan and of The Book
of Mormon may just be the lowest common
denominator in the theory of everything. His
divine design for us is the grand unifying
theorem, and although it is indisputable,
its explanation cannot be challenged in
the classrooms of academia, nor can
it be dissected for examination or
ridicule on a chalkboard.

Secular humanism and other ideologies that extol the virtues of the intellect and demand tangible proof are incompatible with the Spirit. They destroy faith and divert us from following the Plan, whose successful execution hinges upon nourishing the seeds of innocent faith in the revealed word of God, such as we find in The Book of Mormon. "Better had they ne'er been born, who read to doubt, or read to scorn." (Sir Walter Scott).

The Book of Mormon
teaches us how to focus the
powers of heaven, to embrace the
Savior's invitation to be cast off into
flowing streams of revelation, and to be
carried along in quickening currents of
intimate experience with the Holy Ghost.
In wonder and in amazement, we find
that as we internalize the principles
taught in The Book of Mormon, our
nature is transformed, that we
no more have a disposition
to do evil, but to do good
continually.

If
we make
the decision to
no longer accept
the blessings that
had been ours thru a
study of The Book of
Mormon, we will be left
without helm or rudder
upon the sea of life and
will losing our bearings
on the Plan of God. We'll
have drifted into disbelief
because we either deterred or
deferred our response to the
question: "What think ye
of Christ? Whose son is
he?" (Matthew
22:42).

The Book of Mormon can steal our hearts (in a good way!) and stir our imaginations as we contour attitudes, catalyze feelings, capture emotions, crystallize thoughts, congeal passions, compartmentalize actions, and convey sentiments, that lead to spiritual revitalization.

The
Spirit throws
open the windows
to our souls and lets in
more light, so that we might
better understand the power that
that drives the principles of The Book
of Mormon forward and into our hearts.
These are "mysteries" to those who haven't
prepared themselves to receive the streams
of revelation that come from above. The
Lord has assured us, however, that we
"shall know of a surety that these
things are true, for from heaven
will (He) declare it" unto us.
(D&C 5:12).

Without the
sustained power
that is provided in
the Plan of Salvation
by The Book of Mormon,
the ongoing progression of
the children of men can stall
in a flat spin from faith from
which their recovery is often
extremely difficult.

The virtue of
our conformity to
God's great Plan is
a well-trained mind, a
body to match, a love of
achievement, and focused
faith. The Book of Mormon
nurtures these traits, without
which, life can be nothing more
than smoke and mirrors, and
within which we grow old
before our time.

Our acceptance
of The Book of Mormon
commits us to the process of
a spiritual rebirth requiring
us to choose the harder right,
rather than capitulating to
the character-crippling
miscarriage of truth
manifested by the
easier wrong.

Those
who zip along
in the fast lane of
life can far too easily
blow right past the celestial
signals that are posted by The
Book of Mormon that would have
alerted them to slow down, move
over, catch a breath of celestial
air, and take the exit lane
leading to heaven's
gate.

Those without a
clear comprehension of
the elements of The Book
of Mormon may be inclined
to throw up defensive dross that
is designed to deflect, disrespect,
disregard, discourage, or disparage
the uncomfortably penetrating
question: "What think ye
of Christ?"

The
attention and the
adoration of the world is a
satanic seduction that has been
designed in the couture of hell to
influence us to abandon The
Book of Mormon and leave
our coats of many colors
hanging unattended
and unused in the
backs of our
closets.

All
who have
embraced not
only the Plan of
God but also The Book
of Mormon are destined
to become faithful second
milers who are admonished to
run, and not walk, to the end
of their lives, as they seek new
ways to build the Church and
Kingdom of God while they
remain on the earth.

We have firmly
planted both of our feet
upon the path that leads to
celestial glory when we accept
inspired direction from the Holy
Ghost that comes as a product of our
investigation of The Book of Mormon.
Our progression is linked to faithful
consistency in our efforts and to our
resolve to follow the precepts of the
Merciful Plan of our Great
Creator.

All over the world, members of the church have found that the guiding principles of The Book of Mormon make it easier to have bowels that have been moved to compassion for those who are struggling with misfortune or with the heavy weight of unresolved sin.

The Book
of Mormon describes
the quirky contraries of the
gospel, how all of us are tested
and tempted, that we might
show the heavens if we have
the faith that is necessary
for us to go the second
mile; to see what our
spiritually aerobic
fitness level
really
is.

The
Holy Ghost
loves the Plan
of God, and will
disperse the powers
of darkness before us,
and cause the heavens
to shake for our good, if
only to share the joy that
comes as we embrace
the truth.

Disorder
and progression
must ultimately be in
a state of balance, as they
are 'contraries' in the Gospel
Plan. This is why The Book of
Mormon describes how there must
be a healthy juxtaposition between
opposing forces for faith to flourish
as the first principle of revealed
religion.

Through the clarifying lens of The Book of Mormon, we learn how to worship and we discover what to worship, as truth may be recognized by its effects. By rendering unswerving obedience to its principles of action, we may test the claims of the gospel.

With the fragmentation of order, friction is created, which is required to fuel the fires of the Plan of God that warms the world. One could say that opposition, as it is illustrated in The Book of Mormon, is what makes possible our lives on the strait and narrow path that leads to heaven.

We prepare to embrace The Book of Mormon by practicing fast-scale runs through more than half a dozen octaves on all 88 of the glistening black and white ivory keys of experience.

With faith in
The Book of Mormon,
we envision the happiest
place on earth, and realize
that it is only when we return
to our psychological, spiritual,
and emotional sanctuary that
we may rediscover the secret
garden of our spiritual
childhood, where our
dreams really do
come true.

Paul observed of the Athenians, who were in many ways similar to us, that they were inclined to bow down before unknown gods whom they worshipped in ignorance. If that seems to be a problem, The Book of Mormon can help.

We
mustn't
be so bold
as to question
the power of The
Book of Mormon,
not to mention of
the Spirit, Who
testifies of
truth.

The
Book of Mormon
empowers our faith in
God's Plan, so we can
rely upon the horns of
sanctuary, to grasp
them whenever our
yokes seem too
heavy for us
to bear
alone.

Truly, when God said: "Let there be light", it was a simple statement of fact as much as it was a command. It was an invitation to recognize, embrace, and celebrate the light of The Book of Mormon, that dances all around us in as in a revelatory rapture.

Alma
encouraged
us to "try the
virtue of the word
of God." (Alma 31:5)
We do so, that we might
reap its rewards, and thru
our long-suffering and with
the diligence and patience of
faith, harvest the fruit of the
Tree of Life from its low
hanging branches.

Access
to The Book
of Mormon is the
great equalizer. It is
of little consequence to
God that we might retain
a life membership in one of
humanity's most fashionable
ecclesiastical country clubs,
or even that we have paused
to catch our breath on one
of our society's narrow
theological terraces.
All are alike to
Him.

When we are
permitted to look
with the eye of faith
thru the spiritual prism
that is The Book of Mormon,
we can see beyond the limited
horizon of our sight, all the way
into eternity. By the Spirit, our
eyes are opened to understand
the Plan of our God.

The Book of Mormon sensitizes us to recognize the gentle caress of the Master's hand, as our aching spiritual muscles are massaged by faith. We want Him to mold us and to shape us as the Artisan of our destiny.

Our faith
in The Book of
Mormon invites us
to enjoy the influence
of the Holy Ghost, Who,
as a creative consultant,
always stands ready to
offer His constructive
comments relating
to our developing
storyboard.

There is order in The Book of Mormon. Within its pages, we see our obedience as a foundation principle that is anchored in bedrock. The Law of the Lord lies at its heart and shapes our mission. it certifies our success.

Without revelation, there is no student, and as long as we ask the wrong questions, we'll remain at odds with the Holy Ghost, with biblical faith, with revealed truth, with the Plan of God, and with The Book of Mormon. Our rational point of view cannot hope to bridge the gap that exists between the secular and the divine.

Those
who live by
their faith and
embrace The Book
of Mormon fancy its
teachings because they
express the crystal-clear
perspective of a pattern
of heaven that is traced
by the finger of God
upon the fabric of a
telestial tapestry.
He adorns them
in vestments
that are
holy.

The
Book of
Mormon
carries us
to the edges
of eternity, to
the very portals
of heaven, where
"forever" stands
uncovered in a
mind-bending
panorama
that lies
before
us.

The principles and
doctrines of The Book of
Mormon are as pennies from
heaven and a dowry from Deity
that bolster our faith in the
financial stability of His
treasury and facilitate
unwavering fidelity
to the principles
of the Plan.

We
are on the
path to celestial
glory as long as we
accept inspired direction
with dedicated purpose. Our
discipleship is actively linked
to our faithful consistency that
is an expression of our commitment
to obedience to the principles espoused
by the prophets of God who speak to
us from the dust, in the pages
of The Book of Mormon.

The Book of Mormon asks
us to take calculated risks by
exposing our vulnerability to all
the world, but at the same time,
prepares us to be courageously
faithful. It teaches that the
best way to destroy our
fears is by facing
them head
on.

The Book of Mormon's most
zealous professors will not accept
mediocrity. Instead, they align their
behavior with faith, in a harmonious
expression of the balance that can
be achieved with contraries,
so that both honor the
word of God.

We persevere,
as we seek to understand
The Book of Mormon. The only
alternative is to be spiritually starved,
doctrinally dehydrated, or intellectually
inhibited while only inches away from living
bread that could have satisfied our hunger, or
from the fountains of living water that could
have slaked our thirst and healed us of our
worst sins, manifested in the telestial
blemishes that can be so
disfiguring.

The Book of Mormon describes the boundaries that define heaven and that lie beyond the reach of our detection by even the most sophisticated and accurately calibrated instruments utilized by our terrestrial scientists.

We
are given
the gift of the
Holy Ghost to be
our companion after
our baptism, but often
we leave it undisturbed
in its original packaging,
forgetting that He is always
there to bless us with revelation;
namely discernment, insight,
intuition, and inspiration, as
we study the word of God and
the counsel of His prophets
that are found in The
Book of Mormon.

The Book
of Mormon frees
us from incarceration
to confusion, hesitation,
doubt, ignorance, mistrust,
skepticism, suspicion, worry
and uncertainty. It introduces
us to a ladder that has been
set up on the earth, the top
of which rests against
the window sashes
of heaven.

We who have
the faith to believe,
seize the opportunities
that are illustrated by many
examples in The Book of Mormon
to enjoy heavenly intervention. We
have been touched by angels as we are
moved to compassion, mourn with those
who mourn, bear each other's burdens,
comfort those who stand in need of
comfort, witness of God at all
times, and have otherwise
been blessed to walk in
the light of the
Lord.

Disorder
is the contrary
that transports us
far from the influence
of the Plan, whose purpose
is to guide us away from the
precipice of destruction, and to
lead us to a secure sanctuary
where the stability and the
immutability of higher
laws abide.

The Book
of Mormon is as
a star map that was
envisioned by a heavenly
Cartographer to illuminate
the pathway to the promised
land. When we determine to
follow its principles, we will
we receive His endowment
of unearthly power and
walk in the radiant
light of heaven.

The Plan of God teaches us how to view our afflictions, our trials, and our tribulations in a new light, as necessary contraries. We determine to let the Spirit teach us through The Book of Mormon how they can work to our benefit.

The Book of
Mormon blesses us with
the knowledge that our mortal
experience is only a tiny fraction
of a much more expansive reality,
and that our perspective is on
shaky ground only when
we believe it to be
unique.

Heavenly messengers are
as nursemaids to the nations. From the
examples of Nephi, Jacob, Benjamin, Alma,
Mormon, and many others, we learn that they
minister to us according to our needs. They
reach out and lift up the downtrodden
and those who are poor in spirit,
wherever and whenever they
may be found.

Some
explain their
intuitive connection
with The Book of Mormon
as déjà vu, from the French,
literally meaning already seen,
in order to emotionally embrace
and explain the phenomenon of
religious recognition, or a
re-knowing of that which
they've already been
experienced.

We are simply imperfect mortals who are struggling to believe what we can't see. But the reward of our maturing faith is to see what we believe. God's Plan will need to be believed to be seen, until our faith in His divine design, our vision, and our testimony of The Book of Mormon, have been made perfect.

Our happiness is the object and the design of The Plan of God, and his blueprint incorporates The Book of Mormon as one of its central features for those of us living in the Last Days. Our joy "will be the end thereof, if we follow the path that leads to it; and that path is uprightness, virtue, holiness, faithfulness, and keeping all the commandments of God." (Joseph Smith).

Hope is the
inevitable result
of well-founded faith,
when we are meek and lowly
of heart, and we are in control of
our desires and emotions; when our
appetites and our behavior lie within
boundaries that are not only clearly
defined, but also well-established by
many prophet-historians who have
spoken to us out of the dust, in
The Book of Mormon

The
mysteries of
God that are found
in The Book of Mormon
provide the balance we need
in a world that is befuddled
by weights and measures that
have been contaminated by the
evidence-tampering mischief
of he who is the adversary
of all that is good
and true.

No one has a corner on their participation in the Plan of Salvation. Instead, each of us has been hard-wired to respond positively to the entreaties of the Holy Ghost to come unto Christ by way of The Book of Mormon, which boldly testifies of Him.

It is by our
faith to see all
the way to heaven
that the power of the
Holy Ghost is released
to penetrate the barriers
that tend to isolate us from
the sum and substance of our
existence. In turn, with the help
of The Book of Mormon, we are
more accurately able to define
who we are, where we came
from, why we are here,
and where we are
going.

The Book of Mormon endows us with the faith to see all the way to heaven, by responding to our inquiry: "O God, where art thou, and where is the pavilion that covereth thy hiding place?" (D&C 121:1). In the beginning, it was our God who gave the heavens and the earth form and substance by defining the boundaries of not only the temporal universe, but also, of the eternal worlds. (See Abraham 4:1 & 2). It was by the power of faith in the Plan of Salvation that He defined our existence by creating the earth and everything that is therein.

While
The Book of
Mormon invites
us to freely move
about the cabin, it is
always there to guide us
along the path of safety to
find shelter within the sphere
of God's protective influence. It
patiently waits to shield us from
the suffocating storms of Satan,
whose devious doctrines lurk in
the shadows, ready to suck the
life-sustaining marrow from
our bones, if we have left
our seatbelts of faith
unfastened.

The way to
comprehend the hidden
treasures of knowledge that
lie within The Book of Mormon is by
pressing forward with dedication, that
we may feast upon the word of Christ. We
thereby receive the physical and spiritual
strength and nourishment that we need
in order to righteously endure to the
end with continuing responsibility
and accountability. Throughout
the process, we are supported by
our Heavenly Father and we
are sustained by the
Holy Ghost.

Author's Note

The Book of Mormon is a blueprint for our survival in The Last Days. It helps us to become the architects of our own fate and the masters of our destiny; to be as "children coming down like gentle rain through darkened skies, with glory trailing from our feet as we go, and endless promise in our eyes. We are strangers from a realm of light, who have forgotten all - the memory of our former life and the purpose of our call." But with the help of The Book of Mormon, we may learn why we're here, and who we really are. (Doug Stewart, "Saturday's Warrior," adapted).

The Book of Mormon allowed the Restoration to move forward and the Church to be organized. It gave us the gift of a fifth gospel (3 Nephi) that summarizes Christ's ministry in the New World. It fulfilled the prophecies of Isaiah and Ezekiel. (See Isaiah 29:14 & Ezekiel 37:16-17). It has empowered Church members to stand out prominently among their Christian neighbors, and it has endowed them with an element of singularity that distinguishes them from other Christian denominations, allowing the line in the sand separating the faithful from the world to be more clearly defined.

Because of The Book of Mormon, those who make their home in Idumea are differentiated from those who embrace the gospel. It gives its believers symmetry, balance, harmony, clarity, focus, and purpose. It illustrates stories of inspiration that touch them personally and individually, and it blesses them with truth in untarnished majesty that may be proclaimed without qualification or apology to the world. Those who read it unleash the unrestrained power of the Holy Ghost. Their lives are touched by invention, investigation, innovation, insight, intuition, and inspiration, whose catalyst is the Spirit.

Because of The Book of Mormon, we have another witness of Christ, and we learn to rely on Him not only as our protector but also as the generator of life itself. It provides a standard by which we may judge the Bible, and it describes a weapon that is more powerful than military might. Within its pages, the essential ordinance of baptism is re-defined, and the army of God is equipped with superior firepower as it teaches the nations with the word of God. Those who read it draw upon the life experiences of heroes from the past, and learn life-lessons from their own similar challenges.

Because of mentors in The Book of Mormon, we can better understand the saving principles and ordinances of the Gospel. With their profound spiritual insight, we discover who our Savior is, and we learn more about ourselves. With a correct understanding of the Fall, of repentance, and of the Atonement, we are no longer held hostage by guilt, but instead feel the sweet miracle of forgiveness. The Book of Mormon guides us to horns of sanctuary that are our refuge from a violent world, and it shows us how to be born again. It gives us the confidence to feel the tender mercies of God, experience His magnificent grace, find our way home, and obtain His Rest.

Without The Book of Mormon, the Church could not have been organized. So important is The Book of Mormon, that The Church of Jesus Christ of Latter-day Saints was only organized immediately following its publication. Fully ten years earlier, Joseph Smith had communed with The Father and The Son in the Sacred Grove. Three years later, he received several visits from the Angel Moroni. Between 1823 and 1830, he became personally acquainted with all of the important characters in The Book of Mormon and enjoyed additional visits from Moroni. Still, so important was The Book of Mormon to the Restoration of the Gospel, that the Church was not organized until it was hot off the press.

Without The Book of Mormon record, we would have no corroborating evidence that Christ fulfilled His promise to feed His other sheep. "Other sheep I have, which are not of this fold," He had said. "Them also I must bring, and they shall hear my voice; and there shall be one fold, and one shepherd." (John 10:16).

"And if ye shall believe in Christ ye will believe in these words, for they are the words of Christ, and he hath given them unto me; and they teach all men that they should do good. And if they are not the words of Christ, judge ye - for Christ will show unto you, with power and great glory, that they are his words, at the last day; and you and I shall stand face to face before his bar; and ye shall know that I have been commanded of him to write these things." (2 Nephi 33:10-11).

Without The Book of Mormon, prophecy would not have been fulfilled. The words of Christ are made known in The Book of Mormon, as well as in the Bible," and they have been "established in one." (1 Nephi 13:41). As Ezekiel wrote: "Take thee one stick, and write upon it, For Judah, and for the children of Israel his companions: then take another stick, and write upon it, For Joseph, the stick of Ephraim, and for all the house of Israel his companions. And join them one to another into one stick; and they shall become one in thine hand." (Ezekiel 37:16-17).

2,500 years before the visit by Moroni to Joseph Smith, Isaiah prophesied of the Lord's ministry: "I will proceed to do a marvellous work among this people, even a marvellous work and a wonder." (Isaiah 29:14). God did so with the translation, publication, and distribution of The Book of Mormon.

Without The Book of Mormon, Church members would stand out far less prominently as Christians. The great Book of Mormon prophet Benjamin exhorted: "I would that ye should take upon you the name of Christ, all you that have entered into the covenant with God that ye should be obedient unto the end of your lives. And it shall come to pass that whosoever doeth this shall be found at the right hand of God, for he shall know the name by which he is called; for he shall be called by the name of Christ." (Mosiah 5:8-10).

Without The Book of Mormon, the Church would lose much of its prominent singularity. "Take away the Book of Mormon and the revelations, and where is our religion? We have none." (Joseph Smith, Teachings, p. 71). The Book of Mormon sets Latter-day Saints apart as a peculiar people. To be peculiar in a biblical sense is to be "one's very own, exclusive, or special." (Bible Dictionary). Moroni told Joseph Smith: "Wherever the sound (of the Restoration) shall go it shall cause the ears of men to tingle, and wherever it shall be proclaimed, the pure in heart shall rejoice." ("Latter Day Saints' Messenger and Advocate", 2/ 1835, p. 79-80).

Without The Book of Mormon, Joshua's line in the sand would be far less clearly defined. Mormon observed "that after a people have been once enlightened by the Spirit of God, and have had great knowledge of things pertaining to righteousness, and then have fallen away into sin and transgression, they become more hardened, and thus their state becomes worse than though they had never known these things." (Alma 24:30).

Joseph Fielding Smith, Jr. cautioned the Saints: "When you joined the Church you enlisted to serve God. When you did that, you left the neutral ground, and you can never get back on to it. Should you forsake the Master you enlisted to serve, it will be by the instigation of the evil one, and you will follow his dictation and be his servant." (C.E.S. Manual, p. 258).

Without The Book of Mormon, we would have fewer negative examples of those who embrace darkness rather than the Gospel. Mormon said of those who did not belong to the Church, that they "did indulge themselves in sorceries, and in idolatry or idleness, and in babblings, and in envyings and strife, wearing costly apparel, being lifted up in the pride of their own eyes; persecuting, lying, thieving, robbing, committing whoredoms, and murdering, and all manner of wickedness." (Alma 1:32).

Without The Book of Mormon, we would have less symmetry, balance, harmony, clarity, focus, and purpose in our lives. President Ezra Taft Benson told the Saints that a Church member who does not study The Book of Mormon, "is placing their soul in jeopardy and neglecting that which could give spiritual and intellectual unity to their whole life". (C.R., 4/1975).

Without The Book of Mormon, we would have fewer stories of inspiration that touch us personally and individually. From within its pages, we can almost hear Moroni's voice: "Behold, I speak unto you as if ye were present, and yet ye are not. But behold, Jesus Christ hath shown you unto me, and I know your doing." (Mormon 8:35).

Without The Book of Mormon, there would be less truth in the world. The Book of Mormon "was written to be believed. Its one and only merit is truth. Without that merit, it is all that nonbelievers say it is. With it, it is all that believers say it is." (Hugh Nibley. "Of All Things," p. 93). Although it is the rule, as Washington Irving observed, that "history fades into fable; fact becomes clouded with doubt and controversy; the inscription moulders from the tablet; the statue falls from the pedestal," and that "columns, arches, pyramids are but heaps of sand, and their epitaphs, nothing but characters written in the dust," yet The Book of Mormon stands as a shining example of the divine model.

Without The Book of Mormon, we would miss, terribly, its witness of truth. The Book of Mormon "illumines reality, vitalizes memory, provides guidance in daily life, and brings us tidings of antiquity." It is "the evidence of time, the light of truth, the life of memory, the directress of life, the herald of antiquity, committed to immortality." (Cicero, "De Oratore," ii, 36). On its pages, "the centuries roll back to the ancient age of gold." (Horace, "Odes," IV, ii, 39).

Without The Book of Mormon, we would lack a sure witness of Jesus Christ. "For behold, (The Book of Mormon) is written for the intent that ye may believe (the Bible); and if ye believe (the Bible) ye will believe (The Book of Mormon) also; and if ye believe (The Book of Mormon) ye will know concerning your fathers, and also the marvelous works which were wrought by the power of God among them." (Mormon 7:9).

Without The Book of Mormon, we would have fewer opportunities to learn how to rely on the Savior. "No one can lift themselves to celestial glory. Our growth depends on the light of Christ, guidance of the Holy Ghost, and the power of the priesthood that is given us by God and his Son. The religion of Jesus Christ is not just a philosophy of life; it is the generator of life. If you go it alone, you cannot succeed. If you receive His power, you will increase and make it. There is no other way." (Sunday School Course Manual).

Without The Book of Mormon, we would lose an excellent standard by which to judge the Bible and other scriptures. For example, we would not have the Lord's teachings to the Nephites that are similar to His Sermon on The Mount, and we would lack the powerful recitations of Isaiah and of Malachi that are reiterated in its pages. In fact, "The Book of Mormon is the keystone of our religion and the most correct book ever written, and (we) can draw nearer to God by abiding by its precepts than any other book." (Joseph Smith)

Without The Book of Mormon, to what other body of scripture would we turn to emphasize the powerful premise that the pen is mightier than the sword? President Benson urged us to recommit ourselves to a study of The Book of Mormon. "If you do so," he promised, "you will find, as Alma did, that 'the word (has) a great tendency to lead the people to do that which is just - yea, it (has) more powerful effect upon the minds of the people than the sword, or anything else which (has) happened to them.' (Alma 31:5)." (C.R., 4/1986).

Without The Book of Mormon, where would we go to learn so clearly that one must have authority to administer the ordinances of the Gospel? Alma and his sons "preached the word, and the truth, according to the spirit of prophecy and revelation; and they preached after the holy order of God by which they were called." (Alma 43:2). If all churches were equal, then the true Church would not exist anywhere. If, in education, any program were the equal of any other, then receiving any degree would be based upon an indiscriminate course of study that would qualify the recipient in all fields of study. But this is contrary to the order of God.

Without The Book of Mormon there would be confusion regarding the ordinance of baptism. "The first fruits of repentance is baptism; and baptism cometh by faith unto the fulfilling the commandments; and the fulfilling the commandments bringeth remission of sins; and the remission of sins bringeth meekness, and lowliness of heart; and because of meekness and lowliness of heart cometh the visitation of the Holy Ghost, which Comforter filleth with hope and perfect love, which love endureth by diligence unto prayer, until the end shall come, when all the saints shall dwell with God." (Moroni 8:25-26).

Without The Book of Mormon, the soldiers in the army of Christ could not so easily preach, teach, expound, and exhort, as they bear witness of Christ. Mormon explained that The Sons of Mosiah "had given themselves to much prayer, and fasting; therefore, they had the spirit of prophecy, and the spirit of revelation, and when they taught, they taught with the power and authority of God." (Alma 17:3). "God help all honest men," said Marion G. Romney, "to be born again and come to be of sound understanding and to know the word of God and maintain the spirit thereof by study, fasting, prayer, and work, that we may be blessed with His power and authority!" (C.R., 10/1941).

Without The Book of Mormon, we might well lack the confidence to proclaim the Gospel. Through Isaiah, the Lord said: "Then shall ye, who are a remnant of the house of Jacob, go forth among (the nations); and ye shall be in the midst of them who shall be many; and ye shall be among them as a lion among the beasts of the forest, and as a young lion among the flocks of sheep, who, if he goeth through both treadeth down and teareth in pieces, and none can deliver." (3 Nephi 20:16).

Armed with The Book of Mormon, the mighty missionary army of the Lord's Church is "clear as the moon, and fair as the sun, and terrible as an army with banners." (D&C 5:14). "The nations of the earth shall tremble because of her, and shall fear because of her terrible ones." (D&C 64:43). "And it shall be said among the wicked: Let us not go up to battle against Zion, for the inhabitants of Zion are terrible; wherefore we cannot stand." (D&C 45:70). "Fear may seize upon them, and they shall stand afar off and tremble. And all nations shall be afraid because of the terror of the Lord, and the power of his might." (D&C 45:74-75).

Without The Book of Mormon, we would know nothing of the life experiences of so many others of God's children, who are so much like ourselves. "Behold, this is a choice land, and whatsoever nation shall possess it shall be free from bondage, and from captivity, and from all other nations under heaven if they will but serve the God of the land, who is Jesus Christ." (Ether 2:12). Without The Book of Mormon, it would be more difficult to understand that "happiness is the object and design of our existence, and will be the end thereof, if we follow the path that leads to it, and this consists of faith, virtue, uprightness, and keeping all the commandments of God." (Joseph Smith).

Without The Book of Mormon, to whom would we turn for mentors such as Captain Moroni? "Yea, verily, verily ' say unto you, if all men had been, and were, and ever would be, like unto Moroni, behold, the very powers of hell would have been shaken forever; yea, the devil would never have power over the hearts of the children of men." (Alma 48:17). We would never have known men like Nephi, Jacob, Benjamin, Alma, The Sons of Mosiah, Abinadi, Helaman, and Samuel The Lamanite. We would miss the anticipation of striking hands with them when we meet at the pleasing bar of Christ. (See Jacob 6:13, 2 Nephi 33:15 & Moroni 10:27).

Without The Book of Mormon, there would be a conspicuously empty space on the bookshelf of time, instead of a prominently displayed chronicle written especially for our age. Hugh Nibley observed: "It is an exciting thing to discover that the man Lehi was a real historical character ... but it is far more important and significant to find oneself in this Twentieth Century standing as it were in his very shoes." ("The World and The Prophets," p. 196).

Without The Book of Mormon, we would less effectively cope with the mysteries of God, which are the saving principles and ordinances of the Gospel, received by the faithful through personal revelation. They are sacred. It is given unto many to know these mysteries, "nevertheless they are laid under a strict command that they shall not impart only according to the portion of his word which he doth grant unto the children of men, according to the need and diligence which they give unto him." (Alma 12:9). In other words, by judiciously exercising their knowledge of gospel principles that are explained in The Book of Mormon, the faithful can benefit from spiritual insight while at the same time guarding pearls that might otherwise be cast before swine, or trampled underfoot. (Matthew 7:6).

King Benjamin's discourse in The Book of Mosiah is a classic example of a General Conference type of address wherein the saving principles were unfolded to the membership of the Church. When we read his words, faithfully recorded verbatim by the prophet-historian Mormon, it is clear that he was concerned that his people might trifle with the words that he should speak. He recognized the serious nature of his topic, and wanted them to hearken to him, or pay strict attention, and to open their ears to listen carefully, and their hearts to feel the Spirit of his message, and their minds to understand. (Mosiah 2:9). This episode is one of many in The Book of Mormon that illustrate how the mysteries of God may be unfolded to our view. We have the testimony of Christ Himself that The Book of Mormon contains a comprehensive body of doctrine, "even the fullness of (His) everlasting gospel." (D&C 27:5).

Armed with The Book of Mormon, the Lord told Joseph Smith and Sydney Rigdon: "The time has verily come (December 1, 1831) that it is necessary and expedient in me that you should open your mouths in proclaiming my gospel, the things of the kingdom, expounding the mysteries thereof out of the scriptures according to that portion of the Spirit and power which shall be given unto you." (D&C 71:1). Joseph described his subsequent experience in these words: "Our minds being now enlightened, we began to have the scriptures laid open to our understandings, and the true meaning and intention of their more mysterious passages revealed unto us in a manner which we never could attain to previously, nor ever before had thought of." (J.S.H. 1:74).

To the faithful, the Lord promised: "I will reveal all mysteries, yea, all the hidden mysteries of my kingdom from days of old, and for ages to come." (D&C 76:7). Nevertheless, there were certain points of doctrine that were not yet clear. To his son, Alma declared: "Now these mysteries are not yet fully made known unto me; therefore, I shall forbear." (Alma 37:11). He felt that it was always better to keep one's opinion to oneself, rather than to speculate without the foundation of fact or specific revelation. Sometimes it is better to remain silent and be thought a fool, rather than to speak and remove all doubt.

Without The Book of Mormon, we would know far less about the purpose of life. "And now, I would commend you to seek this Jesus of whom the prophets and apostles have written, that the grace of God the Father, and also the Lord Jesus Christ, and the Holy Ghost, which beareth record of them, may be and abide in you forever." (Moroni, in Ether 12:41). Because of this book, we know that "Adam fell that men might be, and men are, that they might have joy," (2 Nephi 2:25), that "wickedness never was happiness," (Alma 41:10), and that we must hold "fast to the rod of iron". (1 Nephi 8:30). We are counseled: "Watch yourselves, and your thoughts, and your words, and your deeds". (Mosiah 4:30). But we also know: "By the power of the Holy Ghost, (we) may know the truth of all things," (Moroni 10:5), and that "when (we) are in the service of (our) fellow beings, (we) are only in the service of (our) God." (Mosiah 2:17).

Without The Book of Mormon, personal accountability would receive far less emphasis. It teaches that we "are free according to the flesh, and all things are given (to us) which are expedient unto men. And (we) are free to choose liberty and eternal life, through the great Mediator of all men, or to choose captivity and death, according to the captivity and power of the devil." (2 Nephi 2:27)

Without the unequivocal teachings in The Book of Mormon that are related to the Atonement of Jesus Christ, guilt might hold our future hostage. "Do ye suppose that ye shall dwell with (Heavenly Father) under a consciousness of your guilt?" asked Moroni. "Do ye suppose that ye could be happy to dwell with that holy Being, when your souls are racked with a consciousness of guilt that ye have ever abused his laws?" (Mormon 9:3).

Without The Book of Mormon, the tender mercies of the Savior, and the sweet miracle of forgiveness might be less lovingly treated. (See 1 Nephi 1:20, 8:8 & Ether 6:12). Fortified by Mormon's discourse on faith, hope, and charity, The Book of Mormon reports that "as oft as (the disciples of Christ) repented and sought forgiveness, with real intent, they were forgiven." (Moroni 6:8)

Without The Book of Mormon, we might be less likely to find peace in a violent world. Its gift is the peace of the Savior of the world, "not the peace of ease, of luxury, idleness, absence of turmoil, and strife, but the peace born of the righteous life, the peace that lifts the soul, that day by day brings us closer to the home of Eternal Peace, the dwelling place of our Father." (J. Reuben Clark, Jr.)

Without The Book of Mormon, we might not clearly understand that we have been born again. Those who enter into the Covenant "are born of him." (Mosiah 5:7). "All mankind ... must be born again, yea, born of God, changed from their carnal and fallen state, to a state of righteousness, being redeemed of God, becoming his sons and daughters." (Mosiah 27:25). A "Born Again Christian" is one who is in a covenant relationship with the Lord, and since only members of Christ's true Church can accomplish that by revelation and through the authority of the priesthood, if follows that the only real Born Again Christians are those who have a testimony of the divine authenticity of The Book of Mormon and follow its revelatory teachings that lead to faith, repentance, baptism, and the receipt of the Holy Ghost.

Without The Book of Mormon, we might not recognize the signs that confirm we have been born again. "And now behold, I ask of you, my brethren of the church, have ye spiritually been born of God? Have ye received his image in your countenances? Have ye experienced this mighty change in your hearts?" (Alma 5:14).

Without The Book of Mormon, finding our way home would be much more difficult. "Think of stepping on shore and finding it heaven. Of taking hold of a hand and finding it God's hand. Of breathing a new air and finding it celestial air. Of feeling invigorated and finding it immortality. Of passing from storm and tempest to the unbroken calm of God's Rest. Of waking up, and finding it Home." (Anonymous).

Without following the teachings and admonitions that are found within the pages of The Book of Mormon, we could not attain God's Rest. "We live in a day and in a world full of doubts and confusion, where people do not know what to believe, where tensions are high, where the pace is frantic and progress in terms of righteousness is not a popular goal. Violence and crudity are everyday patterns all around us. What a blessing it is to know there is a haven, a place of rest from the turmoil of the world. The prophets and the Savior have called upon us to enter into the rest of the Lord, where life has purpose and direction, and where priesthood power is possible." ("Gospel Doctrine Manual," p. 79)

Without The Book of Mormon, we might never know the truth of all things. (See Moroni 10:5). "He that will not harden his heart," taught Alma, "to him is given the greater portion of the word, until it is given unto him to know the mysteries of God, until he know them in full." (Alma 12:10).

The Book of Mormon contains a unique promise, found nowhere else in scripture. Moroni's formula is simple: "And when ye shall receive these things, I would exhort you that ye would ask God, the Eternal Father, in the name of Christ, if these things are not true; and if ye shall ask with a sincere heart, with real intent, having faith in Christ, he will manifest the truth of it unto you, by the power of the Holy Ghost. And by the power of the Holy Ghost ye may know the truth of all things." (Moroni 10:4-5).

Moroni firmly believed that it is the power of God that works miracles in our lives. He knew that the Light of Christ, sometimes called the Spirit of God or the Holy Spirit, and the Holy Ghost have been provided to nurture religious recognition leading to conversion. Therefore, he urged those who would read and study The Book of Mormon to "deny not the gifts of God, for they are many." (Moroni 10:8). All these gifts, he said, "are given by the manifestations of the Spirit of God unto men (and women), to profit them." (Moroni 10:8).

Without The Book of Mormon, there would be less joy in the world. Mormon said of those living after the ministry of the Savior among the Nephites: "Behold, there never was a happier time among the people of Nephi, since the days of Nephi, than in the days of Moroni." (Alma 50:23). Our day is also a wonderful time to be alive. A millennial era approaches. "How do you prepare for the Second Coming?" asked President Gordon B. Hinckley. "Well, you just do not worry about it. You just live the kind of life that, if the Second Coming were to happen tomorrow, you would be ready. Nobody knows what is going to happen. Our responsibility is to prepare ourselves, to live worthy of the association of the Savior, to deport ourselves in such a way that we would not be embarrassed if He were to come among us." ("Church News", 1/2/1999, p. 2).

Without The Book of Mormon, there would be less hope in the world. "Teenagers sometimes ask: "What's the use?" said Boyd K. Packer. "The world will soon be blown all apart and come to an end." That feeling comes from fear, not from faith. No one knows the hour or the day, but the end cannot come until all of the purposes of the Lord are fulfilled. Everything that I have learned from the revelations and from life convinces me that there is time and to spare for you to carefully prepare for a long life. One day you will cope with teenage children of your own. That will serve you right. Later, you will spoil your grandchildren, and they, in turn, will spoil theirs." (C.R., 4/89).

The scripture may yet be written that there never was a happier time among the children of men, than among those who had developed the habit of carefully and prayerfully studying The Book of Mormon, and using the principles taught therein, to guide them with safe passage through perilous times.

Long ago, Cicero wrote that "the first law for the historian is that he shall never dare utter an untruth. The second is that he shall suppress nothing that is true. Moreover, there shall be no suspicion of partiality or of malice in his writing." The accounts in The Book of Mormon abridged by the prophet historian Mormon were true to the mandate of Cicero. Although, as Washington Irving brooded: "It is the rule that history fades into fable; fact becomes clouded with doubt and controversy; the inscription moulders, and columns, arches, and pyramids are but heaps of sand, and their epitaphs nothing but characters written in the dust," yet, The Book of Mormon stands out, without peer, as a shining example of the divine model.

Addendum
A sampling of scriptures
(1 Nephi - Words of Mormon)

"When the Jews heard these things,
they were angry with (Lehi); yea, even
as with the prophets of old, whom they had
cast out, and stoned, and slain; and they also
sought his life, that they might take it away. But
behold, I, Nephi, will show unto you the tender
mercies of the Lord are over all those whom
he hath chosen, because of their faith,
to make them mighty even unto
the power of deliverance."
(1 Nephi 1:20).

"The Lord spake unto my father, yea, even in a dream, and said unto him: Blessed art thou Lehi, because of the things which thou hast done; and because thou hast been faithful and declared unto this people the things which I commanded thee, behold, they seek to take away thy life. And it came to pass that the Lord commanded my father, even in a dream, that he should take his family and depart into the wilderness. And it came to pass that he was obedient unto the word of the Lord, wherefore he did as the Lord commanded him." (1 Nephi 2:1-3).

"I, Nephi, said unto my father:
I will go and do the things which the
Lord hath commanded, for I know that the
Lord giveth no commandments unto the
children of men, save he shall prepare
a way for them that they may
accomplish the thing which
he commanded them."
(1 Nephi 3:7).

"As the Lord liveth, and as we live,
we will not go down unto our father in
the wilderness until we have accomplished
the thing which the Lord hath commanded us.
Wherefore, let us be faithful in keeping the
commandments of the Lord; therefore,
let us go down to the land of
our father's inheritance."
(1 Nephi 3:15-16).

"I also beheld a strait and narrow path, which came along by the rod of iron, even to the tree by which I stood."
(1 Nephi 8:20).

"And they did press forward through the mist of darkness, clinging to the rod of iron, even until they did come forth and partake of the fruit of the tree … The rod of iron … was the word God, which led to the fountain of living waters, or to the tree of life; which waters are a representation of the love of God; and (Nephi) also beheld that the tree of life was a representation of the love of God." (1 Nephi 8:24 & 11:25).

"The Lord hath commanded me to make these plates for a wise purpose in him, which purpose I know not. But the Lord knoweth all things from the beginning; wherefore, he prepareth a way to accomplish all his works among the children of men; for behold, he hath all power unto the fulfilling of all his words."
(1 Nephi 9:5-6).

"The Spirit cried with a loud voice, saying: Hosanna to the Lord, the most high God; for he is God over all the earth, yea, even above all. And blessed art thou, Nephi, because thou believest in the Son of the most high God; wherefore, thou shalt behold the things which thou hast desired. "And it came to pass that the Spirit said unto me: Look! And I looked and beheld a tree; and it was like unto the tree which my father had seen; and the beauty thereof was far beyond, yea, exceeding of all beauty; and the whiteness thereof did exceed the whiteness of the driven snow."
(1 Nephi 11:6 & 8).

"It came to pass that
I beheld that the rod of iron,
which my father had seen, was the
word of God, which led to the fountain
of living waters, or to the tree of life, which
waters are a representation of the love of God;
and I also beheld that the tree of life was a
representation of the love of God."
(1 Nephi 11:25).

The "great and abominable
church, which is most abominable
above all other churches, (has) taken
away from the gospel of the Lamb many
parts which are plain and most precious;
and also, many covenants of the
Lord have they taken away."
(1 Nephi 13:26).

"The time cometh,
saith the Lamb of God,
that I will work a great and
a marvelous work among
the children of men."
(1 Nephi 14:7).

"They shall come to the knowledge of their Redeemer and the very points of his doctrine, that they may know how to come unto him and be saved." (1 Nephi 15:14).

"And I did rehearse unto them the words of Isaiah, who spake concerning the restoration of the Jews, or of the house of Israel; and after they were restored they should no more be confounded, neither should they be scattered again" (1 Nephi 15:20).

"The justice of God did also divide the wicked from the righteous; and the brightness thereof was like unto the brightness of a flaming fire, which ascendeth up unto God forever and ever, and hath no end."
(1 Nephi 15:30).

"And after this manner
of language did my brethren
murmur and complain against us."
(1 Nephi 17:22).

"If God
had commanded
me to do all things,
I could do them. And now,
if the Lord has such great power,
and has wrought so many miracles
among the children of men, how is it
that he cannot instruct me?"
(1 Nephi 17:50-51).

"I have showed thee new things ... even hidden things, and thou didst not know them."
(1 Nephi 20:6).

"Thus saith the Lord God:
Behold, I will lift up mine hand
to the Gentiles, and set up my standard
to the people; and they shall bring thy sons
in their arms, and thy daughters shall be carried
upon their shoulders. And kings shall be thy nursing
fathers, and their queens thy nursing mothers; they shall
bow down to thee with their face toward the earth, and
lick up the dust of thy feet; and thou shalt know
that I am the Lord." (1 Nephi 21:22-23).

"The captives of the mighty shall be taken away, and the prey of the terrible shall be delivered; for I will contend with him that contendeth with thee, and I will save thy children."
(1 Nephi 21:25).

"And now, Zoram, I speak unto you: Behold, thou art the servant of Laban; nevertheless, thou has been brought out of the land of Jerusalem, and I know that thou art a true friend unto my son, Nephi, forever." (2 Nephi 1:30).

"The way is prepared from the fall of man, and salvation is free." (2 Nephi 2:4).

"It must needs be, that there is opposition in all things". (2 Nephi 2:11).

Without opposition
in all things, without entropy,
"righteousness could not be brought to
pass, neither wickedness, neither holiness
nor misery, neither good nor bad."
(2 Nephi 2:11).

At first glance, manipulation
by external forces and free will appear to be
antithetical, but they actually do no violence to the
harmony of our faith, if we think of them as dynamic
counterparts that are the fundamental elements of a process
that leads us through a twisted temporal matrix in the direction
of an expansive, unrestrained, and seamless reality characterized
as "immortality and eternal life." (Moses 1:39). To put it another
way, we realize that control and agency are part of the "opposition
in all thing" that was described by Lehi, and that are absolutely
necessary for the Plan of Salvation to function properly.
As he emphatically put it: "If these things are not,
there is no God." (2 Nephi 2:11 & 13).

"To bring about
his eternal purposes ... the
Lord God gave unto man, that
he should act for himself."
(2 Nephi 2:15-16).

"The Lord God gave unto man that he should act for himself. Wherefore, man could not act for himself save it should be that he was enticed by the one or the other, Wherefore, men are free according to the flesh; and all things are given them which are expedient unto man. And they are free to choose liberty and eternal life, through the great Mediator of all men or to choose captivity and death, according to the captivity and power of the devil." (2 Nephi 2:16 & 27).

"Men are that they might have joy," according to God's "great plan of happiness." For "if there be no righteousness, there be no happiness ... which is prepared for the saints. (2 Nephi 2:25, Alma 42:8, & 2 Nephi 21:13 & 9:43).

"Wherefore,
men are free according to
the flesh; and all things are given
them which are expedient unto man.
And they are free to choose liberty and
eternal life, through the great Mediator
of all men, or to choose captivity and
death, according to the captivity
and power of the devil."
(2 Nephi 2:27).

"And now, my sons, I would that ye should look to the great Mediator, and hearken unto his great commandments; and be faithful unto his words, and choose eternal life, according to the will of his Holy Spirit." (2 Nephi 2:28).

"O how
great the plan of our God!
... The righteous shall have a perfect
knowledge of their enjoyment and their
righteousness, being clothed with purity, yea,
even with the robe of righteousness ... And assuredly,
as the Lord liveth, for the Lord God hath spoken it, and
it is his eternal word, which cannot pass away, that they
who are righteous shall be righteous still ... O the greatness
and the justice of our God! For he executeth all his words,
and they have gone forth out of his mouth, and his law
must be fulfilled." (2 Nephi 9:13-17).

"To be learned is good if they hearken unto the counsels of God."
(2 Nephi 9:29).

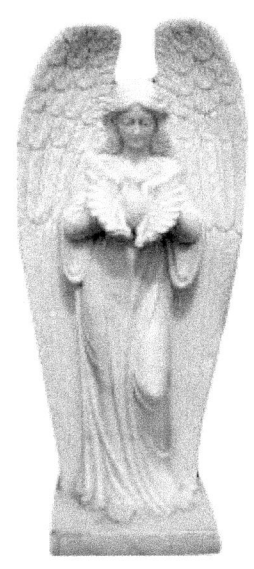

"If there be no Christ, there be no God; and if there be no God, we are not, for there could have been no creation. But there is a God, and he is Christ, and he cometh in the fulness of his own time." (2 Nephi 11:7).

"O house of Jacob,
come ye and let us walk in
the light of the Lord."
(2 Nephi 12:5).

"Wo unto them that call evil good, and good evil, that put darkness for light, and light for darkness, that put bitter for sweet, and sweet for bitter". (2 Nephi 15:20).

"Unto us a child is born, unto us a son is given; and the government shall be upon his shoulder; and his name shall be called, Wonderful, Counselor, The Mighty God, The Everlasting Father, The Prince of Peace."
(2 Nephi 19:6).

2 Nephi 20 is a carefully constructed prophecy organized as a chiasm in 6 parts, in which the destruction of Assyria is a type, or a symbol, foreshadowing the future reality of the destruction of the wicked at the Second Coming of the Lord. So, this prophecy, as are so many of Isaiah's, is dualistic in nature.

"The wolf also shall dwell with
the lamb, and the leopard shall lie
down with the kid, and the calf and the
young lion and fatling together; and a little
child shall lead them. And the cow and the bear
shall feed; their young ones shall lie down together;
and the lion shall eat straw like the ox. And the suckling
child shall play on the hole of the asp, and the weaned child
shall put his hand on the cockatrice's den. They shall
not hurt nor destroy in all my holy mountain,
for the earth shall be full of the knowledge
of the Lord, as the waters cover the sea."
(2 Nephi 21:6-9).

"For the Lord will have mercy on Jacob, and will yet choose Israel, and set them in their own land; and the strangers shall be joined with them, and they shall cleave to the house of Jacob." (2 Nephi 24:1).

"How art
thou fallen from
heaven, O Lucifer, son
of the morning! Art thou
cut down to the ground, which
did weaken the nations!
(2 Nephi 24:12).

"We know that it is by grace that we are saved, after all we can do." (2 Nephi 25:23).

"We
talk of Christ,
we rejoice in Christ, we
preach of Christ, we prophesy of
Christ, and we write according to our
prophecies, that our children may know
to what source they may look for a
remission of their sins."
(2 Nephi 25:26).

In 2 Nephi Chapter 26, Nephi spoke to future generations as if they were present. "And after Christ shall have risen from the dead, he shall show himself unto you ... For behold, I say unto you that I have beheld that many generations shall pass away." (V. 1).

"I prophesy unto you concerning the last days; concerning the days when the Lord God shall bring these things forth unto the children of men." (2 Nephi 26:14).

"Those who shall be destroyed
shall speak unto them out of the
ground and their speech shall be low
out of the dust and their voice shall be as
one that hath a familiar spirit; for the Lord
God will give unto him power, that he may
whisper concerning them, even as it were
out of the ground; and their speech
shall whisper out of the dust."
(2 Nephi 26:16).

"Priestcrafts are that men preach and set themselves up for a light unto the world, that they may get gain and praise of the world; but the seek not the welfare of Zion." (2 Nephi 26:29).

It is only when we have decided to stop living that we
start dying. We live and move and have our being through
sense and perception that blend into a refreshing elixir preventing us
from becoming too set in our ways. These form an unlikely union, that
by intelligent design has been created to upset the status-quo, expand our
experience, weather our storms, and meet our challenges. At the end of the
day, it is "by the experiment of this ministration" that we are able
to "glorify God for (our) professed subjection unto the gospel
of Christ." (2 Corinthians 9:13). It was ordained in the
heavens that as we internalize the doctrine, we feel
the exertion of an equalizing influence,
for "all are alike unto God."
(2 Nephi 26:33).

"The words which are sealed he shall not deliver neither shall he deliver the book. For the book shall be sealed by the power of God, and the revelation which was sealed shall be kept in the book until the due time of the Lord, that they may come forth; for behold, they reveal all things from the foundation of the world until the end thereof. And the day cometh that the words of the book which were sealed shall be read upon the house tops; and they shall be read by the power of Christ; and all things shall be revealed unto the children of men which ever have been among the children of men, and which ever will be even unto the end of the earth." (2 Nephi 27:10-11).

"I will proceed to do a marvelous work among this people, yea, a marvelous work and a wonder."
(2 Nephi 27:26).

In 2 Nephi Chapters 28-30, Nephi gave passionate counsel to those of us who are living in the Last Days. The Spirit had constrained, or compelled, him to do so. (V. 1). He knew that the counsel of future Nephite prophets engraven on plates destined to become The Book of Mormon, would some day "be of great worth unto the children of men." (V. 2). As we read them today, we realize that many of the prophecies in these chapters have already been fulfilled.

"For it shall come to pass in that day that the churches which are built up … the one shall say unto the other: Behold, I, I am the Lord's; and the others shall say: I, I am the Lord's; and thus, shall every one say that hath built up churches and not unto the Lord. And they shall contend one with another, and their priests shall contend one with another, and they shall teach with their learning, and deny the Holy Ghost." (2 Nephi 28:3-4).

"Because of pride, and because of false teachers, and false doctrine, their churches have become corrupted, and their churches are lifted up; because of pride, they are puffed up."
(2 Nephi 28:12).

"Wo be
unto him that
hearkeneth unto
the precepts of men, and
denieth the power of God, and
the gift of the Holy Ghost!"
(2 Nephi 28:26).

"I will give unto the children of men
line upon line, precept upon precept, here a
little and there a little, and blessed are they who
hearken unto my precepts, and lend an ear unto my
counsel, for they shall learn wisdom; for unto him that
receiveth I will give more, and from them that shall say, We
have enough, from them shall be taken away even that which
they have. Cursed is he that putteth his trust in man, or maketh
flesh his arm, or shall hearken unto the precepts of men, save their
precepts shall be given by the power of the Holy Ghost. Wo be unto
the Gentiles, saith the Lord God of Hosts! Fore notwithstanding
I shall lengthen out mine arm unto them from day to day,
they will deny me; nevertheless, I will be merciful
unto them, saith the Lord God, if they will
repent and come unto me."
(2 Nephi 28:30-32).

"Many of the Gentiles shall say: A Bible! A Bible! We have got a Bible, and there cannot be any more Bible." (2 Nephi 29:3).

"Know ye not that there are more nations than one? Know ye not that I, the Lord your God, have created all men, and that I remember those who are upon the isles of the sea; and that I rule in the heavens above and in the earth beneath; and I bring forth my word unto the children of men, yea, even upon all the nations of the earth? Wherefore murmur ye, because that ye shall receive more of my word? Know ye not that the testimony of two nations is a witness unto you that I am God, that I remember one nation like unto another? Wherefore, I speak the same words unto one nation like unto another. And when the two nations shall run together the testimony of the two nations shall run together also."
(2 Nephi 29:7-8).

"I say unto you, as many of the Gentiles as will repent (shall become) the covenant people of the Lord; and as many of the Jews as will not repent shall be cast off; for the Lord covenanteth with none save it be with them that repent and believe in his Son, who is the Holy One of Israel." "For the Lord will have mercy on Jacob, and will yet choose Israel, and set them in their own land: and the strangers shall be joined with them, and they shall cleave to the house of Jacob. And the people shall take them and bring them to their place; yea, from far unto the ends of the earth; and they shall return to their lands of promise."
(2 Nephi 30:2 & 24:1-2; see Isaiah 14:1-2).

"Unless a man shall endure to the end, in following the example of the Son of the living God, he cannot be saved ... and then are ye in this strait and narrow path which leads to eternal life; yea ye have entered in by the gate; ye have done according to the commandments of the Father and the Son; and ye have received the Holy Ghost, which witnesses of the Father and the Son, unto the fulfilling of the promise which he hath made, that if ye entered in by the way ye should receive ... and by the power of the Holy Ghost ye may know the truth of all things."
(2 Nephi 31:16 & 18, & Moroni 10:5).

"Then are ye in this strait
and narrow path which leads to
eternal life; yea, ye have entered in
by the gate; ye have done according to
the commandments of the Father and the
Son; and ye have received the Holy Ghost,
which witnesses of the Father and the Son,
unto the fulfilling of the promise which
he hath made, that if ye entered in
by the way ye should receive."
(2 Nephi 31:17-18).

"Ye have not come thus far save it were by the word of Christ with unshaken faith in him, relying wholly upon the merits of him who is mighty to save. Wherefore, ye must press forward with a steadfastness in Christ, having a perfect brightness of hope, and a love of God and of all men. Wherefore, if you shall press forward, feasting upon the word of Christ, and endure to the end, behold, thus saith the Father: Ye shall have eternal life."
(2 Nephi 31:19-20).

"This is the doctrine of Christ, and the only and true doctrine of the Father, and of the Son, and of the Holy Ghost, which is one God, without end." (2 Nephi 31:21).

This chapter,
together with the discourse by
Lehi in 2 Nephi Chapter 2, is one of
the most important in all scripture. It is
an inspired commentary on Isaiah in which
Jacob approached each subject in terms of God's
goodness and greatness, relating His covenants
to all of the House of Israel, and generalizing
when he referred to the 'Jews". (V. 1-2). Even
though Jacob and Nephi were of Manasseh
thru Joseph, (Alma 10:3), they though
of themselves as 'Jews'. "I say Jew,"
explained Nephi, "because I mean
them from whence I came."
(2 Nephi 33:8).

"And we also had many revelations, and the spirit of much prophecy; wherefore, we knew of Christ and his kingdom, which should come." (Jacob 1:6, see Jacob 4:6).

"I, the
Lord have seen the sorrow,
and heard the mourning of the
daughters of my people in ... all the
lands of my people, because of the
wickedness and abominations
of their husbands."
(Jacob 2:31).

Jacob opened Jacob Chapter 3 by speaking to those who were 'pure in heart'. He encouraged them, exhorting them to "look unto God with firmness of mind, and pray into him with exceeding faith. ...Lift up your heads and receive the pleasing word of God, and feast upon his love for ye may (do so) if your minds are firm, forever." (V. 1-2).

"We search the prophets, and we have many revelations and the spirit of prophecy; and having all these witnesses, we obtain a hope, and our faith becometh unshaken."
(Jacob 4:6).

"The Spirit speaketh the truth and lieth not. Wherefore, it speaketh of things as they really are, and of things as they really will be; wherefore, these things are manifested unto us plainly."
(Jacob 4:13).

"According to the power of justice ... ye must
go away into that lake of fire and brimstone,
whose flames are unquenchable, and whose
smoke ascendeth up forever and ever,
which lake of fire and brimstone
is endless torment."
(Jacob 5:10).

"I soon go to the place of my rest, which is with my Redeemer ... And I rejoice in the day when my mortal shall put on immortality, and shall stand before him; then, shall I see his face with pleasure."
(Enos 1:27).

"What could I write more than my fathers have written? For have not they revealed the plan of salvation? I say unto you, Yea; and this sufficeth me."
(Jarom 1:2).

"There are many among us who have many revelations, for they are not all stiffnecked. And as many as are not stiffnecked and have faith, have communion with the Holy Sprit, which maketh manifest unto the children of men, according to their faith."
(Jarom 1:4).

"The people of Nephi
had waxed strong in the land.
They observed to keep the law of
Moses, and the sabbath day
holy unto the Lord."
(Jarom 1:5).

"After I had made an abridgement
from the plates of Nephi, down to the reign of this
king Benjamin, of whom Amaleki spake, I searched
among the records which had been delivered into my
hands, and I found these plates, which contained
this small account of the prophets from Jacob
down to the reign of this king Benjamin,
and also, many of the words of Nephi."
(Words of Mormon 1:3).

"I chose this things
to finish my record (which) I
shall take from the plates of Nephi;
and I cannot write the hundredth
part of the things of my people."
(Words of Mormon 1:5).

"King Benjamin was a holy man, and he did reign over his people in righteousness; and there were many holy men in the land, and they did speak the word of God with power and with authority … Wherefore, with the help of these, king Benjamin … and also the prophets, did once more establish peace in the land." (Words of Mormon 1:17-18).

"I told the brethren that the Book of Mormon was the most correct of any book on earth, and the keystone of our religion, and (we) would get nearer to God by abiding by its precepts, than by any other book."
(Joseph Smith).

Commentary and Compendium Index

Commentary Volume One
Born in The Wilderness

- 1 Nephi
- 2 Nephi
- Jacob
- Enos
- Jarom
- Omni
- Words of Mormon
- Observations
- Author's Note
- Addendum – A Sampling of Scriptures

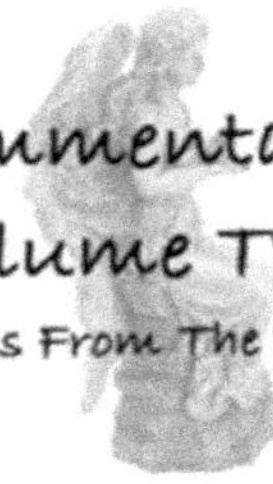

Commentary Volume Two
Voices From The Dust

- Mosiah
- Alma
- Observations
- Author's Note
- Addendum – A Sampling of Scriptures

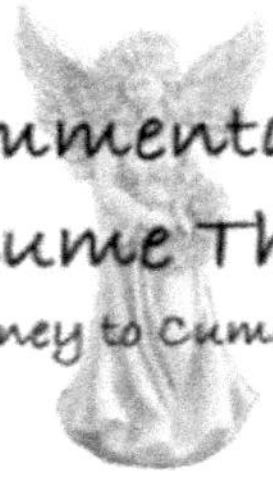

Commentary Volume Three
Journey to Cumorah

- Helaman
- 3 Nephi
- 4 Nephi
- Mormon
- Ether
- Moroni
- Observations
- Author's Note
- Addendum – A Sampling of Scriptures

Compendium
Volume One

- Questions Answered by The Book of Mormon
- Observations
- Familiar Scriptures

Compendium
Volume Two

- Questions Answered by The Book of Mormon
- Without The Book of Mormon
- Observations
- A Few of My Favorite Things
- Familiar Scriptures

Compendium
Volume Three

- Observations
- Essays That Relate to Teachings in The Book of Mormon

Compendium
Volume Four

- Observations
- Essays That Relate to Teachings in The Book of Mormon

Compendium
Volume Five

- Observations
- Essays That Relate to Teachings in The Book of Mormon

Compendium
Volume Six

- Observations
- Essays That Relate to Teachings in The Book of Mormon

Compendium
Volume Seven

- Hebrew Poetry in The Book of Mormon
- Synonymous Parallelism
- Antithetical Parallelism
- Synthetic Parallelism
- Climactic Parallelism
- Chiasmus
- List of Book of Mormon Scriptures That Illustrate Hebrew Poetry
- Observations
- Introduction to The Isaiah Chapters
- "And it came to pass" in The Book of Mormon
- "And thus we see" in The Book of Mormon
- "Behold" in The Book of Mormon

A Book of Mormon Commentary

Born in The Wilderness
Volume One
First Nephi thru Words of Mormon

Voices From the Dust
Volume Two
Mosiah thru Alma

Journey to Cumorah
Volume Three
Helaman thru Moroni

Compendium
Volumes One – Seven

www.ingramcontent.com/pod-product-compliance
Lightning Source LLC
Chambersburg PA
CBHW061400010526
44107CB00012B/1008